THE GRANDFATHER PROFILE
By permission of the author and publishers of "The Carolina Mountains."

A HISTORY OF WATAUGA COUNTY, NORTH CAROLINA.

WITH

Sketches of Prominent Families.

By

JOHN PRESTON ARTHUR.

Written at the request of

Roy M. Brown, W. D. Farthing, W. R. Gragg, G. P. Hagaman,
W. L. Bryan, F. A. Linney, P. C. Younce, A. C. Reese, A. J. Greene,
R. C. Rivers, J. S. Winkler, I. G. Greer, T. E. Bingham,
D. D. Dougherty, M. B. Blackburn, L. Greer,
J. W. Hodges, B. B. Dougherty,
C. J. Cottrell, W. P. Moody,
D. J. Cottrell and
R. L. Bingham

Who guaranteed all costs of publication.

CLEARFIELD

Originally published
Richmond, Virginia
1915

Reprinted by Genealogical Publishing Co., Inc.
Baltimore, Maryland
2002

Library of Congress Catalog Card Number 2002111357

Reprinted for Clearfield Company by
Genealogical Publishing Company
Baltimore, Maryland
2012

ISBN 978-0-8063-1954-4

Made in the United States of America

BIBLIOGRAPHY.

Allison means "Dropped Stitches in Tennessee History," by Hon. JOHN ALLISON, Nashville, 1896.

Asbury means Bishop ASBURY'S Journal, 3 volumes, out of print.

Booklet means "The North Carolina Booklet," published by the State D. A. R. Society, Raleigh, N. C.

Bruce means "Daniel Boone and the Wilderness Road," by H. ADDINGTON BRUCE, McMillan Co., N. Y., 1913.

Cobb means Address by Prof. Collier Cobb before the American Geographical Society in New York City, April, 1914.

Clark means "North Carolina Regiments in the Civil War," by Chief Justice WALTER CLARK, Goldsboro, 1901.

Clark means "The Colony of Transylvania" in the North Carolina Booklet, for January, 1904.

Col. Rec. means Colonial Records of North Carolina, edited by W. L. Saunders, P. M. Hale, printer, Raleigh, 1886.

Crouch means "Historical Sketches of Wilkes County," by JOHN CROUCH, 1902.

DeRossett means "Sketches of Church History of North Carolina," by W. L. DeROSSETT, (Alfred Williams), Raleigh, 1890.

Draper means "King's Mountain and Its Heroes," by Dr. L. C. DRAPER, (Peter G. Thompson), Cincinnati, 1888.

Dugger means "Balsam Groves of the Grandfather Mountain," by SHEP. MONROE DUGGER, Banner Elk, N. C.

Fairchild means Ebenezer Fairchild's Diary of Trip from New Jersey to the Jersey Settlement, now in possession of Col. Wyatt Hayes, Boone, N. C.

Foote means "Foote's Sketches of North Carolina," out of print.

Harper means "Reminiscenses of Caldwell County in the Civil War," by G. W. F. HARPER, pamphlet.

Haywood means "Bishops of North Carolina," by MARSHALL DeLANCEY HAYWOOD, (Alfred Williams), Raleigh, 1910.

Ives means "Trials of a Mind," etc., Boston and New York, 1854.

Kephart means "Our Southern Highlanders," by HORACE KEPHART, Outing Publishing Co., New York, 1912.

Manual means "North Carolina Manual," issued by N. C. Hist. Comm., Edwards & Broughton Printing Co., Raleigh, 1913.

Moore means "The Rhymes of Southern Rivers," by M. V. Moore, M. E. Church, South, Book Co., Nashville, 1897.

Moore means "Roster of North Carolina Troops in Civil War," by John W. Moore, 3 volumes, Raleigh, 1882.

Morley means "The Carolina Mountains," by Margaret W. Morley, Houghton-Mifflin, New York, 1913.

Murphey means "Papers of Arch. D. Murphey," 2 volumes, N. C. Hist. Comm., Raleigh, 1914.

Observer means *Charlotte Daily Observer*, Charlotte, N. C.

Rebellion Records means "The War of the Rebellion," Washington, D. C., 1897.

Rumple means "A History of Rowan County," by Rev. Jethro Rumple, 1881.

Sheets means "A History of Liberty Baptist Church," by Rev. Henry Sheets, Edwards & Broughton Printing Co., Raleigh, 1908.

Skiles means "A Sketch of Missionary Life at Valle Crucis," edited by Susan Fenimore Cooper, 1890.

Smythe means "A Tour of America," by Dr. J. F. D. Smythe.

Thwaites means "Daniel Boone," by Reuben Gold Thwaites.

Warner means "On Horseback," by Charles Dudley Warner, Houghton-Mifflin Co., New York, 1889.

Wheeler means "Historical Sketches of North Carolina," by John H. Wheeler, 2 volumes, 1851.

Williams means "History of the Baptists of North Carolina," by Rev. Charles Williams, Edwards & Broughton Printing Co., Raleigh, 1901.

Worth means "Correspondence of Jonathan Worth, N. C. Hist. Comm." Edwards & Broughton Printing Co., Raleigh, 1909.

CONTENTS.

PAGE

CHAPTER I. The relation of Watauga County and its residents to remainder of the mountains. Early settlers in eastern part of State. Difference between eastern and western settlers. Our Yankee ancestry. Critics eager to find fault. Our annals. Difference between "poor whites" and "mountain whites." Coöperation has ceased. Moonshining an inheritance. Pennsylvania "Whiskey Rebellion." 1

CHAPTER II. Similarity of Indians to Hebrews. A study in ethnology and philology. Speculations as to the beginning of things. Indians never residents of Watauga in memory of whites. Cherokees parted with title to land long ago. Old forts on frontier. Cherokee raids. First white settlers of Watauga. Linville family and falls. 12

CHAPTER III. The greed for land in the eastern section. Bishop Spangenberg sets out to get land for Moravians. He is misled and "wanders bewildered in unknown ways." Reaches delicious spring on Flat Top. Three Forks described. An Indian Old Field. Caught in a mountain snow-storm. Their route from Blowing Rock. Conflicting claims as to locality described. 21

CHAPTER IV. No direct Daniel Boone descendants. Other Boone relatives. Jesse and Jonathan Boone. Their Three Forks membership. Marking the Trail of Daniel Boone. Boone Cabin Monument. Locating Trail. Cumberland Gap pedestal. Boone's Trail in other States. Congress urged to erect bronze statue there. Boone's first trip across Blue Ridge. Probability of relocation of trail. Improbability of the carving on the Boone Tree. Boone's relations with Richard Henderson considered..... 29

CHAPTER V. Backwoods Tories. Samuel Bright, loyalist. Patriots feared British influence with Indians. Bright's Spring and the Shelving Rock. Watauga County once part of Watauga Settlement. Doctor Draper's errors. W. H. Ollis's contribution. No camp on the Yellow. Cleveland's parentage and capture. His rescue, etc. Greer's Hints, of two kinds. The Wolf's Den. Riddle's execution. Killing of Chas. Asher and other Tories. Ben Howard. Marking old graves by United States. Its niggardly policy. Battlefield in Watauga. 53

CHAPTER VI. The Yadkin Baptist Association. Three Forks Baptist Church. List of its early members and officers. A great moral force in the community. Church trials, grave and gay. Other ancient happenings. First churches. Revivals. 71

CHAPTER VII. Order of the Holy Cross. Picture of Watauga Valley in 1840. Valle Crucis as first founded. Rt. Rev. L. S. Ives. Feeble and undignified imitation. Why Ives vacillated. Old buildings. Adobes and humble bees. Easter chapel. Spiritual

v

CONTENTS

starvation on the Lower Watauga. The Mission store. Death of Mr. Skiles. Removal of St. John's. Reinstitution of Mission, and School for Girls. Summer resort, also. 78

CHAPTER VIII. Light on the Jersey Settlement. Meagre facts considered. John Gano, preacher. Fairchild's diary. Adventures on road. Mr. Gano constitutes a church. A colonial document. Other ancient documents and facts. Letter from Morris Town, N. J., Church. The Fairchild ladies. 87

CHAPTER IX. Democracy of the religion of the mountaineer. Our morals, as appraised by others. Pioneer Baptists. The Farthing family. A family of preachers. Rev. Joseph Harrison. Cove Creek Baptist Church. Bethel Baptist Church. Other early churches. Stony Fork Association. White's Spring Church. Methodist Churches. Henson's Chapel. A family of Methodist church preachers. M. E. Churches. Baptists, Presbyterians, Lutherans. 97

CHAPTER X. Formation of county. Councill's influence. Three New England visitors. Doctor Mitchell's geological tour. Tennessee boundary line. Boundary line and Land Grant Warrants. Running State line. Watauga County lines. Watauga County established. Changes in county lines. Avery County cut off. Jails and court houses. To restore lost records. First term Superior Court. Tied to a wagon-wheel. Roving spirit. Legislative and other officers. Watauga's contribution to Confederacy and Federals. Population and other facts. Mexican War soldiers. Weather vagaries. Agricultural and domestic facts. Forests. Altitudes. 114

CHAPTER XI. Boone incorporated. Its attractions. Miss Morley's visit. First residents of Boone. First builders. Saw-mills for new town. The Ellingtons. Other builders. First merchants, J. C. Gaines, Rev. J. W. Hall. Post-bellum Boone. Coffey Bros. Their enterprises. Newspapers. Counterfeiters. 142

CHAPTER XII. Too many troops for limits of book. Keith Blalock. Four Coffey Bros. Danger from Tennessee side. Longstreet's withdrawal. Kirk's Camp Vance raid. Death of Wm. Coffey. Murder of Austin Coffey. Other "activities." Michiganders escape. Camp Mast. Watauga Amazons. Camp Mast surrender. Sins of the children. Retribution? Paul and Reuben Farthing. Battle of the Beech. Stoneman's raid. Official account. A real home guard. Mrs. Horton robbed. No peace. Fort Hamby. Blalock's threat. 159

CHAPTER XIII. Calloway sisters. Pioneer hunters. James Aldridge. His real wife appears. Betsy Calloway. Delila Baird. A belated romance. Colb McCanless, sheriff. His death by Wild Bill. Bedent E. Baird. Zeb Vance's uncle makes inquiry. Peggy Clawson. Other old stories. Joseph T. Wilson, or "Lucky Joe." "Long-Distance." An African romance. James Speer's fate. Joshua Pennell frees slaves. Jesse Mullins' "niggers." Crosscut suit. Absentee landlord. "School Butter." Lee Carmichael. The musterfield murder. A Belle of Broadway. 186

CONTENTS

CHAPTER XIV. Fine Watauga County scenery. Cove Creek. Our flowers. Valle Crucis. Sugar Grove. Blowing Rock. Along the Blue Ridge. Moses H. Cone. Brushy Fork. Shull's Mills. Linville Valley and Falls. The Ollis family. Elk Cross Roads. Banner's Elk. A trip on foot. Meat Camp. Rich Mountain. The "Tater Hill." The Grandfather and Grandmother. Grafting French chestnuts. Beaver Dams. Boone's Beaver Dams trails. Beech Creek and Poga. 209

CHAPTER XV. Ante-bellum education. Peculiarities of speech. We speak the best and purest English. Place-names. Kephart's dissertations. Ante-bellum pedagogues. Our schools. Penmanship. Phillip Church. Jonathan Norris. Eli M. Farmer. Burton Davis. Todd Miller. The "Twisting Temple." Lees-McRae Institute. School-teachers. Normal school at Boone. Skyland Institute. T. P. Adams' long service. Silverstone public school. Walnut Grove Institute. Valle Crucis School for Girls. First agricultural instruction. Prominent in education. Lenoir School Lands. School-house Loan Fund. T. L. Clingman, a teacher. Mount Mitchell controversy. 243

CHAPTER XVI. Gold mines and mining. First owners of Cranberry. Iron forges. Iron bounties. Some old hammermen. Clingman's mining. 263

CHAPTER XVII. First wagon roads. First across Blue Ridge. Caldwell and Watauga Turnpike. Yonahlossee Turnpike. Early road legislation. Earliest stopping places. First paper railroads. First railroad surveys. 268

SKETCHES OF PROMINENT FAMILIES ALPHABETICALLY ARRANGED...... 279

INDEX 357

ILLUSTRATIONS.

THE GRANDFATHER PROFILE. By permission of author and publishers of "The Carolina Mountains."	Frontispiece
COL. WILLIAM LEWIS BRYAN, Historian and Trail Finder	26
DANIEL BOONE CABIN MONUMENT, erected by Col. W. L. Bryan, October, 1912	32
THE OLD PERKINS PLACE, where Cleveland was captured. Photograph by Wiley C. Vannoy, Blowing Rock	60
THE WOLF'S DEN, where Cleveland was rescued. Photograph by Wiley C. Vannoy, Blowing Rock	62
THE THREE FORKS BAPTIST CHURCH. Photograph by Wiley C. Vannoy, Blowing Rock	72
BISHOP L. SILLIMAN IVES, D. D. Photograph by John L. Vest, Forsyth County, N. C.	78
RESIDENCE OF REV. JOHN NORTON ATKINS, and former home of the late Rev. Henry H. Prout	82
REV. REUBEN P. FARTHING	98
COL. JOE B. TODD, Clerk of the Superior Court	134
BOONE, THE COUNTY SEAT OF WATAUGA. Photograph by John L. Vest Forsyth County, N. C.	142
MRS. WILLIAM LEWIS BRYAN, who has lived in Boone since its organization, and for several years prior thereto	146
AUNT DELILAH'S LAST CABIN HOME. Photograph by L. G. Harris, Cranberry, N. C.	192
HORTON FAMILY ARMS, AND EXPLANATION	206
THE BLOWING ROCK. From an oil painting by the late W. G. Randall	214
LAKE AND RESIDENCE OF COL. W. W. STRINGFELLOW, Blowing Rock, N. C. Photograph by Wiley C. Vannoy, Blowing Rock	218
PEAKS OF THE GRANDFATHER MOUNTAIN. By permission of author and publishers of "The Carolina Mountains."	234
THE YONAHLOSSEE ROAD. By permission of author and publishers of "The Carolina Mountains."	238
THE APPALACHIAN TRAINING SCHOOL, AND HOWARD'S KNOB, Boone, N. C. Photograph by John L. Vest, Forsyth County, N. C.	248

ILLUSTRATIONS ix

MISSION SCHOOL AT VALLE CRUCIS, N. C. *Photograph by L. G. Harris, Cranberry, N. C.*.. 254

HON. THOMAS LANIER CLINGMAN. From Clark's "North Carolina Regiments."... 258

THE DEEP GAP, the gateway to Watauga. *Photograph by Wiley C. Vannoy, Blowing Rock*.. 268

MAJ. HARVEY BINGHAM, Soldier and Lawyer...................... 282

HON. E. SPENCER BLACKBURN, M.C., Orator and Statesman.......... 286

DUDLEY FARTHING, Judge of the Court of Pleas and Quarter Sessions.. 308

HON. L. L. GREENE, Judge of the Superior Court.................... 312

COL. JONATHAN HORTON. *Photograph by John L. Vest, Forsyth County, N. C.*.. 322

COL. ROMULUS Z. LINNEY, M.C., Wit, Orator, Lawyer and Statesman.. 328

ADDITIONS AND CORRECTIONS
(Lines are counted from the Top of each Page)

	LINE	PAGE
"it" should be "the inscription"	28	40
"recall" should be "recalls"	22	86
"D. B. Phillips" should be "J. B. Phillips"	last	132
"1858" should be "1859" according to W. Elbert Greene, Esq.	19	138
"Cove Creek" should be "New River"	28	170
"Henry Hamby" should be "Henry Henley"	29	184
"Sharp's Creek" should be "Sawyer's Creek"	15	210
"Harley" should be "Hartley"	1	240
Blank should be filled by "Laura Martin"	35	315
Blank should be filled by "Miss Marilda Ellett first, and then Jane Brown"	36	315
"a Ray" should be "Margaret Duke"	5	316
Blank should be filled by "Jane Ray"	6	316
Blank should be filled by "Catherine Burkett"	7	316
"Ray (?)" should be "Morris"	19	316
"ried a Ray" should be "ried Ella Ray"	22	316
"a Reeves" should be "Winfield Doub"	23	316
"Henry C" should be "Henry W."	26	316
"1829" should be "1827"	30	331
"Eleline" should be "Emeline A."	8	332
"Hiram" should be "Wm. Carroll"	10	332
Instead of two Wilson families, there are two accounts of but one family, both coming from the same ancestor.		352

THE MEN OF WATAUGA.

They told by the sibilant sea of the solemn
  Blue mountains whose summits ascend to the sky,
Where, cradled in solitude, world-weary pilgrims
  Might find perfect rest, undisturbed by a sigh.
They told of savannahs as smooth as a carpet,
  Of golden fruits breaking their branches in twain;
Of vast flocks of wild-fowl, the sunlight obscuring,
  And buffalo haunting the billowy plain.
They told of a land where the sweet-scented wild flowers
  Flash fair as the flame of a taper-lit shrine,
Bedecking the meadows, bespangling the valleys,
  And climbing the mountains, the sun to outshine.
But they told of a cruel foe lurking in ambush,
  For whose treachery nothing but blood could atone,
Of fierce Chickamaugas and Cherokee bowmen,
  Whose swift, stealthy darts sang a dirge all their own.
But the rivers and mountains, the dim, distant mountains,
  Rising range upon range to the ultimate sky—
Could women and children surmount those blue masses?
  Could even strong men those grim rock-cliffs defy?
Yes; North, west of Guilford, and South, west of Cowpens,
  Those mountains had yielded to Boone and Adair;
McDowell and Shelby had led through the passes
  But to find them awaiting the "Hot-spur," Sevier.
'Twas the land that had haunted the dreams of the hunted
  For which all the homeless and hopeless had prayed—
Untrammeled by custom, unfettered by fashion,
  Each man his own master, her mistress each maid.
So, the hunter, his rifle and bullet-pouch bearing,
  Blew a blast on his horn and the hounds thronged around,
The oxen were yoked, and on wheels the small household
  Started out to the West, a new Nation to found!
Through dim, ghostly woodlands and dew-jeweled meadows
  They eagerly followed the track of the sun;
They rafted the rivers and conquered the Smokies,
  From whose peaks they first saw the new homes they had won.
They were men from Old Rowan, Burke, Craven and Chowan,
  Wake, Anson and Surry and Currytuck's lights;
And Mecklenburg sent of her sturdy young yeomen
  Such men as subscribed to our "First Bill of Rights."
They girdled the forests, they drained the morasses,
  They builded of rude logs the Church and the Home—
Through labor and sorrow and sore tribulation—
  Faith for the foundation and love for the dome.
And while these be the Sword of the Lord and of Gideon,
  God's "Chosen" the heathen forever will smite;
And in tears and in blood, with the lead of the rifle,
  The Saxon his deeds will continue to write.
And soon, on the banks of the sparkling Watauga,
  Was cradled the spirit that conquered the West—
The spirit that, soaring o'er mountain and prairie,
  E'en on the Pacific shore paused not to rest.
For the first written compact that, west of the mountains,
  Was framed for the guidance of liberty's feet,
Was writ here by letterless men in whose bosoms
  Undaunted the heart of a paladin beat!   J. P. A.

CHAPTER I.
Several Forewords.

Our Home and Heritage.—Our home is a very small part of that vast region known as the Southern Appalachians, which a recent writer, Horace Kephart, has aptly called Appalachia. This elevated section covers parts of eight States, all of which are south of Mason and Dixon's line. It is in the middle of the temperate zone and, for climate, is unsurpassed in the world. The average elevation is about two thousand feet above tidewater. Blue Ridge is the name of the range of mountains which bounds this highland country on the east, though the western boundary is known by many names, owing to the fact that it is bisected by several streams, all of which flow west, while the Blue Ridge is a true water-shed from the Potomac to Georgia. The various names of the western ranges are the Stone, the Iron, the Bald, the Great Smoky, the Unaka and the Frog mountains. The United States Coast and Geodetic Survey has, however, of recent years, given the name Unaka to this entire western border, leaving the local names to the sections which have been formed by the passage of the Watauga, the Doe, the Toe, the Cane, the French Broad, the Pigeon, the Little Tennessee and the Hiawassee rivers. With the exception of a few bare mountain-tops, which are covered by a carpet of grass, these mountains are wooded to the peaks. Between the Blue Ridge and the Unakas are numerous cross ranges, separated by narrow valleys and deep gorges. Over the larger part of this region are to be found the older crystalline rocks, most of which are tilted, while the forests are of the finer hardwoods which, when removed, give place to luxuriant grasses. The apple finds its home in these mountains, while maize, when grown, is richer in proteids than that of the prairie lands of Illinois.

Character of the Inhabitants in 1752.—Bishop Spangenberg, in the Colonial Records (Vol. IV, pp. 1311-1314), wrote from

Edenton, N. C., that he had found everything in confusion there, the counties in conflict with each other, and the authority of the legislature greatly weakened, owing largely to the fact that the older counties had formerly been allowed five representatives in the general assembly; but, as the new counties were formed, they were allowed but two. It was not long, however, before the newer counties, even with their small representation, held a majority of the members, and passed a law reducing the representation of the older counties from five to two. The result of this was that the older counties refused to send any members to the assembly, but dispatched an agent to England with a view to having their former representation restored. Before any result could be obtained, however, there was "in the older counties perfect anarchy," with frequent crimes of murder and robbery. Citizens refused to appear as jurors, and if court was held to try such crimes, not one was present. Prisons were broken open and their inmates released. Most matters were decided by blows. But the county courts were regularly held, and whatever belonged to their jurisdiction received the customary attention.

People of the East and West.—Bishop Spangenberg, in the same letter, divided the inhabitants of the eastern counties into two classes—natives, who could endure the climate, but were indolent and sluggish, and those from England, Scotland and Ireland and from the northern colonies of America, the latter being too poor to buy land there. Some of these were refugees from justice, had fled from debt, or had left wife and children elsewhere—or, possibly, to escape the penalty of some crime. Horse thieves infested parts of this section. But, he adds in a postscript written in 1753: "After having traversed the length and breadth of North Carolina, we have ascertained that towards the western mountains there are plenty of people who have come from Virginia, Maryland, Pennsylvania, New Jersey and even from New England." Even in 1752 "four hundred families, with horses, wagons and cattle have migrated to North Carolina, and among them were good farmers and very worthy people." These, in all probability, were the Jersey Settlers.

A History of Watauga County 3

The Great Pennsylvania Road.—On the 15th of February, 1751, Governor Johnston wrote to the London Board of Trade that inhabitants were flocking into North Carolina, mostly from Pennsylvania, and other points of America "already overstocked, and some directly from Europe," many thousands having arrived, most of whom had settled in the West "so that they had nearly reached the mountains." Jeffrey's map in the Congressional Library shows the "Great Road from the Yadkin River through Virginia to Philadelphia, Distance 435 Miles." It ran from Philadelphia, through Lancaster and York counties of Pennsylvania to Winchester, Va., thence up the Shenandoah Valley, crossing Fluvanna River at Looney's Ferry, thence to Staunton River and down the river, through the Blue Ridge, thence southward, near the Moravian Settlement, to Yadkin River, just above the mouth of Linville Creek, and about ten miles above the mouth of Reedy Creek. It is added that those of our boys who followed Lee on his Gettysburg campaign in 1863 were but passing over the same route their ancestors had taken when coming from York and Lancaster counties to this State in the fifties of the eighteenth century. (Col. Rec. Vol. IV, p. xxi.)

Our Yankee Ancestry.—As, to Southerners, all people north of Mason and Dixon's line are Yankees, there seems to be no doubt, if the best authorities can be trusted, that we are the sons of Yankee sires. Roosevelt (Vol. I, p. 137) tells us that as early as 1730 three streams of white people began to converge towards these mountains, but were halted by the Alleghanies; that they came mostly from Philadelphia, though many were from Charleston, S. C., Presbyterian-Irish being prominent among all and being the Roundheads of the South. Also that Catholics and Episcopalians obtained little foothold, the creed of the backwoodsmen being generally Presbyterian. Miss Morley says that so many of the staunch northerners—Scotch-Irish after the events of 1730, and Scotch Highlanders after those of 1745— "came to the North Carolina mountains that they have given the dominant note to the character of the mountaineers" (p. 140). Kephart says that when James I, in 1607, confiscated the estates of the native Irish in six counties in Ulster, he planted them with Scotch and English Presbyterians, giving long leases, but that as these leases began to expire the Scotch-Irish themselves came in conflict with the Crown, and then he quotes Froude to the effect that thirty thousand Protestants left Ulster during the two years following the Antrim evictions and came to America. Many of these finally settled in our mountains, among them being Daniel Boone and the ancestors of David Crockett, Samuel Houston, John C. Calhoun, "Stonewall" Jackson and Abraham Lincoln. He might have added, also, those of Cyrus H. McCormick, Admiral Farragut, Andrew Johnson, James K. Polk, John C. Breckenridge, Henry Clay, John Marshall and Parson Brownlow.

Huguenots, Germans and Swedes.—But others came also: French Huguenots, Germans, Hollanders and Swedes, who settled the British frontier from Massachusetts to the Valley of Virginia, the mountain men who counted most coming from Lancaster, York and Berks counties, Pennsylvania. "That was true in the days of Daniel Boone and David Crockett, and also in the days of John C. Calhoun and William A. Graham, of those of Zeb Vance and Jeter C. Pritchard. There has not been one whit of admixture from any other source. Blood feuds have always been absent. The Tiffanys have been able to draw on these mountains for some of their most skilful wood-carvers—a revival of their ancient home industries. I have heard in Pennsylvania within the last thirty years every form of expression with which I am familiar in Western North Carolina, and some of them occur today around Worcester, Mass."[1] Hence, we have in these mountains the sauerkraut of Holland and the cakes of Scotland.

Scum or Salt?—So much has been written in detraction of the Southern mountaineers that ignorant people conclude that they are the very scum of the earth. In all the admirable things Horace Kephart had to say in his "Southern Highlanders," the Northern reviewers found but a few sentences worthy of their notice, and these were, of course, of an unfavorable nature.

---

[1] Dr. Collier Cobb in an address before the National Geographic Society, in New York City, in April, 1914.

These were quoted and commented on by a reviewer in the *Review of Reviews* for July, 1914. In the same number of this periodical (p. 49) there is a picture under which is printed: "Center Peak of Grandfather Mountain, in Pisgah Forest, recently acquired by the Government from the Estate of George W. Vanderbilt." As the Grandfather mountain is at least ninety miles north of Pisgah Forest, the ignorance of the publishers of this magazine of conditions in our mountains is apparent. Kephart's few remarks which caught the eye of Northern reviewers were that "although without annals, we are one in speech, manners, experiences and ideals, and that our deterioration began as soon as population began to press upon the limits of subsistence." An examination of the statistics of population and wealth of Buncombe, Haywood, Jackson, Swain and Cherokee counties in 1880, before the railroad was built, and of 1910, will convince anyone that "population has not yet pressed upon the limits of production." Kephart also said that our "isolation prevented them from moving West . . . and gradually the severe conditions of their life enfeebled them physically and mentally." As opposed to that, Archibald D. Murphey says (Murphey Papers, Vol. II, p. 105) that North Carolina "has sent half a million of her inhabitants to people the wilderness of the West, and it was not until the rage for emigration abated that the public attention was directed to the improvement of" their advantages. This was written prior to November, 1819. Besides, anyone who will read the "Sketches of Prominent Families" in this volume will be convinced that Watauga County at least contributed its quota to the winning of the West. Miss Morley graciously records that, instead of deteriorating, the late George W. Vanderbilt put his main reliance on the native mountaineer in the development of his fairyland estate, Biltmore (p. 149). "They were put to work, and, what was of equal value in their development, they were subjected to an almost military discipline. For the first time in generations they were compelled to be prompt, methodical and continuous in their efforts. And of this there was no complaint. Scotch blood may succumb to enervating surroundings, but at the first call to battle it was ready. Not only did the men do the manual labor, but, as time went on, the most capable of them became overseers in the various departments, until finally all the directors of this great estate, excepting a few of the highest officials, were drawn from the ranks of the people, who proved themselves so trustworthy and capable that in all these years only three or four of Biltmore's mountaineer employees have had to be dismissed for inefficiency or bad conduct."

Won the Revolution and Saved the Union.—Like Tennyson's "foolish yeoman," we have been "too proud to care from whence we came," and it is a singular fact that in spite of all that has been written against us, no Southern mountaineer has taken the trouble to answer our detractors. And, when it is said that we have no annals, Mr. Kephart merely means that we have not written them, for he proceeds to prove that we have annals of the highest order. He credits the mountaineer with having been the principal force which drove the Indians from the Alleghany border (p. 151) and formed the rear-guard of the Revolution and the vanguard in the conquest of the West. He says: "Then came the Revolution. The backwoodsmen were loyal to the American government—loyal to a man. They not only fought off the Indians from the rear, but sent many of their incomparable riflemen to fight at the front as well. They were the first English-speaking people to use weapons of precision— the rifle, introduced by the Pennsylvania Dutch about 1700, which was used by our backwoodsmen exclusively throughout the war. They were the first to employ open-order formation in civilized warfare. They were the first outside colonists to assist their New England brethren at the siege of Boston . . . They were mustered in as the first regiment of the Continental Army (being the first troops enrolled by our Congress and the first to serve under a Federal banner). They carried the day at Saratoga, the Cowpens and King's Mountain. From the beginning to the end of the war, they were Washington's favorite troops." As to the Civil War, he says (p. 374): "The Confederates thought that they could throw a line of troops from Wheeling to the Lakes, and Captain Garnett, a West Point graduate, started, but got no further than Harper's Ferry, when mountain men shot from ambush, cut down bridges, and killed Garnett with a bullet from a squirrel rifle at Harper's Ferry. Then the South began to realize what a long, lean, powerful arm of the Union it was that the Southern mountaineer stretched through its very vitals, for that arm helped to hold Kentucky in the Union, kept East Tennessee from aiding the Confederacy and caused West Virginia to secede from Secession!" There was no Breed's Hill nor Bull Run panic among them in the Revolution or in the Civil War period! Has New England, which has a superabundance of annals, any that will compare with these? And yet, it took an outsider to tell us of them!

Not the Poor Whites of the South.—According to Kephart (p. 356), the poor whites of the South descended mainly from the convicts and indentured servants which England supplied to the Southern plantations before the days of slavery. The cavaliers who founded and dominated Southern society came from the conservative, the feudal element of England. "Their character and training were essentially aristocratic and military. They were not town dwellers, but masters of plantations . . . These servants were obtained from convicted criminals, boys and girls kidnapped from the slums, impoverished people who sold their services for passage to America (p. 357). It was when the laboring classes of Europe had achieved emancipation from serfdom and feudalism was overthrown, that African slavery laid the foundation for a new feudalism in the Southern States. Its effect upon white labor was to free them from their thraldom; but being unskilled and untrained, densely ignorant, and from a more or less degraded stock, these shiftless people generally became squatters on the pine barrens, and gradually sank lower in the scale till the slaves themselves were freed by the Civil War. There was then and still is plenty of wild land in the lowlands and they had neither the initiative nor the courage to seek a promised land far away among the unexplored and savage peaks of the western country."

McKamie Wiseman's View.—This shrewd old mountaineer of Avery County, who is a wise man not only by name, but by nature also, had the true idea of the settlement of these mountains. He said that as population drifted westward from the Atlantic and downwards from western Virginia and Pennsylvania between the mountain troughs, the game was driven into the intervening mountains, and that only the bravest and the hardiest of the frontiersmen of the borders followed it and remained after it had been exterminated. Tradition and early documents bear out this view, the first settlers of the mountains having been almost without exception the men who lived on the mountain-tops, at the heads of creeks and in out-of-the-way places generally, disdaining the fertile bottom lands of the larger streams, preferring the most inaccessible places, because of the proximity to them of the game. Others, with more money and less daring, got the meadows and fertile valleys for agriculture, while the true pioneers dwelt afar in trackless mountains, in hunting camps and caverns, from which they watched their traps and hunted deer, bear and turkeys. The shiftless and disheartened poor whites would soon have perished in this wilderness, but the hunters waxed stronger and braver, and their descendants still people the mountain regions of the South. And he thought, also, that many came down from the New England States because of the religious unrest and dissensions which marked the earlier history of that region, and came where men might worship God in their own way, whether that way were the way of Puritan or Baptist. To use his words, "It was freedom that they were seeking, and it was freedom that they found in these unpeopled mountains." Kephart puts it in another form only when he says (p. 307), "The nature of the mountaineer demands that he have solitude for the unhampered growth of his personality, wing-room for his eagle heart." As another said of the Argonauts, "The cowards never started, and the weaklings died on the way." Mr. Wiseman died in July, 1915.

No Festering Warrens for Them.—Mr. Kephart also tells us (p. 309) that "our highlanders have neither memory nor tradition of ever having been herded together, lorded over, persecuted or denied the privileges of free men," and that, "although life has been one long, hard, cruel war against elemental powers, nothing else than warlike arts, nothing short of warlike hazards could have subdued the beasts and savages, felled the forests and made our land habitable for those teeming millions who can exist only in a state of mutual dependence and cultivation." And, more marvelous still, he adds, "By compulsion their self-reliance was more complete; hence, their independence grew more haughty, their individualism more intense. *And these traits, exaggerated as they were by the force of environment, remain unweakened among their descendants to the present day.*"

Co-operation Has Ceased.—In the early time, co-operation was the watchword of the day. Neighbor helped neighbor, freely, gladly and enthusiastically. But, according to Kephart, all this has ceased, and we have become non-sociable, with each man fighting for his own hand, recognizing no social compact. Each is suspicious of the other. "They will not work together zealously, even to improve their neighborhood roads, each mistrusting that the other may gain some trifling advantage over himself, or turn fewer shovelfuls of earth. Labor chiefs fail to organize granges or unions among them because they simply will not stick together . . ." He quotes a Miss Mills as saying, "The mountaineers must awake to a consciousness of themselves as a people." Including all the Southern highlanders, we constitute a distinct ethnic group of close on to four million souls, and with needs and problems identical. The population is almost absolutely unmixed, and completely segregated from each other (p. 311). The one redeeming feature is a passionate attachment for home and family, a survival of the old feudal idea, while the hived and promiscuous life in cities is breaking down the old fealty of kith and kin (p. 312). "My family, right or wrong" is said to be our slogan, and it is claimed that this is but the persistence of the old clan fealty to the chief and the clansmen.

Moonshining an Inheritance?—Kephart seems to have made a study of blockading and moonshining, and to have reached the conclusion that they are really an inheritance, coming down to us from our Scotch and Irish ancestors, who resented the English excise law of 1659, which struck at the national drink of the Scotch and Irish, while the English themselves were then content to drink ale. Our forebears killed the gaugers in sparsely settled regions, while the better-to-do people of the towns bribed them. Thus the Scotch-Irish, settled by James I in the north of Ireland, to replace the dispossessed native Hibernians, learned to make whiskey in little stills over peat fires on their hearths, calling it poteen, from the fact that it was made in little pots. Finally, these Scotch-Irish fell out with the British government and emigrated, for the most part, to western Pennsylvania, where they brought with them an undying hatred of the excise laws. When, therefore, after they had helped to establish a stable government, an excise law was adopted by Congress, these Scotch-Irish were the very first to rebel. And it was to George Washington himself that the task fell of suppressing their resistance to the United States!

The Pennsylvania Whiskey Rebellion.—Owing to bad roads and the want of markets, there was no currency away from the seaboard. But, condensed into distilled spirits, a ready sale and easy transportation were found for the product of the grain of the mountaineers. For they could carry many gallons on a single horse or in a single wagon and get a fair price from people living where money circulated. When, therefore, they were required to pay a heavy tax on their product, they rebelled. When the Federal excisemen went among them, they blackened themselves and tarred and feathered these intruders on their rights. These "revenuers" then resigned, but were replaced by others. If a mountaineer took out a license, a gang of whiskey boys smashed his still and inflicted bodily punishment on him. All attempts to serve warrants resulted in an up-rising of the people, and, on July 16, 1794, a company of mountain militia marched to the house of General Neville, in command of the excise forces, and he fired on them, wounding five and killing one. The next day a regiment of 500 mountain men, led by Tom the Tinker, burned Neville's house and forced him to flee, one of his guard of United States soldiers being killed and several wounded. On August 1, 1794, 2,000 armed mountain men met at the historic Braddock Field, and marched on Pittsburg, then a village. A committee of Pittsburg citizens met them. The mob of 5,400 men were then taken into town and treated to strong drink, after which they dispersed. The Governor of Pennsylvania refused to interfere, and Washington called for 15,000 militia to quell the insurrection. He also appointed commissioners to induce the people to submit peacefully. Eighteen ring-leaders were arrested and the rest dispersed. Two of the leaders were convicted, but were afterwards pardoned. Even a secession movement was imminent, but as Jefferson soon became President, the excise law was repealed and peace restored. There was no other excise tax till 1812, when it was renewed, only to be repealed in 1817. From this time till 1862 there was no tax, and after that time it was only twenty cents a gallon. In 1864 it was raised to sixty cents a gallon and later in that year to $1.50, to be followed in 1865 by $2.00 a gallon. The result was again what it had been in Great Britain—fraud around the centers of population and resistance in the mountains, the current price of distilled spirits even in the North being less than the tax. In 1868 the tax was reduced to fifty cents, and illicit stilling practically ceased, the government collecting during the second year of the existence of this reduced tax three dollars for every one that had been collected before (p. 163). Since then every increase has resulted in moonshining in the mountains and graft in the cities. The whiskey frauds of Grant's administration invaded the very cabinet itself. So it seems the spirit of resistance makes moonshiners of us all, just as Shakespeare said that conscience makes cowards of us all.

CHAPTER II.
Forerunners of Watauga.

Likeness of the Indians to the Hebrews.—The following has been condensed from the *Literary Digest* for September 21, 1912, page 472: "William Penn saw a striking likeness between the Jews of London and the American Indians. Some claim that the stories of the Old Testament are legends in some Indian tribes. In the Jewish Encyclopedia it is said that the Hebrews, after the captivity, separated themselves from the heathen in order to observe their peculiar laws; and Manasseh Ben Israel claims that America and India were once joined, at Bering Strait, by a peninsula, over which these Hebrews came to America. All Indian legends affirm that they came from the northwest. When first visited by Europeans, Indians were very religious, worshipping one Great Spirit, but never bowing down to idols. Their name for the deity was Ale, the old Hebrew name for God. In their dances they said 'Hallelujah' distinctly. They had annual festivals, performed morning and evening sacrifices, offered their first fruits to God, practiced circumcision, and there were 'cities of refuge,' to which offenders might fly and be safe; they reckoned time as did the Hebrews, similar superstitions mark their burial places 'and the same creeds were the rule of their lives, both as to the present and the future.' They had chief-ruled tribes, and forms of government almost identical with those of the Hebrews. Each tribe had a totem, usually some animal, as had the Israelites, and this explains why, in the blessing of Jacob upon his sons, Judah is surnamed a lion, Dan a serpent, Benjamin a wolf, and Joseph a bough." There are also resemblances in their languages to the Latin and Greek tongues, Chickamauga meaning the field of death, and Aquone the sound of water.

A Study in Ethnology and Philology.—We have seen that the legends show that the Indians came from the northwest. It must be remembered, however, that although they were of one color, they were of different tribes and spoke different tongues or dialects. There is not a labial in the entire Cherokee language, while the speech of the Choctaws, Creeks, Tuscaroras, Algonquins and many other tribes is full of them. They were nomads, wandering from place to place. The Cherokees were admittedly the most advanced of the Indians since the Spaniards decimated the Incas and Aztecs. They were certainly the most warlike. The name "Cherokee" has, however, no significance in their language, as they call themselves the Ani-Kituhwagi and the Yunwiga, or real people. This is likewise true of most of the names of streams and mountains which bear, according to popular belief, Indian names; for in the glossary, given in the Nineteenth Annual Report of the Bureau of Ethnology, 1897, Part I, James Mooney, its author, shows that their meaning has been lost, if, indeed, they ever had a meaning in the Indian tongue. A glance through that collection of Cherokee words will dispel many a poetic idea of the significance of such words as Watauga, Swannanoa, Yonahlossee and others as mellifluous. How came this about? He offers no theory. But Martin V. Moore, who once did business in Boone, has published a small volume, "The Rhyme of Southern Rivers,"[1] in which he makes it appear that most, if not all, of these names of streams and mountains have their roots in the languages of Europe and Asia. He cites an instance when an Indian was asked whether the Catawba tribe took their name from the Catawba River or the river from the tribe? The Indian answered by asking, "Which was here first?" If it was possible for one European or Asiatic tribe or clan to cross into America before Bering Strait divided the two continents, it was possible for many to have crossed also. If one tribe or clan spoke one tongue, other tribes which crossed probably spoke different languages. Thus, America might have become peopled with representatives of many peoples, each speaking a different dialect, and thus giving different names to the several streams and mountains along and among which they for a time abided. If this be so, it is easy to believe that the root or

[1] This was originally published in *Harper's Monthly* for February, 1883, but without its introductory. It was published in complete form by M. E. Church, South, Pub. Co., Nashville, Tenn., 1897.

origin of many so-called Indian words can be found in the Greek, Latin, Hebrew, Persian, African, Chinese and Japanese languages. That many names of Southern rivers show such possibilities is made plain by this little volume.

"**The Other Way About,**" as the English say, would make it possible that these Appalachian mountains being the oldest land in the world—older far than that of the Nile, the Euphrates and the Jordan—were really the birth-place and cradle of the ancestors of the polyglot races which now people Europe and Asia; for, if it was possible for people to come to America from those countries, it was equally possible for people to go from America there. So that, instead of being the New World, America is really the Old World. But, to the proofs:

Words Derived from the Hebrews.—According to Mr. Moore, "te" or "de" in Hebrew means "deep." In its oldest form in Hebrew, it is "te-am," or "te-ho-ma," meaning deep waters—"am" or "homa" denoting waters. "Perpetuity" in Hebrew was denoted by "na." "The fact is illustrated," to quote Mr. Moore's words, "in the Hebrew name 'ama-na'—the river known in Isaiah," lviii, v. 11 (p. 99). Chota, the City of Refuge, as it is called in Cherokee, "was governed by the same laws as those which obtained among the Jewish nations of antiquity" (p. 89).
. . . Telico, Jellico and Jerico (p. 44) are cognate words, and Pocataligo was the title of the river of that name in South Carolina, "long famed as one of the cities of refuge among the aborigines." Likewise, he shows that "toah" or "toe" is from the Hebrew "neph-toah," "the name of a water noted in Jewish history" (p. 29).

Latin, Manchu and Persian.—"The root word of the Mississippi River is traced to the Latin words 'meto' and 'messis,' whence come our words 'meter' and 'measure,' denoting in the original sense a gathering together, tersely characteristic of a stream which gathers to itself the waters of so many different lands" (p. 77). He also traces the root word of "saluda" to the Latin "salio" to leap (p. 41) or a "stream springing out of high places." In "unaka," the name of the mountains south of the Little Tennessee River, unquestionably "a native Indian word,"

A History of Watauga County

he finds a marked likeness to the Latin "unus," "unica" and our English equivalent "unique" (p. 92). "Watauga" has the Latin root "aqua," meaning water. Then, too, "esta" or "aesta," in Latin, refers to summer months, or leisure time, which, combined with the Hebrew "toah" or "toe," makes up our "Estatoe" river (p. 29). "Esseeola" is given as the native name of the river now called Linville, "ola" being from the Manchu dialect word "ou-li," meaning river; and if Miss Morley is right in thinking that it was named for the linden trees on its banks, one cannot help wondering if "esse," in Manchu, means linden! Mr. Moore thinks "catawba" is from the Persian root "au-ba" or "aub," of which the California writing is Yuba, meaning catfish, which is certainly characteristic of our Carolina stream of that name. He also calls attention to the fact that neither the Cherokees nor the Japanese use the letter "r" in their dialects; and that the old Romans used "l" and "r" interchangeably, just as do the Cherokees (p. 50).

First Settlers of Watauga.—The Cherokee Indians were the first settlers of this county, but there is no record that white men ever came into actual contact with them in what is now Watauga county. Boone does not seem to have encountered any on his trip in 1769 until he reached Kentucky. Neither did Bishop Spangenburg on his trip in 1752. James Robertson saw none on his first trip to the Watauga Settlement in 1769, nor in 1770, when he brought his family with him to the new settlement on the Watauga River. Indeed, Virginia had concluded a treaty with the Cherokees in 1772 fixing the top of the Blue Ridge as the eastern boundary, and a line running due west from the White Top mountain (where North Carolina, Virginia and Tennessee join), and the general impression then was that this line included the Watauga Settlement near what is now Jonesboro, Tenn. But in 1771 Anthony Bledsoe extended the Virginia line far enough west to satisfy himself that the Watauga Settlement was not in Virginia territory, and, therefore, not within the treaty limits of 1772. This fact caused those settlers to lease for eight years all the country on the waters of the Watauga River. On March 19, 1775, the Watauga settlers bought in fee simple all the land on the waters of the Watauga, Holston and New Rivers. The western boundary of this tract ran from six miles above Long Island of the Holston, south, to the dividing ridge between the Watauga and the Toe rivers, thence in a southeasterly direction to the Blue Ridge, thence along the Blue Ridge to the Virginia line. This embraced the whole of Watauga, Ashe and Alleghany counties. So that, from 1775 on, the Indians had no right to be in this territory, and, although Wheeler tells us that Ashe was partially settled as early as 1755 by white people—principally hunters—there is nothing to tell us that the Indians ever lived here except arrow heads, broken bits of pottery and so forth.[2]

The Cherokees Kept Faith.—Up to the commencement of the Revolutionary War there is no evidence that the Cherokees lived north of the dividing ridge between the Toe and Watauga clear up to the Virginia line. Thus, whether the lease and deed to the Watauga settlers near Jonesboro were legal or not, the untutored savage stood manfully to this agreement. It is true that war parties were sent through this territory to make trouble for the settlers east of the Blue Ridge, but they had no abiding place west of that divide. Bishop Spangenberg was here in December, 1752, but he saw no Indians, though speaking of an "old Indian field." There is a tradition in the settlement near Linville Falls and Pisgah Church (Altamont), now in Avery County, that William White was the first settler in that locality whose name is now remembered and lived where Melvin C. Bickerstaff now resides, but that another had preceded him at that place, and that while hunting one day he saw from a ridge a party of Indians kill two white men who were "lying out" in that locality in order to escape service in the Revolutionary War, and trample their bodies beyond sight in a mud-hole which then stood near the present residence of Rev. W. C. Franklin. This settler did not reveal himself to the Indians, but, hastening to his own cabin half a mile away, escaped with his wife and child to Fort Crider (which, in 1780, Dr. Draper tells us, p. 185, note, was situated on "a small eminence within the present limits of

---
[2] Rev. W. R. Savage, of Blowing Rock, and W. S. Farthing, of Beaver Dams, have large collections of Indian relics.

Lenoir"), after having been forced to eat while on the journey through the rough mountains the small pet dog which followed them. There is also another tradition that the American forces followed a party of marauding Cherokees to the rock cliff just above Pisgah Church in that locality, but retreated because the savages were too strong for them. These, however, are the only traditions diligent enquiry has revealed. There is, however, other evidence of forays across the Blue Ridge by Cherokees from their towns on the Little Tennessee.

Some Old Forts.—According to Archibald D. Murphey (Murphey Papers, Vol. II, pp. 385, 386), "there was a chain of forts from Black Water of Smith's River in Rockingham near to the Long Island of Holston: 1, the fort at Bethabara; 2, Fort Waddell at the Forks of the Yadkin; 3, Fort Dobbs on the Catawba; 4, Fort Chisholm on New River, and 5, Fort Stalnaker near the Crab Orchard." Just where the fort on New River was located it is now difficult to determine, though it was probably at Old Field or Three Forks, as they were on the road from Wilkesborough to Long Island in the Holston. The Crab Orchard was most likely two miles west of what is now called Roan Mountain, just in the edge of Tennessee. It is now only a flag station, however, the Gen. John Winder road from Roan Mountain station through Carver's gap, three miles southeast of the gap of the Yellow, starting from the latter station to the top of the Roan mountain, where, during the eighties, hundreds of visitors spent the "hay fever months" in comfort. The immense hotel there has been abandoned now, however, and the doors and windows are being carried away every day by marauders, the caretaker having left in 1914.

An Indian Incursion.—The same author says (p. 381, Vol. II) of other forts east of the Blue Ridge: "Forts were erected at Moravian Old Town (Bethabara) by the twelve Moravians first sent out to Wachovia, and by the settlers in the neighborhood two forts were erected: one in the town, including the church, and the other at the mill, half a mile distant. Into these forts the settlers in the neighborhood and even from the Mulberry Fields near Wilkesborough took refuge, about seventy families in all, and here they continued in fort, occasionally, until the general peace of 1763. The people generally went to their homes in the fall or early in the winter, and returned to the forts in the spring, the winter being too severe for the Indians to make such long expeditions for the purpose of mischief. The forts were never attacked. The Little Carpenter, then the chief of the tribe [Cherokees], came at the head of 300 or 400 Indians and killed several of the inhabitants. They [the Indians] remained for six weeks in the neighborhood and then returned. This was in the spring of 1755 or 1756."

Where They Crossed the Blue Ridge.—"They crossed the Blue Ridge at the head of the Yadkin and came down the valley of that river." They killed William Fish at the mouth of Fish's River. One Thompson, who was with him, was wounded with two arrows "while he and Fish were riding together through a canebrake." Thompson escaped and gave the alarm at Bethabara. The people hastened to the forts, two men, Barnett Lashley and one Robison, being killed near the block house the next morning. "Lashley's daughter, thirteen years old," went to her father's house to milk the cows. "Nine Indians pursued her, but she escaped by hiding in the canebrakes until after dark, when she went to the fort, and was not surprised to learn of her father's death." This was in March, 1755 or 1756. The Indians came from the Cherokee towns on the Little Tennessee River. None ever lived in Watauga or Ashe since the whites settled in the piedmont country. In 1759 or 1760 another raid was made to the mouth of Smith's River in Rockingham County (p. 383), where they killed Greer and Harry Hicks on Bean Island Creek, and carried Hick's wife and little son back to Tennessee with them. They, however, were recovered when Gen. Hugh Waddell marched to the Cherokee towns later on. A company of rangers was kept employed by the State, commanded by Anthony Hampton, father of Gen. Wade Hampton, of the Revolutionary War, and greatgrandfather of Gen. Wade Hampton, twice governor of South Carolina (p. 384). Daniel Boone belonged to this company and he buried Fish, who had been killed by Little Carpenter.

First White Settlers of Watauga.—A letter from Lafayette Tucker, of Ashland, Ashe County, states that the descendants of the original Lewis who settled in that neighborhood claim that he came as early as 1730. Thomas Hodges, the first, came during the Revolutionary War and settled in what is now called Hodges Gap, two miles west of Boone, and Samuel Hix and James D. Holtsclaw, his son-in-law, settled at or near Valle Crucis at that time or before. Some of the Norris family also came about that time, but which one or ones cannot be determined now. These were Tories. Ben Howard did not settle in this county, but remained at his home on the Yadkin, though he took refuge in the mountains around Boone during the Revolutionary War, and for ten years prior to 1769 herded cattle in the bottom lands around Boone. He built what is now known as the Boone cabin in front of the Boys' Dormitory of the Appalachian Training School, marked in 1912 by a monument erected by Col. W. L. Bryan.[3] A quarter of a mile north of the knob, looming above Boone village and known as Howard's Knob, is a shallow cave or cliff, called Howard's Rock House, in which he is said to have lived while hiding out from the Whigs. Howard remained loyal to the British crown till 1778, when he took the oath of allegiance. (Col. Rec. XXII, p. 172.) His daughter, Sally, was switched by the Whigs near her home on the Yadkin because she refused to tell where her father was. She afterwards married Jordan Councill, Sr., and settled at what is now Boone, where Jesse Robbins has built a house, called the Buck-Horn-Tree place. Bedent Baird moved to Valle Crucis some time after Samuel Hix went there, but Baird was a Whig. David Miller must have settled on Meat Camp early, for he went as a member of the legislature to Raleigh in 1810. Bedent Baird went to Raleigh as a member of the legislature in 1808. Nathan Horton, ancestor of the large and influential Horton family, was a member in 1800.

Linville Falls.[4]—One often wonders how these beautiful falls get their name of Linville. According to Archibald D. Murphey

[3] Colonel Bryan, however, thinks Howard did not build this cabin, as Jordan Councill the second, Howard's grandson, always called it Boone's cabin. Col. J. M. Isbell, now deceased, told the writer in May, 1909, that Burrell, an old African slave, told him that Howard used it for his herders.

[4] Some suppose that this river takes its name from the lin-tree, or as it is usually spelt, the lyn or linn, but the Linville family is the source of its name. This tree is what the Germans call the linden. It is scarce in these mountains now because of the fact that its branches are among the first to swell and bud in early spring, and great trees were cut wherever found in the forests in order that the cattle might eat the tender limbs.

(Murphey Papers, Vol. II, p. 386), "Two men named Linville from the forks of the Yadkin went to hunt on the Watauga River between 1760 and 1770. They employed John Williams, a lad of sixteen, to go with them, keep camp and cook for them. They were sleeping in the camp when the Indians came on them and killed the Linvilles. They shot Williams through the thigh," but he escaped and rode a horse from the mouth of the Watauga "to the Hollows in Surry" in five days. He recovered from his wound and became a man of influence. It is now almost certain that these falls have taken their name from these two men, who may have visited them before their last hunt and told the people of their location and beauty, for Dr. Draper (note, p. 183) records that the stream itself was named from the fact that in the "latter part of the summer of 1766 William Linville, his son and a young man had gone from the lower Yadkin to this river to hunt, where they were surprised by a party of Indians, the two Linvilles killed, the other person, though badly wounded, effecting his escape. The Linvilles were related to the famous Daniel Boone." It is a matter of record that a family by the name of Linvil—probably an economic way of spelling Linville—were members of Three Forks Baptist Church and lived on what is now known as Dog Skin Creek, or branch, but which stream used to be called Linville Creek. The membership of that church shows that Abraham, Catharine and Margaret Linvil were members between 1790 and 1800, while the minutes show that on the second Saturday in June, 1799, when the Three Forks Church were holding a meeting at Cove Creek, just prior to giving that community a church of its own, Abraham Linvil was received by experience, and in July following, at the same place, Catharine and Margaret Linvil also were so received. Several of the older residents of Dog Skin, Brushy Fork and Cove creeks confirm the reality of the residence of the Linville family in that community. In September, 1799, Brother Vanderpool's petition for a constitution at Cove Creek was granted, Catharine Linvil having been granted her letter of dismission the previous August.

CHAPTER III.
Watauga's First Visitor.

The Greed for Land.—All the land had been taken up in 1752 east of Anson county, which was then the westernmost county of the State. (Col. Rec. Vol. V, pp. 2, 3.) It is now a small county just north of the South Carolina line. "As early as 1754 vacant public lands, as we would call them now, could be found in large bodies only in the back settlements near the mountains, and settlers were coming in there in hundreds of wagons from the northwards . . . The immigrants were said to be very industrious people, who went at once into the cultivation of hemp, flax, corn and the breeding of horses and other stock." (Col. Rec. Vol. V, p. xxi.) The McCulloh lands, consisting of 1,200,000 acres, were granted on the 19th of May, 1737, upon condition that 6,000 Protestants should be settled thereon and four shillings quit rents should be paid for each 100 acres by the 14th of March, 1756. These lands were surveyed and located on the heads of the Pee Dee, Cape Fear and Neuse rivers in 1744, in tracts of 100,000 acres each. (Id. xxxii.)

Bishop Spangenberg's Visit.—"In August, 1752, Bishop Spangenberg and his party set out from Bethlehem, Pa., for Edenton, N. C., to locate lands bought the year before from the Earl of Granville for the Moravian settlement. Leaving Edenton about the middle of September, their route lay through Chowan, Bertie, Northampton, Edgecombe and Granville, to its western border near the Virginia line, and thence along the Indian Trading Path, as near as can now be ascertained, to the Catawba River, thence up that river to its upper waters, thence by mistake over the divide to New River, thence back to the head waters of the Yadkin and thence down the Yadkin to Muddy Creek, where, some ten miles from the river and from 'the upper Pennsylvania road,' they found some 100,000 acres of land in a body unoccupied, which they proceeded at once to take up. In January, 1753, they returned home, having surveyed 73,037 acres of land, to which were added 25,948 acres surveyed by Mr. Churton in the same tract, making in all 98,985 acres. A general deed for the whole tract was made on 7th of August, 1753." (Col. Rec. Vol. V, p. 1146.) The names of the members of Bishop Spangenberg's party were: August Gottlieb Spangenberg, Henry Antes, Jno. Merk, Herman Lash and Timothy Horsefield. Their guides were Henry Day, who lived in Granville county, near Mr. Salis'; Jno. Perkins, who lived on the Catawba River and was known as Andrew Lambert, a well known Scotchman, and Jno. Rhode, who lived about twenty miles from Captain Sennit on the Yadkin road.

The First Visitor to Watauga County.—So far as there is any authentic record to the contrary, Bishop Spangenberg and his party were the first visitors to Watauga county. Following is the record of this visit. (Col. Rec. Vol. IV, p. 10, etc.):

"December 3, 1752. From the camp on a river in an old Indian field, which is either the head or a branch of New River, which flows through North Carolina to Virginia and into the Mississippi River. Here we have at length arrived after a very toilsome journey over fearful mountains and dangerous cliffs. A hunter whom we had taken along to show us the way to the Yadkin, missed the right path, and we came into a region from which there was no outlet, except by climbing up an indescribably steep mountain. Part of the way we had to crawl on hands and feet; sometimes we had to take the baggage and saddles and the horses and drag them up the mountains (for the horses were in danger of falling down backward—as we had once had an experience), and sometimes we had to pull the horses up while they trembled and quivered like leaves.

"Arrived at the top at last, we saw hundreds of mountain peaks all around us, presenting a spectacle like ocean waves in a storm. We refreshed ourselves a little on the mountain top, and then began the descent, which was neither so steep nor as deep as before, and then we came to a stream of water. Oh, how refreshing this water was to us! We sought pasture for our horses and rode a long distance, until in the night, but found none but dry leaves. We could have wept with sympathy for the poor beasts. The night had already come over us, so we could but put up our tent. We camped under the trees and had a very quiet night. The next day we journeyed on; got into laurel bushes and beaver dams and had to cut our way through bushes, which fatigued our company very much.

"Then we changed our course—left the river and went up the mountain, where the Lord brought us to a delicious spring and good pasturage on a chestnut ridge. He sent us, also, at this juncture two deer, which were most acceptable additions to our larder. The next day we came to a creek so full of rocks that we could not possibly cross it, and on both sides were such precipitous banks that scarcely a man, and certainly no horse, could climb them. Here we took some refreshments, for we were weary. But our horses had nothing—absolutely nothing; this pained us inexpressibly. Directly came a' hunter who had climbed a mountain and had seen a large meadow. Thereupon we scrambled down to the water, dragged ourselves along the mountain and came before night into a large plain.

"This caused rejoicing for men and beasts. We pitched our tent, but scarcely had we finished when such a fierce wind storm burst upon us that we could scarcely protect ourselves against it. I cannot remember that I have ever in winter anywhere encountered so hard or so cold a wind. The ground was soon covered with snow ankle deep, and the water froze for us aside the fire. Our people became thoroughly disheartened. Our horses would certainly perish and we with them. The next day we had fine sunshine, and then warmer days, though the nights were 'horribly' cold. Then we went to examine the land. A large part of it is already cleared and there long grass abounds and this is all bottom.

"Three creeks flow together here and make a considerable river which flows into the Ohio, and thence into the Mississippi, according to the best knowledge of our hunters. In addition, there are almost countless springs and little runs of water which come from the mountains and flow through the country, making almost more meadow land than one could make use of. There is not a trace of reeds here, but so much grass land that Brother H. Antes thinks a man could make several hundred loads of hay of the wild grass, which would answer very well if only it be cut and cured at the proper time. There is land here suitable for wheat, corn, oats, barley, hemp, etc. Some of the land will probably be flooded when there is high water. There is a magnificent chestnut and pine forest near here. Whetstones and mill stones, which Brother Antes regards the best he has seen in North Carolina, are plenty. The soil is here mostly limestone and of a cold nature. The waters are all higher than on the east side of the Blue Ridge. We surveyed this land and took up 5,400 acres in our lines. We have a good many mountains, but they are very fertile and admit of cultivation. Some of them are already covered with wood and are easily accessible. Many hundred, yes, thousands—crab-apple trees grow here, which may be useful for vinegar. One of the creeks presents a number of admirable seats for milling purposes.

"This survey lies about fifteen miles from the Virginia line, as we saw the Meadow Mountain and judged it to be about twenty miles distant. This mountain lies five miles from the line between Virginia and North Carolina. In all probability this tract would make an admirable settlement for Christian Indians, like Gradenhutten in Pennsylvania. There is wood, mast, wild game, fish and a free range for hunting, and admirable land for corn, potatoes, etc. For stock raising, it is also incomparable." (From this favored spot they went through the mountains by Reddy's river to the Mulberry Fields and entered land in the neighborhood of what is now Wilkesborough and the Moravian Falls, which took its name from them.)

Where Was This Indian Old Field?—The question arises as to the location of the old Indian field at the head of a prong of New River, where 5,400 acres of land were surveyed and taken up. It will help one to determine this by ascertaining the route by which it had been reached. The entry in the diary immediately preceding that of December 3d, the date on which this spot was described, is November 29, 1752, and was written

A History of Watauga County 25

at the camp "at the upper fork of the second or middle river which flows into the Catawba not far from Quaker Meadows." This indicates that there are three streams which flow into the Catawba at or near Quaker Meadows. There is nothing in the diary to indicate which he calls the first of these "little rivers," but there is no doubt as to the third. It is the entry of November 24th "from the camp in the fork of the third river which empties into the Catawba near Quaker Meadows, about five miles from Table Mountain," now called Table Rock. That could be none other than the Linville River, and, as Johns River is the next below that, it follows that it must necessarily be the "second" or "middle little river." Following up Johns River, he had come on the 25th to the mouth of Wilson's Creek, where he took up 2,000 acres. This is the lower fork of Johns River. The upper fork of this river is at Globe, where the Gragg prong joins the main stream and where Carroll Moore had a mill years ago. It was at this upper fork of middle little river that the following description of the Globe was written:

"With respect to this locality where we are now encamped, one might call it a basin or kettle. It is a cove in the mountains, and is very rich soil. Two creeks, one larger than the other, flow through it. Various springs of very sweet water form lovely meadow lands. Mills may easily be built, as there is fall enough. Below the forks the stream becomes quite a large one. Of wood there is no lack. Our horses find abundant pasture among the buffalo haunts and tame grass among the springs, which they eat greedily, and certainly the settlers of this place can very soon make meadows if they wish. Not only is the land suitable for hemp, oats, barley, etc., but there is excellent wheat land here also. There is also abundance of stone, not on the land, but on the surrounding mountains . . . This survey would contain in itself all the requisites to make comfortable farms and homes for about ten couples."

While there, "A hunter whom we had taken along to show us the way to the Yadkin missed the right path, and we came into a region from which there was no outlet except by climbing up an indescribably steep mountain. Part of the way we had to crawl on hands and feet. Sometimes we had to take the baggage and saddles and the horses and drag them up the mountains . . . and sometimes we had to pull the horses up, while they trembled and quivered like leaves. Arrived at the top, we saw hundreds of mountain peaks all around us, presenting a spectacle like ocean waves in a storm." Could this have been any other place than Blowing Rock?

Their Route from Blowing Rock.—From this point they went down to a stream, where they got water, but no pasturage, and, consequently, they "continued on a long distance" the same day, camping, at last, after nightfall, beneath trees, but without having found pasturage for their horses. This stream must have been either Flannery's Fork—now Winkler's Mill Creek—or the middle fork of New River, but where they camped cannot be determined, though it seems certain that they camped there on the 30th of November. On the first of December they "journeyed on; got into laurel bushes and beaver dams" and had to "cut a way through the bushes," but, being fatigued with this task, they changed their course during this day and "left the river and went up the mountain, where the Lord brought us to a delicious spring and good pasturage on a chestnut ridge." The next day, December 2d, they came to a creek so "full of rocks that we could not possibly cross it, and on both sides were such precipitous banks that scarcely a man, and certainly no horse, could climb them." But there was no pasturage. It was then that "a hunter, who had climbed a mountain and had seen a large meadow," guided them "into a large plain," the spot described with so much particularity. But, on that night of December 2d, a terrible wind and snow storm assailed them and caused them to suffer very much, but it passed, and the next day, December 3d, they made their investigations and described the goodly land to which they thought they had been providentially guided.

Conflicting Claims.—Three forks of New River, near Boone, the old field at the mouth of Gap Creek, and Grassy Creek, in Ashe County, have characteristics similar to those described, but only Grassy Creek has the limestone formation. Unless the

COLONEL WILLIAM LEWIS BRYAN.
Historian and trail finder.

good Bishop knew where the Virginia-North Carolina line was, it is difficult to know why he stated that this spot was "about fifteen miles from the Virginia line," and the reason he gives for this conclusion is still more puzzling, as there is no mountain in Virginia five miles from the line now known as the Meadow Mountain, while the Bald, in Watauga County, is almost directly north of the three forks and apparently about twenty miles away. In reality, it is not over ten, but it is bald and looked like a meadow, at that time, with snow all over it. On the other hand, White Top is about twenty miles from Grassy Creek and four miles from Pond Mountain, the corner between North Carolina and Virginia and Tennessee. As this is bare around its crown of lashorns, it may be that it was called the Meadow Mountain at that time.

Col. W. L. Bryan's View.—After reading Bishop Spangenberg's account of his trip west of the Blue Ridge, Colonel Bryan, of Boone, thinks that the Bishop got to the stream that forms Cone's Lake, near Blowing Rock, and rode north along the top of Flat Top ridge "a long distance" and camped under trees November 30th. That on December 1st he got into laurel bushes and beaver dams on the middle fork of the south fork of New River, which he left and went back on Flat Top range to a spring, still known as Flat Top Spring, and now owned by Thomas Cannon, but which was first settled by Alex. Elrod sometime in the fifties. This spring is on land where there used to be large chestnut trees, and is the most noted spring near. On December 2d the Bishop was on either Winkler's Creek—formerly called Flannery's Fork—or on the middle fork, though the rocks and cliffs and precipices are more marked on Winkler's Creek than on middle fork, especially above or below what is now the Austin place, or where Moses Johnson has a mill. Colonel Bryan thinks that the mountain on which the hunter climbed was Flat Top peak, as from it the meadow in which the three forks join is plainly visible and the bald of Long Hope Mountain, lying almost due north, can be distinctly seen, and this was the mountain which the Bishop mistook for Meadow Mountain in Virginia, now known as White Top. Between the junction of the three creeks, forming Three Forks, and the first bend below that point there used to be a large crab orchard—say, about 1855—and on the new road from Boone to the new electric power dam on south fork whetstones can be found.

Captain W. H. Witherspoon, of Jefferson, thinks that the Meadow Mountain which Bishop Spangenberg saw was the White Top, and that the stream where three creeks meet were the Naked, Ravens and Beaver Creeks, flowing into the south fork of New River, four or five miles east of Jefferson. He thought the Moravians had owned land there; that there is a limestone formation there, and that grindstones are found near. This is about fifteen miles from the Virginia line. White Top is visible from this point, and is about twenty miles distant. Also that there is a pine and chestnut forest south of the south fork of New River and between that river and the Blue Ridge.

CHAPTER IV.
Daniel Boone.

No Direct Daniel Boone Descendants in North Carolina.—According to Thwaites and Bruce, the children of Daniel Boone were James, Israel, Susannah, Jemima, Lavinia, Rebecca, Daniel Morgan, John and Nathan. According to Bruce (p. 87), John was a mere infant in arms when his mother started with her family for Kentucky in September, 1773. John's middle name was Bryan, in honor of his mother's family name. Neither Jesse nor Jonathan Boone, who lived afterwards in Watauga County, were sons of Daniel Boone, nor was Anna, who married William Coffey. So far as the writer knows, there are no direct lineal descendants of Daniel Boone in North Carolina or Tennessee.

Boone's Watauga Relatives.—There is a tradition that Anna, a niece of Daniel Boone, was married in the log house which formerly stood on the site of the present residence of Joseph Hardin, a mile or more east of the town of Boone. Jesse Boone, a nephew of Daniel, certainly lived near the top of the Blue Ridge in a cabin which used to stand in a five-acre field four miles above Shull's Mills, to the right of the old Morganton road. The foundation stones of the old chimney and the spring are still pointed out. The land on which that cabin stood was entered by Jesse November 7, 1814, and the grant for it was made November 29, 1817, the tract containing 100 acres, and beginning on Jesse Coffey's corner. (Ashe County deed book F, p. 170.) By a deed dated July 8, 1823, Jesse Boone conveyed to Wm. and Alex. Elrod 350 acres on Flannery's Fork (now Winkler's Mill Creek) of New River, and on Roaring Branch, two miles from the town of Boone, Mr. J. Watts Farthing now owning the deed. Anna Boone, the wife of Wm. Coffey, and Jesse Boone's sister, talked with this Mr. Farthing about the year 1871 while he was building a house for her grandson,

Patrick Coffey, in Caldwell County. Hannah Boone, another sister of Jesse's, married Smith Coffey, the grandfather of the present Smith Coffey, of Kelsey post office. According to the family history of the Bryan family in the possession of Col. W. L. Bryan, of Boone, it was Morgan Bryan, and not Joseph, as all histories have it, who was the father of Rebecca Bryan, the wife of Daniel Boone. Bishop Spangenberg mentions the fact that Morgan Bryant had taken up land near the Mulberry Fields in 1752. (Col. Rec. Vol. V, p. 13.) According to the same family history, Morgan Bryan was the ancestor of Hon. W. J. Bryan, of Nebraska. Jesse, Anna and Hannah Boone were the children of Israel, a brother of Daniel Boone, not his own children. The same is true of Jonathan Boone, who sold to John Hardin, the grandfather of the present John and Joseph Hardin, of Boone, 245 acres on the 15th of September, 1821, for $600.00, the land being on what was then called Lynch's and Mill Creeks on the north side of New River, and adjoining the lands of Jesse Councill, and running to Shearer's Knob, near the town of Boone. (Ashe County deed book S, p. 509.)

Jesse and Jonathan Boone.—These were members of Three Forks Baptist Church, which speaks well for these relatives of the great Daniel, for he was a religious man himself, his simple creed being: "For my part I am as ignorant as a Child all the Relegan I have to love and feer god believe in Jesus Christ Do all the good to my neighbors and my Self that I can and Do as Little harm as I can help and trust on God's mercy for the rest and I believe god never made a man of my principel to be Lost . . ." What was the creed of Jesse and Jonathan does not appear beyond that implied by their membership of this church. But that each overstepped the rules of that organization is apparent, the minutes revealing the following facts: That in March, 1818, there was a report that Jonathan Boone was drinking too much, but that at the next meeting he came forward and made excuses and was forgiven. However, in May, 1819, there was another report against him for drinking and getting drunk and not attending at church meetings, the result of which was: "We consider him no more a member with us at

A History of Watauga County 31

this time." Before that, however, Jesse and his wife, "Saly," joined this church by letter, as did also his negro girl, Dina, and his brother, Jonathan. In November, 1815, Jonathan was chosen an elder, and in February, 1816, he was ordained by Reuben Coffey and Elijah Chambers. Jesse seems to have kept out of trouble for a long time, but in February, 1820, there was a report that he had requested Brother Jeremiah Green to remove a land-mark—laid over—not proved. But, in "Aprile, 1820, a grievance" took place between Jesse Boone, of this church, and Brother Jesse Coffey, of the Globe church, and James Gilbert and Elisha Chambers, from the Globe church, and Anthony Reese and Robert Shearer, from this church, were appointed to meet at Ben Green's on the second Saturday next ensuing "to set on the business." In June following this committee reported that Jesse Boone had given Brother Jesse Coffey "some cause to be hurt with him." In September, 1820, Jesse Boone and Jonathan Wilson said "the church was not in order," and withdrew therefrom. This did not increase Jesse's popularity with the members, and he was excluded by a committee consisting of John Holtsclaw, Abijah Fairchild, Valentine Reese and Jacob Baker; but, in October, 1821, the terms were fixed upon which he might return, these terms being that he should make acknowledgment for having withdrawn and saying that the church was out of order. At this meeting the church also took up the charges of Brother Wilson and Brother Boone against Brother Shearer, who acknowledged all that had any "wate" (weight) in them; but the church found that Brother Boone was at fault because he said he could "not see his range, and we put him under suspense till he can give satisfaction." Jesse Boone having been excluded "from amonks us," his loyal wife began to absent herself from the meetings, and, accordingly, in January, 1823, she was sent for to come to meetings; but as she refused from time to time to do so, "Sister Poly Green," the messenger sent to secure her attendance, reported that Sister Boone had said that the church would have to "cut her off" for the reason that when she (Sister Boone) had joined the church there were many members in it with whom "she could not fellowship," but that as her husband had joined, she had followed him into the fold. She was excommunicated as a "disorderly member and declared to the world our unfellowship to her." In November following a letter of dismission was given "old Sister Boone," who may have been Jesse's mother, as it was probably not his wife, who wrote from McMinn County, Tennessee, asking for a letter of dismission. But this the church decided to withhold till it got "satisfaction," meanwhile writing "a friendly letter to her." This concludes the residence of the Boones in that part of Ashe which is now Watauga.

Marking the Trail.—On the 23d day of October, 1913, the tablet which had been placed at Boone village as one of the markers on the trail of Daniel Boone through these mountains was unveiled. This is one of six similar markers of iron-bolted-to-stone boulders erected in Watauga County in October, 1913, by the Daughters of the American Revolution. The most eastern of these markers was placed at what is now called Cook's Gap, six miles east of the town of Boone; the next is at Three Forks Baptist Church, three miles from Boone; the third is in front of the court house at Boone; the fourth is in Hodges' Gap, two miles west of Boone; the fifth is at Grave Yard or Straddle Gap, four miles west of Boone, and the sixth and last is at Zionville, near the Tennessee line. The Edward Buncombe Chapter, D. A. R., of Asheville, was in charge of the unveiling of the marker at Boone. The exercises consisted of reading of the ritual of the D. A. R. society by the State Regent, Mrs. W. N. Reynolds, and responses by the audience, introductory remarks by Col. Edward F. Lovill, prayer by Rev. J. M. Downum, and addresses by John P. Arthur, Prof. B. B. Dougherty and E. S. Coffey, Esq., and songs by a choir, led by Prof. I. G. Greer. The county court house was filled. The veil was withdrawn from the marker, at the conclusion of these exercises, by the following little girls: Misses Margaret Beaufort Miller, a niece of Mrs. Lindsay Patterson; Margaret Linney, Alice Councill, Lucy Moretz and Nellie Coffey, all having Revolutionary ancestors. Short addresses were made in the open air to the people who had gathered around the marker by Mrs. W. N. Reynolds,

DANIEL BOONE CABIN MONUMENT

Erected by Colonel W. L. Bryan, October, 1912.

A History of Watauga County 33

State Regent; Mrs. Lindsay Patterson, chairman of the Committee on Boone's Trail, and Mrs. Theodore S. Morrison, Regent of the Edward Buncombe Chapter.

Boone's Cabin Monument.—In October, 1912, just one year previous to the unveiling of the markers along the Boone trail through Watauga, a monument of stone and concrete, far more imposing and substantial than any erected by the Daughters of the American Revolution, had been built on the identical spot on which once stood the log cabin in which Daniel Boone and his companions used to sleep when on their hunting trips through this section. This cabin has long since disappeared, but the stones of the chimney remained in their original bed or foundation till 1911, and were well known by all in the vicinity as having been a part of the old Boone cabin or hunting camp. It was open to all who cared to use it in the old days before the country was settled. Whether Boone actually built it is immaterial. He used it, as did all hunters and herders who found themselves in this locality near nightfall. Just south of it stands the Boys' Dormitory of the Appalachian Training School, a State-supported institution for the education of teachers. In this cabin Benjamin Howard and his herders used to keep their salt and cooking utensils when they visited this section to look after Howard's cattle, which he ranged in the upper valley of the New River. What is now the village or town of Boone stands near by, while over this picturesque little community looms Howard's Knob, 4,451 feet above the level of the sea. Tradition has identified this spot with both Boone and Howard as fully as tradition can identify any fact or place. The mountain was named for Howard and the cabin site for Boone. When Watauga was formed, the legislature called the county-seat Boone because of the location of Boone's cabin within a few hundred feet of its court house. It is, therefore, as certain as anything can be that this is the identical site of Boone's old hunting cabin or camp.[1]

Thanks to Its Builder.—In 1911 Col. William Lewis Bryan began work on this monument, alone and unaided by anyone.

---
[1] While excavating for the foundation of the monument a pair of rusted bullet-molds was found.

He was determined to mark the spot and to have Boone's trail through this county marked also before he died, for he was then well on past his seventieth birthday. The monument was completed in the fall of 1912, but there was no unveiling and no ceremony attending the consummation of Colonel Bryan's dream. When its erection was assured, several people contributed to its cost. When the trail was marked at Boone court house in October, 1913, E. S. Coffey, Esq., a distinguished member of the Boone bar, presented a resolution of thanks to Colonel Bryan for his services in having this spot so appropriately and permanently marked. The resolution was adopted by a rising vote of the large audience which packed the court house to the dome. The monument contains the following inscriptions, chiseled in white marble tablets let in on the western and eastern faces: On the west front: "Daniel Boone, Pioneer and Hunter; Born Feb. 11, 1735; Died Sep. 26, 1820." On the eastern face is the following: "W. L. Bryan, son of Battle and Rebecca Miller Bryan; Born Nov. 19, 1837; Built Daniel Boone Monument, Oct. 1912. Cost $203.37." Thwaite gives these dates as follows (p. 6): Born November 2, 1734; died September 21, 1820 (p. 338).

Information About the Trail.—This same gentleman, Colonel Bryan, supplied the information which led to the location of the trail through Watauga County. He is a direct lineal descendant of a brother of Rebecca Bryan, the wife of Daniel Boone, and has all his life preserved all the traditions he has heard concerning Boone, his wife, his trail and hunting experiences in this section. He originated and inspired the idea of marking the trail through this county, and it is not too much to say that if the Daughters of the American Revolution had not marked it, he would have done it himself. He did, in fact, help place every marker in the county. But, after all the statements of the people living along the trail had been taken down and deposited with the North Carolina Historical Commission, there was never any doubt that these patriotic ladies would see to it that the trail was suitably marked. They took those statements and placed them with Mrs. Lindsey Patterson, as chairman of the Daniel Boone

Trail Committee, and she, as in duty bound, collected all the other evidence available from all sources, and finally agreed to place the markers exactly where Colonel Bryan had recommended that they should be placed. It is not too much to say that but for Mrs. Patterson the trail would not have been marked till it was too late to locate it with any degree of certainty, and posterity will give both Colonel Bryan and Mrs. Patterson their full measure of gratitude for their patriotic work.

The Cumberland Gap Pedestal.—To Mrs. Patterson is also due much of the credit of interesting the chapters of her order to mark the trail in Virginia, Tennessee and Kentucky, till today the entire trail is permanently marked by the Daughters of the American Revolution of those several States. The whole work was crowned on the 30th of June, 1915, by unveiling at Cumberland Gap a substantial stone and concrete pedestal, bearing on its four faces tablets of the Daughters of the American Revolution of these several States. The North Carolina tablet was unveiled by Miss Elizabeth Cowles Finley, of Wilkesborough, N. C., a direct lineal descendant of John Finley; little Margaret Beaufort Miller, Wm. Hamilton Patterson, of Winston-Salem; Elinor Morrison Williamson, of Asheville; Elizabeth Sharp, of New York City, and Elizabeth Shelton, all with Revolutionary ancestors.

Boone's Trail in Other States.—The Tennessee part of the trail traverses the four eastern counties, Johnson, Carter, Washington and Sullivan . . . The first marker on Tennessee soil is at Trade, one mile from Zionville, N. C.; the second is at Shoun's, nine miles due north, through a wild and picturesque gorge along Roan Creek. The third is at Butler, southwest fourteen miles from Shoun's and at the junction of Roan Creek and Watauga River; the fourth is about nineteen miles due north at Elizabethton; the fifth, at Watauga, Carter County; the sixth is placed at Austin Springs, Washington County; the eighth is at Old Fort, south end of Long Island, Sullivan County; the ninth is at Kingsport, opposite the center of Long Island, where Boone gathered his men while the treaty of Sycamore Shoals was being negotiated, two miles from the Virginia line.

The Virginia markers are at Gate City, the county seat of Scott County, one mile from Moccasin Gap; the second marker in Virginia is at Clinchport; the third is at the Natural Tunnel; the fourth is at Duffield; the fifth is at Fort Scott; the sixth is at Jonesville, the county seat of Lee County; the seventh is at Boone Path postoffice. A marker has been placed at two graves between Ewing and Wheeler's Station in Lee County, as probably the place where James Boone, son of Daniel, was massacred by Indians. The eighth tablet was erected to mark the site of Fort Blackmore, where a colonial fort stood in Scott County, and where the Boone party rested in October, 1773, until March, 1775. Mrs. Robert Gray was in charge of marking the trail in Virginia, while Miss Mary Temple had charge of that in Tennessee. The first marker in Kentucky is at Indian Rock, a few miles from Cumberland Gap; the second is at the ford of the Cumberland River at Pineville; the third is at Flat Lick, in Knox County; the fourth is on the farm of C. V. Wilson, near Jarvis's Store; the fifth is on the Knox and Laurel County line, near Tuttle; the sixth is at Fairston; the seventh is a boulder with Boone's name on it, three miles and a half from East Bernstadt. This stone was placed in a churchyard and the marker placed on the stone. The eighth marker is in Rockcastle County near Livingston; the next is at Boone's Hollow, near Bruch Creek, then Roundstone Station and lastly Boone Gap. In Madison County, Berea is the first marker; then Estell Station, the site of Fort Estell, and the place where Boone's party was attacked by Indians and Captain Twitty killed. The last marker is at Boonesboro, there being fourteen markers in Kentucky, all placed under the direction of the State Chairman, Miss Erna Watson.

A National Spot and a National Hero.—Upon this pedestal in Cumberland Gap the Congress of these United States should soon erect a bronze statue of Daniel Boone, clad in hunting shirt, fringed leggings, moccasins, shot pouch, powder horn, hunting knife, tomahawk, etc., with the figure leaning slightly forward while peering from underneath the left hand toward the west, the right hand grasping the barrel of his long flint-lock Kentucky rifle, whose butt should be resting on the ground. The figure should have a coon-skin cap; for, although Thwaites says that Boone scorned the coon-skin cap of his time, it was none the less typical of the head-gear of all the pioneers of the time. Such a statue would identify this historic spot with this historic character and fix forever the costume, accoutrements and arms of the pioneers of America. It is the most significant and suggestive place in America; for, while Plymouth Rock was the landing place of the Puritans, Jamestown of the Cavaliers, Philadelphia of the Quakers and Charleston of the Huguenots, it was through Cumberland Gap that both Roundhead and Huguenot, Puritan and Cavalier passed with the sober Quaker on their way to the Golden West. Boone was their greatest and most typical leader and exemplar. He was colonel and private, physician and nurse, leader and follower, hunter and hunted, as occasion demanded, but he was never a self-seeker or a swindler. His fame is now monumental, for he had no land to sell, no private fortune to make, and his record is one of unsullied patriotism. He was simply a plain man, but a MAN all through. He was neither northerner nor southerner, easterner nor westerner, but all combined, and the men, women and children who followed the glowing footsteps of this backwoods lictor were the ancestors of those who people these United States today and make it the most enlightened, the most progressive and the most democratic nation in the world. That there should be no national monument to this man and on this spot seems incredible. The women and the States immediately concerned have done enough. They have marked every trail leading to this historic gateway. Let the nation act and place there a monument which shall be worthy of the place, the man, and the colossal events which they typify.

History Itself Had Lost the Trail.—For years it had been supposed that Boone's trail from Holman's Ford to Cumberland Gap, especially that part which led through the North Carolina mountains, had been lost beyond recovery. It was known in a vague way that the county-seat of Watauga County, North Carolina, had been named in honor of this pioneer, but the impression prevailed that the little town had no other claims to its name than the empty compliment implied. Bruce (p. 53) records the fact that, after setting out from Holman's Ford, Boone and his companions were "compelled to turn from the beaten road and follow winding, scarcely discernable Indian paths along the ridges and through the valleys of the North Carolina mountains. And history itself soon loses sight of them." All that Boone himself told his biographer, the grandiloquent John Filson, was that "after a long and fatiguing journey through a mountainous wilderness, in a *westward direction*," they came to the Red River in Kentucky. (Id. p. 54.) Bruce adds, what all historians agree upon, that "their route lay across the Blue Ridge and Stone and Iron Mountains, and through the valleys of the Holston and the Clinch into Powell's Valley, where they discovered Finley's promised trail through Cumberland Gap, and, following it, came at last into Kentucky." And this writer tells us something else that is not generally known, which is that each man of Boone's party on that first trip of 1769 rode a horse and led another, which was loaded down with supplies, camp equipment, ammunition, salt, etc. (p. 52). From which it is plain that they never touched the Watauga River or its waters, thus eliminating the Beaver Dams route completely.

Boone Was a Hunter, Not a Farmer.—Boone came to Holman's Ford about 1761. Bruce says he brought his wife back from Virginia at the conclusion of the Cherokee campaign—to use his exact words, "as soon as peace had been made sure"— which could not have been till after the tri-State campaign against the Cherokees of 1761 (p. 43). Now, Holman's Ford is scarcely thirty miles from Cook's Gap on the Blue Ridge, and we are told that Boone's Cherokee campaign "had reawakened all his latent passion for adventure, and, although he brought his family back to the Yadkin as soon as peace had been made sure, he found it impossible to resume the humdrum life of a stay-at-home farmer. More than ever he relied on the products of the chase to supply him with a livelihood, and, since game had become scarce in the Yadkin Valley, he of necessity, as well as choice, embarked on long and perilous hunting trips" (p. 46), sometimes taking with him his oldest son, James, then a boy of eight, though more frequently he journeyed in absolute solitude, pressing restlessly forward on the trail of the retreating beasts of prey. Always, he noted, this led him towards the west, and ere long there recurred to his mind the glowing tales he had heard from the trader Finley in the sad days of Braddock's campaign. It must be to Kentucky, the hunter's paradise, that the wild animals were fleeing. He had vowed to visit Kentucky. Now, if ever, while the Indians were at peace with the whites, was the time to fulfil that vow. But he soon discovered that it was no easy matter to reach Kentucky. In the autumn of 1767 he made his first start, accompanied by a friend named Hill, and, it is thought, by his brother, Squire Boone, named after their brave old father who had died two years before. The route followed was from the Yadkin to the valleys of the Holston and Clinch, and thence to the head waters of the west fork of the Big Sandy. Boone's plan was to strike the Ohio and follow it to the falls of which Finley had told him. But they had only touched the edge of eastern Kentucky when they were snow-bound and compelled to go into camp for the winter. Attempting to renew their journey in the spring, they found the country so impenetrable that they returned to the Yadkin. (Pp. 47, 48.)

Probability of the Re-location of the Trail.—From the foregoing, taken from Boone's latest biographer, it seems most probable that local tradition is correct, to the effect that Boone hunted all through the mountains of what is now Watauga County during several years preceding 1769, and knew the country thoroughly. In Foote's Notes we learn that what is now Watauga, with Alleghany County and that part of the territory still known as Ashe, was settled as early as 1755. Wheeler (p. 27, Vol. II) adopts this statement as true. Cook's Gap and Deep Gap were nearly due west from Holman's Ford. If Boone really followed "a westward direction" from Holman's Ford, he must have passed through one of these gaps, and, as Cook's Gap was the nearer, he probably went through that. If he followed the Holston and the Clinch into Powell's Valley, he must have followed the route marked by the Daughters of the American Revolution Society through Watauga County to Shoun's Cross Roads, and thence via Mountain City and down the Laurel fork of the Holston River. If the country was already settled when he passed through in May, 1769, the people who lived near his trail must have remembered it and told their children where it lay. There is great unanimity among their descendants that it followed the route chosen, except that some contend that it went through the Beaver Dams and across the Stair Gap[1] to Roan Creek in Tennessee. It may have done so, but the route over the mountains between Zionville, N. C., and Trade, Tenn., was much easier, as a buffalo trail led across it, and it was far more direct and practicable than that across Ward's Gap and the Stair Gap. When he got to Shoun's Cross Roads, he probably followed Laurel Creek, just as the little narrow gauge railroad does, over the divide to the Laurel fork of the Holston. He knew this route, having followed it twice before, once in 1761 to the Wolf Hills, and again in 1767 to the west fork of the Big Sandy. But he did not go by Butler, Tenn., wherever else he may have gone, unless he deliberately went many miles out of his westward way.

The Boone Tree Inscription.—The inscription on what is called the Boone Tree, nine miles north of Jonesboro, Tenn., and near Boone Creek, grows more and more apocryphal with time. It never had any sponsor, at best, except the statement of Chancellor John Allison's letter in Roosevelt's "Winning of the West." The picture of it in Thwaites' "Daniel Boone," opposite page 56, shows that the letters were then legible, which could not have been the case if they had been put there in 1760. Bruce, in a foot-note on page 46, says that such a tree stood there until recently, but he gives facts which show it could not have been put there by Boone, for he shows, on page 39, that in April, 1759, the Cherokees forced an entrance into the fertile Yadkin and Catawba valleys, destroyed crops, burned cabins, murdered settlers, and dragged their wives and children into a cruel captivity.[2] So sudden and severe was the blow that the stricken people had no opportunity to rally for an organized resistance,

---

[1] This is called Star Gap by some from particles of mica seen in the bottom of a spring at the base of the mountain, which shine "like stars." But others claim it is really the Stair gap, because a series of stair-like ledges of rock lead down from the gap on the western side. Bishop Asbury confirms this latter view. (Asbury's Journal, Vol. II, p. 189).

[2] The tree, a large leaning beech, was there in June, 1909, and is probably still flourishing, as is many another false witness.

much less undertake an offensive campaign. Abandoning their farms, they hastened for shelter to the strong stockade of Fort Dobbs, or to hurriedly constructed "houses of refuge," or else, if they could possibly find the means to do so, fled with all their belongings to the settlements in the tidewater country. This was the course followed by the Boones, or, at least, by Squire Boone, his son Daniel and their respective families. Squire, it is said, went to Maryland. Daniel took Rebecca and their infant children to eastern Virginia, where he found employment at his old occupation of wagoner.

Boone's First Trip Across the Mountains.—Although Bruce, following the phantom of the Boone Tree legend, states that "as early as 1760 (at the very time when he says elsewhere, page 41, that Boone was with Waddell at Fort Prince George or in Virginia) he (Boone) was threading his way through the Watauga wilds where the first settlement in Tennessee was afterwards established," he cites no supporting facts and is clearly contradicted by every known fact and circumstance of this period. But there is evidence that "in 1761, at the head of a hunting party which crossed the Alleghanies that year, came Daniel Boone from the Yadkin, in North Carolina, and traveled with them as low as the place where Abingdon now stands, and there left them." (Pp. 46, 47.) This visit to the site of the present Abingdon, Va., is still preserved there in a tradition which claims that wolves attacked Boone's party while in that vicinity, which fact gave rise to the first name of that locality, "The Wolf Hills." This trip of 1761 was probably Boone's first visit beyond the Blue Ridge. Bruce says (p. 47) that Boone was again in the Tennessee country three years later, or in 1764, and that in 1765 he went as far south as Florida, and would have settled there but for the influence of his wife, Rebecca Bryan, of the Yadkin Valley. If he had remained in Florida, Bruce adds "assuredly he would never have won fame as the great pilot of the early West." So that, after all, the world owes as much to Rebecca Bryan as to Boone himself!

At Fort Prince George in 1760.—Instead of being on Boone's Creek, carving his name and hunting experiences on trees in

1760, Daniel Boone was with Colonel Montgomery in June of that year, driving the Cherokees from the vicinity of Fort Prince George at the head of the Savannah; while, between then and 1759, he had been in eastern Virginia or about Fort Dobbs, for Bruce tells us (p. 40) that "so soon as he had satisfied himself that his little family would not be exposed to want [in eastern Virginia] he returned to the border, where he found thrilling events in progress. The Cherokees had laid desperate siege to Fort Dobbs, but had been gallantly beaten off by its garrison under command of Colonel Hugh Waddell, one of the foremost Indian fighters of his day. They had then renewed their depredations in small war-parties, ultimately gathering in force to attack Fort Prince George . . ." After driving the Cherokees away from that fort, Montgomery marched his force of 1,200 men, among whom was Daniel Boone, still under command of Waddell, across the mountains to the Little Tennessee, where they were ambushed and forced to retreat to Fort Prince George. From this place Montgomery marched his regulars back to Charleston, S. C., where he embarked with them for New York. "Once more the frontier of Georgia and the Carolinas lay at the mercy of the copper-colored foe (p. 42)." The garrison at Fort Loudon on the Little Tennessee having surrendered, they were allowed to start back for Fort Prince George, but were attacked and many killed, the others being taken prisoners. This forced the three States of Virginia, North and South Carolina to agree on a joint invasion of the Cherokee country, and by June, 1761, two armies were on the march to that country, in the second of which Boone found a place still under Hugh Waddell. This provides for all of Boone's time from 1759 till late in 1761, which shows that he could not have "cilled a bar" on that or any other tree near there in 1760. It is, however, very discouraging to note the persistence of falsehoods, if only they bear a flavor of romance about them.

Richard Henderson.—In a series of brilliant articles entitled, "Life and Times of Richard Henderson," which appeared in the *Charlotte Observer* in the spring of 1913, Dr. Archibald Henderson, then the president of the North Carolina Historical Commission, makes the following claims for his ancestor: "Richard Henderson was recognized everywhere throughout the colony as a fair and just judge," but, notwithstanding that, the Regulators, who fought the battle of Alamance, unjustifiably prevented him from holding court at Hillsboro, visited their "cowardly incendiary vengeance upon" him, and maliciously burnt his home and barn. Also, that but for his illness, Richard Henderson, who was a colonel as well as a judge, would have fought against these Regulators at the battle of Alamance. That the reason Judge Henderson would not comply with the demands of the Regulators at Hillsborough in 1770 was because he would not "yield to the dictates of lawless and incensed anarchists." Also, that "the sentiment which animated the mob at Hillsboro was not one of animosity against Judge Henderson personally," their objection to him having been, seemingly, to the system and that he had been appointed by Governor Tryon and not by the king himself. This, however, was not the case with Judge Maurice Moore, who, according to Dr. Henderson, "was roundly denounced by the Regulators as 'rascal, rogue, villain, scoundrel' and *other* unprintable terms . . ." We are also told that "the demands made upon Judge Henderson by the treasonable mob at Hillsborough, had he attempted to accede to them, which is inconceivable, would have resulted in a travesty of justice." But, even before this, and notwithstanding the proclamation of King George in 1763, forbidding the purchase or lease of lands by individuals from the Indians, Judge Henderson was contemplating the purchase of the very lands the six nations of northern Indians had, by treaty at Fort Stanwix, in 1768, sold to Great Britain. Washington himself was engaged in a like scheme in Virginia, we are told, but Dr. Henderson says: "It is no reflection upon the fame of George Washington to point out that, of the two, the service to the nation of Richard Henderson in promoting western colonization was vastly more generous in its nature and far-reaching in its results than the more selfish and personal aims of Wash-

---

4 The real leaders of the western expansion were James Robertson and the fourteen families from the present county of Wake, who, in 1770 or 1771, had been driven to seek new homes beyond the reach of the exactions of the British tax collectors.

ington." In order to carry out this plan, Judge Henderson in 1769 employed Daniel Boone at Salisbury, while Henderson was actually presiding over the court, to explore these western lands, Boone being "very poor and his desire to pay off his indebtedness to Henderson made him all the more willing to undertake the exhaustive tour of exploration in company with Finley and others."

The Patrick Henry of North Carolina.—Dr. Henderson continues: "From this time forward [the expiration of his term as judge] Richard Henderson, described as the 'Patrick Henry of North Carolina,' sheds the glamor of local fame and enters into national history as one of the most remarkable figures of his day, and indubitably the most remarkable constructive pioneer in the early history of the American people." Elsewhere Dr. Henderson speaks of his ancestor as the "Cecil Rhodes of America." Meantime, however, having returned from his two years' stay in Kentucky, we are told that Boone, grown impatient over the delay caused by Henderson's inability, for whatever reason, to further prosecute his plans at that time, recruited a body of settlers, and, on the 25th day of September, 1773, set out from Holman's Ford with eighteen men and some women and children, his own among the number, but his party was attacked by Indians and were forced to return. From which facts Dr. Henderson draws the following conclusions: "Boone lacked constructive leadership and executive genius.[5] He was a perfect instrument for executing the designs of others. It was not until the creative and executive brain of Richard Henderson was applied to the vast and daring project of western colonization that it was carried through to a successful termination."

The English Spy.—From Judge Clark's article (N. C. Booklet, January, 1904) it appears that Richard Henderson's mother was a Miss Williams, and that he studied law under his cousin, John Williams, who, according to Wheeler (Vol. I, p. 58), was whipped by the Regulators, and was, presumably, the son of his mother's brother, and afterwards married his step-daughter,

---

[5] Richard Henderson's "constructive" genius seems to have resulted in the destruction both of himself and all who put their trust in him, especially Daniel Boone, whom Henderson left penniless in the wilderness of Kentucky.

Elizabeth Keeling. Also, that "the British spy, Captain J. F. D. Smyth, in his 'Tour of America' (Vol. I, p. 124), [states that he] visited John Williams at his home in Granville about December, 1774, where he met Judge Henderson, whom he lauds as a genius, and says he did not know how to read and write till after he was grown. As Henderson became judge at the age of thirty-three, and as, besides, Smyth styles him Nathaniel Henderson and adds that Williams was said to be a mulatto and looked like one, no faith is to be given to any of his statements. He, however, says, probably with truth (p. 126), that Judge Henderson had made a secret purchase of territory from the Indians before his public treaty later on." This Captain Smyth might, therefore, be dismissed without notice if we did not find in Roosevelt (Vol. II, p. 46) that, while Henderson was at Boonesborough in 1775, "a British friend of his" (whom a foot-note shows to have been Smyth) visited him there, indicating his knowledge of Henderson's enterprise, and the further fact that Dr. Henderson himself, in his *Observer* articles of 1913, says: "It is interesting to note that just prior to the public announcement throughout the colony of this vast scheme of promotion [selling the Transylvania lands to unsuspecting frontiersmen], Dr. J. F. D. Smyth, the British emissary, met Richard Henderson at the home of Col. John Williams." But for the facts stated in Dr. Henderson's next succeeding article in the *Observer* on Richard Henderson, one might be tempted to connect this visit with the secret purchase of these lands above referred to, and to guess that it may have been a part of the policy of Great Britain at that time to get Americans interested in these Transylvania lands by low prices, etc., to such an extent that they would, rather than lose their holdings in them, adhere to the mother country in the impending struggle for independence, and thus form a rear-rank which should co-operate with the front rank of soldiers and loyalists in the Atlantic States. It would have been a most powerful and, possibly, successful bar to the achievement of our independence; for, then, Sevier and his Watauga men would have fought against and not for us. But this, probably, was not the scheme that British emissary or scout, as Dr. Henderson also terms him, had in mind, for Dr. Henderson continues: "Though not the first settlement in point of time, for Henderson found several temporarily occupied camps nearby on his arrival, Boonesborough was the first settlement of permanent vitality in the heart of the Kentucky country. No Henderson and there would have been no Boonesborough. No Boonesborough and the American colonies, now convulsed in a titanic struggle, might well have lost to Great Britain, at the close of the Revolution, the vast and fertile possessions of the transmontane wilderness."

Was Even the Treaty a Sham?—Assuming that Dr. Smyth, Richard Henderson's friend and guest, spoke *ex cathedra* when he declared that a secret treaty had been already effected before the 25th of March, 1775, which is the one that was published to the world as the real thing, what shall be thought of the following from Judge Clark's "Colony of Transylvania," before quoted?

"The treaty was debated, sentence by sentence, the Indians choosing their own interpreter. It was only signed after four days' minute discussion and after fierce opposition from a chief known as Dragging Canoe. The goods must have been put at a high valuation, for one brave, who received as his share only a shirt, contemptuously said he could secure more with his rifle in one day's hunting. On the other hand, the Indians received full value, for they had in truth no title to convey, and they plainly told Henderson he would have great trouble to obtain or hold possession on account of other tribes. The territory was not occupied and owned by the Cherokees, nor, indeed, by any tribe, but was a battle-field, where hostile bands met to fight out their quarrels." No wonder then that Dr. Henderson says that these fifty thousand dollars worth of goods were transported across the mountains of North Carolina in six wagons two years before, as other historians agree, any road was opened across them!

The Romantic Side of Boone.—Most of us love to think of him in the light of Kipling's "Explorer," animated by the "something-hidden-go-and-find-it" spirit, rather than as the servant of any man or set of men on his 1769 trip to Kentucky; and while it is no reflection on his character if he was actually employed to spy out the western lands, is it not a reflection upon Richard Henderson to say at this late day that he was actually scheming while a judge on the bench to violate the law?[6] As well as can be gathered from the *Charlotte Observer's* articles (Life and Times of Richard Henderson), it appears that when in 1773 Henderson's term as judge expired by limitation of the judiciary act of 1767, he learned "through the highest English legal authorities . . . according to the most recent legal decision rendered in England on the subject, purchases by individuals from Indian owners were legally valid. Without royal grant, Patrick Henry in Virginia, in 1774, was negotiating for the purchase of part of the very territory Henderson desired. Two years earlier the Watauga settlers leased from the Cherokees the lands upon which they resided—a preliminary to subsequent purchase . . . The opinion handed down by the Lord Chancellor and the attorney general cleared away the legal difficulties."[7] This, apparently, was Henderson's justification for proceeding to violate the Royal Proclamation against purchasing lands from the Indians. His plea that the Cherokees really owned the land seems to be based on the sole claim that "their title to the territory had been acknowledged by Great Britain through her Southern agent of Indian affairs, John Stuart, at the Treaty of Lochaben in 1770." Dr. Henderson told H. Addington Bruce that Judge Henderson, "in developing his Transylvania project and purchasing Kentucky from the Cherokees, acted under the advice of an eminent English jurist, 'in the closest confidence of the King,' and that he, therefore, regarded the enterprise as having the royal sanction," which view of the case Mr. Bruce understood Professor Henderson would soon set forth in a biography of Richard Henderson. That promise was

---

[6] There can be no doubt that Doctor Henderson claims that it was Judge Henderson's purpose to carry out this plan at the time he is said to have employed Boone in 1769; for he says Judge Henderson saw the significance of the Fort Stanwix treaty, and realized that the lands could be acquired only from the Indians, and that his plan was temporarily "frustrated by the exciting issues of the Regulation."

[7] How Richard Henderson, then a private citizen, could have had knowledge of these facts when the Governors of Virginia and North Carolina, the accredited representatives of Great Britain, were ignorant of them, is not explained. They were ignorant, for both denounced Henderson and his associates as land pirates, engaged in an unlawful undertaking.

evidently made during or prior to 1910, when Bruce's "Daniel Boone and the Wilderness Road" was first published. The proof is still not forthcoming because Dr. Henderson's book is not yet printed. When it is published to the world it will undoubtedly surprise many historians and others who consider themselves well informed about the history of these times and events. It is a great pity that it could not have been presented to the world a hundred years ago, before such erroneous ideas of Richard Henderson became prevalent. It is also hoped that it will then be shown that Richard Henderson and his associates devoted the 400,000 acres of land which they obtained from Virginia and North Carolina to the making whole of all those who bought land from them, including the 2,000 acres which Boone received as compensation for his services, but to which he got no valid title. What Virginia did for Boone is not pertinent. What did Richard Henderson do? When these matters shall have been cleared up, North Carolina, no doubt, will be proud to erect a monument to his memory.

Forehanded "for Once."—It seems that it was Boone's business to recruit a party of roadmakers before he started from Sycamore Shoals, with the understanding that they were to meet at Long Island, in the upper Holston, just south of the Virginia line. "Thirty guns" or riflemen were secured, who, according to Felix Walker, afterwards congressman from this State, explicitly agreed to put themselves "under the management and control of Colonel Boone, who was to be their pilot through the wilderness." Then, March 10, 1775, began the making of the Wilderness Road, by way of Clinch and Powell's Rivers and Cumberland Gap and Rock Castle River to the mouth of Beaver Creek where it empties into the Kentucky River.[8] This spot had been selected years before by Boone as an ideal place for the settlement, and there he began the choice of locations for himself and his companions. When Henderson and his larger party

---

[8] As the Sycamore Shoals Treaty was not ratified till the 25th of March, Boone's departure on the 10th for the purpose of cutting the Wilderness Road, shows a degree of cock-sureness on the part of Henderson & Co., which gives additional force to the suggestion of the spy, Smyth, that a secret treaty had been already concluded; which, if true, merely makes the public treaty a farce and fraud, and lends a still more sinister aspect to this affair.

A History of Watauga County 49

arrived three weeks later he made the "distinctly embarrassing discovery that Boone and his companions had preempted the choicest locations for themselves. Rather than have trouble, the tactful proprietor decided to leave them in undisturbed possession and appease the rest by locating the site of the capital of Transylvania, not in the sheltered level chosen by Boone, but some little distance from it, on a commanding elevation overlooking the Kentucky." (Bruce, p. 117.)

Henderson's and Washington's "Continental Vision."—Dr. Henderson does not hesitate to give Richard Henderson what he considers his true place in the westward movement: "Washington expressed the secret belief of the period when he hazarded the judgment that the royal proclamation of 1763 [forbidding individuals to buy or lease lands from the Indians] was a mere temporary expedient to quiet the minds of the Indians, and was not intended as a permanent bar to the Western civilization. Some years earlier, Richard Henderson, with the continental vision of Washington, had come to the conclusion that the unchartered West offered unlimited possibilities in the shape of reward to pioneering spirits, with a genuine constructive policy, willing to venture their all in vindication of their faith. George Washington, acquiring vast tracts of Western land by secret purchase, indirectly stimulated the powerful army that was carrying the broad-axe westward; Richard Henderson, with a large-visioned constructive policy of public promotion, colonization and settlement for the virgin West, conferred untold benefits upon the nation at large by his resolution, aggressiveness and daring. Washington and Henderson were factors of crucial importance in the settlement of the West and the advance of the pioneer army into the wilderness of Tennessee, Kentucky and Ohio." Elsewhere (Neale's Monthly, p. 211) Dr. Henderson says: "George Washington and Richard Henderson, as landlords, were vital factors in the development of the West."

Dr. Henderson's Original Discoveries.—Dr. Henderson promises to furnish not only documentary evidence to support all these statements, but photographic fac-similes in proof of the claim that Boone was indebted to Richard Henderson for legal services[9] for a number of years prior to 1769, which had not been paid off prior to that date. Also, that the merchandise which was to be paid for the title of the Cherokees to the Transylvania lands was transported by Richard Henderson, *not* accompanied by Boone, "in six wagon loads of goods from Hillsboro, N. C. (really from Fayetteville—then Cross Creek), to Sycamore Shoals, by wagon over the North Carolina mountains" by a route "discovered through researches made for me among old maps, showing wagon roads of North Carolina, dating as far back as 1770. The stages of the route I hope to give in my published book when it appears. Henderson also carried the goods from Sycamore Shoals to Martin's Station in Powell's Valley by wagon also; from there to the future site of Boonesboro the goods were transported by pack-horses."[10] Dr. Henderson very properly "scrupulously omitted citation in my 'Life and Times of Richard Henderson' to authorities other than known or accessible books, such as the North Carolina Colonial Records, etc.," as upon these new authorities rests his "claim to original research and discovery."

Misconceptions About Colonel Henderson.—Assuming that Dr. Henderson shall be able to establish these facts, which is not questioned, there is no one who has suffered more at the hands of historians than his ancestor, Richard Henderson. For the general impression of him is that he and his father had been part and parcel of the office-holding oligarchy or "ring" that dominated county government under Governor Tryon, Henderson's father having been sheriff and himself under-sheriff; also, that, as a judge, Richard Henderson was personally obnoxious to the Regulators because he at least had not prevented "the legal tyrannies and alleged injustices of county officials," and was "so terrorized that during the night he mounted a fast horse and galloped out of town,"[11]

---

[9] This must have been a large fee that required Boone to go in debt to get supplies for his journey (Bruce, p. 62) and to spend two years of his life in the wilderness.

[10] From Doctor Henderson's letter to J. P. A., June 11, 1913. The new material, discovered by Doctor Henderson, after laborious investigation extending over years, "was not accessible to or even known to R. G. Thwaites, biographer of Daniel Boone, or to H. Addington Bruce, author of "Daniel Boone and the Wilderness Road."

[11] Bruce, p. 97.

when in the fall of 1770, while hearing cases at Hillsborough, his court room was invaded by a mob and minor officials were beaten. People generally believe that the grievances of the Regulators were genuine wrongs from which they, at great risk, were seeking to escape; that these Regulators were not anarchists,[12] but American patriots making the first stand for American liberty, bravely and openly and against great odds. They do not believe that Judge Henderson refused the demands of these oppressed people out of any high regard for the law, but because he wished to carry out the mandates of Tryon, by whom he had been appointed to the bench. Nevertheless, they were willing to believe that he was incapable of deliberately planning to violate the proclamation of 1763 against the purchase of lands from the Indians by individuals while he himself was presiding over a court of justice and drawing the pay of the colony or of the Crown of England for discharging the duties of a judge of the Superior Court of the colony of North Carolina. They supposed that Daniel Boone went to Kentucky in May, 1769, not because he had been paid to aid Henderson to violate the law he was sworn to uphold, but because John Finley had spent the winter before at Holman's Ford and had persuaded Boone that he could guide him to Kentucky by crossing the mountains to the westward. It was the general belief, also, that it was not in consequence of the Treaty of Fort Stanwix of 1768, but of the victory over the northwestern Indians at the Great Kanawha, September 10, 1774, which prompted Henderson and Hart to visit the Otari towns the following October for the purpose of getting from the Cherokees what was a worthless paper title to the Transylvania lands, and that Henderson especially, who was a lawyer, knew that "neither the British government nor the authorities of Virginia or North Carolina would recognize the authority" of the Cherokees to convey title thereto, and that instead of being a worthy scheme of national expansion, it was really a "bold, audacious dash for fortune." (Walter Clark in North Carolina Booklet, January, 1904, p. 7.) And, unfortunately, it is also the

---

[12] It seems strange to have a North Carolinian write in such terms of the Regulators, whom we have been taught to revere as heroes and patriots.

general belief that Henderson at least cared little for the ruin that he must have known would follow the failure of his title to the lands which he was trying to sell to the untaught pioneers."[*] For he speaks of them in his journal as "a set of scoundrels who scarcely believed in God or feared the devil." Certain it is that when all hope of profit disappeared, so did also Henderson and his associates, leaving Daniel Boone, with his helpless family, in the wilderness with a worthless title to two thousand acres of land, which had been his sole compensation for risking his life and cutting out the Wilderness Road for Henderson and his followers to travel over. And the claim upon which so much stress is laid, that Henderson shared "with Washington the vision of Western expansion," is made ridiculous when the Watauga Settlement of 1769 is remembered and it is recalled that Harrodsburg, only thirty miles southwest from Boonesboro, had been settled in 1774; also, that two weeks before Boone's arrival at Boonesborough (April 1, 1775) this same Harrodsburg, after having been abandoned in 1774, had been re-occupied by as hardy pioneers as any who came with Boone, and that about the same time two other settlements nearby were made at Boiling Springs and Logan's Station. Roosevelt says that with the failure of his title in both Virginia and North Carolina, "Henderson, after the collapse of his colony, drifts out of history." (Winning of the West, Vol. II, p. 64.) To some people of simple minds it might almost seem that it would have been better that Richard Henderson should be allowed to *remain* out of history, unless, indeed, it can be shown that he restored to poor, deluded Daniel Boone the 2,000 acres he had been duped into accepting as his share of the enterprise, for both Virginia and North Carolina together donated outright to Henderson and company 400,000 acres of land, out of which it does seem that Boone should have been made whole. Daniel Boone, penniless, remained in the wilderness and was the real leader of the great western expansion.

---

[13] A largely signed memorial was sent to the Virginia Convention in 1776 by these settlers, from which it appears that the price of the land had been advanced from twenty to fifty shillings a hundred acres, all of which was to be paid down; that 70,000 acres at the Falls of the Ohio (Louisville) had been reserved to the proprietors and their friends. It implored His Majesty, the King, to vindicate his title from the Six Nations; and asked to be taken under the protection of Virginia.

CHAPTER V.
During the Revolution.

Backwoods Tories.—Roosevelt (Vol. II, p. 70) says: "The backwoodsmen, the men of the up-country, were, as a whole, ardent adherents of the patriotic or American side. Yet there were among them many loyalists or Tories, and these Tories included in their ranks much the greatest portion of the vicious and disorderly elements. This was the direct reverse of what obtained along portions of the seaboard, where large numbers of the peaceable and well-to-do people stood loyally by the king. In the up-country, however, the Presbyterian Irish, with their fellows of Calvinistic stock and faith, formed the back-bone of the moral and order-loving element, and the Presbyterian Irish were almost to a man staunch and furious upholders of the Continental Congress . . . The Tories were obnoxious under two heads (pp. 72, 73); they were allies of a tyrant who lived beyond the sea, and they were the friends of anarchy at home. They were felt by the frontiersmen to be criminals rather than ordinary foes. They included in their ranks the mass of men who had been guilty of the two worst frontier crimes—horse-stealing and murder . . . and the courts sometimes executed summary justice on Tory, desperado and stock-thief, holding each as having forfeited his life."

Samuel Bright, Loyalist.—We should not be surprised, therefore, to learn that there is a tradition still preserved at Ingalls and Altamont post offices, in what is now Avery County, but which formerly was a part of Watauga, that Samuel Bright, along whose "trace," according to Draper (p. 177), Sevier's men passed on their way to King's Mountain, September 27-28, 1780, was a Tory of the Tories, and while he might have claimed the Crab Orchard,[1] a mile below the confluence of the Roaring Creek

---
[1] Owing to the several counties in which this land has been it is impossible to get record evidence of Bright's ownership, if he ever held title. Local tradition claims that the Crab Orchard was embraced in both the Cathcart and Waight-

with the North Toe River, his home was two miles northeast of Alta Pass, where the C. C. & O. R. R. crosses the Blue Ridge, and stood near what is now a tram-road for lumber hauling. Joe Lovin now lives one-fourth of a mile southwest from the old Bright chimney mounds, which are still distinguishable. Indeed, Robert Lee Wiseman, a direct descendant of William Wiseman, the first settler of that locality, has the original grant and knows the location of the old Bright place not only from tradition, but from having surveyed the lands originally granted to Samuel Bright. One of these grants is numbered 172 and calls for 360 acres in Burke County. The grant is dated March 5, 1780, though the land was processioned June 28, 1774, by Will Davenport, who owned "the noted spring on the Davenport place, since Tate's, and now known as the Childs place," spoken of by Dr. Draper (p. 178). The grant is registered in book No. 3 of Burke County, and was signed by J. C. Caswell, Governor, and countersigned by "In Franck, Pri. Sec." The land was surveyed by C. W. Beekman, county surveyor of Burke, August 10, 1778, while the chain carriers were Thomas White, afterwards Major White, of McDowell's regiment, and James Taylor White. The land granted lies on both sides of Toe River, and a part of it is now owned by W. H. Ollis as part of his home tract, and the balance by J. L. Wiseman. The seal attached is of chalk or plaster of Paris and bees wax, one-quarter of an inch thick and three inches in diameter. On one side is a female figure with staff and liberty cap in one hand and an open scroll in the other. The obverse face contains a female figure, a cow and a tree, while beneath these figures are "Independence MDCCLXXVI." This seal is not impressed upon the paper, but is detached from it, being connected with it by a double tape ribbon. Around the border is what appears to be *E Pluribus Unum* and *Sua Si Bona*, though a defacement of the wax renders some of the letters uncertain. Tradition is here borne out by the State and Colonial Records in Volume XXII (p. 506), which records that Samuel

---

still Avery grants, and that the representatives of these two claimants compromised the matter by Avery paying John Brown, Cathcart's representative, 12½ cts. per acre for the tract, and taking possession. John Ollis, father of W. H. Ollis, helped to clear it "back in the Forties."

Bright, after having witnessed the trial and conviction at Salisbury before Judge Samuel Spencer, March 6, 1777, of one William Anderson, of having stolen from one Jowe, and the branding of the said Anderson on the ball of the thumb of his left hand with the letter T, signifying thief, was brought before the same stern judge to answer the charge of having committed sundry misdemeanors against the State by encouraging the enemies of said State. But Samuel evidently knew on which side his bread was buttered, and took the benefit of the governor's proclamation, promising amnesty to all who would come in and take the oath of loyalty to the patriot cause, and got off scottfree.

Thirty-Nine Lashes on the Bare Back.—Now William Wiseman, who had been born in London, England, on St. James Street, Clarkville or Clarkwell Park, February 2, 1741, and apprenticed to a joiner, fearing service in the British army, stowed himself away on a merchant vessel in 1761, and, after lying concealed three days and nights, revealed himself to the captain, and upon arrival at a port in Connecticut was sold to pay his passage money; was bid in by a master joiner, who gave him his liberty and a box of tools upon proof that Wiseman could make as good a chest as he could himself. "What those old fellows were after," said an old citizen in speaking of Wiseman, "was freedom;" and as there was much religious persecution in the northern colonies about that time, William Wiseman took his tools aboard a sailing vessel and finally settled at the place at which W. H. Ollis now lives. Here he married a Davenport, sister, no doubt, to the Davenport of Davenport Place spoken of by Dr. Draper. He was the very first settler in that locality, and became a justice of the peace. To him was brought one day the wife of Samuel Bright, charged with having stolen a bolt of cloth from a traveling peddler. She was convicted by him, and as the peddler insisted that he should pass sentence upon her, he did so, and as there was no sheriff to inflict it, he enforced it himself— "thirty-nine lashes, well laid on."

Patriots Feared the Indians.—Now, the Cherokees had ceded the lands on the Watauga and its waters to the Watauga settlers, but Roosevelt tells us (Vol. II, p. 74) that they "still continued jealous of them," and that the Cherokees "promptly took up the tomahawk at the bidding of the British" (p. 75). As Bright and Wiseman lived south of the ridge which divided the Toe from the Watauga, their homes were within Indian territory at this time. Therefore, Magistrate Wiseman had been afraid to lay the lash on Mrs. Bright's bare back during the absence of her husband, who was on a hunting expedition at that time, lest upon his return he should incite the Indians to burn his cabin and scalp him in the bargain. But he was worse afraid of the peddler, who threatened to report him to the great judge, Samuel Spencer, at Salisbury, if he did not carry out the sentence he had himself imposed. He was, therefore, much perturbed till Bright and a family named Grant left the country, passing over the Bright Trace and by the Bright Spring on the Bald place of the Yellow into Tennessee. Aunt Jemima English, who was born Wiseman, daughter of the original William, justice of the peace, etc., May 6, 1804, but lived to a green old age, not only preserved these traditions, which she had at first had from her father, but she believed that the Grant family which left with the Brights were the family from whom Gen. U. S. Grant, of the U. S. army, sprang.

Bright's Spring and the Shelving Rock.—We must not forget that "the gap between the Yellow Mountain on the north and the Roan Mountain on the south" (Draper, p. 177) was once a part of Watauga County (see chapter X on Boundary Lines). It was here that two of Sevier's men, James Crawford and Samuel Chambers, deserted and went ahead to tell Ferguson of Sevier's approach. It was here also, according to local tradition in the mouth of everyone in May, 1915, that one of Sevier's men froze to death and was buried in the edge of the bald of the Yellow. Draper, however, says nothing of such an occurrence, though he does say (p. 177) that the "sides and top of the mountain were covered with snow, shoe-mouth deep, and on the summit there were about one hundred acres of beautiful table-land, in which a spring issued [Bright's], ran through it and over into the Watauga." This latter fact, not generally known, coupled with the still more important fact that all of Watauga County on the waters of Watauga River was once a part of Washington County—formerly Washington District—of the famous and immortal Old Watauga Settlement of Sevier, Robertson and Tipton, may well "stir a fever in the blood of age and make the infant's sinews strong as steel." For Col. Henry H. Farthing, of Timbered Ridge of the Beaver Dams, and Col. Joseph C. Shull, of Shull's Mills, have each a grant from the State to lands in their neighborhood, described as being in Washington County, North Carolina. Shull's grant is numbered 841 to Charles Asher for 300 acres in the county of Washington on both sides of Watauga River, and dated 11th July, 1788. It is signed by Samuel Johnston, Governor, and countersigned by Jas. Glasgow, Secretary of State. On it is a certificate from the county register, Samuel Greer, dated May 28, 1819, that it is a true copy from the records. The Farthing grant is to John Carter for 300 acres in the county of Washington, beginning on two white oaks standing near the path that leads across Stone Mountain to Cove Creek and on the west side of the Beaver Dam Creek. It is dated November 17, 1790, and is numbered 947, and recorded in the office of the Secretary's office, page 234. For, when the Watauga settlers set up house-keeping on their own hook, they had named the territory they had acquired from the Indians by lease and purchase Washington District, and in 1777, before they tried to secede, calling the new State Franklin, North Carolina converted Washington District into Washington County. (Laws 1777, ch. 126.) Dr. Draper continues: "Thence from Talbot's Mill to its head, where they bore somewhat to the left, crossing Little Doe River, reaching the noted 'Resting Place,' at the Shelving Rock, about a mile beyond the Crab Orchard, where, after a march of about twenty miles that day, they took up their camp for the night. Big Doe River, a bold and limpid mountain stream, *flowing hard by,* afforded the campers, their horses and beef cattle abundance of pure and refreshing water. Here a man of the name of Miller resided who shod several of the horses of the party."

Even Homer and Dr. Draper Sometimes Nod.—Notwithstanding all the pains Dr. Draper took to get the facts for his excellent "Kings Mountain and Its Heroes," his failure to visit the actual scenes along the route of the King's Mountain men is responsible for the error in the statement that the Big Doe River, *flowing hard by,* afforded the campers, etc., abundance of pure and refreshing water." The nearest point from the Shelving Rock to the Big Doe River is at least one mile and a half where that stream flows through the Crab Orchard, and the route to it is over a rather high ridge and by a rough trail. But the Little Doe, with enough pure and refreshing water for all the men and stock then in what is now Tennessee, flows within one hundred yards of the Shelving Rock, on which there has been placed a bronze tablet about two feet square with the following inscription:

First Night's
Encampment of
KING'S MOUNTAIN MEN
SEPTEMBER 26, 1780.

———

They Trusted in God and
Kept Their Powder Dry.

———

Placed by John Sevier Chapter, D. A. R.,
1910.

A Busy Forge.—But he was right in stating that a man of the name of Miller resided at the Shelving Rock and shod their horses, for Squire W. H. Ollis, of Ingalls, N. C., furnished this identical information to the Historical Society of New Jersey in 1872, saying that "Absalom Miller told me that his father lived at Shelving Rock in September, 1780, and shod the horses of some of the King's Mountain men while they camped under the Shelving Rock." As most of Sevier's men were practical blacksmiths, we may well imagine that Johnson's forge was a busy place early on the morning of September 27, 1780, and well up into that day, and that, while some were shoeing the horses, others were busy at bellows and anvil, hammering out horseshoes and nails, thus leaving none of the available tools idle for a moment. For the way up what is now called Hampton's Creek to the gap of the Yellow was even steeper in those days than it is now, with rocks galore to wrench the shoes from the best shod horses. Dr. Draper tells us that on this day the men, weary of driving the herd of cattle with which they had started, killed such as were necessary for a temporary supply of meat and abandoned the rest, thus considerably delaying the march of the day, "following the well-known Bright's Trace, through a gap between the Yellow Mountain on the north and the Roan Mountain on the south. The ascent was not very difficult along a common foot-path." But, for three miles at least, it was *very* steep and rocky, as the same old Trace, now used as a "near cut," still bears witness most eloquently. Arrived at the gap, now grown up with trees, they had a parade on the Yellow and fired off their short Deckard rifles "for fun." This was but a short day's march—seven miles—making twenty-seven miles from Sycamore Shoals in two days. Here, at a conference of the officers, Colonel Campbell was appointed to the chief command. (Note on page 178.) On the 28th they descended Roaring Creek by Bright's Trace, then following the bank of the stream very much as does the rude and rough wagon road of today, to its mouth in North Toe River, one mile from the North Carolina Crab Orchard, or Avery's Quarter, as it is now known. Here, at the mouth of Roaring Creek, lives Tilmon McCurry, who thinks that the Samuel Chambers who had deserted the night before, finally settled in Buncombe County, North Carolina, but what became of James Crawford seems not to be known. Only a short distance from the mouth of Roaring Creek is that of Powder Mill Creek, a short distance up which latter stream Dorry and Loddy Oaks made enough powder in the dim and distant past with which to buy a negro man, and, no doubt, obtained the bounty referred to in Wheeler's History of North Carolina (Vol. II, p. 52). From the mouth of Roaring Creek, however, Bright's Trace is now no longer followed, the Cranberry and Spruce Pine Road having usurped its usefulness, but it can be traced still as it takes its almost straight course to the crossing of Toe River, almost a mile above Spruce Pine, at which place a small monument marks Sevier's route.

They Did Not Camp on the Yellow.—Bright's Spring in North Carolina is a mile north of the gap between the Yellow and the Roan. It is in a field that in 1780 contained a bald place of about 100 acres, though the Humps, lying near, have since been cleared and the bald place is now much larger than it was then. There is also another spring on the Tennessee side, near the gap, called also Bright's Spring. It is true the ground is said to have been covered with snow when they camped there, but that 1,040 men [2] and horses could have supplied themselves with water on the top of that mountain would have been an impossibility. Dr. Draper says in unmistakable language that they "passed on a couple of miles, descending the eastern slope of the mountains into Elk Hollow—a slight depression between the Yellow and Roan Mountains, rather than a gap—and here at a fine spring flowing into Roaring Creek they took up their camp for the night" (p. 178). Yet, the general impression is that these men camped on the Yellow Mountain that night!

Oliver Cromwell's Descendant.—Dr. Draper records the fact that Col. Benjamin Cleveland claimed direct descent from Oliver Cromwell, from a liaison with Elizabeth Cleveland, "a beauty of the time of Charles the First" (pp. 425, 426), but this story is doubted by the eminent historian. Cleveland was mistaken in acting as though cruelty was Cromwell's chief virtue.

Cleveland's Capture at Old Fields.—Dr. Draper says that this doughty warrior was captured at this place, which he is said to have owned, on the 22d day of April, 1781, while on a visit to his tenant, Jesse Duncan, at the lower end of the Old Fields— probably the very spot at which the late Nathan Waugh lived and died. Captain William Riddle was the leader of the gang which captured him, they having stolen his horses from Duncan's barn the night before and led them up south fork of New River

---

[2] The force which started from Sycamore Shoals consisted of: Colonel Campbell's men, 200; Colonel Shelby's, 240 men; Lieutenant-Colonel Sevier's, 240 men; McDowell's party, who had retreated from Cowen's Ford, 160 men; (Draper, p. 149); Arthur Campbell, with 200 men (Id. p. 175), making in all 1,040 men.

Photo. by Vannoy.

THE OLD PERKINS PLACE.
Where Cleveland was captured.

into a laurel thicket just above the house then occupied by Joseph and Timothy Perkins, about one mile distant. There were six or eight men with Riddle, and when they reached Benjamin Cutbirth's home the day before, four miles above Duncan's home, and failed to get any information from him, they abused him shamefully and left him under guard. Cleveland ran into the ambush prepared for him and was captured and taken into the Perkins house, which stood on the site of the house in which Nathan Waugh's son, Charles, now resides. The illustration shows the present house and apple tree in its front under which it is said Cleveland was sitting when captured. Into this house of the Perkinses, Zachariah Wells followed Cleveland and attempted to shoot him, but that brave(?) man seized Abigail Walters, who was present, and kept her between him and his would-be assassin (p. 440). Cleveland was then taken up New River to the mouth of Elk Creek, and thence to "what has since been known as Riddle's Knob." (See illustration.) This is some fourteen miles from Old Fields and in Watauga County. Here they camped for the night (p. 441). But they had been followed by young Daniel Cutbirth and a youth named Walters,* Jesse Duncan, John Shirley, William Calloway, Samuel McQueen and Benjamin Greer, while Joseph Calloway mounted a horse and hastened to notify Captain Robert Cleveland, Ben's brother, on Lewis' Fork of the Yadkin. Five of these in advance of Robert's party fired on Riddle's gang at the Wolf's Den early the next morning, and Cleveland dropped behind the log on which he had been sitting slowly writing passes for the Tories, fearing that when he should finish doing so he would be killed. Only Wells was wounded, the rest escaping, including Riddle's wife. As it was thought that Wells would die from his wound, he was left on the ground to meet his fate alone. But he survived. About 1857 Micajah Tugman found a curious knife in the Wolf's Den, supposed to have been Riddle's.

Greer's Hint.—This "hint" is thus accounted for by Dr. Draper in a note at foot of page 442: "Greer was one of

---

* These boys had planned to rescue Cleveland, but they thought better of it when Riddle's force came in sight.

Cleveland's heroes. One of his fellow soldiers stole his tobacco from him, when he threatened he would whip him for it as soon as he should put his eyes on him. Cleveland expostulated with Greer, telling him his men ought to fight the enemy and not each other. 'I'll give him a hint of it, anyway,' said Greer, and when he met the tobacco pilferer he knocked him down. Greer's hint was long a by-word in all that region.—Col. W. W. Lenoir." It is claimed that Greer killed Colonel Ferguson at King's Mountain. If so, Greer's hints were rather rough.

Greer Gets Another Kind of Hint.—Just twenty years after the memorable capture and rescue of Cleveland by Greer, to wit: on the first Saturday of April, 1801, the Three Forks Baptist Church, of which he was a member, gave Cleveland's "hero" a "hint" to appear at the next meeting of that organization and answer to the charge—not of having looked upon the wine cup when it was red—but of having partaken of the apple juice after it had been distilled. Brother and Sister Wilcoxen were cited to appear as witnesses against him. But Ben did not take the hint, neither did he continue his membership with that church!

The Wolf's Den Tradition.—There is still a tradition in the neighborhood of the Wolf's Den that Ben Greer killed or wounded Riddle at that place soon after Cleveland's rescue, one version saying that Riddle was only wounded and then taken to Wilkes and hanged. Indeed, the place in the gap between Pine Orchard and Huckleberry Knob, through which the wagon road from Todd to Riddle's Fork of Meat Camp Creek now runs, is still pointed out as that at which Greer and his men camped in the cold and wind, without fire or tent, till they saw the campfire on Riddle's Knob flame up, after which they crept up to that lonely spot and either killed or wounded the redoubtable Tory. But Dr. Draper has an altogether different story to tell about Riddle's capture and execution.

Cleveland Hangs Riddle.—Dr. Draper says (p. 444) that soon after Cleveland's rescue Riddle and his men made a night raid into the Yadkin Valley, where, on King's Creek, they captured two of Cleveland's soldiers, David and John Witherspoon, and "spirited them away into the mountain region on the Wa-

Photo. by Vannoy.

THE WOLF'S DEN.

Where Cleveland was rescued.

tauga River in what is now Watauga County," where both were sentenced to be shot, when it was proposed that if they would take the oath of allegiance to the king, repair to their home and speedily return with the O'Neal mare—a noble animal—and join the Tory band, their lives would be spared. This the Witherspoons agreed to, and returned with not only the mare, but with Col. Ben Herndon and a party also, when they captured Riddle, Reeves and Goss, "killing and dispersing the others." These were taken to Wilkesboro, court-martialed and executed" on the hill adjoining the village, "on a stately oak, which is yet (1881) standing and pointed out to strangers at Wilkesboro." Wells, too, his wounds still unhealed, was captured and taken to Hughes' Bottom, one mile below Cleveland's Round About home-place, and hanged by plow lines from a tree on the river bank, without trial and in spite of the protestations of James Gwyn, a lad of thirteen, whose noble nature revolted at such barbarity. But Cleveland's cruelty was too well known to need further comment, for it is recorded of him that he once forced an alleged horse-thief to cut off his own ears with a dull case knife to escape death by hanging—all without trial or evidence of any kind whatever (p. 447). Cleveland moved to South Carolina at the close of the Revolutionary War, where he died while sitting at the breakfast table, in October, 1806, in the sixty-ninth year of his age. Cleveland County in this State was named in his honor. Dr. Draper says he was buried in the forks of the Tugalo and Chauga, Oconee County, South Carolina, but his grave with a stone marking it is in the churchyard of New Hope Baptist Church, near Staunton, Wilkes County, North Carolina, according to several recent statements of Col. J. H. Taylor, the father of Mrs. John Stansbury, of Boone. However, some claim that this is Robert Cleveland's grave-stone. So much for two versions of Riddle's death.

But there is still another, for Col. W. W. Presnell, for many years register of deeds for Watauga County and a brave one-armed Confederate soldier, still points out at the foot of a ridge north of James Blair's residence, on Brushy Fork Creek, two low rock cliffs, between which and the hollow just east of them stood until recently a large white-thorn tree upon which W. H. Dugger and other reputable citizens of a past day said Cleveland had hanged Riddle and three of his companions. Certain it is, according to Dr. Draper (p. 445), that "Colonel Cleveland was active at this period in sending out strong scouting parties to scour the mountain regions, and, if possible, utterly break up the Tory bands still infesting the frontiers." Others say that two of these men were named Sneed and the third was named Warren.

The Killing of Charles Asher.—Col. Joseph C. Shull has among his papers grant No. 841 to Charles Asher to 300 acres of land in the county of Washington, on both sides of the Watauga River, dated the 11th day of July, 1788. Charles Asher located this land at what was afterwards and still is known as Shull's Mills in Watauga County, North Carolina, after having married one of the daughters of Samuel Hix, the Tory who settled first at Valle Crucis and afterwards hid out at the Lybrook place near Banner's Elk. His son was surprised in his new log cabin in what is now Colonel Shull's orchard, by Joseph White's men soon after the close of the Revolutionary War.[4] Asher ran, but was shot and killed, his body falling where it was buried, near Colonel Shull's cow barn in the meadow in front of his residence.

Benjamin Howard.—This gentleman was the first transient boarder in the vicinity of Boone, for he built the cabin which stood in front of the Boys' Dormitory of the Appalachian Training School and on the site of which Col. W. L. Bryan has erected a substantial monument. Howard's home was near Elkville on the Yadkin, but as he herded cattle in the valley of New River, he built this hut for the accommodation of himself and his herders. When too hotly pressed by the Whigs or American Patriots, Howard sheltered himself in a cave at the base of a long, low cliff a quarter of a mile north of the knob above the

---

[4] Joseph White was a major in Col. Joseph McDowell's regiment after the Revolutionary War (Col. Rec., Vol. XXII, p. 460), and went on three tours with small detachments on the north-west side of the Blue Ridge. (Id., p. 99.) In "North Carolina: A History," published by Edward Buncombe Chapter D. A. R., it is erroneously stated (p. 100) that White also was killed. White is mentioned by Doctor Draper, pp. 149-199 and 257, while on page 474 it is stated that White probably commanded a company at King's Mountain.

town of Boone which has borne his name for years. His daughter, Sallie, when still a child, is said to have endured a severe switching rather than reveal his whereabouts when met in the road one day by a band of men in search of her parent. She married Jordan Councill the first. Her father took the oath of allegiance to the United States in 1778, however (Col. Rec. Vol. XXII, p. 172), and Miss Sallie soon afterwards became a staunch American herself.

Edward Moody, Patriot.—Under a large white-oak tree, two feet in diameter, on a sunny ridge overlooking the site of his earthly home, is a rather small, white marble stone bearing the following meager inscription:

> EDW'D MOODY,
> HOWE'S, VA.
> MIL. REV. WAR.

When one reflects that this memorial was erected by the government of the United States on the Fourth day of July, 1910, in the presence of the largest gathering of people that has ever taken place in Watauga County, and remembers that the stone is intended to mark the grave of one of the heroes of the American Revolution, one's heart does not swell with any great amount of pride or gratitude. Yet, that is all there is to mark the last resting place of a brave man who shed his blood that these United States might be free! That is all to tell coming generations that here lies the dust of a patriot and a gentleman. Even the dates of his birth and death have been forgotten. But while he lived no man stood higher in the love and respect of all who knew him. He was the husband of "the Widow Moody" to whom the Rev. Henry H. Prout paid a glowing tribute in the "Life of W. W. Skiles."

William Jonas Braswell, Hero.—In a lonely field now owned by W. H. and Harstin Ollis, under two hickory trees, a third of a mile above the old Gen. Albertus Childs' place on Three Mile Creek, is another one of those "monuments" at the unveiling or dedication of which our great government occasionally invites its citizens to be present. It contains an even more economical inscription than that of poor Edward Moody. It follows:

WM. BRASWELL,
N. C. MIL.
REV. WAR.

"That's the crap," as our farmers say in derision of a small offering. This was unveiled to the light of day and to the indignation of all right-thinking people in 1913, the crowd in attendance numbering nearly five hundred. That seems to be all this great and powerful government could find out about this dead hero, now without a vote. But others remember something else of him, John Wise, born May 9, 1835, relating that Braswell lived on Lower Creek in Burke County, and hunted through the country lying between that locality and Black Mountain, in what is now Yancey. He had relatives in Pensacola, near Big Tom Wilson's old home, "under the Black." When a very old man, Braswell, his wife and a girl named Yarber started late one fall from Lower Creek to Pensacola to visit people named Mace, relatives of his wife, probably. They had to spend the night in camp under a rock on a high ridge leading up from Burke to the Linville country, then and now a much used highway for local travel, a wagon road now replacing the former trail. They could not procure fire, and a cold-snap coming on, the old man "froze down," to use Captain Wise's forceful phrase. When the chill morning dawned his wife and the Yarber girl met Jacob and William Carpenter at the ford of Linville River, to which point they had hastened through the darkness, seeking aid. The women went on to Carpenter's house in the meadow in front of Captain Wise's present residence, while the two Carpenter men hastened on to the camp rock, where Braswell was found, very low, but still alive. Placing him on a horse, they managed to keep him there by walking on each side of him and holding him in the saddle till they reached home. There he died after having revived for a short time, and was buried where the so-called "monument" now stands. His name was William

Jonas Braswell, but to have spelled all that out on a tomb-stone would have required, at five cents a letter, at least fifty cents more! Hence, etc. The present wagon road does not pass very near the old camp rocks, but they are still remembered, while the high ridge on which they stand have preserved that part of a hero's name which a niggard nation consigned to oblivion, for it has been called ever since "Jonas's Ridge."

William Davis—What?—Hero? Patriot? Let us see. His grave is near the road in front of the Gen. Albertus Childs' house on Three Mile Creek, now owned and occupied by Robert Moseley. Two common "mountain rocks" mark the place of his burial. Two other graves beside his are similarly designated. No munificent government, proud of his record, has "sought his frailties" or his virtues "to disclose." Why? For he was a soldier of the Revolutionary War as well as those over whose ashes grave-stones have been erected. Who knows? Probably a bit of red-tape was missing somewhere. Maybe his name does not appear on any roster or muster roll. Yet, in the Congressional Library, at the nation's capital, is an allegorical painting called "History." It represents a gray-haired sire telling the story of the past to his son, and this son telling the same story with additions to *his* son, and so on down the line till the printed page is reached. The name of that oral story is "Tradition." Well, tradition says that William Davis was not only a brave soldier, but a mighty hunter as well, when the wilderness was to be conquered and weaklings stayed at home and sneered at the illiterate and the lowly. Davis came to America with William Wiseman and William Penley long before the Revolution. He settled first in Virginia and afterwards came to Ashe County, where he married Frances Carpenter, sister of the first Jacob Carpenter. Then he moved to what is still called Davis Mountain, near Crossnore, on the upper waters of Linville River. When the game was exhausted there, he moved to Three Mile Creek and built four log houses "all in a row," with communicating doors between and a chimney at each end. Standing before a blazing fire in one end of the house, with the three intervening doors open, one looks through four large, low-ceiled, comfortable rooms to cherry-red flames leaping up the chimney at the farther end—one of the "fairest pictures of calm content that mortal ever saw." The date of the building of this old structure is recorded on one of the inside logs, but it has been ceiled over and cannot now be seen. But it was made there many, many years ago. The present Jacob Carpenter, his greatnephew, of Altamont, knows the date of his birth and death, but they would cost the United States some "good money" to have them carved on a 12 x 24-inch stone. Davis died November 18, 1841, when 114 years of age. Still, as he had no middle name, it does seem that the Government, with a big G, might "sort of look after" Uncle Billy, who fought his battles for him before Uncle Sam was born, he having been shot through the hips at King's Mountain. His wife, who sleeps beside him, was certainly a heroine, whether Uncle Billy was a hero or no, for on one occasion, in February, while in a sugar camp on Davis Mountain, he had to be away from her on a cold night. One of her cows found a calf that night, and Mrs. Davis brought it to camp with her and fought off the wolves with fire-brands till morning.

A Revolutionary Welshman.—On the south fork of New River, on Harvey Phillips' farm at McGuire post office, is the grave of a soldier of the Revolutionary War. His name is Jones, but the given name has been lost. That he was a Welshman is implied by his name. Close by him sleeps Benjamin Blackburn, another Revolutionary soldier, from whom has descended a long line of useful and honored citizens.

Moses Yarber.—The United States has also been equally generous to her dead and gone soldiers of the War of 1812, for, in the same graveyard which holds the ashes of Edward Moody, our great government has erected another monument, which, at five cents a letter, including apostrophes, must have cost at least thirty cents more than did Edward Moody's. But it managed to spell out his full name, instead of contracting it as it did with the latter's given name, recording it as Edw'd, instead of Edward, thus saving at least five cents, assuming that the comma cost a nickel. As the enduring marble embalms his name and record, we have the following:

MOSES YARBER
McNEIL'S CO.
S. C. MIL.
WAR 1812.

These abbreviations stand for whatever the reader may elect to attribute to them, the punctuation rendering the following story as intelligible as any: "Moses Yarber McNeil's County, saw cow Millie Warranted 1812."

Two of Yarber's daughters live within two miles of his grave, Jemimah and Catharine, the former having been born April 27, 1825, and the latter February 18, 1830. Moses was blessed with other children also—William, born February 23, 1810; Annie, born July 15, 1816; Mary Ann, born June 9, 1818—but they have been dead a number of years. Moses himself died November 30, 1867. But just think what an unheard-of sum it would have cost our Government—again that big G—to have recorded that fact—with every abbreviation possible, sixty-five cents! His daughters knew the date of his death when, on the 4th day of July, 1910, this stone was erected. They knew also that Moses had married Elizabeth Edwards, a daughter of Henry Edwards, of Darlington District, South Carolina, and a soldier of the Revolutionary War. Thus, these two old ladies, in poverty and alone, have the proud consciousness that their father's full name will be preserved as long as that gravestone endures, if only posterity has the intelligence to guess that his name was Yarber and not McNeil, but what interpretation it will give to the balance of the inscription must always be problematical. Moses and his family moved to Flat Top, now Linville City, about 1838, and from there to their present home in 1855. They have no votes, these good women; if they had, it is likely that they would have also a pension apiece. *Sic transit!*

Two Old Tory Knobs.—On Riddle's Fork of Meat Camp are two knobs or peaks which are known, one as Hagaman's Knob and the other as Wiley's Knob, from the fact which tradition still maintains, that at their bases two Tories, hiding out during the Revolutionary War, made their headquarters. They were, doubtless, a part of Riddle's gang.

Old Battle in Watauga?—In Robert Love's pension papers it is said that "he was in command of a party of Americans in 1780 against a party of Tories in July of that year." This band of Tories was composed of about 150 men, and they were routed up New River at the Big Glades, now (1833) in Ashe County, North Carolina, as they were on their way to join Cornwallis." Col. W. L. Bryan says that the Big Glades were on the south fork of New River, near Deep Gap.

Guarded Major Andre.—Nathan Horton, whose grave-stone in Three Forks churchyard records the fact that he was a soldier of the Revolutionary War, according to a tradition still preserved in his own family, guarded Major Andre when the latter was executed for treason, at which time he carried a shotgun loaded with one ball and three buck-shot. A fine old Grandfather clock of mahogany, with elaborate face and works, brought by Nathan Horton from New Jersey when he emigrated to Ashe soon after the Revolution, is now in the home of J. Crit. Horton, on New River, five miles from Boone.

Following are the names of other Revolutionary soldiers who lived and died in Watauga: Benjamin Bingham, great uncle of Hon. Thomas Bingham, who is said to have fired the last gun at Yorktown, Va.; John Adams, born in France and came over with Lafayette's soldiers as a drummer-boy of sixteen years, remaining, concealed in a flour barrel, at Philadelphia, when Lafayette returned to France; the brothers, George, Absalom and William Smith, were in the Virginia army and at Cornwallis's surrender at Yorktown.

CHAPTER VI.
Three Forks Association.

Yadkin Baptist Association.—This association constituted the Three Forks association in 1790. From it many other churches had been organized east of the Blue Ridge.[1]

In 1779 King's Creek Church, in Caldwell, and Beaver Creek, in Wilkes, were organized. A few years later Brier Creek, in Wilkes, was constituted. It had many "arms,"[2] and from it grew Lewis Fork, in Wilkes, and Old Fields Church, in Ashe County. Three Forks was constituted by the Yadkin Baptist Association. It became an association itself in 1840.

"In 1790 Three Forks Church, the first in Watauga, was constituted. Part of the original members of this church came from the Jersey Settlement Church. Cove Creek was the second church in Watauga, being organized in 1799. At first these churches had only log houses in which to worship. The floors were rude, and large cracks were in the walls, so that they were often uncomfortable in winter. But the praises of God rang out from the lips and hearts of these old Baptist fathers. These churches first joined the Strawberry Association in Virginia, but in 1790 withdrew to organize the Yadkin Association. The first ministers of this body were George McNeil, John Cleveland, William Petty, William Hammond, Cleveland Coffey, Andrew Baker and John Stone . . . Later on the Mountain, Catawba and Brier Creek Associations were formed, and so the Yadkin Baptists continued steadily to grow."

Three Forks Baptist Church.—This was the first church established west of the Blue Ridge, excepting only the one established at the Old Fields, which, according to Mr. Williams, was established "a few years after"—1779. It was organized No-

---
[1] Williams' History of the North Carolina Baptists.
[2] According to Rev. Henry Sheet's History, "arms" were church communities which had not been regularly organized into constituted churches.

vember 6, 1790, according to the records now in the keeping of the clerk, Mr. John C. Brown, of New River. These records show that "the Baptist Church of Jesus Christ in Wilkes County, New River, Three Forks Settlement," was organized by James Tomkins, Richard Greene and wife, Daniel Eggers and wife, William Miller, Elinor Greene and B. B. Eggers. This soon became the mother church, from which went out "arms" to the Globe, to Ebeneezer and to South Fork and other places. Attendants came to Three Forks from all this section, many coming even from Tennessee. Among the first pastors of this mother church are: Richard Gentry, of Old Fields; John G. Bynum, who died in Georgia; Mr. Barlow, of Yadkin; Nathaniel Vannoy, George McNeil, of Wilkes; Joseph Harrison, of Three Forks; Jacob Greene, D. C. Harmon, Smith Ferguson, Brazilla McBride and Jacob Greene, of Cove Creek; Jackie Farthing, Reuben Farthing and A. C. Farthing, William Wilcox and Larkin Hodges. They earned their bread in the sweat of their faces and worked in the Master's vineyard without money and without price. They have all gone to their reward in heaven.

Membership from 1790 to 1800.—James Tompkins, Richard Green, Daniel Eggers, Ellender Green, William Miller, Mary Miller, Phoebe Eggers, Sarah Coleman, Avis Eggers, Elizabeth Tompkins, Ben. Cutbirth, Anna Wilcoxon, Lidia Council, Benj. Baylis, Eliz. Cutbirth, Sarah Baylis, James Chambers, Anna Chambers, John Faugerson, Ebineezer Fairchild, James Jackson, Catharine Hull, Joseph Sewel, Ezekiel England, Ruth Tompkins, Christeana Reese, Valentine Reese, Samuel Ayers, Elijah Chambers, Moses Hull, Joseph Ayers, William Tompkins, Benj. Green, Sam'l Wilcoxon, Sr., Garsham Tompkins, John Reese, Hodges Counsel, Mary Fairchild, Sarah Green, Sarah Reese, Charity Ayers, James Proffitt, James Calloway, Jeremiah Green, Sarah Hull, Joannah Eggers, James Faugerson, Elizabeth Hull, Martha Chambers, Landrine Eggers, Nathan Horton, Mathew Counsel, Nancy Chambers, Rachel Chambers, Jesse Counsel, Comfort Wade, Edward Stocksdale, Edieth Stocksdale, Joseph Tompkins, Susannah Brown, Sam'l Wilcoxon, Jr., Thomas Wade, Samuel Baker, John Ayers, Sam'l Castle, Martha Castle, Abraham

THE THREE FORKS BAPTIST CHURCH.

Photo. by Vannoy.

A History of Watauga County 73

Eaton, Jno. Parr, Mary Parr, Jonathan Allen, Jas. McCaleb, Mary McCaleb, Anne Doneky, Catharine Allen, Wm. Davis, Rebekah Fairchild, Richard Orzgathorp, Jno. Vanderpool, Ellen Vanderpool, Catharine Hull, Sam'l Vanderpool, Sam'l Pitman, Winant Vanderpool, Jr., Anna Vanderpool, Winant Vanderpool, Naomi Vanderpool, Keziah Pitman, Abraham Vanderpool, Sarah Davis, Abraham Linvil, Susannah Vanderpool, Peter Regan, Rebekah Regan, Catharine Linvil, Margaret Linvil, Maryann Isaacs, Mathias Harmon, Mary Harmon, Jno. Holesclaw, Jane Vanderpool, Jacob Reese, Catharine Brown, Hannah Phillips, Jeremiah Buck, Sarah Shearer, Jno. Shearer, Valentine Reese, Jr., Mary Eggers, Jonathan Buck, John Brown, Hannah Reese, Elisha Chambers, David Coleman, James Jackson, Jr., Elizabeth Horton, Henry Chambers, Rachel Brown, Anna Reese, Mary Reese, Eliz. Reese, Isaac Reese, Landrine Eggers' negro man by name of George, Anthony Reese, Asa Chambers, Comfort Stocksdale, Samuel Northern, Susanna Fairchild, Mary Owens, William Owens, Daniel Eggers, Jr., Henry Earnest, Gracy Shearer, Susannah Brown, Debby Lewis, Benj. Brown, Mahala Eggers, Elizabeth Morphew, Margaret Chambers, Robert Shearer, Jane Triplet, Richard Lewis, John Ford, Benj. Tompkins, Lyon Wilcoxon, Benj. Greer, Barnet Owens, Susannah Owens.

Of these there were received by experience: Three in 1790, three in 1791, twenty-nine in 1792, seven in 1793, none in 1794, two in 1795, none in 1796, one in 1797, one in 1798, sixty in 1799. Received by letter in 1790, one; in 1792, eight; in 1793, one; in 1795, four; in 1796, seven; in 1797, two; in 1798, six; in 1799, nine. The following were dismissed by letter: Jeremiah Green, in 1793; Samuel Ayers, Benj. Bayless, Sarah Bayless, Joseph Sewel, Garsham Tompkins, Ruth Tompkins, Joseph Tompkins, Wm. Tompkins, in 1794; Jesse Counsel, Lydia Counsel, Mathew Counsel, in 1795; Elijah Chambers, Samuel Wilcoxon, Anna Wilcoxon, Sam'l Wilcoxon, Jr., in 1797; Jonathan Allen, Catharine Allen, James McCaleb, Mary McCaleb, Thomas Wade, Comfort Wade, Mary Reese, in 1798. Elizabeth Tompkins died in 1796. The following were excommunicated:

Sarah Hull, Ezekiel England, Susannah Brown, Jesse Counsel, in 1794; James Callaway, Samuel Ayers, in 1795; William Miller, James Jackson, Landrine Eggers, Hodges Counsel, in 1796; Mary Miller, in 1797; Samuel Wilcoxon, Jr., Moses Hull, in 1798; Jno. Ayers, Daniel Eggers, Phoebe Eggers, Mahala Eggers, Martha Chambers, in 1799; William Owens, in 1801. It must not be concluded, however, that these had been guilty of very serious offences, for most, if not all, of them were restored to full membership by recantation.

The One Great Moral Force.—In the early days, when courts were few and far between and settlers scattered here and there, the only influence for good in pioneer communities was the church. This proved to be the case in this portion of Ashe County from 1790 to 1800. Nothing seemed too trivial for the correction of the church. What now appear very venial offences, were tried, frequently with the result of expulsion, but always with the assurance of restoration upon proper submission and repentance. Among the more serious offences thus punished were one case of adultery in 1794, one case of drinking to excess in 1795, one case of disposing of property to defraud creditors in 1798, and in 1799 a man confessed to fornication. This is a fine record for ten years in this far-away community. Among the more trivial matters of which the church took notice in the first thirty years of its existence were John Brown's confession of "being so overcome by passion as even to strike a man;" Comfort Wade was excommunicated for having told Phoebe Eggers that a certain piece of cloth was cross-barred and others that it was tow linen, but at the next meeting her husband obtained a new hearing, when she was acquitted (April, 1801). In January, 1853, Burton and Damarcus Hodges were cited to appear and answer to the charge of having joined the Sons of Temperance. In December, 1801, Brother Parr was tried and acquitted for letting his children "go naked," and at the same meeting Polly Owens was publicly excommunicated for allowing her daughter to "request a certain young man to meet her, and accordingly he did, when they spent the whole time of public worship talking and laughing," but soon afterwards, the mother "having acknowledged her transgression," she was restored to full membership. In April, 1802, Benj. Brown was acquitted of having attended the races at Elizabethton, and in July, 1802, Brother John Brown was cited to answer the charge of having joined the Masons, and in August was excommunicated therefor.* At the same meeting an unnamed charge against Brother Hull was tried, and it was found that he had done nothing "worthy of death or bonds." A second protest was also then entered against the subject of double marriages "as being against the word of God." "Cathern" Hull was excommunicated because her conduct at Cove Creek had not been agreeable to the gospel and not giving the church satisfaction. Sister Eggers had a grievance against Brother Hull and Brother Reese "for refusing to talk with her about her distress, and for saying her daughter had a fambly and had not." Hull was reproved for this. But in March, 1803, Brother Hull was excommunicated for not complying with his bargain, whatever that might have been. In April of the same year it was shown that the report was proven false that "Sary Reese had said that it took three persons to complete a sermon delivered by Brother McCaleb, to wit: Brother McCaleb, Brother Richard Green and the devil." Again, in May, 1807, James Proffitt was excommunicated for having joined the Masons, while in July, 1811, Henry Chambers was acquitted of the charge of not having paid a just debt. In the following month Jeremiah Green was cited to appear to answer to the charge of having allowed "his daughter to go with a married man," and a letter of dismission was refused him till he should debar her from his home. This daughter, however, was restored to full membership in June, 1812. As this was before Noah Webster had established a uniform system of spelling, each man spelt "according to the dictates of his own conscience," just as they worshipped, and so, in July, 1816, we find a complaint that was "throad out of doors." In July, 1802, Brother

---

* The language of the minute shows the frequent use of "of," not now so common: "first, of joining of them (the Masons); second, of denying of it, and third, of refusing to obey the church." Again, in July, 1802, it is recorded that "we enter our solemn *test* against its (double marriage) being agreeable to the Word of God." Our modern expression is "*protest against*," which seems a contradiction in terms.

Shearer's name is spelt Shirrow. In April, 1801, "a letter was received from Brother Wade, requesting a re-hearing of his wife's excommunication, and stating that "he stood with her except she got another." At the June meeting following she was acquitted. There are several instances of male members having been chosen to act as singing clerks, though it is probable that then, as now, the female members did most of the singing and made the best music.

Other Ancient Happenings.—The last Saturday in April, 1792, was set apart as a day of fasting and prayer, and at the same meeting James Chambers was "approbated to exercise his gift in preaching." In August, 1793, James Chambers, Ebenezer Fairchild and Samuel Wilcoxon were sent as delegates to the assembly at Eaton's Meeting House, Dutchman's Creek, near Daniel Boone's old home, while in February, 1793, James Tompkins and Richard Green were sent to the association at Brier Creek to "seek for union." In January, 1795, a brother was suspended for "drinking to excess, using profane speeches, singing vain songs and dancing." In March, 1800, the first "solemn protest was entered against double marriage," and in July following James Chambers, James McCaleb and Shadrack Brown were sent to the association at Fox Creek, Grayson County, Va. In November, 1800, John Brown and Elisha Chambers were elected singing clerks, and in August, 1802, Brother Hull was "cited for going to law contrary to an act of this church." In January, 1815, Brother Boone laid an allegation against Brother Hartley for "not giving good usage at his mill," and in February following and again at a called meeting during same month Hartley was admonished.

First Churches.—There seems to be no record of the building of the first church which stood on the site of the present structure, though tradition says it was merely a log cabin, without chimney or windows. The first Robert Shearer in 1790 lived on the hill above the present site of Three Forks Church, and it was in his home that the church was constituted. Robert's grandfather is said to have lived just below the dam of the A. T. school on New River. Certain it is that within the memory

A History of Watauga County

of men now living, in the fall of 1856 and in 1857 services were held in the second or third log house which stood there, and that the worshippers had frequently to leave the church and warm themselves by a fire under the tall oaks which grow near by. There is a tradition that a heavy fall of snow crushed the roof of the building in about 1830, but it is certain that in October, 1805, James McCaleb and James Morphew were appointed trustees to "form a plan of a roof for our Meeting House, and divide three-fourths of the work between the male members, leaving one-fourth part for the Jenerosity of those that are not members . . ." In the following December four dollars in Brother Shearer's hands were spent for nails for the roof. There is a record, however, of the building of the present structure, for on November 3, 1866, Robert Shearer, Eli Brown and Ransom Hayes were appointed commissioners to build a new church, which was completed in the summer of 1867.

Revivals.—There was a protracted meeting in January and February, 1853, which continued for thirteen days, Larkin Hodges and John Cook being the ministers in charge. There were seventy-seven conversions and admissions by letter. There was another great revival in September, 1866, with Joseph Harrison and A. C. Farthing as ministers, at which there were forty-three conversions. But there were "lean seasons" also, for, though the church flourished from its foundation in 1790 till 1800 and afterwards, there was no business recorded from October, 1808, till March, 1809, nor in May and June and August and December of the latter year. Again, in April and May, October and December, 1811, and in January, February, April, May, June, September, October and November, 1812, and from September, 1823, till July, 1824, there seems to have been no business. In February, 1807, the only instance on record, there was no meeting on account of the weather. The first pastor was Brother Chambers, elected in September, 1792.

CHAPTER VII.
Order of the Holy Cross.

A Graphic Picture.—In 1840 a botanist from New York visited what is now Valle Crucis, and on his return interested Bishop L. Silliman Ives, then bishop of the Episcopal Church of North Carolina, in this locality. Following is a description of the country at that time:[1] "In 1840 the valley of the Watauga, in North Carolina, was a secluded region, isolated and forgotten, a mountain wilderness, showing only here and there the first rude touches of civilization. The narrow, winding trail or foot-path, the rough sled-road, often dangerous for wheels, here and there a log cabin, with a narrow, rough clearing about it, or at long intervals a rude saw-mill or grist mill, with perchance a small, unpainted frame dwelling, or a blacksmith shop and a humble backwoods store, marking the beginning of a hamlet, such were the only traces of human habitation to be found on the banks of the stream. But the highland valley was magnificent in natural beauty. It lay in the elevated country between the Blue Ridge and the Alleghanies, nearly three thousand feet above the sea, while grand old mountains of successive ranges, broken into a hundred peaks, rose to nearly double the height on either hand, many so near that their distinctive features could be clearly seen, while others were only dimly outlined in the distance. These mountain ranges were peculiarly interesting, differing in some particulars from those of any other parts of the country. The vegetation was singularly rich and varied. The valley, entirely shut in by forest-clad mountains, was watered by three small, limpid streams, two of them leaping down the hillsides in foaming cascades; the principal stream, formed by the junction, after a short course of two miles, passing through a narrow gorge, threw itself into the Watauga."

---

[1] From William West Skiles' "A Sketch of Missionary Life at Valle Crucis, 1842-1862." Edited by Susan Fenimore Cooper, 1890, pp. 5, 6.

Photo. by Vest.

L. SILLIMAN IVES, D. D.
Bishop of the Protestant Episcopal Church of the Diocese of North Carolina.

Valle Crucis.—There is, perhaps, more interest in this place and its romantic history than in any other in Watauga County. It is called the Valley of the Cross because of the fancied resemblance to that symbol of our faith caused by two creeks, each flowing from an opposite direction into Dutch Creek— Clark's, which rises under the Grandfather and flows into the right bank of Dutch Creek, which has its sources in Hanging Rock, while nearly opposite the mouth of Clark's Creek, and coming in from the left, is Crab Orchard Creek, flowing from the neighborhood of Banner's Elk.[2] There is a dreamy spell which hangs over this little valley, lending its charm to the story of the spiritual doubts that once perplexed the soul of a good man in his struggles to see the true light of Christianity. He was not the first, nor will he be the last, to grope in semi-darkness, turning hither and thither in his bewilderment; loving and clinging to past ties, yet dreading to follow where they led; adventuring by fits and starts on uncertain paths, and, like a frightened child, returning again to the known ways of his childhood and earlier manhood, till, at last, the final step was taken beyond all recall.

Rt. Rev. L. Silliman Ives.—Second bishop of North Carolina, from May, 1831, to December 22, 1852,[3] was born September 16, 1797, in Meriden, Conn., and in his youth was a Presbyterian. In his young manhood he became an Episcopalian, while in later years he made his submission to the Catholic Church of Rome. He is said to be the only bishop of the Protestant Episcopal Church of America who ever went over to the Roman Catholic Church. He became rector of St. Luke's Episcopal Church in New York City, married Rebecca Hobart, daughter of the Rt. Rev. John Henry Hobart, Episcopal bishop of New York State, to which union was born one child who did not live to maturity. While quite young he served a short time with the troops under General Pike in the War of 1812, after which he determined to study for the ministry of the Presbyterian Church, and for that

---

[2] According to DeRossett's Church History of North Carolina, Valle Crucis was named in honor of an old English abbey by that name. Its altitude is 2,726 feet.

[3] He published "The Trials of a Mind in Its Progress to Catholicism," 233 pages, Boston and New York, in 1854.

purpose, in 1816, entered Hamilton College, New York, at Clinton, where he remained but a year, when, his health failing, he changed his faith and, in 1819, began to study for the Episcopal ministry. After his visit to Italy in 1852, he became professor of rhetoric in St. Joseph's Theological Seminary, New York, and lectured in the convents of the Sacred Heart and Sisters of Charity and in public. He established in New York City two charitable institutions for the protection of destitute Catholic children, of both of which he was president. He published many works. He died in Manhattanville, N. Y., October 13, 1867, and was buried in the Catholic Protectory, Westchester County, New York. His wife, who was born February 6, 1803, died August 3, 1863. Bishop Ives served the Catholic Church only as a layman, being barred from the priesthood on account of his marriage.

"**A Feeble and Undignified Imitation.**"—From "The Bishops of North Carolina," from which most of the above was taken, we learn (p. 112) that by "1849 the Mission at Valle Crucis had begun to drift away from the teachings of the Church, and was fast becoming a feeble and undignified imitation of the monastic institutions of the Church of Rome," but, with the exception of this error, we are told in "Sketches of Church History in North Carolina" (p. 337) that "Whatever we may think of the strange ideas and practices which Bishop Ives engrafted on to the associate work which he established at Valle Crucis, his conception that this was the most practical and efficient way to reach the scattered populations of the mountains was fully justified in the results which remain to this day." On page 80 of the same work we read that there had been three ordinations, one priest and two deacons, at Valle Crucis, while at least eight young men had there prepared for the ministry. William R. Gries, William Passmore, George Patterson, Frederick Fitz Gerald, Joseph W. Murphey, Richard Wainwright Barber, Charles T. Bland, William West Skiles, Thomas F. Davis, Jr., and others were at one time or another connected with this mission. So concerned was the Church throughout the State by the rumors which came from the mountains as to this brotherhood, or "Order of the Holy Cross," that United States Senator George E. Badger issued a booklet on the Doctrines of Bishop Ives, and that this interest has not subsided is shown by the very interesting account of Valle Crucis which was published in the *Messenger of Hope* for February, 1909.

Cause of His Vacillation.—In the spring of 1848 Bishop Ives had a severe attack of fever while in attendance upon the general convention in New York City. From this, it is claimed, he never recovered his mental poise. It is also stated (p. 132) in the "Bishops of North Carolina" that his father died from a self-inflicted wound while temporarily insane, while Bishop Ives' own brother wrote, February 25, 1853 (p. 133), that there was a tendency to insanity in the family. It is stated in the "Life of W. W. Skiles" (p. 91) that at the convention of the Church, held at Fayetteville in 1851, the committee of inquiry reported the bishop as being "in a high state of nervous excitement, arising either from bodily disease or constitutional infirmity, in which he admitted that he had been insensibly led to teaching and believing opinions on matters of doctrine, of the impropriety of which he was then fully satisfied. He mentioned having tolerated the Romish notion of the Invocation of Saints, Auricular Confession and Absolution, but had always abhorred the doctrine of Transubstantiation, while the spiritual presence of Christ in the Eucharist was the doctrine our church teaches," and he signed a paper to the above effect.

The Old Buildings.—These were a saw mill, a log kitchen and dining room, a log dwelling containing four rooms and a frame building (60' x 20') with a room at each end for teachers, together with a large hall for school purposes in the center, all on the ground floor, while over the whole was a dormitory for boys. All of these were ready for use and occupancy in 1845. "The adobes used in the buildings were made of clay and straw as usual, and were considered to be of good quality. But they soon began to crumble away, and in the course of the summer they were attacked by an unforeseen enemy—the humble bees took possession of them, burrowing into the fresh clay to such an extent that the walls in many places looked like honey-combs, and were so much weakened that they gave way in places under the weight above them." From which it was concluded by the students that there could have been no humble bees in Egypt in the time of the Pharoahs (p. 37).

Easter Chapel.—Less than a mile below the home of the Widow Moody, on the left bank of the Watauga River and two miles above Shull's Mills, is the site of this old chapel, now gone. A "man in affliction" had given Mr. Prout $300.00, out of which he built Easter Chapel on a large rock two hundred yards from the Watauga River, with a spring at its base. It was of logs, hewn by Levi Moody, the widow's son, "a good, guileless man." It was fifteen feet wide by forty feet long, and had a little chancel at the east end, with oaken altar beneath a narrow window. The roof was steep, and each side wall contained a small window. The rafters showed from the inside, while rude benches afforded seats for those who came to worship. It was called Easter with especial reference to the doctrine of the resurrection and in connection with the devotion of the mountaineers in keeping that great festival. The Grandfather Mountain looms in the distance. But a limb from an overhanging tree crushed in the roof of the chancel, and the balance of the building, after the Civil War, went rapidly to decay. A wind-storm on the 4th of March, 1893, threw the walls to the ground, all except two of the sills, which still remain, slowly passing into dust and decay. The logs out of which these walls had been built were of poplar, and were three feet broad by four or five inches thick. Thus, three of them sufficed to make a wall nine feet high. If this be doubted, a small cabin now (1915) standing near will substantiate the fact of the possibility of such a thing, as one of its walls has but three logs in it, each log being three feet broad. Rev. J. Norton Atkins now owns the house formerly built by Rev. Henry H. Prout which stands near,* though Mrs. J. F. Coffey owns the rock on which the chapel used to stand. The perennial spring, however, spoken of in a note on page 96 of Skiles' Life, has disappeared, blasting for a new road, which was never built, having caused it to sink.

---

* Rev. W. R. Savage purchased this tract from Isabella Danner, or Dana, she having "heired" it from her father, Larkin Calloway. (Deed Book 6, p. 209.) Mr. Savage sold it to Mr. Norton.

RESIDENCE OF REV. JOHN NORTON ATKINS
Former home of the late Rev. Henry H. Prout.

The Widow Moody.—Among those spoken of with affection by Mr. Prout was Mrs. Edward Moody. She was a sister of Col. John Carter, for whom Carter County, Tennessee, was named and in honor of whose wife Elizabethton, the capital of that county, was called. She and her husband came from Augusta County, Virginia, soon after the Revolutionary War, in which he had fought and where he was seriously wounded. Of her Mr. Prout said: "The house of the Widow Moody was long a sort of social center on the Upper Watauga. Here the missionary [himself] first learned, in 1842, that a log cabin may shelter happy people. More generous, sweeter Christian hospitality, more glad, more cheerful kindness are seldom met with than this worthy family showed me when a stranger and alone. There was a native refinement and a balance of judgment about the character of the mother of the family. I shall not soon forget her invariable reply to the inquiries of her friends when asking after her welfare—she was blind, with many infirmities, and yet the answer of Christian faith never failed: 'Thank God, no reason to complain.' There was in that far-off settlement a simplicity of manner, a generous tone, not often excelled, a graceful modesty, an unassuming dignity, very rare, but in harmony with the grand and beautiful scenery of the region" (p. 87). This house was two stories high, with two shed-rooms, and contained six rooms in all. It stood in the old orchard between the Grave Yard Ridge, where Edward Moody is buried, and the former residence of Sheriff Calloway.

The Lower Settlement.—Rev. W. W. Skiles had most to do with the establishment of a school and church at this point, which is at Ward's store, several miles below Valle Crucis. The first service was held in a small log cabin. "Men and women came in, many on foot, some on horseback, the wife in sun-bonnet and straight, narrow gown, riding behind her husband. Here and there a woman was seen mounted on a steer, with a child or two in her arms, while the husband, walking beside them, goad in hand, guided the animal over the rough path. The women all wore sun-bonnets or handkerchiefs tied over their heads. Some were bare-footed. There were many more feet than shoes in the congregation. The boys and girls, even when full grown, were often bare-footed. This was, no doubt, the first service of our church held in that region. And it was declared to be the first religious service of any kind held on the Watauga for seven years" (p. 13). This statement was confirmed by Rev. L. W. Farthing, who then lived on Beaver Dams, near by, but now lives within a few hundred yards of the site on which old St. John's Chapel first stood. Owing to the inaccessibility of the place and the fewness of preachers, no service had been held there during the time stated.[5] The log house soon became too small, and a larger one was obtained. "The pupils tried very hard to learn their lessons well. Occasionally some of the parents would come in and pore intently over the spelling book" (p. 14).

At the Store.—Mr. Skiles kept store at Valle Crucis for the Mission, as well as practiced medicine and taught school. "Or a load of goods, brought with great toil over the mountain roads from Morganton or Lenoir, consisting of tea, coffee, sugar, mustard, pepper, salt, farm tools, nails, screws, etc., a few packages of the more common medicines . . . boots and shoes, school books, paper, pens, ink, with a very modest supply of general stationery; needles, pins, thread, tape, buttons, with perchance a few pieces of calico, flannels and shirting . . ." "Some few, very few, in fact, came in rude wagons, others on horseback, some on steers, many on foot. Most of them carried a gun, a backwoods custom very common in that region; frequently a hound or two followed. The sack of grain was carried on the shoulders by those on foot. The men were, many of them, clad in home-spun tow shirts and short trousers, without coat or shoes even in winter. They were rarely in a hurry, the movement of the country people of that region almost always being slow and deliberate. They were strong, healthy, quiet and composed, frequently ruddy from exposure. A number smoked

---

[5] There was only a trail from Beaver Dams to the Hix Settlement. A chopped-out way, known as Daniel Boone's trail, led from Elizabethton up Watauga river, via Beech Creek and Windy Gap. It was by this trail that Rev. James Eden came to the Hix Settlement to preach the sermon of Andrew Harman when he was killed some six years before Mr. Prout came. Mr. Harman had been killed by a tree which fell on him.

A History of Watauga County 85

corncob pipes; even women rode on steers with children in their arms (p. 111). Seven deer within limits of Valle Crucis were killed in 1854" (p. 114).

After the Civil War.—From the death of Mr. Skiles, there was no minister in this section representing the Episcopal Church till Rev. George H. Bell was ordained in 1883. At his instance St. John's was moved from its beautiful situation near Ward's Store, on Lower Watauga, six miles below Valle Crucis, to its present location on the right bank of Watauga River, two miles higher up the stream. Its location is fine, but the change was made not so much for a better site as for the purpose of serving both the upper and lower communities, there then being no mission or chapel above that point. Now, however, that there is a chapel at the Mission School at Valle Crucis, it would be better if St. John's were on its former site. Rev. Milnor Jones succeeded Mr. Bell, coming in 1895 and remaining three years. This was made a missionary district in 1895, and work was resumed that year under Bishop Cheshire. Then, in September, 1902, Rev. Wm. Rutherford Savage came and has been in this section ever since. He is located at Blowing Rock. Serving with him were Rev. Hugh A. Dobbin, who was ordained August 6, 1909, and Rev. John Norton Atkins, who was ordained December 22, 1907. In 1914 Mr. Dobbin left Valle Crucis to take charge of the Patterson School for Boys on the Yadkin, after which time Rev. Floyd W. Tomkins, son of the distinguished Rev. Dr. Tomkins, of Philadelphia, took charge of Valle Crucis, St. John's and Dutch Creek Mission. Mr. Savage has charge of Blowing Rock. The chapel at Todd was built in 1910, and is in charge of Mr. Atkins, with Boone, Easter Chapel and other chapels in Ashe County. Rt. Rev. Junius M. Horner was consecrated bishop of the Missionary District of Asheville December 28, 1898. The house now used as the rectory was built by Mr. Jones, and was then called the Mission House. The log house just across the Banner Elk road was built by Bishop Ives, and is the only one of the old Ives buildings now remaining. Bishop Horner bought back the upper part of the Valle Crucis property from E. F. Lovill, Esq., administrator of James P. Taylor, who had obtained it from his father, Henry Taylor, June 2, 1893. The deed is dated December 4, 1903, and the consideration is $3,500.00 for the 525 acres conveyed. (Book 1, p. 592.)

Rev. William West Skiles.—This good man was born in 1797, came to Watauga County soon after the school was started at Valle Crucis, studied theology and medicine, and made himself generally useful and helpful to all with whom he came into contact. He died at the home of Col. John B. Palmer, on Linville River, December 8, 1862, and his remains were buried first in the graveyard of the first St. John's, but moved in 1889 to their present resting place in the graveyard of the present church of that name a few miles below Valle Crucis. He taught school, kept store and practiced medicine among the poor people of this county for many years. He never married. He is still remembered by many of the older people of Watauga and vicinity. His life was full of good deeds.

"The Angelus."—Although a bugle was used to summon the little Valle Crucis family to work and to worship, there is, nevertheless, something about the story of this old institution, combined with the name of the valley and its atmosphere and surroundings, which recall the lines of Bret Hart's famous poem, "The Angelus:"

> "Bells of the past, whose long forgotten music
>   Still fills the wide expanse,
> Tingeing the sober twilight of the present
>   With color of romance;
> I hear your call, and see the sun descending
>   O'er rock and hill and sand,
> As, down the coast, the mission voices blending,
>   Girdle the sunny land."

CHAPTER VIII.
Ebenezer Fairchild.

First Light on the Jersey Settlement.[1]—From a sketch of the Greene Family of Watauga, by the late Rev. G. W. Greene, Baptist missionary to China, we learn that "about the middle of the eighteenth century a colony moved from New Jersey and settled in Rowan County, North Carolina. This "Jersey Settlement" is now a part of Davidson County, and lies near the Yadkin River, opposite Salisbury . . . H. E. McCullough, of England, had secured grants to large tracts in North Carolina, tract No. 9 containing 12,500 acres, including much of the land of the Jersey Settlement. Jeremiah Greene bought 541 acres of this tract. This land is described as lying "on the waters of Atkin or Pee Dee," on Pott's Creek. This creek passes near the village of Linwood, within a mile of the Jersey church, and empties into the Yadkin, not far away. This land was bought in 1762. Some years later, when this tract of land was divided between his two sons, Richard and Isaac, the new deeds were not registered, but the names of the new owners were written on the margin of the page where the old deed was registered. The Yadkin becomes the Pee Dee in South Carolina. In his "Rhymes of Southern Rivers" M. V. Moore says that Yadkin is not an Indian name, but a corruption of Atkin or Adkin. If Atkin's initials were P. D., then P. D. Atkin might very easily have become P. D. Yatkin, just as "don't you know" becomes "doncher know." Henry Eustace McCulloh was doubtless the "H. E. McCullough, of England," referred to by Mr. Greene, as he was the agent of the province of North Carolina in December, 1771, and was commended for good conduct (Col. Rec.,

---

[1] Rev. Henry Sheets, author of "A History of Liberty Baptist Association," the successor of the Jersey Settlement Church, says that the McKoys, Merrills, McGuires, Smiths, Moores, Ellises, Marches, Haydens, Wisemans and Tranthams are the names of some of the leaders of the Jersey Settlement, but that letters to prominent men in New Jersey failed to secure any information as to this colony. Governor Ellis's ancestors were among these settlers, and many residents of Ashe, Watauga and Alleghany claim the same distinction.

Vol. IX, p. 206), and he surrendered land in Mecklenberg, claimed by John Campbell, Esq., of England, without authority, as Campbell claimed, although there was a direction in the minutes of the council journals that the attorney-general directing McCulloh was to surrender it.² (Id. p. 790.) It seems that land in large tracts had been granted to certain persons of influence on condition that they be settled within certain dates, for G. A. Selwyn, of England, appointed H. E. McCulloh to surrender any part of three tracts of 100,000 acres each, which had been granted to him upon the above conditions. (Id. Vol. VI, pp. 996-7.) This was in November, 1763, only a year after Jeremiah Greene bought his 541 acres from H. E. McCullough. This would seem to account for the reference by Bishop Spangenberg to the 400 families from the North which had just arrived in 1752, and for the fact that most of the land east of Rowan County had been already taken up at that time. (Id. Vol. IV, p. 1312.)

Meager Facts Concerning.'—This settlement consisted of about ten square miles of the best wheat land in the South, and was located in Davidson County, near Linwood. It was composed of many people from New Jersey who had sent an agent there to locate and enter the best land still open to settlement. According to Rev. C. B. Williams in his "History of the Baptists in North Carolina" (p. 16), "The exact year in which the Jersey Settlement was made on the Yadkin is not known. It is probable that this settlement left New Jersey and arrived on the Yadkin between 1747 and 1755. Benjamin Miller preached there as early as 1755, and the facts indicate that there were already Baptists on the Yadkin when Benjamin Miller visited the settlement. The Philadelphia Association has in its records of 1755 the following reference: "Appointed that one minister from the Jerseys and one from Pennsylvania visit North Carolina." But Miller appears to have gone to the Jersey Settlement still earlier than 1755 . . . (p. 17). Another preacher

---

² See, also, Col. Rec. Vol. V, p. xxxii.

¹ The first mention of this settlement is probably by Bishop Spangenberg (Col. Rec., Vol. IV, p. 1311 to 1314), in which he spoke of 400 families with horses and wagons and cattle having emigrated from the North to North Carolina.

A History of Watauga County

who visited the Jersey Settlement was John Gano. He had been converted just before this time, and was directed by Benjamin Miller, pastor of Scotch Plains Church, New Jersey, to take the New Testament as his guide on baptism. He became a Baptist, and, learning of Carolina from Miller, decided to visit the Jersey Settlement on his way to South Carolina. This he seems to have done in 1756. During his stay at the settlement he tells us in his autobiography that "a Baptist Church was constituted and additions made to it." He left the colony early in the year 1759, and so the church must have been organized between 1756 and 1758. There is a tradition that while there Gano married a Bryan or a Morgan, one of the antecedents of the Bryan family of Boone.

John Gano.—It appears from Rev. Henry Sheets' History of the Liberty Baptist Association (Raleigh, 1907), that the Rev. John Gano had been a Presbyterian, but met Rev. Benjamin Miller, the pastor of the Scotch Plains Baptist Church in New Jersey, who induced him to take the New Testament on the mode and subjects of baptism. In a short time he joined the Baptists and became a minister. On his way to South Carolina, Mr. Gano visited the Jersey Settlement on the Yadkin, and soon after his return home was induced to make a second trip, when he was strongly solicited to move among them. It was on this second journey that he was accompanied by Ebenezer Fairchild, and, by traveling about eight hundred miles, arrived after a journey of five weeks. We have most of Ebenezer Fairchild's diary of their trip to and from the Yadkin, though the first few pages are missing. Fairchild was in a wagon, while Gano and his wife and child were in a chair or chaise, which turned over on one occasion, though no one was hurt.

Ebenezer's Diary.—It begins October 21, 1757, at some unnamed place along the road, where he got up and wrote a letter to his wife, Mr. Gano preaching on the 23d, after which they drove to a Mr. Winchester's, where they remained till Tuesday morning on account of the rain. It was on the day following that Mr. Gano upset the chair, "but they wasn't hurt." Mr. Gano preached that night on "What will ye that I should do unto you?" after which Fairchild smoked a pipe and went to bed. The next day they crossed Menoe Crosse Creek and came to Frederick Town, stopping at Arthur Charleston's, "where they did a little business." They soon forded the "Patomoc," and put up all night at Mr. Nolens. The next day "we see a wench that said she was a negroe to Mr. [undecipherable] son." They then crossed "Goos" Creek and turned out of the Bell Haven Road to a tree marked with a B, where they slept in the woods that night. All the next day they drove in the rain and crossed Bull's Run, and, going on seven "milds furder," came to "one powel ordnari, or powel town." This was Saturday night, and they found forty-five travelers already there, but they remained all night. Having a house to themselves, did not, however, prevent their being kept awake till after ten o'clock by the fiddling and dancing of seven men. The next day Ebenezer was so upset by the want of rest the night before that he could "hardly get any ease lying in the wagon" till he remembered the cause of his restlessness. On the Sabbath John Gano preached from Galatians—chapter and verse undecipherable. "They behaved quite od—talked in meeting and did not sing with us, except two or three of them." The next day they crossed Seder [Cedar?] Creek and came to a "taverne," but passed on to the "Rapahannock and crost it." As it was then night, they went to James Alieson, "but he would not let us stay there, so we drove on again about half a mild and campd in the woods." There Mrs. Gano was quite unwell, but they got her some sage tea and got her to bed also. The next day was November 1st, and they drove ten miles before taking breakfast, going nine miles further on to the south branch of the Rappahannock "and foarded it and ate supper at John Bannon's," where Mrs. Gano spent the night, Fairchild and her husband camping out. There they bought half a bushel of apples for a shilling. Later on they reached Porter's tavern, where they "drank a dram," and then went on again, Mr. Gano buying a turkey on the way, which they dressed and ate at camp that night. The following day they killed a deer by the way and had steaks for supper that night. At a tavern kept by someone unknown to Ebenezer, he got a quart of cider, and ate his dinner alone. Mr. Gano left him at the next tavern, and Fairchild "lay alone that night." But "as there were a bought (about) sixteen Irishmen or there a bought, there was noise all rownd." The next day he got up early and crossed a prong of the James River at Tucker Woodles'. On Saturday they reached Jacob Micaux's, on the south side of the James River, where Fairchild went hunting, but got nothing. At night he and Micaux's family sang psalms, hymns and said poetry till bed time, when he "went to his duty." That is, he had to go out and stay with the wagon, near which several "Irishmen" were camping, who usually "made a noise." The next morning he went early to what seems to be "Guglin" Court House to meet Mr. Gano, who preached from I Peter, 9th chapter, verse 18, "If the righteous scarcely be saved," etc. On the fifth they bought two hens and "made broth, ate supper and went to bed." The next day Ebenezer killed a pilot (snake), and they "past by a smith's shop and a taverne." Then they "crossed Allen's Creek and went two mild furder and campt." On Friday, November 11th, they reached "ronoak and fared over," meaning probably that they ferried over. They bought corn at David Michels, where Gano again left Ebenezer and "he shifted for himself." The 13th was the Sabbath, when Fairchild salted the horses. Gano overtook Fairchild after crossing the Tar or the Haw River, the word being uncertain, bringing with him John Shurman, but Shurman went on to his own home that night. They proceeded on to Orange, but how do you suppose he spelt it? "Orring!" The next day Uriah Carl and another, whose name cannot be deciphered, "being weary of traveling so slo, set out for themselves at high speed, but Tuesday we overtook them, but they set out again." Mr. Gano bought two more hens a short time afterwards, which Fairchild is careful to state that they "cooked." As it rained, Mrs. Gano got into the wagon "and rid till we came to Little Creek, where she got out and maid tea." They came at length to John Hunt's and then drove two miles to Colonel Smith's, where they took out the teams, "unloaded the waggin, and maid it our home." Subsequent disclosures show that they made Colonel Smith's their home—not the "waggin"—where they remained till three days after Christmas, when they set out for their New Jersey home again; not, however, before Fairchild had recorded the fact that "John Stits Gano this day walked half acrost the room all alone—a bat came into the room tonight." While at Colonel Smith's, also, it seems that Fairchild was converted by Mr. Gano's sermon of November 26th, for he writes: "Blessed be God, it was a good day for my sole." While out hunting there they saw "a man on horseback with a woman behind him a straddle." During their stay there Fairchild went to visit Ephriam Coxe, where a woman told him she had lived there six years and had been but to three houses in that neighborhood. On Christmas Day Mr. Gano preached a sermon at Colonel Smith's house, but spent the night at John Hunt's, taking breakfast with Isaac Thomas. There Fairchild "tuned my fiddel, and maid ready to start homeward the next day." But that night he records the fact that he hopes things will grow better; that "men and women do try to preach. Some men do preach with the Bibel wrong end up; sometimes two or three are preaying at once, two or three exhorting at same time." Mr. Marshal McLean, Mr. Breed, Mr. Stain, McMulkey, Mr. Bentin, and how many more separately ministered there I do not know. John Hunt and Benjamin Marvel separately, but preaching; but I believe they are three good men. Mr. McDaniel ———— (name undecipherable), Mr. Swetens, Mr. Wilson, Mr. Minten—these all separately ministered, besides Mr. Marshall. These "are from round about—all but nineteen within fifty mild of Mr. Gano at the Jersey Settlement." They had intended to start back on the 27th, but the weather being bad, they went instead to look at a piece of land. He did not like this as well as land on Muddy Run, with a "sand spring" near the door. To this spring after dinner he took Mrs. Gano, who liked it. He adds forebodingly: "How it will sute my wife I don't know, but I hope well, and my wife to come and see for herself." "After we rid about awhile we went to John Hunt's, there staid till dark, then came home." On the 28th of December they set off on horseback for New Jersey, and reached there on the fifteenth or sixteenth of January, 1758, after crossing the "sus ka hannar" on Friday, the 13th. This was a quick trip, compared with their journey down. The most notable thing that occurred on their return journey was a receipt for a sore backed horse: A pint of salt and a quart of wheat flour, mixed with water in a stout bag or sack. This is then placed on "a clean place in the fire, where it is baked to a hard or firm lump." Then it is gritted up into a powder and poured on the sore place on the horse's back. It was prescribed by "John poepper, hoarse doctor, Mary Land."

Mr. Gano Constitutes a Church.—In Mr. Sheet's history (p. 75) Mr. Gano said that before he left the Yadkin a Baptist Church was constituted and many additions made to it. But he left it in 1758 because of war with the Cherokee Indians. A second son was born to him November 11, 1758. And the new church did not survive his departure very long (p. 76). In a note (p. 76) Mr. Sheets thinks they never had another pastor, and that the records were destroyed or carried off, and the church finally scattered and became extinct. The settlement was on the Yadkin River in what is now Davidson County, and mainly on the south side of what is now the Southern Railway track, near what has always been known as the Indian Trading Ford.

A Colonial Document.

By His Excellency JONATHAN BELCHER, ESQ.,

Captain-General and Commander-in-Chief of the Province of Nova Caesarea, or New Jersey, and Territories thereon depending in America, CHANCELLOR and VICE-ADMIRAL in the same, etc.:

To EBENEZER FAIRCHILD, ESQ.:

Reposing especial trust and confidence in him, he was "under the broad seal of Great Britain" appointed "insigne of that company whereof John Brookfield is captain. You are, therefore, to take the said company to your charge and care as insigne. Done at Elizabethton in New Jersey the 14th day of July in the 31st year of His Majesty's reign, Anoque Domini, 1757. Seal. J. BELCHER."

Lincoln a Plagiarist?—On a blank discharge from Sir Henry Clinton, K. B., General and Commander-in-Chief of all His Majesty's forces within the colonies, lying on the Atlantic Ocean, etc., is written:

Cyrus Fairchild, his hand and pen;
He will be good, but God knows when.

As this is attributed to Abraham Lincoln by some of his biographers as an example of precocious literary ability, it may surprise them to learn that it was current in Watauga County before Lincoln was born.

An Ancient Document.—Among the papers of the late Ebenezer Fairchild is an agreement dated May 23, 1761, by which John Stevens and Alexander Rutherford, for themselves and the devisees of Mary Alexander, undertake to convey to Ebenezer Fairchild, of Newtown, in the county of Sussex, eighty acres of "rights for unappropriated land in the Eastern Division of New Jersey, except Romopok, upon the payment of sixty pounds Proclamation Money of New Jersey."

Carpenter and Yeoman.—There is also a deed from Peter Dukerson, carpenter, of Morristown, province of East New Jersey, to Ebenezer Fairchild, yeoman, of the same place, for fifty acres in Morristown, for seventy-two pounds, dated May 16, 1754, and in the 27th year of His Majesty King George the Second of Great Britain.

On Bound Meadows Run.—There is a warrant for the survey of fifty-three and three-tenths acres of land in the county of Sussex on the head of a southwest branch of Wall Kill, called the Bound Meadows Run, for the devisees of Mary Alexander at the request of Ebenezer Fairchild, by virtue of a warrant to her and Robert Hunter Morris for 1,600 acres of land to be taken up in any part unappropriated in the Eastern Division of New Jersey. It is dated December 9, 1757, and recorded in Book W4, page 14, by virtue of her last will and testament, which is recorded in Book A5, page 9. All recorded in the Public Records of the Proprietors of New Jersey, in the Surveyor General's office at Perth Amboy, in Book S, page 389. John Smyth, Jr., Surveyor General.

AN OLD LETTER.

Morris Town, August 23d, 1771.

The Church of Jesus Christ in this place holding Believers Baptism Laying on of Hands Eternal Election & Final Perseverance of the Saints in Grace &c

To the Church of Christ in Roan County in North Carolina of the same Faith, or to any one of the sister churches to whom These Presents may Come, Greeting:

Whereas our Brother Ebenezer Fairchild has Been Baptized in a Regular Way and Received by Us in Full Communion who for some time gave Good Satisfaction to this Church, But after faling into some Sensorious Errors was Laid under Suspension, And is now Removed from us without a Regular Dispensation has Sent us a Letter Dated September 28, 1770, wherein he seems to make very humble Confession of his Sins and Grievance to the Church and Desires Forgivness for it which, as he Confesses, was Drinking too hard, Loose Living, and also not keeping his Place in the Church which he Acknowledges and Begs our Prayers to God for him that he may be Enabled to Live up to the Profession he has made, which may the Lord help him to do.

Wherefore as his Life and Conversation is now better Known to you than to us, Although by what we Hear from him we do hope he is a Humble Penitent, Therefore, if you do Receive him, he is Dismissed from us, and the God of all Grace Bless you all.

Amen.

Brother Ebenezer Fairchild	James Goble
we rejoice to hear from you	Daniel Walling
such agreeable News may the	John Brookfield
Lord grant you Grace and live	Ezekiel Goble
Agreeable to the profession	Sam'l Parkhurst.
you have made . . . Pray for us.	
Signed by us at our Meeting	
Part for All.	

The Fairchild Ladies.—These ladies, whose names were Rachel and Clara, lived in Watauga County during the first quarter of the nineteenth century on Howard's Creek, where

William Hardin now lives. Rachel Fairchild had married a man named Smith, but he died soon afterwards, and she and her sister were generally known as Fairchilds. They were the daughters of Cyrus Fairchild, son of Ebenezer Fairchild. They reared Wyatt Hayes, and after his marriage deeded to him their land, he having agreed to support them the remainder of their lives. In Deed Book F, page 497, is the record of a deed from "Cirous" Fairchild to Rachel and Clary Fairchild, showing that Rachel did not continue to be known by her late husband's name at that time. The consideration named is "for divers good and causes and considerations for the service of my daughters, Rachel and Clary Fairchild, for the last fifteen years and longer." The land was the 200 acres which Ebenezer Fairchild had entered on Howard's Creek when he first came to this country. The deed is dated April 26, 1843. It is probable that their father died soon afterwards, for when Wyatt Hayes was four years old his mother died, and he was taken to the home of the Misses Fairchild in 1846, where he remained till they died, excepting the time when he was in the Civil War, where he had part of one of his feet shot off at Mechanicsville in the first of the Seven Days Fight around Richmond in 1862.

CHAPTER IX.
Various Churches.

True Democrats.—According to Kephart (p. 268), "the mountaineer is intensely, universally Protestant, and, as John Fox says, 'he is the only man in the world whom the Catholic Church has made little or no effort to proselite.' Dislike of Episcopalianism is still strong among the people who do not know, or pretend not to know, what the word means. The first settlers among the Appalachians were, mainly, Presbyterians, as became Scotch-Irishmen, but they fell away from that faith, partly because the wilderness was too poor to support a regular ministry and partly because it was too democratic for Calvinism, with its supreme authority of the clergy . . . This much of the seventeenth century Calvinism the mountaineer retains: a passion for hair-splitting argument over points of doctrine and the cocksure intolerance of John Knox; but the ancestral creed itself has been forgotten. The circuit rider, whether Methodist or Baptist, found here a field ripe for his harvest. Being himself self-supporting and unassuming, he won easily the confidence of the people. He preached a highly emotional religion that worked his audience into an ecstacy that all primitive people love. And he introduced a mighty agent of evangelization among outdoor folk when he started the camp-meeting."

Our Morals.—"As for the morals of our highlanders," continues Kephart (p. 274), "they are precisely what any well-read person would expect, after taking their belatedness into consideration. In speech and conduct, when at ease among themselves, they are frank, old-fashioned Englishmen and Scots, such as Fielding and Smollet and Peppys and Burns have shown us to the life . . . I have seen the worst as well as the best of Appalachia . . . but I know that between the two extremes the great mass of the mountain people are very like persons of similar station elsewhere, just human, with human frailties, only a little more honest, I think, in owning them . . . The worst have not been driven into a war against society, and still have good traits, strong characters, something responsive to good treatment. They are kind-hearted, loyal to their friends, quick to help anyone in distress."

Pioneer Baptists.—Roosevelt says (Vol. III, pp. 101, 102): "Presbyterianism was not, however, destined even here [in the Watauga Settlement] to remain the leading popular creed. Other sects, still more democratic, still more in keeping with backwoods life and thought, largely supplanted it. Methodism did not become a power until after the close of the Revolution, but the Baptists followed close on the heels of the Presbyterians. They, too, soon built log meeting-houses here and there, while their preachers cleared the forests and hunted elk and buffalo, like other pioneer settlers. To all the churches the preachers and congregation, alike, went armed, the latter leaning their rifles in their pews[1] or near their seats, while the pastor let his stand beside the pulpit." True to the above account, the Baptists were the first to penetrate to what is now Watauga County. Three Forks Church was started in November, 1790, but, while it was the first in what is now Watauga County, it had been preceded in the territory west of the Blue Ridge by the Beaver Creek and Old Fields churches. From Rev. Charles B. Williams' "History of the Baptists in North Carolina" (p. 121) we learn that Three Forks Baptist Church became an association by that name in 1840, and that "like the Yadkin and Catawba associations, the Three Forks had a sharp struggle with antimissionism. But its churches are now taking their stand in the regular lines of the convention's advanced work. It numbers thirty-three churches, with a membership of 2,728, and contribued in 1900 to all objects $1,457.00." Col. Thomas Bingham, for several terms a member of the State legislature and clerk of the Superior Court of Watauga County, was born 1845, and remembers that as late as 1854 or 1855 two Missionary Baptists appeared at the Cove Creek Baptist Church, near which his father then lived, but were not made welcome in the church.

---

[1] These "pews" were simply split logs, with pegs for legs or support, and without backs of any kind.

REV. REUBEN P. FARTHING.

However, they preached in the grove that night, and moved their subsequent meetings to the house of his father, G. M. Bingham's, where they held protracted meetings, one that summer and another the following winter. But a few years later Three Forks itself became a Missionary Baptist association, as did also Cove Creek.

Farthing Family.—The coming of the Farthing family to Beaver Dams gave a fresh impetus to the cause of the Baptist Church in this section. They arrived in the fall of 1826, having come from Orange, close to the Wake County line, two brothers, William W. and John, having been first here. But William soon died, and John, having lost his wife, returned to Wake, where, having married again, he reappeared in Beaver Dams settlement in 1831 and settled where Zionville now flourishes. They organized Bethel Church, on Beaver Dams, July 4, 1851, getting their constitution from the Cove Creek Church, and having a membership of ten. Three other churches were constituted from Bethel, viz: Beaver Dams, in September, 1874; Forest Grove, about 1889, and Timbered Ridge in 1906.

A Family of Preachers.—The first Dudley Farthing, father of Rev. William W. Farthing, who came to Beaver Dams in October, 1826, was a public speaker of note in his home county, but he always said that as he could blow only a ram's horn and not a silver trumpet, he would not be a preacher. But his son, William, was a preacher of force and fame, and, although his health was such after his removal to this county that he did not preach often, he left four sons, upon whose shoulders his mantle fell and with whom it abided. They were Reuben P., John A., Stephen*and Abner C. Farthing, who for years were the captain jewels in the Baptist carcanet. And their descendants still wear the armor they laid aside, and are still battling in the vanguard of the army of the Lord as preachers and leaders, while still others, feeling that in the pulpit they would be as helpless as David would have been in the armor of Saul, in their own way and in God's good time are striking mighty blows in the sacred cause of righteousness. No family in Watauga County have done more for the general uplift than that of the Farthings.

A History of Watauga County

Rev. Joseph Harrison.—This "just and faithful knight of God" was the son of Joseph Harrison, and was born February 4, 1799, in Iredell County, close to Black Oak Ridge, now Alexander County. Joseph, Sr., came from England with his brother, Benjamin, Ben going to Indiana and Joseph to Iredell. There he married Mrs. Nancy Price, whose father was John Caldwell. They had five children: Nathan, born in 1824, married Polly Harrison, his cousin; Joseph, born February 2, 1843, married, first, Elizabeth Hamlet, second, Carolina Wolff, third, Alice Baird, and fourth, Albertine Bond; Malinda, born in 1822, married Wilson Bradshaw; Mary, born in 1834, married John Cook, and Martha, born August 24, 1836, married Emanuel Van Dyke. He preached from 1825 till his death in 1884. He was repeatedly elected Register of Deeds of Watauga County, but during the Civil War he remained loyal to the Union, refusing to take the oath of allegiance to the Confederacy, with the result that Rev. D. C. Harmon served during that time.

Cove Creek Baptist Church.—There was such a strong representation in the Three Forks Baptist Church from the Cove Creek section that in April, 1799, it held its meeting there, and again in June, when Sarah Davis, Abraham Linvil and Susannah Vanderpool were received by experience, while in the following July Catharine Linvil, Margaret Linvil, Mathias Harmon, John Holsclaw and Morgan Isaacs were received by experience. These were followed in August, 1799, by Sarah Davis (probably daughter of the Sarah who had been received in June), Phoebe Vanderpool and George Davis, who were likewise received by experience. The first Saturday in September Three Forks Church again met at Cove Creek and chose Brothers Chambers and Samuel Vanderpool to attend the association at King's Creek on the fourth Saturday in that month. At this meeting also Brother Vanderpool's petition for a church at Cove Creek was granted, while in December, 1799, the newly constituted Cove Creek Church asked Three Forks for ministerial help for ordination, and it was granted, the constitution having been granted already. The first church was of logs and tradition says stood on the creek, but was washed away with the bridge over which the road then crossed, half a mile above Sugar Grove. The road was then changed so as to go around the hill and ford the creek below the site of the old log bridge which the freshet had carried off. This church was then moved to the site of the present Walnut Grove Academy, but was still of logs, and Hugh M. Isaacs, who was born in 1839, attended this church with his mother when he was six years of age, and remembers distinctly that the birds flew around inside the church, feeding their young in their nests in the roof and eaves, the logs being open, without chinking of any kind. It then stood where the Academy now stands and where there are yet two or three graves.

Bethel Baptist Church.—This church was constituted July 4, 1851, from Cove Creek Baptist Church. The members were Wm. B., Abner C., Stephen J., Ann, widow of Wm. B., Anne W., Rachel W., Mary N. and Margaret Farthing, and Madison Johnson and Nancy Johnson. The first church was of logs and stood on the knoll across the road from the site of the present church, which was erected in 1872 or 1873, and was probably the best in the county at that time. It has constituted three other churches which have drawn their membership mainly from Bethel: Beaver Dams Baptist Church, constituted in September, 1874; Forest Grove Baptist Church, constituted in 1889, and Timbered Ridge Baptist Church, in 1906.

South Fork Baptist Church.—This was the third church constituted in Watauga County, and stood at what was known as Elk Cross Roads.

Ebenezer was perhaps the fourth church to be constituted, and was built at what is now called Zionville. Later on three churches were merged into this and called Mt. Zion, but afterwards took the name of the place at which it stood, Zionville.

Other Early Churches.—Laurel Springs Church was constituted before the Civil War, with Joseph Brown and Riley Norris as prime movers. The Blowing Rock Church began about 1900 with the Hartleys, Greens and Browns as chief supporters. In 1885 or thereabout the church at Shull's Mills was begun, with the Robbins, Shulls and Browns active in its interest. In 1890 or thereabout George and Isaac McGinnis and Marion Story constituted the church at Mt. Lebannon, while about 1895 James Perry and Carroll Adams started Pleasant Grove at Silverstone. Andrew J. and Eli Harman began the Zion Hill Church about 1880, and at about the same time Elias Isaacs and the Phillips family were active in constituting Mount Gillead. Bethany, near the top of Beach Mountain, began about 1895, and Gap Creek about 1875, with Larkin Michael zealous in the interest of the former and John Hopkins in that of the latter. Rich Mountain Church was constituted about 1900, and 'Doe Ridge, on Stony Fork, about 1900.

Brushy Fork Baptist Church was constituted February 26, 1858, by Elders D. C. Harman and Joseph Harrison, with eleven members, to wit: M. C. Harman, Moses Hateley, John A. Hagaman, Sarah Reece, Sally Hagaman, Sarah Hagaman, Susan Danner, Elvira Holsclaw, Elizabeth Hix, Melissa Harman and Sarah Monday. Elder D. C. Harman was the first pastor and served the church in succession for about twenty-five years, except eight or ten months, when he was in the Civil War. The following elders have served the church as pastors: D. C. Harman, A. C. Farthing, E. F. Jones, J. J. L. Sherwood, David Green, J. F. Eller, E. M. Gragg, J. F. Davis, Sidney King, Omey Triplett, S. L. Fox and J. M. Payne. The church has ordained the following ministers: John A. Hagaman, J. F. Davis, I. J. McGinnis, Thos. C. Holsclaw, S. L. Fox and John P. Hagaman.

The Boone Baptist Church.—This church was constituted in 1882 (Deed Book J, p. 502), by W. L. Bryan and Thomas J. and W. C. Coffey and others. This congregation is now erecting a large and handsome brick church on the corner of Main and School House Streets, to cost over $5,000.00.

Other Early Churches.—The South Fork Baptist Church at Elk Cross Roads was the third church to be constituted in this county, and among the finest and best beloved of its pastors was William Wilcox. Ebenezer was the fourth church, and it with two others were merged into one, called Mount Zion, which afterwards took the name of the town which grew up about it—Zionville. It was here that John Farthing had settled on his re-

A History of Watauga County 103

turn to this country in 1831. Antioch was organized largely through the influence of the Rev. D. C. Harman, with the assistance of Messrs. Dyer and Wiley Harman, as well as members of the Hix and Ward families. In it the Rev. L. W. Farthing has been a factor of great good. It was constituted in 1848, and a log house which stood in a meadow near the left bank of the Watauga River, from which position it was washed away in the May freshet of 1901. In 1904 the original site of the first St. John's, surrounded by young white oaks, was bought from the Episcopal Church and a large and attractive frame structure erected there.

Stony Fork Association Churches.—Among the Baptist Churches belonging to this association are Poplar Grove, Mount Vernon, Laurel Fork in the Storie settlement, Boone's Fork, Yadkin Elk and Doe Ridge.

Bishop Asbury's Journal.—It is generally supposed that this good man did not travel through Watauga in his trips through these mountains, but the following excerpts show the contrary: "Monday, April 28, 1788 (after preaching the day before at the Globe on John's River [p. 31]), after getting our horses shod, we . . . entered upon the mountains, the first of which I called Steel, the second Stone, and the third Iron Mountain; they are tough and difficult to climb. We were spoken to on our way by most awful thunder and lightning, accompanied by heavy rain. We crept for shelter into a little dirty house, where the filth might have been taken from the floor with a spade. We felt the want of fire, but could get little wood to make it, and what we gathered was wet. At the head of Watauga we fed, and reached Ward's that night.[2] Coming on the river next day, we hired a young man to swim over for a canoe, in which we crossed, while our horses swam to the other shore. The waters being up, we were compelled to travel an old road over the mountains. Night came on . . . About nine o'clock we came to Greer's . . .

---
[2] This was probably Ben Ward, whose descendants are among Watauga's best citizens. There is a tradition that while at Ward's the Bishop needed a better light than that afforded by the open fire, and that Ward supplied it by throwing deer bones on the live coals from a heap of all sorts of bones kept in the chimney jamb for that purpose. It is not mentioned in the Journal, however.

"Monday, April 5, 1790 (p. 78). After worming the stream (John's River) for awhile, we took through the Laurel Hill and had to scale the mountains, which in some places were rising like the roof of a house. We came to the head of Watauga River; a most neglected place. Here the people have had their corn destroyed by frost, and many of them have moved away. It was thus we found it in Tyger's Valley. We passed by W—'s, a poor lodging, and slept at the Beaver Dam in a cabin without a cover, except what a few boards supplied. We had very heavy thunder and lightning, and most hideous yelling of wolves around, with rain, which is most frequent in the mountains. Tuesday, 6th. We were compelled to ride through the rain, and crossed the Stone Mountain . . . We came on to the dismal place called Roan's Creek, which was pretty full . . . Reaching Watauga, we had to swim our horses, and ourselves to cross in a canoe . . . At length we came to Greer's, and halted for the night.

"Wednesday, March 27, 1793 (p. 189, Vol. II). We began our journey over the great ridge of mountains. We had not gone far before we saw and felt the snow . . . We came to the head of Watauga River. Stopped at Mr. S—'s . . . My soul felt for the neglected people. It may be, by my coming this way, that I shall send them a preacher. We hasted on to Cove's Creek; invited ourselves to stay at C—'s, where we made our own tea, obtained some butter and milk and some most excellent Irish potatoes. We were presented with a little flax for our beds, on which we spread our coats and blankets, and three of us slept before a large fire. Thursday, 28th. We made an early start, and came to the Beaver Dam; three years ago we slept here in a cabin without a cover. We made a breakfast at Mr. W—'s,[3] and then attempted the Iron or Stone Mountain, which is steep like the roof of a house. I found it difficult and trying to my lungs to walk up it. Descending the mountain, we had to jump down the steep stairs,[4] from two to three and four feet.

---

[3] This was probably Benjamin Webb, the first settler on Beaver Dams, and who sold out to Rev. W. W. Farthing in 1826.

[4] This gap is commonly called Star Gap, though many insist that its true name is Stair Gap because of the steps mentioned by Bishop Asbury.

At the foot of this mountain our guide left us to a man on foot; he soon declined, and we made the best of our way to Dugger's Ford, on Roan's Creek. We came down the river where there are plenty of large, round, rolling stones, and the stream was rapid. Wednesday, April 22, 1795 (p. 263, Vol. II). Crossed the ridge and kept on to the westward. We went Major J. White's path, and found it abundantly better than the old one. We reached the top of the ridge in about six miles. Here we found ourselves among fruitful hills; then we had a good path for six miles more, except where there were some laurel branches and roots. We stopped at S—'s, and it was well we did, or we would have been well nigh starved, both man and horse. I went on to D—'s, and thence to Nelson's, where I met with Brothers B—, A— and W—, ancient men among us. I stood the fatigue and sleeping three in a bed better than I expected. From White's to Nelson's is eighty miles. We crossed the Watauga about twenty times. At supper we ate of the perch that are taken in great plenty from Smith's fish spring. I judge there must be a subterraneous communication from that to the river.[5] Wednesday, March 22, 1797 (p. 340, Vol. II). After preaching at John's River on the 21st, "I set out on my journey for the west . . . It began to rain violently before we came to Henley's. I took shelter in a house from the rain, and talked and prayed with a poor woman. We dined at Mr. Henley's, calling at Wakefield only to talk and pray. I cannot well pass by my friends without calling. We hastened across Linville Mountain, which is awfully barren, and came on to Young's Cove . . ."

White's Spring Church.—Whenever Bishop Asbury visited John's River he was entertained by Major Joseph White, as the Bishop's Journal shows (Vol. II, pp. 31, 78, 189). By April, 1795, Major White had constructed a good road over the Blue Ridge, probably through what is now called the Coffey Gap, as the Bishop speaks of following the "Major J. White's path, and found it abundantly better than the old one" (Vol. II, p. 263).

---
[5] This is what is now known as Fish Spring, four miles below Butler, Tenn. But there is nothing separating the spring from the river, and no fish are found in the spring, floods having washed the intervening bank away.

Major White had a camp near this old path, and the fine spring there, and just below the Coffey Gap, still goes by the name of White's Spring. This is the same White who was a major in Colonel McDowell's regiment. A good building for the accommodation of the Methodists was erected near this spring about 1895, and commands a fine view. According to Draper (note on page 149), Captain Joseph White was wounded at Cowan's Ford in a skirmish September 12, 1780, and was at King's Mountain (Id. p. 474).

Methodist Churches.—According to Mr. Cyrus A. Grubb, of Laxton Creek, Methodism began in this county about 1809 when an itinerant minister, whose name he has forgotten, traveled through what is now this county in the interest of Charles Wesley's newly founded church, Bishop Asbury having preceded him at various times between 1788 to 1798, but passing through only a small corner and holding meetings in this section and in other sections, notably in Buncombe County, from 1800 to 1813. This unnamed pioneer in Methodism is said to have stopped first at the home of Gwyn Houck on Old Fields Creek, next at Risden Cooper's on Cranberry, then at James Jackson's on the ridge between Grassy Creek and Meat Camp, afterwards going to Edward Moody's on upper Watauga, followed by a visit to a man named Davis on Cove Creek. No visit seems to have been made to Boone, or what was probably nobody's home at that time, for, unless the first Jordan Councill had moved here then, this locality was probably "all in woods." At each place he "left an appointment," as the saying went in those days and as it still goes in many parts in these days. Out of the visit to Cooper's grew what is now Cranberry Church, on the ridge between Cranberry Creek and Meadow Creek. The Cooper family has always stood for this branch of the Christian religion, and its influence has been powerful and efficacious in that cause. James Jackson was so much interested in the necessity for some edifice in which all the people might come and worship, go to school or discuss public affairs, that he conveyed to Edmund Blackburn, a brother of Levi, David Miller and Ephraim and William Norris, as trustees, a tract of land for a school house, meeting house or church, as was desired by those using it, to be open at all times to all alike. It was at this house that the first Methodist preacher first preached, but his name has been forgotten. Levi Blackburn lived near Jackson Meeting House at that time, but soon afterwards sold out to Jonathan Norris and moved to Riddle's Fork of Meat Camp—a section then and since known as Hopewell. Here a log school house was used as a church when the congregation proved too large to be accommodated in Levi's hospitable home, where for many years preaching was held whenever there chanced to be a preacher in the neighborhood. About that time another appointment was left at Elk Cross Roads, to which Levi Blackburn soon moved and where he died, and where he started another church, using his home or a log school house for the purpose for many years. This is as far as Brother Grubb's information extends, but others state that when Henry Taylor came to live at Valle Crucis he became active in the cause of Methodism, and his family have since followed in his footsteps. He is said to have induced preachers to hold meetings in the orchard in rear of the present store house of W. W. Mast at Valle Crucis, in his own home and at Franklin Baird's home, a mile down the Watauga. As interest increased he acquired the home that had been occupied by "Old Man" Christoffle,[*] a chairmaker, who lived on the right hand side of the road going from Valle Crucis to Charles D. Taylor's present mill, inside a field. This house was enlarged and was the first Methodist Church in that community. This was in the fifties. This small house was used only three or four years, when another was built where the present edifice now stands, long before the Civil War. The present large frame church was built in 1895. Among the more active pioneers in Methodism in this place were Joel and Levi Moody, Sally Tester, Franklin Baird, Andrew Mast and the first Joseph Shull. But its growth was slow for a long period. Among the first elders and preachers were Elder Haskew, who came from

---

[*] Tradition says that this man was judicially and *judiciously* whipped at Boone for having stolen "hawgs." One who saw the thirty-nine lashes "well laid on" remembers that the licks were struck with small willow switches, which made first white and then red stripes. Christoffle left the country after this disgrace.

Tennessee long before the Civil War; Archelus Brooks and a Mr. Allspaw. Since the Civil War the church has grown to be the largest and most influential of the denomination in the entire county, most probably.

Henson's Chapel.—According to Col. Thomas Bingham, Elizabeth Whitlow was the first Methodist who ever came to what is now Watauga County. She came with her family when they were on their way to Tennessee in 1810 or 1811, and, becoming snow-bound on Brushy Fork, became acquainted with Golston Davis, whom she afterwards married. Golston followed her to Tennessee, where they were married, and soon returned and started a Methodist community. This is probably the Davis with whom the first itinerant left an appointment, as stated by Cyrus Grubb. But there was no Methodist Church for a long time, the first Methodist preacher who passed up Cove Creek using the log Baptist Church which formerly stood on the site on which the present Walnut Grove Academy now stands. But he preached largely, if not entirely, to Baptists, and when he offered to leave another appointment there objection was made. Whereupon, this Methodist preacher asked if there was not some member of the congregation who would open the doors of his home for the next appointment, and Golsten Davis offered his own home for that purpose. It is said that Davis was not a very prepossessing looking man, and that up to that good hour his wife had been more charmed with the beauty of his heart than with the pulchritude of his person. But when he rose and made this offer, tradition says she declared that he was "pretty," using a generic word for good looks which is still common with our people. At that meeting at Davis's house only two or three were present. This was near Amantha and that preacher's name was Greer. From this nucleus grew the present large Methodist community which worships at Henson's Chapel, built about 1868, the widow of Charles Henson having donated the land for that purpose. Her name was Elizabeth, and she came with her husband from Iredell County about 1829 or 1830. The present house, replacing the one built in 1868, was built about 1885. This congregation is credited with paying more money for all purposes than any other Methodist Church in the county, having contributed this year $563.00, of which $360.00 is for the pastor's salary. It has 196 members, of whom J. B. Horton, Don Horton, Thomas Bingham and J. C. Henson are very active and earnest. Among those most prominent in the past are recalled the names of George M. Bingham, John Combs, Thomas Harbin and wife, Charles Henson and his wife, Elizabeth, George Moody, Mrs. Eli Farmer and Golson Davis and wife. Among those who preached here in the distant past were Messrs. Miles, Joshua Cole, Tillett, Blackburn and Martin. Sheriff A. J. McBride was for a time a Methodist preacher, but toward the close of his life became a Baptist minister, dying in that faith.

The Boone Methodist Church.—This was organized soon after the close of the Civil War, meetings having been held prior to that time in the court house and elsewhere. But about 1873 land was bought on the hill on which now stands the residence of J. M. Moretz and a church seating 600 erected. This was used till September, 1897 (Deed Book T, p. 369), when M. B. Blackburn sold them the small lot on which the present church was built. The Hardin, Winkler, Blair, Norris, Blackburn, Lovill, Bingham, Councill, Critcher, Rivers and Linney families are prominent in this church.

Other Churches.—After the Civil War the third church was built at Elk Cross Roads, after which J. N. and his wife, Nancy, Norris conveyed land to G. W. Norris and C. A. Grubb and others, as trustees in April, 1886, at Fairview, where a large congregation worships (Deed Book L, p. 575). On the 4th of February, 1882, George W. Dugger conveyed to Thomas Proffitt, R. N. Culver, E. H. Banner, J. H. Perry and A. J. Proffitt, as trustees, land for a Methodist Church at Banner's Elk, which church was soon afterwards erected. In this community the church is quite strong, its members having worshipped before acquiring this land in a common meeting house used by all denominations. On the 19th day of April, 1902, John W. Hodges and wife and Robert L. Bingham conveyed to L. H. Michael and others, as trustees, land at Rutherwood for a

Methodist Church, which was soon afterwards erected (Deed Book Z, p. 142). The first Methodist Church at Hopewell was a small log house which stood in rear of the present home of Wiley W. Blackburn on the land of Joseph Miller. It had been built by Levi Blackburn and his sons about 1850, but afterwards a frame church was erected 100 yards above the site of the first log structure. This stood till about 1900, when the present house was built about 300 yards from the former. As well as Rev. Lorenzo Dow Cole, who for years has been the chaplain of the Nimrod Triplet Camp, Confederate States Veterans, now recalls, the first Methodist preacher in this county found Aunt Elizabeth Cooper on Meadow Creek, away back in the earliest days, and left an appointment at her house, and when Cyrus A. Grubb was a boy they were preaching in an out-house in her yard. Out of this in 1885 grew the present Cranberry Church. One of the earliest churches built was at John Morphew's, and later on near Laxton's Creek. About 1875 the Blackburns and Grahams built a church at Todd. It is called Blackburn Chapel. Rev. James Daly, Joseph Haskew and ———— Clawton were presiding elders prior to the Civil War. Among the preachers who have served the Methodist Churches since the war are Messrs. George Stewart, G. W. Miles, L. L. Cralock, B. W. S. Bishop, Taylor, Wheeler, Cook, Cordell, Blair, Bagley, Vestal, Jones and Bennett.

A Family of M. E. Church Preachers.—William Matney and John Wright with their families came from England to America just after the close of the Revolutionary War and settled in Virginia, near the James River, William finally locating in Pittsylvania County, where he spent the remainder of his life. He was a strict John Wesley type of a Methodist. Two of his children, John and James, are remembered yet by his North Carolina descendants, John having married Nancy Wright, a daughter of John Wright above named, and after a few years removed from Pittsylvania to a farm near the Moravian Falls, in Wilkes County, and, after most of his children were grown, he sold this farm and moved to Caldwell. He had a large family of children, was a scholarly man for his day, taught school, conducted religious services and was an effective, old-time Methodist exhorter. All of his five boys married except one who died at fourteen, while all of his seven girls followed their example, one of them marrying Adam Hampton, of Watauga, and the others Caldwell and Wilkes County men. John Matney's eldest son, William, settled in Missouri; John was killed at the battle of Gettysburg, while James and Thomas became itinerant Methodist preachers of the M. E. Church. Thomas came to Watauga County just after the close of the Civil War, and James followed in 1871, both preaching in the bounds of the Blue Ridge circuit. James Matney organized six of the churches of this circuit, the first having been in 1865 and in the home of Samuel Brown, the grandfather of R. M. Brown. Thomas Matney had eight boys, six of whom were preachers. Two have died and two others have gone to other States, while two still remain members of the Blue Ridge Atlantic Conference. Thomas Matney died at Montezuma, now in Avery County, while James Matney died at his home in Watauga, February 28, 1914, aged ninety-one years, his widow and three children still residing here. One son, Prof. W. W. Matney, resides in Asheville. The men of this family seem specially called to preach, and all are law-abiding citizens and friends of education, temperance and progress.

Methodist Episcopal Churches.—This branch of the Methodist Church did not begin its work in this section till after the close of the Civil War. There is a church of this denomination on the Blue Ridge, known as Brown's Chapel, and others at the mouth of Grassy Creek, on the head of Valley Creek and at Silverstone, and the Pine Grove Methodist Church one mile from Antioch Baptist Church on lower Watauga.

Primitive Baptists.—For years this church, also called Hard Shells, Anti-missionary, etc., Baptists, were the prevailing denomination of this entire mountain country. They were the pioneers and fought the first battles with sin in this wilderness, led by preachers who refused all compensation for their services as ministers of the gospel. A church of that faith is still flourishing on the upper Watauga, near Shull's Mills. It seems that the real name of this denomination is simply "Baptists."

The Presbyterian, Southern.—There is a flourishing church of this denomination at Banner's Elk, which was established there about 1900, and another at Blowing Rock, established in 1898. That there are schools with both these churches goes without saying, as with this denomination beside the foundation stone of Christ and Him crucified is always laid still another foundation stone, EDUCATION. The good work these churches are doing is simply incalculable. With them, faith without works is dead, while to be in true fellowship with them, one must prove his faith *by* his works. Schools, hospitals, orphanages, domestic science and other practical and helpful enterprises, signalize this denomination wherever it is found. Gradually the descendants of the old Scotch Covenanters are returning to the home of their great-great-grandfathers, always to remain.

The Lutherans.—This church is the Protestant Church of Germany, having been founded long before Henry the Eighth established the Church of England. Martin Luther believed that the people were entitled to read and interpret the entire Bible, and to that end defied the Diet at Worms with words that will live forever: "Here I stand, God helping me. I can do no otherwise." The large German and Dutch element of our population required a church of this character, and one was established at Valle Crucis before Bishop Ives arrived in 1842. Among these were William Van Dyke, Andrew and Alexander and James Townsend, Harvey Hollers, Samuel Lusk, members of the Herman family, and David Shook, all Lutherans. Their church stood to the left of the road going from Mast's store at Valle Crucis toward the Mission School, in a little flat above Dr. Perry's, nearly opposite the site of the first Methodist Church. It was here that Christian Moretz preached, while others came occasionally. It is mentioned in the "Life of W. W. Skiles" that members of this church worshipped with the Valle Crucis Mission during the time of Bishop Ives. Timothy Townsend is now a vestryman of the Episcopal Church at Valle Crucis. Prior to the establishment of this church at Valle Crucis, about 1845,

A History of Watauga County

according to Alfred J. Moretz, his father, John Moretz, established the first Lutheran Church in the county, near Soda Hill, in a small school house. This church was visited in summer months by Lutheran ministers from Lincoln, Iredell and Catawba counties. These preached at first in German. Among the first of these preachers were Alfred J. Fox, of Lincoln; Jonathan and Timothy Mosers, of Catawba, and Father Henry Goodman, of Iredell, and Adam Elfird, of Lincoln. The first sermon was preached at Lookabill school house. The Lutheran Church was not built there till after the Civil War, say, 1866 or 1867. A new church replaced the first about 1890. Another Lutheran Church was built about 1900 at the head of Meat Camp Creek. There is also one on Dutch Creek at Valle Crucis, while there is a small congregation at Gap Creek. The Moretz, Winebarger, Woodring and Davis families, of Meat Camp, were attendants of these churches. There is a German Reformed Church at Blowing Rock, with Rev. John Ingle as pastor. The Lutherans, under the leadership of Rev. Mr. Carpenter, are preparing to build a church edifice in Boone.

The Episcopalians.—In addition to the facts stated in Chapter VII, it should be recorded that on June 26, 1882, the late D. B. Dougherty conveyed to the Diocese of North Carolina a lot in Boone opposite the late Dr. W. B. Councill's home place. (Deed Book "J," page 488.) Shortly thereafter George W. Councill was given the contract to build the present St. Luke's Church. After Mr. Savage's arrival, in 1903, a vestibule and chancel were added to the original building.

CHAPTER X.
County History.

Formation of the County.—In 1848 George Bower, called "Double Head" because of his wisdom and farsightedness, was in the State Senate from Ashe, and Reuben Mast in the House. Bower lived in Jefferson, while Mast lived near Valle Crucis, thirty-five miles from the county-seat, which rendered it very inconvenient for him and his neighbors to attend court. As Ashe County embraced in its limits not only what is now Watauga, but the present county of Alleghany also, it could very well spare the southern portion, which was too remote for convenience. Besides, Jordan Councill, Jr., lived in the territory which it was sought to detach from the mother county, and his influence, which was great, was thrown for the new county. As he was the brother-in-law of Senator Bower, he naturally "had the ear of the court." A bill for a new county was, accordingly, introduced in the legislature and passed in 1849.

Jordan Councill, Jr.'s, Influence.—This gentleman for years kept the only store in this section. He fixed prices of all things in which he dealt. He bought large steers for as low as nine dollars each, and drove them and the larger cattle to the Valley of Virginia, frequently accompanied by his brother-in-law, George Bower. From Virginia they went north and bought their stocks of goods, shipping them by water to Richmond, Va., and from there by canal boat to Lynchburg, from which point they were brought by wagon to Boone and Jefferson. Other goods were shipped by water to Fayetteville, from which they were brought by wagon to Boone. Councill would load wagons with deer hams and hides, butter, cranberries, dried fruit, beeswax, tallow, etc., and, drawn by six horses, these wagons were hauled to Charleston, S. C. With the wagon train went droves of mules and horses, which were sold along the road to planters and goods purchased with the proceeds. He unwittingly hauled a rat in a goods box from Charleston to Boone on one occasion. He drove cattle—fat cows and heifers—to Charlotte and Concord. Large droves of cattle, horses and mules passed through Boone from Kentucky to the South and East before and since the Civil War. Hogs were driven through before, but not since, the Civil War. When the location of the county seat was to be determined it was the influence of Jordan Councill, Jr., that fixed it near his store and dwelling. Some wanted the court house at Brushy Fork and others at Valle Crucis. It would most probably have been located at the Muster Ground, half a mile east of Boone, if Benjamin Councill, Sr., had been willing to donate the ground for that purpose, but as Ransom Hayes and Jordan Councill, Jr., were willing to donate twenty-five acres each, it was determined to locate the court house where F. A. Linney's residence now stands, Hayes deeding twenty-five acres between the branch above Blackburn's hotel, then called Upper Branch, and the branch that flows by the new post office, then called the Middle Branch, and Councill a like amount of land between the Middle and Lower Branches, as the stream that flows west of the Critcher hotel—the old Coffey hotel—was called.

Three New England Visitors.—Watauga has had three distinguished visitors from New England: Dr. Elisha Mitchell, of the North Carolina University; Charles Dudley Warner, and Miss Margaret W. Morley. To our everlasting regret, we pleased only that last of these, but, as she was the most recent, it is hoped that we had improved since the visits of the other two. "Faithful are the wounds of a friend," said Solomon thousands of years ago. If so, then Dr. Mitchell and Mr. Warner were our friends indeed, for they "spoke right out." As Dr. Mitchell's remarks were in letters to his wife and not intended for the public, nothing he wrote rankles, but while we are anxious to attribute the Warner strictures to dyspepsia, he certainly "stuck to what he said," having preserved what he wrote for *Harper's Magazine* in 1884, and repeated it in book form (On Horseback) in 1888.[1] He certainly flayed us, sparing

---
[1] "On Horseback."

nothing and nobody. And if, in this Land of the Sky, he saw a bird or a bee or a sunbeam; if a single pleasant odor from the chalices of the wild flowers was wafted to his nostrils, if a bird sang within his hearing or a child's prattle appealed to him once during the whole of that two hundred miles' journey through the mountains of Tennessee and North Carolina in the liquid gold of our summer sunlight, he left no record of it in the saturnine account of his trip which he published to the world. On the other hand, Miss Morley, who passed over a part of this same route a few years later, saw the sunshine imprisoned in our flowers, heard the strains of invisible choirs in babbling brook and singing bird, and recognized angel faces in the countenances of little children clinging to those whom Mr. Warner called their "frowsy" mothers.² Mr. Warner's chief trouble seemed to be flies. Whenever he stopped, there seemed to him to be nothing but flies. They were not only in the ointment, but in the amber also. And no wonder, for on leaving Abingdon, Va., the saddle he rode was discovered to have been smeared the previous winter with tallow. Seat, pommel, cantle, stirrup leathers and saddle skirts, all had been covered with tallow, which had been well rubbed in when they were put away the winter before. Mr. Warner discovered this before he started on his journey, and bought white overalls, which served to protect his trousers from the grease. This grease, mixed with the dust of the road, attracted the flies, and *hinc illæ lacrimæ*, or words to that general effect.

Dr. Mitchell's Geological Tour.²—In July, 1828, this gentleman of New England birth and North Carolina adoption, for he was then a slave-owner, made a tour of the mountain counties at the expense of the State, and "determined" several specimens of minerals that were submitted to him. He passed over the Ballou iron mines, the Ore Knob copper mines, the mica mines near Beaver Creek, the porcelain clay on Howard's Creek, and was near the Elk Mountain copper vein; he visited the

---
² "The Carolina Mountains," Houghton-Mifflin Co., Boston, 1913.
² This diary was published by the University of North Carolina in its James Sprunt Historical Monograph, No. 6, 1905. It should be widely read.

A History of Watauga County

Grandfather and did not recognize the tamarack tree nor the great age of the rocks of that ancient pile, thinking they "belonged to the transition of Tennessee," whatever that may or may not mean. But he made no report of his journey and seemed never to have suspected that copper, iron and mica of great wealth and abundance existed at the points indicated. But he did find fault with one of our ladies because she wiped her soiled hands on her clean apron just before she began to mix the meal for his bread, and called some of the women with whom two hunters were living illicitly "schquaws, very pretty ones, but schquaws notwithstanding." He visited Robert Shearer's, where he met his "pretty daughter and her husband, a good-hearted fellow, not half good enough for her." He preached at Three Forks Baptist Church, stopped at Jordan Councill's store, which he found open on Sunday, and visited Noah Mast, David Miller and several others.

The Tennessee Boundary Line.—In 1784 North Carolina passed an act to give Congress twenty-nine million acres lying between the Alleghanies and the Mississippi River. Congress needed the money with which to pay off debts incurred during the Revolutionary War, but that was not the principal reason for the cession of this great territory, much of the best portions of which had been already granted to settlers. Up to that time the people of the ceded territory had presented many claims for compensation for military services, supplies, etc., in campaigns against the Cherokees, in the strict justness of which the mother State did not altogether believe. On the score of poverty North Carolina had refused to establish a Superior Court in this territory, called the Watauga Settlement, or to appoint a prosecuting officer. The four counties comprising the settlements west of the mountains were Davidson, Washington, Sullivan and Greene, and their representatives voted in the legislature for the cession. The act of cession provided, however, that the sovereignty and jurisdiction of North Carolina should continue over the ceded territory until it should be accepted by Congress, and made the act void if Congress should not accept the gift within two years. As most of the Watauga settlers were originally from Virginia, the majority were anxious for an excuse to withdraw from North Carolina and set up a government of their own. The result was the attempt to establish the independent State of Franklin, with John Sevier at its head. This attempted secession failed and North Carolina resumed full jurisdiction over the disputed territory before March, 1788. Congress accepted the cession of the territory, and in 1796 the State of Tennessee was organized. In 1796 North Carolina ordered a survey of the boundary line between the two States.

Boundary Line and Land Grant Disputes.—Any map of North Carolina will show that the line between it and Tennessee runs due south from the Hiawassee River, instead of following the general southwestern direction with the trend of the mountains. The case decided by the Supreme Court of the United States in 1914, between Tennessee and North Carolina, grew out of a dispute over the line at the head of Telico and Citico Creeks, just north of the Hiawassee River, being what is called the Rainbow Country. Telico and Citico Creeks rise much further east than the points at which the State line crosses those streams, the mountain range bending eastward instead of following the general southwestern course of the range. The Supreme Court decision is to the effect that, as it was originally run and marked there, and both States adopted that line soon thereafter as being in accord with the Act of Cession, each State is bound thereby. Why Tennessee consented to this loss of territory may be accounted for by the fact that the line runs due south from the Hiawassee River to the Georgia line.[4] There is, however, no evidence that the commissioners agreed to exchange what North Carolina gained in the "Rainbow" country for what Tennessee gained south of the Hiawassee. But, in making that trade, North Carolina lost the Ducktown copper mines!

Military Land Warrants.—When the Tennessee territory was ceded to Congress the act provided that all military land warrants that had been given to soldiers of the Revolutionary War, and all entries previously made in the ceded territory,

---

[4] Archibald D. Murphey anticipated trouble on this account because of the claim Tennessee was making in November, 1819, that the mountain range did not extend south of the Hiawasse river. Murphey's papers, Vol. II, p. 190.

should be reserved for the satisfaction of those warrants and entries in case the holders of the same might not be able to satisfy them out of land fit for cultivation in North Carolina. Many of these warrants had not been so satisfied. Congress accepted these conditions. However, in 1803, at the request of Tennessee, North Carolina granted Tennessee power to issue grants and perfect titles in this reserved territory as fully as could North Carolina, except that North Carolina reserved the right to issue military warrants exclusively, which act Tennessee ratified August 4, 1804, and Congress April 18, 1806. But, as time went on, very little territory was left in Tennessee except Indian lands, to which the Indian rights had not been extinguished. As, however, North Carolina had executed to Tennessee title to all the Tennessee territory by deed dated February 25, 1790, Congress, in order to make this power effective, had to cede to the latter State nearly half of the vacant lands within its limits, which it did by the same act by which it had ratified North Carolina's grant in 1803 to Tennessee of equal power with herself to issue grants and perfect titles, except military warrants, namely the act of April 18, 1806. All the territory to which title still remained in Congress was the Chickasaw Indian Reservation, which by treaty of 1818 vested in Congress. Congress then empowered Tennessee to satisfy North Carolina claims out of lands lying west and south of the line prescribed in the act of April 18, 1806. North Carolina notified holders of her military warrants of this, and caused the muster roll to be published and transcribed, but went on thereafter to issue additional military warrants until the muster roll had been filled. But, in 1840, some of these military land warrants and some entries also remained unsatisfied. Tennessee, claiming that she had already provided for all valid military land warrants, refused to made provision for those still outstanding. But this provision had required the submission of such claims to a commission which had been appointed by Tennessee alone, and had ceased to exist from October 22, 1822, so that no North Carolina military land warrants issued after that date could be submitted to that commission. Under these circumstances Robert Love, of Haywood County, prepared and submitted to Congress a memorial in 1816, and succeeded, apparently, in getting these claims satisfied, and another memorial was drawn up and sent to Congress by Archibald Murphey January 29, 1824, according to Murphey's Papers (Vol. II, pp. 320, 328). Many of these military land warrants were held by the descendants of Revolutionary soldiers in Ashe, afterwards Watauga County.

Running the State Line.—As the Cherokees occupied the territory southwest of the Big Pigeon River in what is now Haywood County, no provision was made for running the line beyond that point. Generally speaking, the line was to follow the tops of the Stone, the Smoky and the Unaka Mountains from Virginia to Georgia, but to be surveyed and marked only from Virginia to the Pigeon. The surveying party consisted of Col. Joseph McDowell, David Vance, Mussendine Matthews, speaker of the House, commissioners. John Strother and Robert Henry were the surveyors. The party met May 19, 1799, at Captain Isaac Weaver's, near what is now Tuckerdale, a station on the new Virginia-Carolina Railway, in Ashe County. The chain bearers and markers were B. Collins, James Hawkins, George Penland, Robert Logan, George Davidson and J. Matthews. James Neely was commissary. In addition, there were two pack horse men and a pilot. The survey began on the 20th of May and ended the 28th of June, 1799. They camped on the night of the 23d of May in the Cut Laurel Gap, whence they sent John Strother down to David Miller's on Meat Camp to get a young man to act as pilot, but Strother failed to do so, and then went on "to Cove Creek, where I got a Mr. Curtis and met the company in a low gap between the waters of Cove Creek and Roan's Creek, where the road crosses the same." This road must have been the Indian trail which passed over the low gap between what is now Zionville, N. C., and Trade, Tenn. Traces of this trail can still be seen to the right of the present wagon road. It was this trail that Boone followed on his first trip into Kentucky. The new pilot was discharged on the 28th because he proved "not to be a woodsman;" and on June 1st they came to the Wattogoo River. This was a short distance above Watauga Falls, where they killed a lean bear, just out of winter quarters, which they ate "with bacon and johnny cake on Sunday morning." As the act of cession required the line to be run from the "place where the Watauga River breaks through the mountain a direct course to the top of the Yellow Mountain where Bright's Road crosses the same," and as the Yellow was not visible from the river bed, the surveyors had to go back to the peak overhanging the Falls and get the bearing of the Yellow from that point. The diaries of Strother and Henry show that the line was actually run and marked from the Watauga Falls to the top of the Yellow, though a local tradition maintains that the party simply found the easiest path to the top of the Yellow, without surveying or marking a straight line from the point where the river breaks through the mountain. It was here that the Cranberry vein deflected their compasses. It was on Saturday, June 1st, that they came across a very large rattlesnake, which Strother called a rattlebug. They tried to kill it, but "it was too souple in the heels for us." In Robert Henry's diary he mentions Gideon Lewis as the guide from White Top Mountain to the place where they sent for another, when they got to the head of Meat Camp. One of his descendants, David Lewis, lives near Ashland, and Rev. Gideon Lewis, a Dunkard minister, lives now in Taylor's Valley, Tenn. Most of the Lewises of Watauga are descended from the same Gideon who piloted these surveyors along the State line in 1799.

Watauga County Lines.—In order to determine the lines of Watauga County it is necessary to give the various calls of several counties, as follows:

Of Burke: Beginning at the Catawba River on the line between Rowan and Tryon Counties; thence running up the meanders of said river to the north end of an island known by the name of the "Three Cornered Island;" thence north to the ridge that divides the Yadkin and Catawba waters; thence westerly along the ridge to the mountain which divides the eastern and western waters, commonly known by the name of the Blue Mountains(sic). All that part of Rowan County which lies west and south of the said dividing line shall thenceforth be erected into a new county by the name of Burke, while that part east of the dividing line shall remain Rowan County. Laws of 1777.

Of Buncombe: Beginning on the extreme height of the Appalachian Mountain where the southern boundary of this State crosses the same; thence along the extreme height of said mountain to where the road from the head of Catawba River to "Swannanoe"(sic) crosses; thence along the main ridge dividing the waters of South Toe from those of "Swannanoe" unto the Great Black Mountain; thence along the mountain to the northeast end; thence along the main ridge between South Toe and Little Crabtree to the mouth of said Crabtree Creek; thence down Toe River to where it empties into the Nollechucky River(sic);[8] thence down the said river to the extreme height of the Iron Mountain and Cession Line; thence along the Cession Line to the southern boundary; thence along said boundary to the Blue Ridge, and thence to the beginning. Laws of 1791.

Of Ashe: "That all that part of the county of Wilkes lying west of the extreme height of the Appalachian Mountains shall be and the same is hereby erected into a separate and distinct county by the name of Ashe." Potter's Revisal, Vol. II, p. 98, Laws 1799. This is the shortest act creating a new county on record, and the supplemental acts required to make it clear shows that while brevity may be the soul of wit, it is not that of perspicuity.

In 1814 (Rev. Stat. Vol. II, p. 98) an act was passed to establish permanently the dividing line between the counties of Burke and Ashe, which was to be as follows: Beginning at the Yadkin Spring (which is fifty yards southeast of Green Park Hotel, Blowing Rock); thence along the extreme height of the Blue Ridge to the head spring of the Flat Top Fork of Elk Creek (on the right of Linville River after passing Linville Gap); thence down the meanders of said creek to the Tennessee State line, shall be and the same is hereby declared to be the permanent dividing line between the counties of Burke and Ashe.

---

[8] This river is now called the Toe or Estatoe till after it passes into Tennessee, when it becomes the Nollechucky, or simply "the Chucky."

Of Yancey: That all that part of Burke and Buncombe included within the following bounds, to wit: Beginning on the extreme height of the Black Mountain, running thence along said mountain to Ogle's improvement; thence along the dividing ridge to Daniel Carter's Fork field; thence a direct course to the mouth of Big Ivy Creek; thence with the Warm Springs Road by Barnard's Station to the Three Forks of Laurel; thence a direct line, so as to include James Allen's house to the Tennessee line; thence with said line to the county of Ashe; thence with the line of said county to the Grandfather Mountain; thence a direct course to the extreme height of the Hump Backed Mountain [just east of Linville River above the Falls]; thence with the Blue Ridge to where it intersects the Black Mountain; thence with the ridge of said mountain to the beginning, be and the same is hereby erected into a separate and distinct county by the name of Yancey. Laws of 1833.

A Supplemental Act, passed in 1833 (Rev. Stat. Vol. II, pp. 170, 171), provided that the county courts of Buncombe and Yancey should appoint commissioners to ascertain the dividing line between said two counties whenever the same shall be necessary, and that they should commence their survey at Daniel Carter's Fork field and run a direct line from thence to Barnard's Station, from which point the line shall run along the old Warm Springs Road to James Allen's Road, so as to include his house, and thence to the Tennessee line.

Watauga County Established.—"That a county be and is hereby laid off and established by the name of Watauga, to be composed of parts of the counties of Ashe, Wilkes, Caldwell and Yancey, beginning at the State line in Lemuel Wilson's plantation and running with the State line in a northern direction two miles; thence running as near as may be in a direct line, so as to include Thomas Sutherland in the county of Ashe, to the top of the Big Bald Mountain; thence to the mouth of Elk Creek (now Todd or Elkland) on the South Fork of New River; thence down the river to the mouth of a creek [now called Meadow Creek] that runs through Samuel Cooper's plantation; thence to the Deep Gap of the Blue Ridge between the waters of Stoney Fork and Lewis Fork waters of the Yadkin River, to where the road leading from Wilkesboro to the Deep Gap crosses the top of Laurel Spur; thence to Elk Creek at the Widow Hampton's; thence to the top of the White Rock Mountain [between Joe's Fork and Dugger's Creek]; thence to the top of the Blue Ridge at the nearest point of the Yadkin Spring; thence along the extreme height of the Blue Ridge to the top of the Grandmother Mountain; thence with the lines of Burke County to the corner of McDowell County; thence to the State line where it crosses the Yellow Mountain; thence with the State line to the beginning. Ratified the 27th day of January, 1849, Laws of North Carolina, 1848-49, pp. 66, 667, Ch. 25.

Mitchell County: It was established out of portions of Yancey, Watauga, Caldwell, Burke and McDowell Counties, with the following boundaries: Beginning at the top of Grandfather Mountain; thence with the top of the Blue Ridge to the Bear Wallow Gap; thence to the Three Knobs; thence to Big Crabtree Creek; thence down said creek to Toe River; thence down said river to the Tennessee line; thence with the Tennessee line to Elk River; thence to the place of beginning. Laws of 1860-61, Ch. 8, p. 14.

Changes in Watauga County Lines.—By the laws of 1876-77, chapter LXVII, page 341, the lines between the counties of Watauga, Wilkes and Ashe were changed so as to run from the top of the Wolf Knob, near the Widow Tempy Mikels, where the Watauga and Wilkes County lines intersect, and thence running a north course to the top of the Blue Ridge at the dividing line between the lands of Leander Robbins and Enoch Triplett, and thence a north course to the top of Henson's Ridge; then a north course to the ford of Gap Creek, near the mouth of Alexander Green's lane; thence a northwest course to the top of the Big Ridge to the Ashe County line. All of Ashe and Wilkes counties within these lines was to be a part of Stony Fork township, Watauga County.

By the laws of 1870-71, page 319, "all that portion of Caldwell County comprised within the following boundaries, viz: beginning at the Fairview on the Caldwell and Watauga turn-

A History of Watauga County

pike road on the top of the Blue Ridge; thence a straight line to the top of the Grandfather Mountain," was annexed to Watauga County. In a suit between Levi Morphew and Elisha and Joseph Tatum concerning the county line between the mouth of Meadow Creek and the high knob near Cranberry Methodist Church, about 1883, it was decided that there should be a resurvey, the first survey having been made by Reuben Mast, county surveyor when the county was first formed. It is said that Mast guessed that Deep Gap was south sixty degrees east from the mouth of Meadow Creek, but that when he got to the first high knob from which he could see Deep Gap he found he had been wrong. Instead, however, of turning back and running a new line, he continued the line to Deep Gap, leaving much land that legally belonged to Ashe in Watauga County. The court ordered a new survey, to be run on the true degree, and Rev. L. W. Farthing ran and marked it. (Levi Morphew v. Joseph Tatum and others, Minute Docket B, page 172, July Term, 1883, Superior Court, Watauga County.)

Avery County Established.—By the Public Laws of 1911, chapter 33, page 63, Avery County, named in honor of Col. Waightstill Avery, of Revolutionary fame, the one hundredth county of North Carolina, was established, with the following boundaries: "Beginning at the highest point of the Grandfather Mountain, the corner of Watauga, Caldwell and Mitchell Counties, and running a direct line to the Hanging Rock Mountain; then with the dividing ridge to the Turnpike Road in the gap of Bower's Mountain; then a direct course to the eastern prospect on the eastern end of Beech Mountain; then a direct course to the Buckeye Spring; then down and with the meanders of Buckeye Creek to Beech Creek; then with the meanders of Beech Creek to Watauga River; then with the meanders of Watauga River to the Tennessee line; then with the Tennessee line to the Grassy Ridge Bald; then a direct line to Spear Top; then with the main height of Yellow Mountain to the highest point on Little Yellow Mountain; then a direct line to Pine Knob; then to the mouth of Gouge's Creek on Toe River; then south forty degrees east to the Bald Ground on Humpback

Mountain at the McDowell County line; then with the McDowell County line to the Burke County line; then with the Burke County line to the Caldwell County line; then with the Burke and Caldwell line to the highest point on Chestnut Mountain; then a direct course to Anthony's Creek so as to include all of Carey's Flats; then to the beginning." Ratified 23d of February, 1911.

Last Change in County Line.—The act creating Watauga County provided that the line should run from the top of the Big Bald Mountain to the mouth of Elk Creek. As long as men remember there has been a settlement at the mouth of Elk Creek, called at first Elk Cross Roads, and later on, for the sake of brevity, and in honor of the Todd family, Todd. When, however, the Virginia-Carolina Railroad reached that place, it was found that Todd was too brief for euphony or the terminus of a great railroad, and changed to Elkland. But the post office still remains Todd. Then, too, it was found that a part of Todd or Elkland was in Watauga and part in Ashe County, owing to the fact that the line between the two counties did not follow Elk Creek, while the boundary line of the town did follow that stream. So, in order to avoid confusion and for other reasons, Hon. Robert L. Ballou, State Senator, had the line changed so as to run from the top of the Big Bald to the ford of Elk Creek near the residence of Alex. Blackburn, just above the town, from which point it follows the creek to its mouth in the South Fork of New River. (Ch. 34, Public Laws, 1915.)

Jail and Court House Changes.—The land for the first court house was donated by Jordan Councill the second. It was on the hill now occupied by F. A. Linney's and J. M. Moretz's residences. The court house was burned on the 29th day of March, 1873, according to Col. W. W. Presnell, and while he was register of deeds.* It was thought by some that one of the county officers, against whom judgments were docketed, caused it to be burned, but this theory is not generally believed now. Later on, during that year, a new court house was built on the lot now occupied by the Watauga County bank building, but a deed therefor was not made till April 12, 1875, when Joel Norris

---

* A wind-storm blew in the gable end of the court-house January 28, 1886.

A History of Watauga County 127

conveyed to the county commissioners one half of an acre on the corner of King and Water Streets for $300.00 (Deed Book G, p. 208), Thomas J. Coffey and W. C. Coffey having the contract for $4,800.00, the building committee having been Henry Taylor, Dudley Farthing and Jacob Williams. It seems that there must have been some doubt as to the power of the county commissioners to build "the court house on a lot other than the one on which the old one stood when it was burned," for chapter CVII, Laws 1873-74 (p. 143), made that action legal. The county commissioners, consisting of J. E. Finley, Thos. J. Coffey and W. H. Calloway, sold the lot on which the jail then stood to Coffey Brothers for $555.00. The deed was dated June 1, 1888 (Deed Book N, p. 330). On May 22, 1889, Coffey Brothers sold to J. E. Finley, W. W. Presnell and Joseph H. Mast, county commissioners, for $200.00, half an acre of land on Burnsville and King streets, and running with Burnsville street across the branch to a back street. This is the lot on which the present jail stands.

The First Jail.—This was built by a Mr. Dammons for $400.00, and stood in front of the present Murray Critcher barn, west of the street leading from the Critcher Hotel to the side street in front of the present Baptist Church. It was of brick, with a steel cage inside. But the brick were of poor quality and could be easily removed from around the windows and doorways, and, after standing a few years, Elisha Green got the contract to build another of white pine logs, the same steel or iron cage which had been in the first being used in the second. This stood till Stoneman's raid, when it was burned. After the close of the Civil War, Jack Horton, who had built the first court house, got the contract to build a new jail, which was also of heavy logs, the second story timbers being twelve inches square and crossed with heavy iron bars three inches broad and bolted to each log by heavy iron bolts. This was removed when the jail lot was sold. The present jail was built by William Stephenson, of Mayesville, Ky., in 1889, for $5,000.00.

Court Records of Ashe.—Some of our heroes of the past suffer when subjected to the fierce light of history, among whom are Benjamin Cleveland, Richard Henderson and Judge Spruce McCay, the last of whom was denounced by Chancellor John Allison, of Tennessee, in his "Dropped Stitches" (pp. 51, 52) as a "heartless tyrant." This gentleman (McCay) married a daughter of Col. Richard Henderson, according to Wheeler's History (Vol. II, p. 384), and not a daughter of Gen. Griffith Rutherford, as erroneously stated in "Western North Carolina" (p. 374). He presided over the Superior Court of Ashe County in September, 1807, but his record there was unobjectionable. It was only when he was in Jonesboro, in August, 1782, presiding over the court of Oyer and Terminer, that he won for himself such condemnation. It was Judge Francis Locke, at the March term, 1809, who passed such a cruel and bloody sentence upon Carter Whittington, at Jefferson, after his conviction of perjury. This sentence was that he be fined £10, stand one hour in the pillory, have both ears entirely severed from his head and nailed to the pillory.

To Restore Lost Records.—Laws to "restore the records of Watauga County . . . carried away and lost by Kirk, in 1865," and when "the court house and all the records therein were burned," were passed in 1873-74 (Ch. XIX). Chapter 38, Laws 1874-75, makes the certificate of the clerk of the late county court and of the Judge of Probate competent to secure reregistration of destroyed record of deeds.[7]

To Encourage Sheep Raising.—The laws of 1850-51, chapter 184, page 497, authorized a majority of the justices of Watauga County to lay a tax on the citizens for the purpose of paying any person or persons who kill any wolf or red fox that is caught in said county, which was amended by chapter 121, Laws 1874-75, page 121.

To Protect Fish.—Chapter 285, Laws 1899, provided penalties for the destruction of fish in waters of Watauga County, while chapter 639 provided for fish-ways over dams on the South Fork of New River, and chapter 319 of the same laws forbade the use of dynamite to destroy fish; chapter 345 of same laws regulated fishing in Elk, while the laws of 1907 prohibits saw dust in streams.

---

[7] See, also, Chapter 162, Laws of 1874-'75.

A History of Watauga County

First Term of Superior Court.—There is much confusion as to where the first term of court was held in Watauga County. It is generally conceded that it was held in a barn in rear of what was then the home of Henry Hardin and is now the residence of Joseph Hardin, a mile or more east of Boone. It is also generally admitted by those who were there that "hawgs"—not hogs, be it understood!—had held several terms of court there before Watauga County was formed. That should tell the entire story of what followed, but lest it fail to do so, it may be added that if an elephant had as much power in his or her hind legs as each denizen of that barn had before court met, he could jump around the world in one jump. But these facts are insignificant compared with the question as to what court was held there and then. If it was the County Court, then Dudley Farthing, Esq., presided over his first court as the presiding justice thereof—a position he held with dignity and honor till the constitution of 1868 substituted the Board of County Commissioners therefor. If it was the Superior Court, then Judge Anderson Mitchell presided and E. C. Bartlett acted as clerk. It is contended by those who insist that it was the Superior Court which was then held there that there are yet living several men who were jurors at that term, and that jurors belong exclusively to the Superior Court. This is a mistake, grand and petty jurors having been a part of every other term of the County Court of Pleas and Quarter Sessions, according to the recollection of Col. W. L. Bryan, who served as a justice of the peace several years before that court was abolished. Besides, unless it was, there was no county court from the formation of the county in 1849 until some time in May, 1851, for by an act which was ratified January 28, 1851, it was expressly provided that "there shall be a Superior Court of Law and Equity opened and held for the county of Watauga, at the court house in Boone on the sixth Monday after the fourth Monday in March and September, in each and every year, . . . at which time the judge holding the said court shall appoint the necessary court officers." Watauga was then placed in the seventh circuit, and all suits pending in the Superior Court of Ashe in which both parties were citizens of Watauga, and all criminal proceedings against citizens of Watauga were transferred to this court. And it was further provided that the "spring and fall, now jury terms, of the Courts of Pleas and Quarter Sessions shall be held in . . . Watauga County, at the same time and on the same week on which the Superior Courts of Law and Equity shall be holden," etc.[3] This seems also to make still more doubtful another disputed point, viz: as to when the first sheriff was elected by the people. For if he was elected first in 1852, then the general impression that D. C. McCanless absconded during his second term is established, and if he was elected in 1850, then McCanless must have been serving his third term, which some still insist was the case. But this seems to establish another fact, viz: that the court house was far enough advanced by May, 1851, to be used by the court, for all who were present at the first court held in that building agree that it was far from finished at that time. The act expressly provides that the first term shall be held "at the court house in Boone." If there was no such building then, it is likely that the act would have been differently worded. Still, it may have been held elsewhere, as many contend.

A Snap-Shot in Passing.—Mr. Skiles, in his "Life," leaves us this (p. 79): "I was at Boone Tuesday [before May 21, 1850] and saw a great crowd; it was court week, and I witnessed an amusing scene. There was a man intoxicated who was very rude and treated the court with contempt. For want of a jail to put him in, the court ordered him taken out and tied to a wagon wheel until he became civil. They took him out, tied him, and left him tied."

A Happy and Homogeneous People.—Many think that Watauga has the best dwelling and farm houses in the State; that its inhabitants are of a more homogeneous character than any other; that there are almost as few tenants as in any other county, except Alleghany; that there are fewer very poor and fewer very rich people than elsewhere; that the average of in-

---
[3] This was repealed, (Laws 1852, Ch. XLVI, p. 100) and the terms of courts of Pleas and Quarter sessions were required to be held on the third Monday in February, May, August and November of each year.

telligence and education will compare with those of any other county most favorably; that there is as little crime per capita as in any other; that there is as great church attendance and as many churches and school houses per capita as in any other county; that the apples, cabbages, beets, buckwheat, stock of all kinds, and dairy products surpass all other counties in the State.

That Roving Spirit.—The same influences which brought our ancestors to America and their sons into the unexplored mountains, sent their grandsons across the plains in 1849, and since then into every State and territory of the vast West. When Missouri was first opened to settlement many left this county and tried their fortunes there, some to remain, others to return. It was probably this "trek" which caused so many families to disappear from the church rolls of Three Forks Baptist Church. For them, there was still something else to find, and they went and sought it, some of them to realize that they had already chanced upon it in Watauga County (then Ashe), and to return to enjoy it. Among those going to Missouri were the Whittingtons. Dr. Whittington, of Asheville, is a descendant of Benjamin, and his wife, who was a Wilson, of Yancey. Wiley Whittington, a brother of John and Cromwell, who went to Missouri, passed on still farther westward, only to be killed at last by Indians in the Rocky Mountains while on his way to California. It is said he had shot an Indian, and when the rest of the Indian band demanded his surrender by his party, they gave him up to the savages, who robbed him and stripped him of all clothing and then left him to perish in the mountains. Jonathan Lewis left Zionville for California in 1849, settled in Fresno and got rich. He went from Watauga County alone, joining a party in Missouri. Alexander Thomas, Andrew J. McBride, Marion Wilson, Jesse Bradley and Wm. Isaacs, of the Cove Creek section, went to California in 1849, and McBride left a diary, but it has been misplaced within the last few years. It is said that his brother, Carroll, went with him, and that on their return Carroll stopped in Tipton County, Tennessee. While in the West they killed a deer, but Indians took it from them and forced them to run for their lives and to hide in a ravine. It

A History of Watauga County

is also said that they made money in California, but spent it all buying a waterproof cloth with which to make a pipe to draw off the water in a creek above the point at which they had discovered gold, hoping to gather much from the bottom of the bed, not realizing that it was being washed down from above till too late.

Legislative Representatives.[9]—Alexander B. McMillan, in 1850, and Benjamin C. Calloway, in 1852, both of what was and still is Ashe County, represented Watauga in the House, and George Bower, also of Ashe, in the Senate, but from and including 1854 Watauga has had its own citizens as representatives in the House:

	Senators.	Representatives.
1854.	George Bower, of Ashe.	Jonathan Horton.
1856.	A. M. Bryan, of Ashe.	George N. Folk.
1858.	Joseph H. Dobson, of Surry.	Mark Holdsclaw.
1860.	Joseph H. Dobson, of Surry.	George N. Folk.
	G. N. Folk having resigned, his place was filled by	Thomas Farthing.
1862.	Isaac Jarratt, of Ashe.	William Horton.
1864.	Jonathan Horton, of Watauga.	William Horton.
1865.	A. C. Cowles, of Yadkin.	Charles Potter.
1866.	A. C. Cowles, of Yadkin.	William Horton.
1868.	Edmund W. Jones, of Caldwell.	Lewis B. Banner.
1870.	W. B. Council, of Watauga.	W. F. Shull.
1872.	J. W. Todd, of Ashe.	J. B. Todd.
1874.	A. J. McMillan, of Alleghany.	L. L. Greene.
1876.	Hervey Bingham, of Watauga.	W. R. Council.
1879.	J. Bledsoe, of Ashe.	W. R. Council.
1881.	F. J. McMillan, of Alleghany.	Thomas Bingham.
1883.	E. F. Lovill, of Watauga.	W. W. Lenoir.
1885.	J. W. Todd, of Ashe.	E. F. Lovill.
1887.	W. C. Fields, of Alleghany.	Thomas Bingham.
1889.	W. S. Farthing, of Watauga.	J. A. Crisp.
1891.	Benjamin P. Griggsby, of Ashe.	D. B. Phillips.

[9] From the "North Carolina Manual."

A History of Watauga County 133

1893. W. C. Fields, of Alleghany.   E. F. Lovill.
1895. W. H. Farthing, of Watauga.   L. H. Michael.
1897. J. M. Dickson, of Ashe.   Thomas Bingham.
1899. W. C. Fields, of Alleghany.   W. B. Councill, Jr.
1901. L. H. Michael, of Watauga.   William H. Calloway.
1903. H. M. Wellborn, of Ashe.   Lindsay H. Michael.
1905. S. A. Taylor, of Alleghany.   C. W. Phipps.
1907. E. F. Lovill, of Watauga.   W. D. Farthing.
1909. Robert L. Doughton, of Alleghany. Smith Hageman.
1911. John M. Wagoner, of Alleghany. Smith Hageman.
1913. E. S. Coffey, of Watauga.   John W. Hodges.
1915. Robert L. Ballou, of Ashe.   A. W. Smith.

Superior Court Clerks.—The first clerk was probably appointed by Judge Anderson Mitchell, who held the first court. A fine cherry tree stands alone in the field near where the old barn stood. The fleas which attended as witnesses, jurors and spectators are still remembered for their cordial reception of their human rivals. The first clerk elected by the people was George M. Bingham, of Cove Creek, but owing to an impediment in his speech, he resigned at the first term, Mr. ———— McClewee, an attorney resident in Boone at that time, being appointed to fill the unexpired term. This was probably in 1850. Then followed Col. J. B. Todd, Henry Blair, W. J. Critcher, appointed to fill the term for which Col. J. B. Todd had been elected in 1868, but which he could not fill because he could not take the "iron-clad oath" of Reconstruction. Owing to the destruction of the records when the court house was burned in 1873, it is impossible to give the dates accurately prior to that time, but from then on the records show that J. H. Hardin served from 1874 to 1882; J. B. Todd from 1882 to 1894; M. B. Blackburn from 1894 to 1898; John H. Bingham from 1898 to 1902; Thomas Bingham from 1902 to 1910, and W. D. Farthing from 1910 to the present time, 1915.

The registers of deeds were Rev. Joseph Harrison, from about 1850 to 1860, or thereabout; Rev. D. C. Harman, till 1865; Joseph Harrison, till 1870; W. W. Presnell, from 1870 to 1886;

Eugene Blackburn, from 1886 till his death, when W. W. Presnell was appointed to fill out his term; then came M. B. Blackburn, from 1888 to 1890; then Calvin J. Cottrell, from 1890 to 1894; then John W. Hodges, from 1894 to 1898; then J. M. May, from 1898 to 1908, followed by W. Roy Gragg, from 1908 till now, 1915.

Sheriffs.—Michael Cook, 1849 to 1852; John Horton, 1852 to 1856; D. C. McCanless, 1856 to 1859 (January); Sidney Deal, till 1860; A. J. McBride, from 1860 to 1866;[10] Jack Horton, from 1866 to 1876; A. J. McBride, from 1874 to 1882; D. F. Baird, 1882 to 1886; J. L. Hayes, 1886 to 1890; D. F. Baird, 1890 to 1894; W. H. Calloway, 1894 to 1900; W. B. Baird, 1900 to 1904; J. W. Hodges, 1904 to 1908; D. C. Reagan, 1908 to 1912; E. R. Eggers, for part of Reagan's unexpired term; Asa Wilson, elected 1912, but resigned, and E. R. Eggers appointed by county commissioners to fill out term to 1914; W. P. Moody, elected in 1914. Sidney Deal lived where J. W. Farthing now lives, and was elected sheriff by the people in 1860, but joined the army, and the remainder of his term was filled by Jack Horton. Deal moved across the Blue Ridge after the close of the Civil War.

Financial.—The debt of Watauga County is too small to be mentioned, there being only a few hundred dollars still due for the new court house. Real estate is assessed at about one-third of its real value. The tax rate for State and county combined is one per cent. of assessed value, being twenty-seven and two-thirds mills for State and seventy-two and one-third for county, and $2.30 on each poll. This is equivalent to about thirty-three cents on each hundred dollars. The towns have no debts and raise little or no money for street or other improvements, what is collected for any purpose being largely voluntary contributions in many cases from the more progressive citizens and licenses from "shows," etc. County affairs are keenly looked after not only by the county commissioners, but by many citi-

---

[10] Some claim that A. J. McBride was sheriff during the Civil War, and others that Jack Horton held the office from 1862 till 1876. Owing to the loss of the records 1873, it is impossible to ascertain the exact facts now. Some claim that Sidney Deal was elected sheriff in 1860, and served till he entered the Confederate Army, while this is denied by others.

COLONEL JOE B. TODD.
Clerk of the Superior Court.

zens who are eager to find a seam in the political armor of anyone offending in the way of extravagance, carelessness or fraud. Every dollar collected is applied as the law requires.

Watauga's Contribution to the Confederacy.—Company D, First Cavalry, was organized in Boone May 11, 1861; first captain, Geo. N. Folk; first lieutenant, Joe B. Todd; second lieutenant, James Councill; third lieutenant, J. C. Blair.

Company B, 37th Regiment, organized September, 1861, in Boone. First captain, Jonathan Horton; first lieutenant, A. J. Critcher; second lieutenant, David Greene; third lieutenant, Jordan Cook.

Company E, 37th Regiment, was organized at Sugar Grove August 8, 1861. First captain, W. Young Farthing; first lieutenant, Paul Farthing; second lieutenant, W. F. Shull; third lieutenant, Isaac Wilson, Jr.

Company I, 58th Regiment, reorganized in Boone in July, 1862. First captain, Wm. Miller; first lieutenant, Wm. M. Hodges; second lieutenant, Jordan C. McGhee; third lieutenant, James Horton.

Company D, 58th Regiment, organized at Valle Crucis July 7, 1862. First captain, Rev. D. C. Harman; first lieutenant, Ben. F. Baird; second lieutenant, W. P. Mast; third lieutenant, Wm. Howington.

Company M, 58th Regiment, organized early in the winter of 1863 from Ashe and Watauga. First captain, Leonard Phillips; first lieutenant, Geo. W. Hopkins; second lieutenant, Thomas Ray; third lieutenant, J. Riley Norris, with about fifty of the men from Watauga.

Company A, 6th Cavalry Regiment; Captain B. Roby Brown, with twenty to twenty-five men from Watauga.

There were other companies made from Ashe and Watauga by William G. Bingham and Thomas Sutherland, who joined a Virginia regiment of cavalry, there being about twenty-five men from Watauga. There were five full companies that went from Watauga, each of which must have contained 150 men, from first to last, and parts of three additional companies that had at least 100 Watauga men, besides the men from Watauga County who joined other regiments. By Moore's Roster, Watauga County actually furnished 671 men, and the Home Guard at Camp Mast must have contained 250 men. Col. W. W. Presnell, adjutant of the Nimrod Triplett Camp of Confederate Veterans, estimates that there must have been 900 men from this county in the service of the Confederacy, but there were most likely nearer 1,000.

Col. Presnell estimates that there were at least 100 men from Watauga County who went through the lines and joined the Federals, or remained in Watauga and worked for them in Watauga County during the closing months of the war.

He also says that Companies D, B and E were in the eastern or Virginia army, while the other companies were in the western army.[11]

Population and Other Facts.—The population since 1850 follows:

1850	1860	1870	1880	1890	1900	1910
3,400	4,957	5,287	8,160	10,611	13,417	13,423

But for the pigeonholeing of a bill which Marcus Holtsclaw had passed by the House of Commons in 1858, the court house would have been changed from Boone to Brushy Fork, Holtsclaw having been elected over Thomas Greene and William Horton by one vote on the issue of making that change. But Joseph Dobson, of Surry, represented Watauga in the Senate that year, and he put Holtsclaw's little "bill to sleep."

That our pioneer ancestors spun, wove, knitted, made rope, tanned hides, dyed, made shoes, boots and moccasins; made pails, buckets, cradles, bee-gums, ladles, chairs, plows, sleds, wagons, knives, guns, and almost every tool then in use goes without saying, for they were cut off from the world and markets of all kinds. Dyes were obtained from yellow oak, from hickory, which dyes yellow; butternut dyes brown, black wal-

---

[11] By joint resolution No. 56, of the General Assembly of North Carolina, 1915, the State Historical Commission was authorized to correct and amend Moore's Roster of Confederate troops from North Carolina so as to include all who were actually in the service of the Southern Confederacy, the present list being faulty and incomplete.

nut dyes dark brown, sumac dyes yellow, alder dyes reddish, dogwood dyes red, madder dyes red, bedewood dyes purple, dye-flowers and snuff weed dye yellow, copperas dyes yellow, and burnt copperas red. To "set" dyes they used laurel leaves, copperas, alum, salt, etc. Honey and maple sugar and syrup were the sole "sweetening" we had before sorghum came in shortly before the Civil War. Reaping hooks preceded scythes and cradles many years. Grain was threshed out on cloths by the use of flails made of hickory sapplings beaten soft two feet from the large end.

Soldiers of Mexican War.—The government does not place "monuments" over the graves of dead Mexican soldiers, presumably, else George Wright, whose body lies near that of Moses Yarber, would be similarly honored. He has a son living in the Beech Mountains who doubtless could furnish full information for a tombstone, but, jemooney Christmas! just think what it would cost! How many other dead Mexican soldiers are buried in these mountains is unknown, and the government does not seem to care. A few are still living, here and there, among them being Benjamin Pritchard, now living on Roaring Creek, still neat and soldierly, and Nehemiah P. Oaks, who lives within a mile or so of Elk Park. Pritchard was born on the Blue Ridge, near the McKinney Gap, about 1825, and remembers that on one occasion a Mexican threw every man in his regiment in wrestling contests. Then Pritchard was sent for and threw the Mexican three straight falls. He was a member of Captain John Blalock's company, of which A. T. Keith was a lieutenant. Blalock had to resign because of bad health, and when the men elected a man named Constable, who lived on Cane Creek, captain, Keith also resigned, feeling that he had been slighted. John Payne was the colonel and Montford Stokes lieutenant-colonel of the regiment, which was the First North Carolina. Nehemiah P. Oaks was born on the Humpback Mountain, December 28, 1828, and belonged to the same company and regiment. He was also a member of the 13th Tennessee Cavalry, and draws two pensions. Pritchard also draws a pension for service in the Mexican War.

Assessments for Taxation in 1915.—It will be interesting to compare the assessments of property this year with those for the years following the building of a railroad through this county. The increase in population between now and then will also be of interest.

Total real estate assessment in 1915 amounts to.. $1,783,983.00
Total personal property assessments for 1915....   948,866.00

Total assessments $2,732,849.00

The highest average assessment per acre was in Cove Creek, $14.17. The lowest average value per acre was Elk Township, $3.91.

The Weather.—It is colder in Watauga both summer and winter than in any other county of the State, probably, with the exception of Ashe, Alleghany, Avery and Haywood. The "cold Saturday" was February 8, 1835. The date of the Big Snow cannot be fixed, except that on the 2d and 3d days of December, 1886. But old people remember hearing of a snow that was so deep that all fences were obliterated from the landscape, and deer were slaughtered by the score. On the 5th of June, 1858, corn knee-high was killed in this county and all fruits and vegetables, while white-oak trees between Boone and Jefferson were killed outright, some of their stumps being still visible. There was a frost at Blowing Rock July 26, 1876, while on February 13, 1899, the thermometer went to fourteen degrees below zero. On the 15th of May, 1835, there was snow while land was being laid off for corn and sugar water was being boiled for maple syrup on Brushy Fork.

Agricultural.—Patch farming was the rule for years, only small clearings being possible because of the sparseness of the population. Corn could not be raised at all for many years till the land was opened up to the sunlight. Owing to the stumps and roots, it was difficult to plough the ground at first, and the planting was done with the hoe. Gradually the land became warm enough to produce and mature corn or maize. Cabbages and all root crops flourished from the first settlement. Buckwheat and rye did well long before wheat, oats and other small grain began to thrive. Stock were fed on Irish potatoes and buckwheat, as is still the case in some places. Long, red Irish potatoes were carried in the arm as are ears of corn, and horses got fat on them. Hogs were kept in the mountains all winter, as the mast rarely failed. When a very cold or snowy time came, corn was carried to these hogs, beds were made for them in sheltered places, under cliffs and in caves of rocks, but for many it was literally a case of "root hog or die." Col. W. L. Bryan has a bronze medal and a diploma which were awarded to him at the Columbian Exposition for the best buckwheat. If a colony of Swiss could be induced to try their lot with us, they could demonstrate the fact that on our mountain slopes, properly terraced, we could raise grapes, fruit of all kinds, and goats and cattle without number. Cheese factories have been already established at Sugar Grove, June 5, 1915, and elsewhere. The factory at Sugar Grove was the first established in the South. It is already thriving. With a little harder work and more scientific methods, wealth would follow agriculture in Watauga.

Mountain Forests.—In his address before the American Geographical Society in New York in April, 1914, Prof. Collier Cobb, of the University of North Carolina, said that seventy-six per cent. of this section is still forest cover, or a little more than three million acres of forest land is found in the sixteen mountain counties; that the mountains of North Carolina are the oldest forest land on the continent, and the botanists and plant geographers are agreed that the deciduous forests of eastern North America have been derived from the forests of these mountains, in which they reach their greatest development; that while the hardwoods of the northern United States have migrated from the mountains since the last glacial period, it seems equally certain that the coniferous growth on the Balsams and other high mountains was forced south at the time of the greatest extension of the ice sheet, and is able to survive now only in the cooler atmosphere of our high mountains, where the mean annual temperature is forty-eight degrees, and, in the valleys they enclose, fifty-four degrees Fahrenheit; while the rainfall of the region, most of which comes in the growing season, is seventy inches, being greater than that of any other portion of the United States, except the Puget Sound region. The United States has recently acquired an immense reserve in the neighborhood of Blowing Rock. The Lenoir timber lands were sold in 1915 for $40.00 per acre. They are near the Grandfather.

Banks and Banking.—Watauga has three banks, one, the Watauga County Bank, Boone, was organized in 1904 with $10,000.00 capital. This was increased in 1908 to $12,000.00, in 1914 to $16,800.00, and in 1915 to $17,000.00. It has never declared a dividend of less than twelve per cent. since George P. Hagaman became cashier, and once declared eighteen per cent. The Blowing Rock Bank was organized about 1904 with $5,000.00 capital, which has been increased to $16,000.00. It has thriven also. The Valle Crucis Bank was organized in 1914 with a capital of $8,000.00. The cattle industry requires much money, and all kinds of stock thrive in this county.

Altitudes.—The following heights have been taken from S. M. Dugger's "Balsam Groves of the Grandfather Mountain" (p. 286): Blowing Rock, 4,090; Boone, 3,332; Valle Crucis, 2,726; Shull's Mills, 2,917; Cook's Gap, 3,349; Banner Elk, 3,900; Beech Mountain, 5,522; Hodges Gap, 3,376; Hanging Rock, 5,237; Sugar Mountain, 5,289; Grandfather, 5,964; Dunvegan, 4,924; Howard's Knob, 4,451; Bald of Rich Mountain, 5,368; Sugar Loaf, 4,705; Snake Mountain, 5,594; Elk Knob, 5,555; Flat Top, 4,537; Deep Gap, 3,105; Elk Park, 3,180; Cranberry, 3,160; Montezuma, 3,882; Linville, 3,800; Yonah Lossee Road, from 4,000 to 5,000; Beacon Heights, 4,650; Grandmother, 4,686; Linville Gap (Guyot), 4,100; United States, 4,081; McCanless Gap, 4,250; White Top, 5,530; Toe River Gap, 5,188; High Pinnacle, 5,690; Mount Mitchell, 6,711; Clingman's Peak in Blacks, 6,611; Roan Mountain, High Knob, 6,313; Big Yellow, 5,500; Cold Spring Balsam, 5,915; Caney Fork Divide, 6,370; Double Spring Mountain, 6,380; Enos Plott Balsam, 6,097; Amos Plott Great Divide, 6,278; The Pillar of the Smoky, 6,255; Mt. Henry, 6,373; South Peak,

6,299; Thermometer Knob, 6,157; Mt. Guyot, 6,636; Mt. Alexander, 6,299; Mt. LeConte of the Bullheads, 6,612; Mt. Stafford, 6,535; Mt. Curtis, 6,566; Master Knob, 6,013; Mt. Love of the Smoky, 6,443; Clingman's Dome, 6,619; Mt. Buckley, 6,599; Mt. Collins, 6,188; Thunderhead, 5,520; Devil's Court House in Whitesides, 6,049; Rocky Bald of the Nantahalas, 5,822; Tusquittee Bald, 5,314. Watauga is probably the highest county in general altitude in North Carolina, being over 3,000 feet above sea level.

Mount Washington, of New Hampshire, is 6,286. There are, therefore, twenty-three peaks in North Carolina which are higher. There are twenty-three other peaks over 6,000 feet, but less than 6,286. There are seventy-nine which exceed 5,000, but fall a little short of 6,000 feet. It should be borne in mind, however, that all these measurements are barometric, and, therefore, inexact, according to Horace Kephart's "Southern Highlanders."

CHAPTER XI.
The Town of Boone.[1]

Incorporation.—This town was not incorporated till the session of the legislature of 1871-72 (Ch. 50), when it was regularly chartered and its boundaries defined. But this act was amended in 1872-73 (Ch. XXXI, p. 411) by extending the corporate limits so as to begin at a stake half a mile north of the court house and running thence to a stake half a mile east of the court house; thence to a stake half a mile south of the court house; thence to a stake half a mile west of the court house, and thence to the beginning. W. L. Bryan was its first mayor and has held that office intermittently for twenty-five years.

Its Attractions.—As Boone is on no large stream, it is far distant from the moisture arising from rivers and creeks. It is not high enough to be caught in low-hanging clouds, and is free from their damp and clinging mists. The town is 3,332 feet above tidewater, with a spring, summer and autumn climate unsurpassed in the mountains. It is picturesquely situated at the base of Rich Mountain and almost directly under Howard's Knob. Its population consists of a homogeneous citizenship, with no very wealthy and no very poor people in its make-up. Its death rate is less than that of any other town of its size in the State. Its schools, both primary and normal, afford abundant opportunity for the education of all. The school population of the Appalachian Training School is better behaved and more appreciated by the citizens of Boone than that of any other school or college town in the State. Boone has a public library of its own, and access to many thousands of volumes in the library of the Appalachian Training School. It has three churches, one bank, a Masonic hall and three hotels. There is no

---

[1] Most of the facts for this chapter were furnished by Col. and Mrs. Wm. Lewis Bryan, the oldest residents of the place. I am also indebted to them for so much other information which I have embodied in this book, that to credit them with each item would be almost impossible. Colonel Bryan, indeed, is almost as much the author of the work as I am myself. J. P. A.

BOONE, THE COUNTY SEAT OF WATAUGA, 1915.

reason why Boone should not become the best and largest summer resort in the State. Inexhaustible springs on Rich Mountain afford more pure water than a population of twenty thousand could consume. Boone has electric lights and garages and livery stables. Its population is about 700 souls. It has local and long-distance telephones, several physicians, and a drug store. The view from Howard's Knob is unsurpassed in the State.

Miss Morley's Visit to Boone.—From her "Carolina Mountains" (pp. 355 to 360) the following detached sentences and paragraphs are taken:

"Leaving Blowing Rock one day in mid-June, you perhaps will walk away to Boone, some ten miles distant, three miles of the way a lane close-hedged on either side with gnarled and twisted old laurel trees heavily-laden with bloom so that the crisp flower cups shower about you as you pass and the air is full of their bitter, tonic fragrance. Large rhododendrons stand among the laurel, but their great flower clusters are as yet imprisoned beneath the strong bud-scales. When the laurel is done blooming, you will perceive that you must come this way again for the sake of the rhododendrons. Little streams of crystal clearness come out from under the blossoming laurel, flash across the road, and disappear under the laurel on the other side. How sweet the air where all the odors of the forest are interwoven with the bitter-sweet smell of the close-pressing flowers! How the pulse quickens as one steps along. Is that a bird? Or is it your own heart singing?

"Before the first freshness of that laurel-hedged road has begun to dim from familiarity, you emerge into the open where the view is of wide, rolling slopes, green hills and valleys dotted with roofs, and beyond these the great blue distant mountains soaring up into the sky. That steep hill to your left is bright red with sorrel, a sorry crop for the farmer, but a lovely spot of color in the landscape. You climb up this sorrel-red hill to the top of Flat Top Mountain, up over the rough stones and the dark red sorrel to where the view is wide and fine. But Flat Top Mountain offers you more than a view. It is noon when you get there, for you have not hurried, but have stopped every moment to smell or to see, or just to breathe and breathe as though you could thus fill your bodily tissues with freshness and fragrance to last into your remotest life. As you climb up Flat Top, you detect a fragrance that does not come from the flowers, a warm, delicious fragrance that makes you look eagerly at the ground. Seeing nothing, you go on half disappointed, half buoyant with the certainty of success—ah, it comes again, that delicious warm fragrance. You abandon yourself to primitive instincts and trusting your senses turn about and walk straight to where the ground is red with ripe strawberries. You sit down on the warm grass and taste the delectable fruit. A bird is singing from a bush as though sharing in your pleasure. When you have gathered the best within reach, you lie back and watch the clouds sailing like white swans across the sky. Then you take out the bread you have brought, the most delicious bread ever baked, for it has in some magical way acquired a flavor of blossoming laurel and rippling brooks and blue sky and the joy of muscles in motion, of deep-drawn breath, of the lassitude of delicious exercise, with a lingering flavor of the spicy berries whose fragrance is in the air about you. Such bread as this is never eaten within the walls of a house. And then you rest on the warm hillside fanned by the cool breeze, for no matter how hot the summer sun, there is always a cool breeze in the high world at the back of the Grandfather. Before starting on, you must taste again of the exquisite feast spread for you and the birds, whose wings you hear as they come and go, fearless and ungrudging, for there is enough for all.

"Further along on the mountain stands an old weather-boarded house whence you see Boone in the distance lying so sweetly among its mountains. A path here leads you down to a deserted cabin in a lovely hollow. That well-worn path at the door-step leads to the spring only a few steps away, such a spring as one is always looking for and is always finding at the back of the Grandfather. Its water is icy cold and it is walled about with moss-covered, fern-grown stones. This cabin in the lovely hollow, with its ice-cold spring, the surrounding fruit trees, the

A History of Watauga County 145

signs of flowers once cultivated, gives you a strange impulse to stop here, like a bird that has found its nest, but you go on along a woodsy by-road, whose banks are covered with pale green ferns, and where the large spiræa in snowy bloom stands so close as almost to form a hedge. The velvety dark-green leaves of wild hydrangea crowd everywhere, its broad flat heads of showy buds just ready to open. Enormous wild gooseberries invite you to taste and impishly prick your tongue if you do. The blackberries make a great show, but are not yet ripe. The roadside now and then is bordered with ripe strawberries. This shady way brings you again into the 'main leadin' road' you left some distance back when you climbed the sorrel-red hill to the top of Flat Top Mountain, and which now also has its wealth of flowers, among which the pure-white tapers of the galax shine out from the woods, while here and there a service tree drops coral berries at your feet.

"Soon now you cross the deep, wide ford of Mill River on a footbridge, substantial and with handrail, and where you stop of course to look both up and down the stream overhung with foliage, and just beyond which is a pretty house with its front yard full of roses. It is only two miles from here to Boone, and you breathe a sigh of regret at being so near the end of the day's walk; yet when you find yourself in Mrs. Coffey's little inn with its bright flowers you are glad to sit down and think over the events of the day.[2]

"Boone is at the foot of Howard Knob; is a pretty snuggle of houses running along a single street. Boone says it is the highest county seat in the United States [she should have added: 'east of the Rockies'] and that Daniel Boone once stayed in a cabin near here, whence its name. However all that may be, the lower slopes of Howard Knob are pleasantly cultivated and valleys run up into the mountains in all directions, as though on purpose to make a charming setting for Boone the county seat.

"That first visit to Boone!—what a sense of peace one had in remembering that the nearest railroad was thirty miles away [it is now at Todd, only ten miles north]; and then—what is

---

[2] This is the identical inn that in 1884 was to Charles Dudley Warner, Anathema and Maranatha.

that?—a telephone bell rings its insistent call and Boone is talking with Blowing Rock, or Lenoir, or New York City, or Heaven knows where! For though this part of the country was last to get into railroad communication with the outer world, it was by no means the last to grasp the opportunities within reach.

"With what delicious weariness one sinks to sleep after the day's walk over the hills! Your eyes seem scarcely to have closed when a loud noise wakens you with a start—what is it? Nothing excepting that the day's work has begun, broad daylight flooding in at the window. Breakfast is ready, coffee, cornbread, fish from some near sparkling stream, rice, hot biscuit, eggs, wild-plum sauce, honey and wild strawberries—you can take your choice or eat them all. And what a pleasant surprise to find everything seasoned with the wonderful appetite of childhood that reappears on such occasions as this!

"Your body seems borne on wings, so light it feels as you leave the inn and again take to the road. Back to Blowing Rock? No, indeed; not even though you could return, part way at least, by another road. The *wanderlust* is on you—the need of walking along the high valleys among the enchanted mountains. That seems the thing in life worth doing. As you leave Boone you notice a meadow white with ox-eyed daisies, and among them big red clover-heads, and, if you please, clumps of black-eyed Susans—for all the world like a summer meadow in the New England hills. Ripe strawberries hang over the edge of the road.

"From Boone to Valle Crucis you must go the longest way, for so you get the best views, the people tell you. And so you go a day's walk to Valle Crucis, where the Episcopal settlement lies in the fine green little valley."[*]

Old Map of the Town of Boone.—When the town was formed the county court, with Judge Dudley Farthing as its chairman, laid it off into streets and lots, the main street running east and west being called King Street, the first street to the north of it and parallel with it was named Queen Street, while the street running between the present Watauga County Bank

---

[*] In her "Carolina Mountains" Miss Morley says that even our roosters crow with a Southern accent.

MRS. WILLIAM LEWIS BRYAN.

Who has lived in Boone since its organization, and for several years prior thereto.

A History of Watauga County 147

Building and the law office of E. S. Coffey, Esq., was designated as Water Street. The broad street running south from King Street and between the present residence of Mr. R. C. Rivers and Fletcher and Lovill's law offices and passing down in front of the present jail was called Burnsville Street, as it led to the Burnsville road.

First Residents of Boone and Vicinity.—The land on which Boone stands, from about the present Methodist parsonage to the forks of the road near I. W. Gross's residence, belonged originally to John and Jerry Green, two brothers. One of them lived in a large log house between the present Judge Green's residence and the storehouse just west of it, and the other in the orchard on the lot where Dr. J. W. Jones now lives. One of them sold to Jordan Councill, Jr., and the other to Ransom Hayes. Then Jordan Councill, Jr., built the present large old Councill house and the store in which Richard Green now lives. These were the first houses in Boone proper, if we except the log residence of Jordan Councill, Sr., which stood a few hundred yards east, at the Buck Horn Tree place. There was another house which stood in the orchard near the present Blackburn hotel. It was a small clapboarded house, with only one room. Ben Munday and family occupied it first and afterwards Ellington Cousins and family, dark of skin, lived there till Cousins ilt a house up the Blackburn branch in rear of the Judge Green house. It is still known as the Cousins Place. Then B. J. Crawley built the store and residence across the branch in rear of W. R. Gragg's house and above the Watauga County Bank. The next house, now occupied by R. C. Rivers and family, was ı st occupied by Jesse McCoin. Prior to 1857 Jesse McCoin and Robert Sumter moved away and Col. J. B. Todd rented the Rivers house from Jordan Councill, Jr., after he was elected clerk. Then Captain J. L. Phillips moved in and remained till Dr. J. G. Rivers came in 1865. Next was the James Tatum storehouse, which stood where W. L. Bryan now lives.

The First Builders.—Soon after Boone was formed Jordan Councill, Jr., built a residence on the lot now occupied by R. C. Rivers as a home. Indeed, the front rooms of that residence are the same that Jordan Councill, Jr., had erected there. He also built a house on the site now occupied by the new post office, just west of the middle branch. This house was afterwards moved to the rear of the residence and used as a kitchen. It still stands to the south of the wing added to the front by Mr. Rivers. Mr. Councill also built, between the dwelling and the last named house, a small room for Solomon Crisp, where the latter made boots and shoes and sold whiskey. He came from Caldwell County, and continued in business in that store from about 1850 till about 1857, when Myrick and White took it. Crisp was in the Civil War and still lives near Patterson. The residence which Jordan Councill, Jr., built was used by his tanner, Jesse McCoin, and the house he erected on the present post office site was used as a residence by Robert Sumter, another tanner. They lived there till about 1856, when they returned to the east of the Blue Ridge, from which they had come. B. J. Crawley came from Forsythe County early in the fifties, and built a storehouse and dwelling on Water Street, just across the branch from the Watauga County Bank. He soon afterwards let M. T. Cox have the buildings. Cox after leaving Boone had a store at Soda Hill also, where Joel Norris sold goods for him. Crosby returned to Forsythe before the Civil War. Cox then closed out and went into business at Rutherwood, now Virgil, with Henry Blair, under the firm name of Cox & Blair. J. C. Blair, Henry's son, was chief clerk. But the firm became involved and Cox left some of his creditors in the lurch and went to Arkansas. The Soda Hill store was sold out by the sheriff. Elisha Green, however, followed Cox to Arkansas and succeeded in collecting some money for a few of his creditors, while Henry Blair, at great sacrifice, succeeded in paying off the firm debts of Cox & Blair. Allen Myrick and Noah White, of Guilford, moved into Crisp's store about 1857, and ran till about 1862, when they married, closed up their business and moved to Texas. Both had been widowers, but Myrick married a Miss Coffin, of Guilford County, the marriage being performed at High Point, while White married Titia Moore, a daughter of Reed Moore, of Three Forks.

Then was built the James W. Council house and store, opposite the Blair hotel. Next came the house just east of the Blair hotel. It was built by Levi Hartley, of near Lenoir, for a whiskey saloon. His sons, Nathan and Samuel, conducted the business, however, Levi never having moved to Boone. His sons carried on the rum business there till just before the Civil War. Nathan Hartley married Louisa McGhee and died in the Civil War. Samuel Hartley married a daughter of a man who lost his mind trying to invent an augur which would bore a square hole. Sam died in Lenoir after the Civil War. He was a good citizen and much respected. T. J. Coffey and brother bought the property and added to it, and T. J. Coffey lived there after his marriage till he moved to the Hall house. George and Phillip Grubb then built a residence on the corner now occupied by the law offices of Lovell and Fletcher, and a blacksmith shop near the present jail. They swapped this property to John Fraser for property in Taylorsville, N. C. Frazer moved in, went to the War of 1861, returned to Boone, and afterwards moved to Caldwell County. George Grubb quit the blacksmith business and went to carpentering. His brother, Phillip, left this country about 1860 and never returned.

Saw Mills for Boone.—Jordan Councill, Jr. bought a saw mill from David Sands on the east prong of New River, two miles from George H. Blair's present home. Councill afterwards sold it to Michael Cook, the second. William Elrod built a saw mill over the north or Boone fork of New River, near where the bridge now crosses that stream on the turnpike, two miles southeast of Boone, and in front of J. Watts Farthing's present home. Thomas Blair, who lived where William Trivett now lives, near where the three forks of New River join, built a saw, grist and carding mill near where the Turnpike turns up the Middle Fork of New River. He swapped to Harrison Edmisten for a farm on John's River soon after the Civil War. These three mills were bought or built for the sole purpose of producing lumber with which to build the new town of Boone, and must have been in operation about 1849 or 1850.

John and Ellington Cousins.—These brothers came from near East Bend, Forsythe County, soon after Boone was formed, bringing white women with them. Ellington's wife was Margaret Myers and John's was named Lottie. Ranson Hayes sold Ellington an acre of land up the Blackburn branch, where he built a house and lived in 1857, having moved from the house in the orchard below the road near the present Blackburn hotel. He had two daughters. Sarah married Joseph Gibson and moved to Mountain City, Tenn., where he carried on a tannery for Murphy Brothers, but he afterwards returned to this State and lived at or near Lenoir, finally going West, where he remains. Ellington died at Boone and his widow and daughter, nicknamed "Tommy," went with Gibson and his wife to Mountain City, where she also married. John lived near Hodges Gap and at other places, dying at the Ed. Shipley place, near Valle Crucis. He had several children.

Other Builders.—Joseph C. Councill built the brick house now used as the office of the *Watauga Democrat* long before the Civil War. The workmen employed in its construction were Bartlett Wood and J. C. McGee. Wood was a mason, carpenter and cabinet maker. Councill moved to Texas after the Civil War, where he married, but he returned to Boone and died there. Bartlett Wood helped build the first court house and a dwelling house which stood between the present residence of W. L. Bryan and what is now the Blair hotel, among the first houses built in Boone. Wood resided in this house till shortly before the Civil War, when he took a contract and moved to Shouns Cross Roads, Tenn., where he remained till his death.

Hotels.—Jordan Councill, Jr., and Ransom Hayes, who lived where Mrs. L. L. Green now lives, kept boarders before the Civil War and took care of such travelers and court attendants as came to Boone till about 1870, when T. J. and W. C. Coffey opened their hotel, soon followed by W. L. Bryan, who built and conducted the present Blair hotel in December, 1870. It is not generally known, but Squire James W. Councill and Elisha Green built the frame of a large hotel on the site of the Blair hotel at the beginning of the Civil War, but were not able to complete it. When Kirk's regiment came in March or April, 1865, they took the timbers and made a stockade around the court house, using also for the same purpose the timbers of the incomplete house built by William F. Fletcher and which then stood on the lot where M. B. Blackburn now has a bee yard. J. J. Horton built a store and dwelling where the Blackburn hotel now stands about 1880 and where he carried on merchandising for several years. When M. B. Blackburn was elected clerk of the Superior Court in 1894, he moved to Boone and occupied the dwelling which now stands above and to the north of the new residence of Dr. H. McD. Little, which was completed in 1913. Then M. B. Blackburn sold goods in a store near Mrs. L. L. Green's residence and bought the hotel property, having exchanged his Meat Camp farm for it. He enlarged and improved the original house considerably, and has conducted a mercantile establishment and hotel there ever since.

One of the first houses built in Boone was that which stands above Dr. Little's present residence. The frame of that house was cut and put together by Jacob Cook at Cook's Gap about 1850, when Sheriff Jack Horton bought it and moved it to its present location. Jack Horton married a Mast and lived on Cove Creek, where his son, James Horton, now lives, but when he was elected sheriff in 1852 he came to Boone, Michael Cook having been appointed sheriff by the court when the county was organized. Horton and Cook tied in the race before the people and the tie was cut by the casting vote of Squire James Reagan, a justice of the peace, who voted for Horton in the contest before the county court. Horton then moved into the house above Dr. Little's.

The First Merchants of Boone.—Jordan Councill, Sr., lived where Jesse Robbins has recently built two cottages, and near which stood the old Buck Horn oak. Jordan Councill, Jr., son of Jordan, Sr., built and occupied the old frame residence which still stands north of the road to Jefferson. It was probably the first frame house built in the county, and was for years the finest house in this section of the State. The store house used by Jordan Councill, Jr., stood west of his residence and between the office building erected by Dr. W. R. Councill and the road. The store house was afterwards moved across the road to its present location, and is now occupied as a residence by R. M. Greene.

What is now Boone was for years known as Councill's Store, and as early as 1835 a post office was in existence there. Sheriff Jack Horton had a store house which stood on the present court house lot, fronting what is now M. B. Blackburn's hotel. It stood on the same side of the street as the present new court house and nearly in front of where that building now stands. In this store Horton sold whiskey, goods and kept a sort of harness and saddlery shop. He also conducted a tan-yard on the lot near the branch which runs below Blackburn's present upper barn, where traces of the vats are still visible. James Todd, of Rowan County, was the saddler, and William F. Fletcher, of Lenoir, was the tanner and harnessmaker. Fletcher is said to have been related to William Lenoir and married Sarah Dula, of Yadkin Valley. He lived till ten or twelve years ago, when he died in poverty. He had neglected the hides which were being tanned in 1857, and Col. W. L. Bryan was employed to make such hides as had not been too badly damaged into shoes. These hides had been removed from the Horton vats to those of Henry Hardin, which stood where they still stand, in rear of the present residence of Joseph Hardin, one mile east of Boone and on the north side of the Jefferson road. Here these damaged hides were finished. It was soon after this that Jacob Rintels, who had been in copartnership with Samuel Witkowsky above Elkville on the Yadkin River, came to Boone and rented Sheriff Jack Horton's store room, where he remained for about one year, removing his stock of goods to the store room and residence which had been built by Jordan Councill, Jr., for his son, James W. Councill, on the land now occupied by the residence of J. D. Councill, opposite the Blair hotel. James W. Councill had kept goods in this store for awhile, but closed out and rented the store room to his cousin, Joseph C. Councill, son of Benjamin Councill. Rintels got Milly Bass, a respectable white woman, to keep house there for him, and W. L. Bryan boarded there while he clerked for Rintels. He occupied this building for a year or two, when Rintels moved to Statesville. W. L. Bryan bought the debts due Rintels and then, with Moretz Wessenfeld, opened a store in the same building. But Wessenfeld soon had to go to

A History of Watauga County 153

the army, when W. L. Bryan bought him out and continued to sell goods there till Stoneman's raid, March 28, 1865. This building was burned late in the fall of 1878, and the present dwelling was erected by Jas. W. Councill, father of J. D. Councill, assisted by his sons, the following spring. James H. Tatum, of Iredell, came soon after Boone was established, and built a store on the lot now occupied by the residence of W. L. Bryan, part of the foundation of that store still serving as part of the foundation for the residence. Tatum ran a store there several years and then rented it to Joseph C. Councill, who sold goods there till shortly before the Civil War, when he moved his goods across the street to the store and residence built by Jordan Councill, Jr., for his son, James W. Then Allen Myrick kept store there for Shilcutt & Bell, of Randolph County. Bell came to Boone several times, but soon closed out and went to Texas. Then Gray Utley, who married Tatum's daughter, got an interest in the land and sold it to Col. Wm. Horton and E. S. Blair shortly after the Civil War. Blair was the brother-in-law of Wm. Horton, and sold his interest in the land to him, Col. Jonathan Horton obtaining a one-half interest therein also. Jonathan Horton and Mrs. Rebecca Horton, widow of William, sold the land to W. L. Bryan about 1889. Sheriff Jack Horton occupied this store awhile as an office, and then E. S. Blair sold goods there for Rufus L. Patterson & Co., of Patterson, for a few years after the Civil War. Then Col. William Horton and Blair sold goods there for awhile. The old storehouse was removed and a large new store erected in its place. It was well built and greatly admired. Colonel Bryan kept a large stock of goods there till the night of July 4, 1895, when the store and goods, with a dwelling which stood between the store and what is now the Blair hotel, and a large barn in rear, were burned by James Cornell and Marion Waycaster, who had been hired to burn this property by Lloyd, Judd, Tyce and Mack Wagner. Their object was to burn the evidence which Colonel Bryan, who was United States Commissioner, had locked in his safe against Tyce Wagner for robbing the mail. Judd, Lloyd and Mack were sentenced to the State penitentiary for ten years each,

Waycaster got twenty years and Cornell five years, the latter having turned State's evidence. They were convicted by a jury at Boone, at the spring term, 1896, of Superior Court, presided over by Judge Geo. W. Brown (Minute Docket D, p. 102). Tyce was convicted in the United States Court of robbing the mail and sent to Sing Sing for five years. Governor Russell pardoned all who had been sent to the State penitentiary. By the first of March, 1870, W. L. Bryan had completed the store room at the west end of what is now known as the Blair Hotel, now used as the parlor, and carried on business there till September, 1873, for M. V. Moore, of Lenoir, when he bought Moore out and continued the business there till 1889, when he moved into the new store room he had built on the site of the Tatum store.

Joseph C. Gaines, of Caldwell, built the Ransom Hayes brick house about 1851 or 1852. It was one story high, with a ground plan of forty by twenty feet, with brick partition through center. It had a chimney at each end, and both gables ran up to the rafters. Hayes' boys waited on Gaines and the latter laid all the brick in eight days. He was paid $70.00 for his work, besides board. This house stood on the north side of the road from Brushy Fork just before it reaches Boone, and its foundations are now the foundations of the two-storied brick house occupied by Mrs. L. L. Green, the Hayes house having been burned. Calvin Church, of Wilkes County, built the brick house occupied by Judge L. L. Green till his death, and since then by his widow. It is two stories high. Church lived on the Watauga River at the Franklin Baird place below Valle Crucis, and died there, and Henry Taylor was executor of his estate.

Post Bellum Boone.—Rev. J. W. Hall was a Baptist preacher and performed the marriage ceremony when Judge L. L. Green was married to Miss Martha Horton, daughter of Sheriff Jack Horton, and when J. Watts Farthing was married to Miss Rivers, daughter of Dr. J. G. Rivers, both marriages having been solemnized in the Masonic Lodge of Boone on the first day of March, 1876. Mr. Hall was also a carpenter and cabinet maker. He did the wood work on the second court house. After going to McDowell County, he went to Clay County and thence to Georgia, where he remained. But before leaving Boone finally he went for a time to Mountain City, Tenn., where he learned to frame dwelling and other houses by nailing the uprights to the sills, instead of mortising and tenoning them, as had been the universal practice before that time. On his return from Mountain City to Boone he built the dwelling now owned and occupied by W. Columbus Coffey in accordance with the new method. Squire D. B. Dougherty built a small house for the post office just east of the Critcher hotel soon after the Civil War. It was enlarged and improved and used by D. Jones Cottrell as a store room about 1909 and since. St. Luke's, the Episcopal Church, was built about 1882 or 1883. The residence now owned and occupied by J. C. Fletcher, Esq., was built by Dr. L. C. Reeves, of Alleghany County. He married Sallie Councill, daughter of J. W. and Mollie Councill. Dr. Reeves moved to Blowing Rock, where he died. J. C. Fletcher bought this property about 1896, and has occupied it ever since. He married Miss Carrie H. Bryan, daughter of Mr. and Mrs. W. L. Bryan, December 16, 1896. In 1913 he was appointed examiner of land titles under the Week's law for the acquisition of national forest lands. Soon after the Civil War, in which he had served, Major Harvey Bingham bought the lot of land where Brannock's residence now stands, and laid the foundation for a home there, but Rev. J. W. Floyd, a retired Methodist minister, from east of the Blue Ridge, bought and finished the house and lived there several years, dying there about 1888. Then Joseph F. Spainhour, Esq., a lawyer, now living in Morganton, bought and enlarged the house and lived there till he sold the place to the Hinckels, of Lenoir (Deed Book N, p. 63). Benjamin Brannock then bought the place and has lived there since.

Thomas Greer built the Beech house in rear of the residence of W. C. Coffey, between 1865 and 1868, and died there, having moved there from the head of Elk after the marriage of his daughter with T. J. Coffey. Although weatherboarded now, it is really a hewed log house, in the hewing of the logs for which Captain Cook, a son of Michael Cook, took a large part.

156   A History of Watauga County

J. G. Rivers came from Bluff City, Tenn., in 1863 to Cove Creek, N. C., on account of his Southern principles. In the spring of 1865 he moved to Boone and bought the residence now occupied by his son, R. C. Rivers, from Captain J. L. Phillips, who had owned the property, having bought it from Jordan Councill, Jr., about 1860, and having moved there from Todd. Phillips was a most estimable gentleman, and was a captain in the 58th North Carolina Regiment, under Col. John B. Palmer. He was shot in the forehead by a pistol bullet during a battle in Tennessee, and while in a hospital his brains actually oozed out of the wound. Notwithstanding, he got well apparently and returned to his old home at Todd, where he taught school and made shoes, but in two or three years died from the effects of the old wound. His wife was a sister of the Miss Greer who married T. J. Coffey. Phillips was a brave and honorable citizen.

Coffey Brothers.—Thomas J. and W. C. Coffey, two brothers, had carried on business at what is now Butler, Tenn., but on the left bank of Roan Creek, before the Civil War. They had to leave on account of their Southern principles after the war commenced. They returned to their old home in Caldwell County and remained till after the close of the war, when, in 1866, they moved to Boone and opened a store in the store room which stood where J. D. Councill's residence now stands. But W. C. Coffey opened a branch store at Zionville and moved there about 1867. T. J. Coffey lived in the Brown cottage just east of the Blair hotel after his marriage to Miss Curtis, of Wilkes County, till the Coffey hotel and store, now occupied by Murray Critcher, was completed in 1870.

Coffey Brothers' Enterprises.—Thos. J. Coffey and brother used to operate a wagon, harness and saddle business in Boone for years after the Civil War. These wagons were taken to Kentucky and exchanged for horses and mules which were driven South and sold. The wagons were made about two hundred yards east of the house now occupied by Wilson A. Beech; the saddles and harness were manufactured in rooms on the second story of the present Brick Row, east of the Critcher hotel. John Allen made the wagons and Joshua Setzer made the harness and saddles. They also tanned hides in front of what is now the residence of W. A. Beech. They bought hides in the South, in bales, besides tanning hides for local farmers.

Newspapers.—The *Watauga Journal* was the first paper in Boone; was started by a man named McLaughlin, of Mooresville, and was Republican in politics. McLaughlin left and went to Johnson City, where he became chief of police. The *Enterprise* succeeded the *Journal* in 1888 and was conducted by Judge L. L. Greene and Thomas Bingham during the Harrison campaign, stopping soon after his election in 1888. The *Watauga Democrat* was also begun in 1888 by Joseph Spainhour, Esq., and the Democratic party. John S. Williams also was connected with it, but R. C. Rivers and D. B. Dougherty took charge July 4, 1889, and it has been conducted since then by R. C. Rivers. The *Watauga News* was established in January, 1913, by Don H. Phillips, as an independent paper, but it suspended after having existed for about a year.

Population.—The town has grown so much since the census of 1910 that the figures there given would be misleading now. Within the corporate limits, without including the school population of about 300, it is thought there are something over 400 people. This is a pretty constant quantity, as there are but few visitors to the town in the summer season, almost all stopping at Blowing Rock and seemingly unconscious of the fact that Boone is on the map at all.

Counterfeiters.—From about 1857 and till 1875 or thereabouts a gang of counterfeiters and horse thieves carried on their business from Taylorsville to Cincinnati, Ohio. Boone was one of their headquarters. Dark and blood-curdling stories are still told of the secret murders and robberies which occurred in a house near Taylorsville, which stood near a body of water. It is said that the owner of this house enticed travelers to stop over night with him and that they were never heard of again. When, years afterwards, the pond was drained saddles and bridles were found at the bottom, heavily weighted with stones. It was supposed that the horses were hidden in the woods till a favorable opportunity offered, when they were driven across the mountains to Cincinnati, Kentucky and Tennessee and sold. The basement of an old, unfinished house which had been built by W. F. Fletcher, framed and covered, was used as a hiding place for the horses as they passed through Boone, being tied under that dilapidated building during the nights they stayed in that town. When the dwelling of the man living near Taylorsville was removed after his death, skeletons of human beings were found underneath the floor. A woman saw a man chasing another near this house at dusk one evening, and reported the facts to the sheriff. Investigation revealed nothing but tracks, but when the road was changed later on, a human skeleton was found buried near a ford under the bank of a creek. About 1872 or 1873 Watauga County was flooded with counterfeit ten-dollar bills on the Bank of Poughkeepsie, of New York. They were thick, badly printed bills and were far too green in color to deceive experts, but they passed current here for some time. The house in which these men congregated at intervals stood near the present site of the county court house till about 1883, when it was removed.

CHAPTER XII.
War Times and Afterwards.

A Hopeless Task.—It would take several volumes the size of this to give the history of the troops sent from Watauga County into the Civil War. Their record is partially preserved in Clark's North Carolina Regiments, Moore's Roster and elsewhere. Only some of the principal events which occurred in this county and in those portions of this section which were once a part of Watauga County can be given. There were at least one thousand men from Watauga in the Confederate army and one hundred in the Federal, Company I of the Thirteenth Tennessee Cavalry having no less than thirty-three Wataugans in its ranks. Col. George N. Folk was the first to enlist volunteers in this county, and the response which his call met with was but the forerunner of many more enlistments soon to follow. Many men composing the Fifty-Eighth North Carolina Regiment, Col. J. B. Palmer's, went from this county, though a large part of it was then embraced in the newly formed county of Mitchell. Indeed, Colonel Palmer's home on the Linville River had been in Watauga from the time it was purchased and the residence built in 1858 till the new county was formed in 1860-61. The old county line then ran below his residence along Pisgah Ridge, and a voting precinct, at Levi Franklin's house, now the upper part of Potter Brown's meadow, is still remembered by some of the older residents of Boone and vicinity. It was the most remote of all in the county, and the messenger bearing the returns usually did not arrive at the court house in Boone till after midnight. That he managed to get here even as late as that was due to the practice prevailing at the time, of keeping "tab" on the votes as they were cast, removing them from the hat into which they were usually deposited, examining them, and crediting each candidate for whom they had been cast with the vote to which he was entitled. Thus, the count was kept as rapidly as the ballots were deposited. But, and this seems to have been an important legal feature of the matter, some ballots were always left in the hat to show that the voting was still going on, or that the precinct had not closed. Consequently, when the sun set on the first Thursday in August of election years, there were but a few ballots remaining to be counted, which was soon done and the messenger dispatched with the result to Boone. Captain William M. Hodges, still hale and active at the age of eighty-three, remembers attending that precinct in 1850 or 1852 in the contest between Michael Cook and Jack Horton for sheriff. He took some of the juice of the peach with him, a gallon and a half, to be exact, and carried the precinct overwhelmingly for Cook, his uncle, or, to be exact again, thirty-eight out of forty votes. The dancing which took place at Franklin's house during that day, in which barefoot girls and women joined, was the most vigorous, if not the most graceful, he ever witnessed. He still wonders how it was that those bare feet did not wear through to the quick.[1]

"Keith" Blalock.—It might seem almost as if the history of the Civil War in Watauga were inextricably interwoven with the life and adventures of W. M. Blalock, commonly called 'Keith" Blalock, a nic-name given him because of the fact that Alfred Keith, of Burnsville, was a great fighter during Blalock's youth, and as he was something of a fighter himself, his boy companions called him "Keith." Keith and his wife, born Malinda Pritchard, lived "under the Grandfather" when the Civil War commenced, and both became members of Zeb Vance's 26th Regiment, he as W. M. and she as Sam Blalock. She wore a private's uniform and tented and messed with Keith. She watched the men "when they went in swimming" near Kinston, but never went in herself. Keith was a Union man and joined only to avoid conscription and in the hope that opportunity might offer for him to desert to the Union lines. But the fortunes of war did not afford this chance as speedily as he wished, so he went into the bushes and covered himself with poison oak. When this took effect the army surgeons were puzzled as to the nature

---

[1] He also wonders if one of the Franklins, who had his tax list there, ever got it straightened out after the dance was over and the peach-juice exhausted.

of his complaint, but they agreed that he was then unfit for service and discharged him. Then "Sam" presented himself and convinced his colonel, Zeb Vance, that he was no longer fit for duty either, his lawful tent and messmate having been discharged. They returned to their home under the Grandfather, but it was not long till Keith had cured his infirmity by the frequent application of strong brine to the affected parts, brine being nothing more or less than strong salt water. Then Confederate sympathisers wanted to know why he did not return. Keith showed his discharge, and they answered by trying to arrest and conscript him. He and "Sam" retreated still further up under the Grandfather and lived in a rail pen. But they were followed even there, and on one occasion Keith was so hotly pursued that he was shot in the left arm, and had to take refuge with some hogs which had "bedded up" under the rocks. Keith then went through the lines into Tennessee and became recruiting officer for a Michigan regiment stationed in Tennessee. Whether true or not, Blalock believed that Robert Green, who then lived in the Globe, but had also a place at Blowing Rock, was in the party that had wounded him. Accordingly, when he and some of his comrades met Green one day while he was driving his wagon from the Globe to Blowing Rock, he shot Green as he ran down the side of the mountain, breaking his thigh. Green's friends say that Blalock's crowd left him lying as he had fallen, and that he managed to regain his wagon, turn it around and drive back home. Blalock's friends say that after he had wounded Green, shooting him through his wagon body and afterwards bragging on his marksmanship, he went to him, and finding him unconscious, took him to his wagon, put him in it, turned the wagon around and started the team in the direction of Green's home. This is doubted by Green's friends, however. Robert Green was the father of the late Judge L. L. Green, of this county.

Four Coffey Brothers.—To go back a little, Keith Blalock's mother had married Austin Coffey, while Keith was a very little boy, and Coffey reared him to manhood. Austin Coffey lived almost in sight of the home of his brother, McCaleb Coffey, in the Coffey Gap of the Blue Ridge and on the old Morganton Road.

McCaleb was rather a Confederate sympathiser, having a son, Jones, in the Confederate army. Austin was rather a Union man, though too old to be drafted into the service. Of course, he sheltered and fed Keith and his comrades whenever he or they came to his home. But William and Reuben Coffey were pronounced Southern men, and active in forcing out-lyers and others subject to conscription into the ranks of the Confederate army. Meantime, Blalock was taking recruits through the lines into the Union army in Tennessee. Thus, a natural antagonism sprang up between him and William and Reuben Coffey.

Danger from Tennessee.—Up to the spring of 1864 the Union element in the mountains had been rather timid, but as the tide of battle turned against the Confederacy, and recruiting officers, of whom James Hartley was a conspicuous example, increased throughout the mountain region, Union men and women grew bolder. Then, too, there had been numerous desertions from the Southern army, and men not only from these mountains, but from Tennessee, Georgia and Virginia, were lying out in the mountains almost everywhere. Of course, they had to live, and if those who could would not feed them, they naturally tried to feed themselves. To do this they had to pilfer, steal and finally, in bands, to rob outright. A state of guerrilla warfare was thus imminent, when an event occurred which almost revolutionized matters in the mountains. This was Kirk's raid through the mountains to Camp Vance, six miles below Morganton. That it had been successful was almost a miracle, and the leaders of the Southern Confederacy realized the vulnerability of its piedmont region to like incursions from East Tennessee. It should be remembered that General Burnside had long been in possession of Knoxville, Tenn., and that he might at almost any time send a large force through the mountains and destroy the railroad from Richmond to Columbia, the main artery of the Confederacy. To guard against this contingency, General Robert B. Vance, of Asheville, had been placed in command of the Military District of Western North Carolina, as it was officially designated. Also, that on the 7th of July, 1863, the General Assembly of North Carolina had provided for the organization and equipment of the Home Guard, officially designated as "The Guard for Home Defense," to be composed of all males between eighteen and fifty years of age. In April, 1864, Gen. John W. McElroy, commanding the forces around Burnsville, wrote to Governor Vance that "the county is gone up," and that there was a determination on part of the people generally "to do no more service in the cause."[2]

Longstreet's Withdrawal.—General Longstreet had been detached from Lee's army in Virginia and sent to East Tennessee in 1863, where, after the Battle of Chickamauga, he drove the Federals back into Knoxville and besieged that place. But Lee could not long do without Longstreet, and so, in January, 1864, Longstreet tried to withdraw from Knoxville and return to Richmond with his army. No sooner, however, had Longstreet started than Burnside started after him. In anticipation of this, General Vance was ordered to cross the mountains through Haywood County and attack Burnside in flank as he pursued Longstreet. Vance, however, was captured as soon as he reached the western slope of the Smoky Mountains, and sent to prison, his force of about 1,200 men of all arms retreating back to Buncombe as best they might. Thus the Military District of Western North Carolina was left without a general. But Col. J. B. Palmer, of the 58th North Carolina, asked to be placed in command, and he was accordingly transferred early in 1864 from his regiment in the western army and placed in command. But General Lee wanted a West Point man in charge of this most important region, and assigned General James G. Martin to that position. Meantime, Keith Blalock was passing back and forth between the lines and keeping the Federal authorities informed of conditions around his old home "under the Grandfather." The mountains were at that time practically defenseless. Camp Vance with a few hundred recruits was the only force of moment between Knoxville and Salisbury, where were confined thousands of Federal prisoners. Blalock had grown up with Joseph V. Franklin, who was reared near Linville Falls and knew the country like a book. Col. George W. Kirk was

---

[2] Rebellion Records, Series I, Vol. LIII, p. 485.

then in command of the Third North Carolina Mounted Infantry, United States Army, and persuaded the military authorities to allow him to make a raid to Camp Vance, release the conscripts there, steal an engine and train, cut the wires, go on to Salisbury, release and arm the prisoners there and turn them loose on the country. It was a daring scheme, and the wonder is that Kirk was allowed to make the venture.

Kirk's Camp Vance Raid.—With 130 men, including twelve Cherokee Indians, on foot and carrying their rations and arms and blankets, Kirk left Morristown, Tenn., June 13, 1864, and marched via Bull Gap, Greenville and the Crab Orchard, all in Tennessee, crossed the Big Hump Mountain and went up the Toe River, passing the Cranberry iron mine, where from forty to sixty men were detailed by the Confederate government making iron, when they camped near David Ellis' house and where rations were cooked for Kirk's men. On the 26th they scouted through the mountains, passing Pinola and crossing Linville River. The following day they got to Upper Creek at dark, where they did not camp, but keeping themselves in the woods all the time, got to Camp Vance at daylight. Here they demanded its surrender, which was agreed to. It had been Kirk's plan to take a locomotive and cars and such arms as he might find at the Camp and go to Salisbury, where the Federal prisoners confined there were to be released. Failing in that, he wanted to destroy the bridge over the Yadkin, but a telegram had been sent before they could cut the wire and that part of their scheme was abandoned. They captured 1,200 small arms, 3,000 bushels of grain, 279 prisoners, thirty-two negroes and forty-eight horses and mules. Kirk also got forty recruits for his regiment, and then, after destroying the locomotive he found there, three cars, the depot and commissary buildings, he started to return. R. C. Pearson shot Hack Norton, of Madison County, one of Kirk's men, at Hunting Creek, but Kirk got over the Catawba River and camped that night. The next day they crossed John's River and Brown's Mountain, where they were fired into by pursuing Confederates at 3:30 p. m. Kirk put some of his Camp Vance prisoners in front, and one of them, B. A.

Bowles, a drummer, was killed and a seventeen year old boy wounded. Colonel Kirk was himself wounded here with several others of his command. This was at Israel Beck's farm. They camped that night at top of the Winding Stairs Road, where they were attacked next morning. Col. W. W. Avery and Phillip Chandler were mortally wounded, Col. Calvin Houck was shot through the wrist and Powell Benfield through the thigh. The attacking party then retreated and Kirk continued his retreat, passing by Col. J. B. Palmer's home and burning it that morning. Kirk and all his men escaped without further mishap. On July 21, 1864, General Stoneman, wiring from Atlanta, thanked and complimented Kirk, but instructed General Scofield at Knoxville not to allow him to undertake another such hazardous expedition. Joseph V. Franklin, now living at Drexel, N. C., was the guide. A man named Beech, who had been wounded, was left at John Franklin's, near Old Fields of Toe, where he was attended by Eleazer Pyatt. At Henry Barringer's, on Jonas's Ridge, some of Kirk's men threw off some of the plunder they had captured, lest its weight should retard their retreat. In his "Reminiscenses of Caldwell County" (p. 51), G. W. F. Harper gives an account of an attack upon Kirk's retreating men by ten men, including himself, at Moore's Cross Roads, where they captured one prisoner, two mules and some arms. No mention of this is made in the official report. (See Rebellion Records, Series 1, Vol. XXXIX, Part I, p. 232.) Harper also states that the detachment which attacked Kirk at the head of the Winding Stairs was under command of Col. Allen Brown, from the garrison at Salisbury, with militia and volunteers from Burke County, and was well armed. The pursuing party was composed of about 1,200 men.

Death of William Coffey.—Kirk's raid in 1864 emboldened the Unionists in Watauga County, and Blalock went about in Federal uniform, fully armed. Between August, 1864, and February, 1865, the people of this section were harassed beyond measure, for not only had the deserters and outlyers to be fed by submitting to their thefts and robberies, but a body of men calling themselves Vaughan's Cavalry, and claiming to be Confederates, came from Tennessee to Boone on their way to Newton for the purpose of recruiting their horses, it was alleged, but to keep out of danger also, most probably. These men were worse than Kirk's or Stoneman's men, according to old people still living, stealing horses and mules and everything else they fancied. What they did not like they destroyed, throwing out of doors many of the household goods of the defenceless women and children. Col. W. L. Bryan and J. W. Councill followed them to Newton and recovered two horses they had stolen from the latter in 1865. In these circumstances, there is no wonder that Blalock hunted out his enemies. Reuben Coffey was first sought, but he was not at home when Keith called. He and his aids then went to William Coffey's field, forced him to go half a mile with them to James Gragg's mill, and to sit astride a rude bench, where he was shot, Blalock turning over that act to a man named Perkins, because of the fact that William Coffey was the brother of Austin Coffey, Keith's step-father. In 1864 Keith also had what he called a "battle" with Jesse Moore in Carroll Moore's orchard, in which Jesse was wounded in the heel and Keith had an eye shot out. Pat, a son of Daniel Moore, had a thigh broken in same fight. This was in the Globe, in Caldwell, however.

The Murder of Austin Coffey.[3]—These activities soon brought some of Colonel Avery's battalion on the scene, and a party of Captain James Marlow's company went to McCaleb Coffey's house in the Coffey Gap. There they found Austin Coffey, who was recognized by John B. Boyd, and arrested. Boyd left his prisoner with Marlow's men and went on home in the Globe. That was Sunday, February 26, 1865. Nothing was seen of Austin Coffey after that till his body was discovered a week later in the woods by searchers sent out by his widow. All sorts of stories have been circulated as to what really happened to Austin, and it was only recently that what is probably the true account was obtained from J. Filmore Coffey, of Foscoe. This gentleman is a son of Austin Coffey, having been born in 1858. When he became a man and had married he stopped one

---

[3] Austin Coffey was the son of Jesse Coffey, and was born in 1818, and died on the 27th of February, 1865.

night in 1882 at the house of a man named John Walker, near Shelby. When Walker learned Coffey's name and that he was the youngest son of Austin Coffey, Walker told him that he, Walker, had been a member of Marlow's company when Austin was turned over to them; that they had taken him to a vacant house about half way between Shull's Mills and Blowing Rock, known then as the Tom Henley place, where Nelson Coffey now lives, one-half mile west of the Blowing Rock Road. There a fire was kindled and Coffey went to sleep on the floor before it. While he was sleeping this John Walker was detailed to kill Austin Coffey, but refused. It was then that a base-born fellow, named Robert Glass, or Anders, volunteered to do the act, and while the old man slept shot him through the head. The body was taken to a laurel and ivy thicket near by and hidden. One week later a dog was seen with a human hand in his mouth. Search revealed the body. Glass, after suffering much mental torture, died long before 1882 in Rutherford County. J. F. Coffey acquits both John Boyd and Major A. C. Avery of all complicity in his father's death.

Other "Activities."—About this time Levi Coffey, a son of Elisha, threw in his fortunes with Blalock and his companions, and when Benjamin Green and his men tried to arrest Levi at Mrs. Fox's house, above what is now Foscoe, the latter ran out of the house and was shot in the shoulder, but he escaped. This was during the autumn of 1864, as well as can now be determined. This caused the bushwhackers, as Blalock and his followers were called, when they were not called robbers outright, to turn against the Greens, and finding that Lott Green, a son of Amos, was at his home near Blowing Rock, they went there at night to arrest or kill him. Lott was expecting a physician to visit him that night, and when someone knocked at his door, he, thinking that the doctor had arrived, unsuspectingly opened it. Finding who his visitors really were, he drew back, slamming the door to. It just so happened that there were at that time in the house with Lott his brother, Joseph; his brother-in-law, Henry Henley, the latter of the Home Guard, and L. L. Green, afterwards a judge of the Superior Court, then but seventeen years old, but also a member of the Home Guard. The bushwhackers are said to have been Keith Blalock, Levi Coffey, Sampson Calloway, son of Larkin, Edmund Ivy, of Georgia, a deserter from the Confederate army, Adolphus Pritchard, and ——————— Gardner, of Mitchell. Blalock demanded that all in the house surrender, whereupon Henly asked what treatment would be accorded them in case they surrendered, and Blalock is said to have answered: "As you deserve, damn you." Henley then slipped his gun through a crack of the door and fired, wounding Calloway in the side. The bushwhackers then retired, and the Green party, who followed, saw blood. Calloway was left at the house of John Walker, two miles above Shull's Mills. Henly led the party at Green's house, excepting L. L. Green, to Walker's, and surrounded it. Henly was at the rear and shot Edmund Ivy as he ran out, killing him. Blalock called to a woman to open the gate, and Mrs. Medie Walker, born McHaarg, did so. Through this gate Blalock and his company escaped. A little later on, February 26, 1865, Captain James Marlow's infantry, expecting to unite with a detachment of cavalry under Nelson Miller at Valle Crucis, went to Austin Coffey's house and arrested Thomas Wright and Austin, Alex. Johnson, who claimed to be a recruiting officer for Kirk, having just left and gone to McCaleb Coffey's house.' The infantry followed, taking Wright with them, but Wright's wife and Blalock's mother, then Mrs. Austin Coffey, went a nigh-way and gave warning to the inmates of McCaleb's house before the infantry arrived by calling out in a loud voice that the "rebels" were coming. Thereupon, Johnson dashed out of the door, and although fired on, escaped unhurt. Most of the infantry followed Johnson, but John Boyd, in charge of four or five men, entered the house, where they found Sampson Calloway, he having been removed from the Walker house which Henly had attacked. Calloway got into bed and was not arrested, but Austin Coffey was arrested, as before related. All now agree that Austin Coffey did not deserve his fate: that he was a big-

---

Brooks and Smoot, "two preacher men," also engaged in piloting Union men through the lines to Tennessee, via Elk Cross Roads, Sutherland and Cut Laurel Gap, were killed on the left of the road to Blowing Rock, beyond where Kilby Hartley lives, by the Home Guard.

hearted man, who had fed Confederates as well as Union men at his house. He was a Union man, but not active in arresting Southern sympathizers, and had tried to prevent the raids on Lott Green's and Carroll Moores' houses.

Two Michiganders Escape.—Reuben Coffey, sick of living in a turmoil with his neighbors, had left the Globe and moved to a house on Meat Camp, but needing some household articles he had left at his Globe home, returned during this winter, accompanied by his daughter, Millie, who was riding a white horse. The robbers had taken all of McCaleb Coffey's horses, and when the white horse appeared McCaleb threw a "grise" of corn over his back to be taken to Elisha Coffey's mill by Miss Millie. On their way down the mountain Reuben and his daughter met two men, who said they were from Michigan and had escaped from prison. They were not in uniform, neither were they armed. Reuben had a gun and arrested them, after which he took them by McCaleb Coffey's house to David Miller's, one mile away, hoping to get Miller to go with him and them to Camp Mast on Cove Creek, but Miller excused himself, and Reuben went on alone with his prisoners. When they got to the intersection of the turnpike with the old Morganton Road, about two miles above Shull's Mills, one of the prisoners called Reuben's attention to some rude benches standing on one side of the road, and when he looked in the direction indicated the other seized his gun, while his companion struck Reuben a blow on the back of his head with a heavy stick. In the ensuing scuffle the two overcame Reuben and took his gun away from him. At that moment, after having tried to shoot him and failing only because the cap snapped, they heard Wilson Beech, a boy, returning at a gallop from the mill, when they ran off and escaped. This boy, now an elderly man, remembers that he was working in the field at McCaleb Coffey's, with Polly Hawkins as a helper, when they saw James C. Coffey coming down the road on foot. He said, "Hurrah! the war is over." This, however, was in April, 1865.

The Sins of the Children.—Leading up to the surrender of this camp are several very distressing circumstances. Levi Guy, who lived on Watauga River near its falls and its passage into

Tennessee, was an old man during the Civil War. His three sons, Canada, Enoch and David, were active Union men. Their enemies called them robbers. There were near the head of North Fork of New River several men of the name of Potter and others named Stout. Thomas Stout, another old man, had three sons, Abram, Daniel and John, who, with the Potters and Guys, were charged with many depredations throughout this region. One night in 1863 a band of men, among whom were supposed to have been the three Guy "boys," as they were called, went to the home of Paul Farthing on Beaver Dams, where Lewis Farthing now lives, and after demanding his surrender, fired into the log walls of his residence. It had been agreed by the people of this neighborhood that, in case any house should be attacked, horns or trumpets should be blown, so that all who heard the signal might hasten to the assistance of those in trouble. This alarm was sounded from the upper story of Paul Farthing's house by his women folk, while he fired at the attacking party from the rooms below. Several neighbors heard the alarm and started to the rescue. Among these was Thomas Farthing, and he was shot dead as he approached the house, the robbers taking flight immediately thereafter. Some time later Levi Guy was captured by some of the Confederate Home Guard and hanged, although he protested that he had done nothing more than shelter his own sons when they came to his house for food and beds. Paul Farthing was falsely charged with having been concerned in this deed.

While Isaac Wilson, son of Hiram, was ploughing in his field at the head of the North Fork of Cove Creek, bushwhackers, among whom are supposed to have been Potters and Stouts, slipped up on him and shot him dead. Soon thereafter Canada Guy and a boy named Jacob May, a son of Jeff May, of Roan Creek, Tenn., were captured by Daniel Sheppard and some of Captain Price's men of Ashe County, near Sutherland, and hanged, though it is said that May was innocent and was exhonorated from all complicity by Guy before he was killed.[5]

---

[5] It is said that Sheppard was afterwards captured and hanged on a dogwood in Johnson County, Tenn., but that the rope broke. Jeff May, his captor, then took the halter from Sheppard's horse and strangled Sheppard to death with it.

A History of Watauga County 171

After this it is claimed that Paul Farthing's house was again attacked at night, but that he returned the fire and wounded or killed one of the assailants, as blood was seen on the road leading away from the dwelling. Then, sometime afterwards—dates are lacking all through this period—Old Man Thomas Stout, father of the Stout boy or boys charged with having been concerned in the killing of Isaac Wilson, was captured by Confederate Home Guards in the spring of 1864 and taken to Hiram Wilson's on Cove Creek, where he was kept all night. Big Isaac Wilson, a cousin of "Little" Isaac, the slain man; Jay or Jehu Howington and Gilbert Norris are said to have started with Stout next day for Camp Vance, below Morganton, and after having been told to go "the nigh-way." Thomas Stout was never seen alive again. Two months later James H. Presnell was cow-hunting on Rich Mountain and found a shoe. He reported this to his brother, Col. W. W. Presnell, when he got back to their home on Brushy Fork. The next day the two brothers went back to the place at which the shoe had been found, and within fifty paces they found what remained of the body of Thomas Stout, including his gray hair. It had been placed in the cavity formed by the blowing down of an oak tree; logs had then been placed beside the body and the whole covered with brush and leaves. Not far off, dangling from a leaning white oak, was the hickory thong by which he had been hanged, with the noose still in a circular form, though it had been cut in two when the body was removed. Colonel Presnell reported these facts to Abram Lewis, an officer at Camp Mast, and soon afterwards Thomas Stout's widow had the remains removed and buried near her home.⁶ Thus was the Bible promise reversed, that the sins of the fathers should be visited upon the children; but, alas, the sins of the children are much oftener visited upon their fathers!

Retribution?—It became necessary sometime in the fall of 1864 to gather the crop of Big Isaac Wilson on the head of the

---

⁶ E. B. Miller, of Meat Camp, says that on the 10th of April, 1865, he was near the Little Cavit of the Rich Mountain, and hearing some one sobbing, went to the place from which the sound came. There, at the root of the tree, stood Mrs. Tom Stout with the bones of her husband in her apron, crying as if her heart would break.

North Fork of Cove Creek. Friends of Thos. Stout knew of this and were lying in wait when the men came with fell purpose. They shot and killed Howington[7] and James Norris, a son of Gilbert's, while Big Isaac himself was severely wounded, but recovered. It is said that Gilbert Norris afterwards went blind. All concerned in the death of old Levi Guy are said to have speedily come to a bad end, also.

Some Watauga Amazons.—In "the course of human events" it so happened in John Walker's lifetime, as it had in the Declaration of Independence, that things had got past all endurance. He was a soldier in Camp Mast, but he was sick and tired of it all. John wanted to be well out of it, but he did not wish to desert. Therefore, when it came time for him to spend a week at the home of his father, Meredith Walker, he got Levi Coffey and Erwin Calloway, a brother of W. H. Calloway, afterwards sheriff, to "capture" him at the end of his week at home. But it would never do for Levi to be known in the matter, as he was John's best friend, and for Calloway to capture him unaided might seem to smack of complicity. But it had so chanced that, some time before, Henderson Calloway had brought in from Tennessee a full United States officer's uniform, shoulder-straps, belt and sword. Adorned in these, it was hoped that Erwin would not be recognized, but where were the "assisting force" to come from? Levi was not long in answering. His own wife, Edith and Elvira Taylor, Catharine and Jemima Yarber and Frankie Danner were "force" enough for the occasion. So he got them to assume male attire and armed them with "stick guns." At night Erwin Calloway, panoplied in full regimentals, marched his squad into the Walker yard and halted them at the front door, himself rapping for admittance. John and his women folk, with white faces, appeared and opened the door. Erwin demanded his surrender, the female guard, with sergeant Levi Coffey remaining in the dark, but still dimly visible. There was a parley, John's women pleading for him, with tear-bedimmed

---

[7] Dr. J. G. Rivers lived at the Swift place on Cove Creek and was the first to hear of the killing of these men. He ran his horse to Camp Mast and reported the facts, and the entire camp hastened to the scene. Doctor Rivers was with Howington toward his end and Howington asked him why it was so hard for him to die. Rivers asked if he had anything on his mind. He said he had helped hang old man Thomas Stout, and had never known any peace since. He then died.

eyes. Erwin went inside, leaving Levi to keep the sentinels outside alert and watchful, which he did by gruff commands. But Erwin was obdurate, and tore John away from the arms of his family and marched him to the squad outside. For effect Jonathan McHaarg was also captured at the same time and place, the women of the family alone being ignorant of the deception practiced. Meantime, however, it had become bruited about that Yankees were in the gap of the mountain, and France and Wilts Beech, two boys, were started on horses for Camp Bingham to bring assistance. These were met by Erwin's squad and turned back, while John Walker was taken on to a ridge and rock cliff just above Elisha Coffey's Mill, afterwards known as Lenoir's Stonewall Mill, where he was fed by Elisha whenever he went out to feed his hogs. It was about one week later that John walked into his home, apparently much crippled up and sorely distraught, but bearing an iron clad paper-writing with his signature attached, a duplicate of one he declared the Yankees in Tennessee had compelled him to sign while in captivity in order to secure his parole. Of course this was merely a fake, but it worked, for when Bingham sent for John the messenger advised John to respect his parole, and he was left at home till the surrender at Appomattox and ever thereafter.

Camp Mast at Sugar Grove.—Captain Price had a company of the Home Guards at Jefferson, while Major Harvey Bingham had two companies at a camp on Cove Creek, four miles above Valle Crucis, which had been named in honor of the Mast family. It was just below the old Mast Mill, now called Pete Mast's Mill. Geo. McGuire was captain of one company and Jordan Cook of the other. The land on which it stood is now occupied by the residence and grounds of Boone Deal. Only one-half of the force was in camp at any one time, the other half being at their homes every alternate week. The camp consisted of wooden shacks and tents. There were also some fortifications around it. Many wounded Confederate soldiers formed part of the garrison of Home Guards stationed there. The men were rather poorly armed, and Major Avery's battalion was on its way to supply them with better weapons in February, 1865, when it was surrendered, as will more fully appear later on.

The Battle on the Beech.—In the fall of 1864 nine men went to James Farthing's home, a mile and a half below what is now Ward's Store on lower Watauga River, robbed him, shot him and left him for dead. They then went a mile further up, to Reuben P. Farthing's, claiming to be Confederates. Thomas Farthing was up stairs in Reuben's house, wounded. But he had a pistol, and hearing what was passing below, put his head out of the window and ordered the nine men to leave. They did so, but took several horses from one of Thomas Farthing's brothers as he was going with them to the pasture. Word was sent to Major Bingham, who immediately came with eighteen men. Rations for three days were then cooked by the Farthings for these men, and they followed the horses to Cranberry and recaptured them, returning to the old Joel Eggers place near Balm, where they stayed that night. Captain James Hartley was notified of their presence there, and supposing that they would return to Valle Crucis by the Bowers' Gap, secreted himself and thirteen of his men there and awaited Bingham's approach. But Bingham had decided to return to Reuben Farthing's below Ward's Store for the purpose of returning the recaptured horses. There is a wagon road there now, but then there was only a trail. One of Hartley's runners informed him of Bingham's purpose, and Hartley, taking a near way up the ridge, arrived in time to confront them at the place now owned by Lee Gwaltney, seven miles from Ward's Store and one mile from what is now Balm. This spot is about half way between the Hanging Rock and the South Pinnacle of the Beech, but then known as the Abe Baird land. In the fight which ensued Richard Kilby was killed and Elliott Bingham, a brother of the Major's, so badly wounded that he died afterwards. These men belonged to Major Bingham's battalion. None of Hartley's men was hurt. The Confederates retreated, although they greatly outnumbered the attacking force. A. J. McBride, of Bingham's command, although a preacher, cursed and swore when ordered to retreat.

Surrender of Camp Mast.—It is difficult to get the exact date of the fall of this mountain stronghold, for weak as it was, it was all there was at that time, but T. P. Adams, of Dog Skin

A History of Watauga County 175

Creek, says it was the 5th of February, 1865. As he was one of the captured garrison, he probably knows. Assuming that this is the correct date, on the 4th of February of that year Captain James Champion, of Indiana, a recruiting officer for the Federals, gathered at Banner Elk about one hundred Union men, most of whom were armed after one fashion or another, but many of them had no weapons at all. He marched them that day to Valle Crucis, where they halted, killed one of Henry Taylor's beeves, cooked it and had supper. This dispatched, Captain Champion made them a speech, in which he told them of his plans. But, he added, that if there was any man in the party who expected to loot or rob or burn or destroy any property not strictly contraband, he must fall out, as all he expected to do or allow to be done was to burn the camp, capture the garrison and disable the arms found there. Out of 123 men in his command, twenty fell out, indicating that they had joined in the hope of plunder only. With James Isaacs for guide, the residue started, following the public road to the old Ben Councill place at what has been called Vilas since Cleveland's first post-master general was in office. They crossed Brushy Fork Creek at this point and took the ridge between that stream and Cove Creek, and came down upon Camp Mast just before a chill dawn. It seemed, however, as they passed over the frozen ground, that the clang of their horses' shoes had aroused every dog in Christendom, and just before reaching the camp a flock of sheep became frightened and fled helter-skelter down the ridge toward the camp, with bells jingling and sheep bleating, thus making a veritable pandemonium. But the camp was still asleep, and Champion's men were placed at regular intervals around it, each second man being required to build a fire. When the palid dawn gave way to a roseate sunrise and reveille sounded, the sleepy garrison looked out upon the frozen hills but to discover that they were indeed encompassed round about, if not by an army with banners, at least by an apparent wall of smoke and fire. Champion had divided his force into three companies, one under I. V. Reese, the second under Aaron Voncannon, while he remained in charge of the third. General Franklin, General being his baptismal name and not a mere empty title of military rank, was sent forward with a flag of truce, returning soon afterwards with Captain George McGuire, who was native and to the manner born, but afterwards suspected by some to have conspired with Champion for the surrender of the Camp, as the latter had selected a time when Major Harvey Bingham had gone to Ashe to confer with Captain Price as to some desired co-operation between the two forces. McGuire reported that he had taken a vote and found that about sixty of his men favored surrender, while eleven voted to fight. He was sent back for the names of those on each side of the question, and soon returned with them. The minority was overruled and the garrison surrendered, all being over by nine o'clock that winter morning. They were taken down Cove Creek, crossing Watauga River at the old Ben Baird place, and followed the old Bedent Baird Road over Beech Mountain to George Dugger's, and thence to where Sam Banner lived, where Keith Blalock's son joined them, taking charge of the prisoners. When these reached Ham Ray's at Shell Creek in Tennessee most of those who had voted to surrender were paroled and discharged, while all of those who had voted to fight, except T. P. Adams, were sent on to Camp Chace. McGuire went on, but not to Camp Chace. He rode with the officers and never returned to this State.

Paul and Reuben Farthing.—When the question of surrendering was put to the garrison at Camp Mast, Paul Farthing declared that the surrender of the Camp meant the surrender of his life. Miss Sophronia Mast, a daughter of the venerable Joseph Mast, of Sugar Grove, and Miss Melinda Williams, now the wife of Mr. Wesley Holtsclaw, were returning at dawn from having sat up all night with a sick neighbor, when they discovered that they were within the lines of Champion's men encircling the camp. They were detained there, and while waiting to be allowed to proceed to their homes advised Paul Farthing and his nephew to escape by following the stream under the bushes growing on the bank of the creek flowing hard by, but they said it had grown too light and that they would be discovered and killed. Paul Farthing, however, gave Sophronia his pistol, knife and pocket-book,

A History of Watauga County

and Dr. J. G. Rivers, who was also of the surrendered garrison, entrusted some things to Miss Williams, and these articles were afterwards faithfully delivered by these two young girls, Miss Mast afterwards becoming the wife of Captain Newton Banner. The two Farthings, Paul and his nephew, Reuben, did die at Camp Chase, just as they had predicted would be the case if surrendered.

Stoneman's Raid.—General Stoneman reached Boone in the forenoon of March 28, 1865. The day was fair. Some men in the house which stood where J. D. Councill's residence now stands, among whom was W. Waightstill Gragg, fired on the head of the column as it came down the road from Hodges Gap. This was enough: Warren Green was killed; so were Jacob M. Councill and Ephraim Norris. The following were wounded: Calvin Green, son of Alexander Green; Sheriff A. J. McBride, Thomas Holder, son of Elisha; John Brown, son of Joseph Brown, of Gap Creek, and W. Waightstill Gragg, of the First North Carolina Cavalry, who was then at home on a furlough. The house from which the shooting had been done, now J. D. Councill's, was converted into a hospital and the Federal surgeon did his best for the wounded. Calvin Green was taken to the old Jordan Councill house. He had been badly wounded, but recovered. McBride had been shot in the breast, but the ball followed a rib and lodged near his spine, from which the Federal surgeon removed it, while McBride lay on his stomach on the floor, without anaesthetics of any kind. Holder's wound was in the hip and groin. He lived on Howard's Creek, but is now dead. Brown had his ankle broken. Gragg's wound was not very severe. He lived a short distance above the house now occupied by Benjamin Brannock. After the firing from the Councill house, Stoneman's men charged, and all who were in that house or near it ran through the fields toward the foot of Howard's Knob. Hence, all were wounded in the rear, except McBride, who was hit in the breast. The house in which Jacob M. Councill was killed is called the Mark Hodge house. It still stands, in rear of Benjamin Councill's home, though untenanted now. Jacob had been ploughing and was putting his harness up when one of Stoneman's men came to the door and shot him dead, notwithstanding his protestations. A colored woman, Phoebe by name, who had been at work with him, saw the deed.

Official Account.—Major-General George Stoneman's command, consisting of a cavalry division and a battery of artillery, left Knoxville March 21, 1865, and camped at Strawberry Plains, and by the 27th forded Doe River and crossed the Smoky Mountains into North Carolina, moving out at 5:00 a. m. March 28th and reaching Boone about eleven o'clock that morning. Here the division divided, the first brigade taking the route to Yadkin River, while part of the remainder went through Deep Gap to Wilkesboro. Col. George W. Kirk, in command of the second and third North Carolina Mounted Infantry, United States Army, left Taylorsville, Tenn., on the 5th of April and came to Boone, where he was joined next day by Brigadier-General Davis Tillson. On the morning of the 7th Major Bahney left with the second North Carolina Mounted Infantry for Deep Gap, and Major W. W. Rollins, with 200 men of the third North Carolina Infantry, went to Blowing Rock Gap, called by army officers Watauga Gap, while Colonel Kirk, with 406 men, remained in Boone. General Tillson gave instructions for building rough but formidable field works and the collection of as large a supply of forage and subsistence as possible, while Kirk was instructed to barricade the Meat Camp road leading through State Gap and also a road not then on General Tillson's military map, leading through Sampson Gap, between Deep and Watauga Gaps, a few miles from the latter. On the 27th of April the second and third North Carolina Mounted Infantry were moved toward Asheville, reaching there on the 30th. (Rebellion Records, Series I, Vol. XLIX, Part 1, pp. 323 to 337.) Signal stations on mountain tops were established from Butler, Tenn., to Lenoir, N. C.

Obeyed Orders.—Boone court house was pierced with holes to fire through, while a barricade was made around it of timbers taken from an unfinished building which then stood where the Blair hotel now stands, and from another half finished house then standing near Blackburn's present hotel. Deep Gap and

A History of Watauga County

Blowing Rock also were fortified, traces of both fortifications being still visible. William P. Welch, now living at Deep Gap, recalls the fort and many incidents connected with the fortification of that place. It was a palisaded fort enclosing about one acre and ditched around. The J. D. Councill house stands now on the site of his father's residence, destroyed by fire in the fall of 1878, which was used as a hospital for the wounded soldiers who fell in that skirmish.

Other Details.—From the same source (p. 330) it is learned that when camped ten miles west of Jonesboro, Tenn., the train came up and "the First and Second Brigades drew all the rations the men could carry conveniently. On the 26th of March the command moved, cutting loose from all incumbrances in the way of trains. One wagon, ten ambulances and four guns with their caissons were the only wheeled vehicles that accompanied the expedition . . . On the 27th a portion of the command moved up the Watauga River, and after halting for a short time at the mouth of Roan Creek to feed, marched until 12:00 p. m., when we bivouacked on the eastern slope of the Iron Mountain until daylight, when the march was resumed. About 10:00 a. m. on the 28th, when approaching the town of Boone, it was learned that there was a meeting of the home guard in that town to take place on that day. Major Keogh, aide-de-camp to Major-General Stoneman, went forward with a detachment of the Twelfth Kentucky Volunteer Cavalry and surprised and routed the rebels, killing nine[8] and capturing sixty-eight. . . . At Boone the command separated, General Stoneman, with Palmer's Brigade (First), going by way of Deep Gap to Wilkesborough, whilst I, with Brown's Brigade (Second) and the artillery, moved toward the place by the Flat Gap road. . . . At 9:00 p. m. Brown's Brigade arrived at Patterson's factory, at the foot of the Blue Ridge, and found an ample supply of corn and bacon. I remained in rear to give my personal attention to the artillery, which did not arrive at the factory until 7:00 a. m. on the 29th. After feeding and resting, the march was resumed at 11:00 a. m., a guard having been left in charge of the forage and subsistence

---

[8] Only three men were killed, and five wounded.

until the arrival of Colonel Miller, who had orders, after supplying his command, to destroy the remainder and burn the factory. The order was executed . . ."* According to General Stoneman's report (p. 324), his command was detained on the Yadkin River three days by a freshet, but the tithing depots along the route traversed by their various parties furnished them with supplies in the greatest abundance. "The number of horses and mules captured and *taken* along the road, I have no means of estimating. I can say, however, that we are much better mounted than when we left Knoxville. Have a surplus of led animals and sufficient besides to haul off all of our captures, mount a portion of the prisoners and about a thousand contrabands [negroes], and this after crossing Stone Mountain once and the Blue Ridge three times and a march made by headquarters since the 20th of March of 500 miles and much more by portions of the command. The rapidity of our movements has in almost every instance caused our advanced guard to herald our approach and made the surprise complete."

A Real Home Guard.—The men who met in Boone on the day Stoneman arrived were Confederate soldiers at home because of wounds or illness or on parole. They had met to form a real home guard, not against the Federals, but against the robbers and marauders of both sides. Soon after the close of hostilities the Federal authorities at Salisbury authorized some of the Confederate soldiers who had been officers in the army to organize a home guard for Watauga County. Col. Joseph W. Todd, who then resided in this county, was made captain, and he soon restored order in and about Boone. He moved to Jefferson, where he became a practicing attorney. He was born September 3, 1834, at Jefferson, and died there January 28, 1909. He married Miss Sallie Waugh, of Shouns. For his ancestry, see sketch of Jos. W. Todd, his cousin.

Robbing Mrs. Jonathan Horton.—While Kirk's men were stationed in Boone, about the first part of April, 1865, John

---

* Clem Osborne, of North Fork, was at the factory for the purpose of buying thread. He was chased to the top of the factory, and when about to be killed, gave a Masonic sign, which saved his life. Some time afterwards when apparently "tipsy" he was urged to tell what sign he had given and what words he had used. He gave a sign, and mumbled certain words indistinctly, but which turned out to be "Calf rope." He wasn't nearly so drunk as he pretended to be.

Ford, William Thomas Benson and John Roland were said to have been concerned in the robbery of Mrs. Jonathan Horton, on Shearer's Hill, near Three Forks Church, and taking from her clothing a purse containing some jewelry. She was made to dismount and give up her horse, but as she got down she gave the horse a lick with her riding switch and he ran away home, thus escaping capture. Later on Ford and some of his companions stopped at the home of Ransom Hayes, at what is now known as the Green Brick House, and one of Hayes' daughters, now Mrs. W. L. Bryan, noticed that he was wearing on the lapel of his coat a gold brooch, containing a miniature of Mrs. Horton's husband, Col. Jonathan Horton. She asked him what he was doing with it, and he said he had no use for it, and gave it to her and requested that she return it to Mrs. Horton, which was done. In the "Worth Correspondence" (Vol. II, p. 267), Colonel Carr, of the commission to investigate oppressions of Union people, claims that Benson, who, with two others, was indicted for highway robbery from the person of Mrs. Horton, was of the Union army and had been ordered to impress horses, to which Solicitor Bynum replied that the evidence before him showed that if Benson "ever had belonged to the Union army he had deserted, and the robbery was under no authority, but for his own private gain and done under circumstances of wanton outrage and cruelty." It cannot be determined from the court records what the facts were as to the indictment, but several old men yet living were at the trial of John Ford at least, and remember that Judge Buxton, who presided, held that the evidence showed that the robbery had been committed before Lee's surrender and was not indictable under Andrew Johnson's proclamation of amnesty. It is not at all certain that John Roland was even charged with that offense, and it is well established now, from the general opinion of his neighbors near Cook's Gap, that Benson had nothing to do with the robbery, even if he was indicted for it. The facts about Benson are said to be about as follows: William Thomas Floyd Benson was a member of a regiment in the Confederate army and lived near Wilmington, N. C. He, with several others, deserted and got to Buck's Ridge, near where Jordan Hampton's residence now stands. Here they camped and rested a week, buying a heifer of William Cook and paying for other rations they consumed while there. They then went to Carter County, Tennessee, where Benson enlisted in Stoneman's command as William Thomas Floyd, enlisting at Jonesboro. He now draws a pension in that name. When some of his relatives some years ago came from Wilmington to Blowing Rock and enquired for Thomas Benson, they were directed to go to Cook's Gap, where they identified him as their kinsman. He is said also to have drawn his share of his father's estate some years ago. His character is good.

"Peace, Peace, When There Was No Peace."—The great Civil War was over at last, and the harassed and impoverished people of Watauga County hoped for a cessation of hostilities and the burial of all animosities, feuds and misunderstandings. Most men and women "took heart of hope" and began all over again. Ploughshare and reaping-hook took the place of sword and rifle. But others were completely discouraged and inclined to move away and seek homes elsewhere. Among these was Jordan Councill, the second, who had been the foremost and only merchant in this section from about 1820 till Boone was formed into the county seat. He decided to sell out before the United States government confiscated all he had. Squire Daniel B. Dougherty, however, took a more hopeful view of the future. Councill offered to sell out to Dougherty for half the value of his land, and Dougherty, who is said to have had little or no money, agreed to buy. Accordingly, on the first day of August, 1865, Jordan Councill gave D. B. Dougherty his bond for title to all his land and property in and around Boone when Dougherty should pay him $3,000.00 cash. (Deed Book M, p. 248.) Councill moved away, but returned and recovered all the property Dougherty had not sold, the proceeds of that which had been sold having been applied on the bond. But that had not been all. In the May and June following Appomattox, a sort of guerilla warfare had been going on "below the Ridge," and the returned Confederate soldiers at the request of the Federal authorities formed themselves into a Home Guard for the protection of such little personal property as had escaped the robbers during the war, for the country was for months infested with all sorts of roving characters, returning soldiers, adventurers and desperadoes of all kinds. Henry Henly, who lived just below Blowing Rock, was killed at the capture of Fort Hamby, and anarchy seemed to have "come down on us like night."

Fort Hamby.—Even after the surrender the trouble continued. "Several worthless characters deserted Stoneman's command along this march and formed with native bushwhackers bands under the leadership of two desperate men, Wade and Simmons. Wade's party located in a log house on a high hill half a mile north of Holman's Ford of the Yadkin River, in Wilkes County. Being heavily armed with army rifles and pistols, they made daily raids into the surrounding country, robbing, plundering and terrorizing the citizens, taking everything they could find to eat, as well as horses, etc. Their practice was to ride up to a house, dismount and enter, pointing loaded guns at any persons occupying the house, threatening to shoot if they opened their mouths, while others were searching closets, trunks, drawers, etc., taking what suited them. The people for miles and miles in the country surrounding lived in constant dread of them, as they seemed filled with a spirit of hatred and revenge, treating all persons not in sympathy with them with the greatest cruelty. The house they used was finely located for offensive as well as defensive operations. On a high hill, facing the Yadkin River on the south and front, and Lewis' Fork on the west, their guns could sweep the country for a half a mile each way up and down the river. The house was two stories, with portholes cut in the upper story. It was formerly occupied by a family named Hamby, and after being fortified was known as Fort Hamby. The robbers, numbering probably twenty-five or thirty, made several raids into Caldwell and Alexander Counties . . . insulting in the grossest manner the women and children . . . Major Harvey Bingham, with a small home guard, followed the raiders out of Caldwell County on May 6th (1865) . . . surprising the defenders in the fort at night. . . . The men begged for their lives, and no arms being in sight, Major Bingham gave them time to dress. The prisoners . . . rushed for their guns and fired on the attacking party, killing two, Robert Clark, son of General Clark, and Henry Henly . . . the others . . . made their escape, leaving the dead bodies on the ground. The next week they raided the home of Rev. J. R. Green in Alexander County. But his son was home from the army and fired on the robbers, driving them off. Col. Washington Sharp, of Iredell County, gathered about twenty men, pursued . . . and rushed up to within a few yards of the fort, when Wade's men opened fire and killed two, Mr. James Linney, brother of Hon. R. Z. Linney, and Mr. Jones Brown . . . the others made a hasty retreat, leaving the two dead bodies. Colonel Sharp then collected a squad of about twenty returned soldiers, and sent a message to Caldwell County for help . . . Among those who went were A. S. Kent, T. L. Norwood, Jas. W. Norwood, George H. Dula, Robert B. Dula, and S. F. Harper. They collected others along the way . . . and waited at Holman's Ford for the Alexander company about May 18th. The robbers had killed a woman at the ford the day before. The fort was surrounded, and at nightfall a kitchen near the fort was set on fire and from it the fort itself caught. Sharp was in command. The besieged asked what would be done with them if they surrendered, and were told that they would be killed. They came out, with Wade in front holding up his hands as though he intended to surrender, but kept running and escaped. His comrades, four men, then surrendered and were tied to stakes and shot, after the Rev. W. R. Gwaltney had prayed for them. This ended the marauding and robbing in that section. Henry Hamby was from Watauga County. The above was condensed from "The Capture of Fort Hamby," by S. Finley Harper (p. 45); "Reminiscenses of Caldwell County, North Carolina, in the Great War of 1861-65," by G. W. F. Harper.

Blalock's Threat.—When Keith Blalock was told that John B. Boyd had arrested Austin Coffey and that Coffey was dead, he swore he would kill Boyd if it took forty years after the war to do so. It did not take nearly so long, for on the evening of February 8, 1866, when Boyd and William T. Blair were going

A History of Watauga County 185

from a house on which they had been at work they met Blalock and Thomas Wright in a narrow path at the head of the Globe. Blalock asked, "Is that you, Boyd?" and Boyd answered, "Yes," at the same time striking Blalock with a cane, the blow being aimed at his head. Blalock caught the blow on his left wrist, ran backwards a few steps and shot Boyd dead with a seven-shooting Sharp's rifle. Keith made Blair turn Boyd's body over, and finding that all life was extinct, turned and left the scene, stopping at Noah White's house to tell him what had been done. Blalock was examined before the Provost Marshal at Morganton, and he sent the case to Judge Mitchell at Statesville, but Governor Holden pardoned him before trial.[10]

Post Bellum Echoes.—From "Correspondence of Jonathan Worth," published by Edwards & Broughton Printing Co., Raleigh, 1909 (Vol. II, p. 725, etc.), we learn that Major Frank Walcott, one of the military commissioners sent to investigate alleged persecutions of Union men in Watauga County, wrote that "Union men were pursued with malicious persecutions;" that Austin Coffey was murdered by the Home Guard and that no steps were taken to prosecute his slayers, and that "a clearer case of self defense than Blalock's killing of John Boyd could not be made out." To these charges W. P. Bynum answered that Blalock had killed Boyd since the war, but not in the discharge of any military duty or order, and that the grand jury found true bills against all implicated in the killing of Austin Coffey, and that the case would be tried at the fall term of the Superior Court of Watauga County. The destruction of the records by fire in March, 1873, precludes any record evidence from that source, but tradition says that the solicitor failed to make out a case and the men were acquitted.

---

[10] John Boyd was born in Caldwell County. Blalock was born June 21, 1836, and died near Montezuma, N. C., August 11, 1913, the result of an accident on a hand-car.

CHAPTER XIII.
Some Thrice-Told Tales.

The Calloway Sisters.—Benjamin Calloway was one of the pioneers of this section, having his home on the upper Watauga. Two of his daughters, Fanny and Betsy,[1] must have been women of unusual physical charm. That each was possessed of a character of motherly devotion which halted at no sacrifice can never be doubted by anyone who knows their true story. It was the fate of one of these women unconsciously to supplant another woman in the affections of her husband, and of the other to be supplanted by a "mere strip of a girl." But the time came when each was widowed while yet the father of her children lived. Still, notwithstanding the ruin of their affections, each "found a way out of the wreck to rise in, a sure and safe one," through her children, each emerging from the fiery furnace of affliction without the smell of fire upon her garments, nay, glorified and almost apotheosized beneath her crown of martyrdom.

Pioneer Hunters.—There was much in the wild, free life, no less than in the picturesque costume of the backwoods hunter of this period, garbed in hunting shirt, fringed leggins, moccasins, powder horn and bullet pouch, to attract the fancy of young girls in this mountain wilderness. Light-hearted, care-free, debonair, they sang and danced and frolicked when they came in from their traps and camps in the peaks and crags of the wilder mountains. For they had regular huts or homes at different places on their "ranges," where they lived in solitude, often, for months at a time. One of them is thus described in the "Life of W. W. Skiles" (p. 53, etc.).

"They pushed bravely on, however, and at nightfall came to a small clearing in which stood the solitary cabin of a hunter. It

---

[1] Ben Calloway was closely related to Col. Richard Calloway, of the Kentucky pioneers, and named his daughters for the two daughters of Richard Calloway, Fanny and Betsy, who, on the 17th of July, 1776, were captured by Indians with Jemima, second daughter of Daniel Boone, while boat-riding on the Kentucky river, one of whom, Betsy, married Samuel, a brother of Richard Henderson.

was built of unhewn logs; the chimney consisted of sticks, crossing one another, well daubed inside and out with clay. The roof was shingled with oak boards three or four feet long, kept in place by logs laid lengthwise, well pinned down, with here and there a heavy stone to give additional strength against winds. The floor was of hewn lumber, three or four inches thick. There was but one room in the cabin, with a rude bed or two in one corner, three or four rough chairs of home make, a bench or two, a table to match in the center, and a huge fireplace where logs of six or seven feet could be piled together. Over the door, on wooden pegs, lay the rifle, always within reach and always loaded. Against the outer wall of the cabin were hung antlers of deer, while skins of wolf, bear and panther were hung up there to dry. Here, in the heart of the forest, lived Larchin Calloway, a famous hunter, and here the party from Valle Crucis was made heartily welcome. They were hungry and dripping wet from head to foot, but the latch-string of a mountain cabin door always hangs outside in token of welcome."

James Aldridge.—This hunter and pioneer has been, of late years, somewhat overshadowed by the fame of his son, Harrison, probably as great a marksman, trapper and backwoodsman as his father. As well as can be now ascertained, James Aldridge came to what is now called Shull's Mills about the year 1819 or 1820, his first son by Betsy Calloway having been born December 15, 1821. James claimed to be a single man, and soon persuaded Betsy Calloway to marry him. He must then have been at least thirty-five years old, for he had left a wife and five children in Virginia on the Big Sandy River,[2] his first wife having been born a Munsey, according to James A. Calloway, one of James' grandsons. It is claimed that he married Betsy, but as such a marriage would under the circumstances have been a nullity, it is immaterial whether he did or not. Certain it is that she always went by the name of Betsy Calloway and that she bore him seven children: Harrison, who married Jensey Clark; Tempe, who married Benton Johnson; Jane, who married Ensley

---

[2] The Big Sandy separates Kentucky from old Virginia, now West Virginia, and rises about 100 miles north of Abingdon. It was visited by Boone in the autumn of 1767, accompanied only by a man named Hill, according to Bruce (p. 48), who says he then visited the West Fork of that stream. Aldridge may have lived on the Virginia or the Kentucky side of the Big Sandy, but his descendants in Watauga always speak of his home as having been in Virginia.

Issacs, Perrin Winters, Henry Shull, of Virginia, and John Calhoun; Ellen, who married Frank Fox; Benjamin, who married Millie Burleson and yet lives, Crossnore being his post office; Waightstill, who married Polly Johnson and lives near Benjamin, and Emeline, who married Abram Johnson. Harrison, in memory of a faithful dog which saved his life from wild hogs, had that dear friend buried on a ridge above the home of his son, James A. Aldridge, and requested that he be buried there also. His tombstone, surrounded by a substantial stone wall, records the fact that he joined the Baptist Church October 22, 1870, and died January 11, 1905.

James Aldridge was seen and remembered by very few men or women who are living today. Those who saw him say he was slightly above the average in stature, with dark hair and blue eyes. He was a great fiddler and hunter and of a happy disposition. He first lived near where G. W. Robbins' hotel now stands, but after the birth of Harrison moved to the Hanging Rock Ridge, near Nettle Knob, a mile from James A. Aldridge's present house, for it seems that he had been "squatting" where he first settled, but entered and obtained grants to land in 1828. There he built two substantial cabins, with large fireplaces, so deep, in fact, that the dogs frequently went behind the fire and between it and the back of the chimney, where they sat and blinked at the people in front of the hearth. There is a cleared place in the "swag" of the ridge above Robbins' hotel which is still pointed out as the place where James Aldridge burnt willow logs and limbs to make charcoal for powder, which he manufactured for his own use.

The Real Wife Appears.—The exact date of the coming of the real wife into the life of Betsy Calloway is not certain, but shortly after the birth of Waightstill, her last child, which must have been about two years after the birth of Benjamin, he having been born about 1834, say, 1836, a fur peddler of the name of Price, as Levi Coffey remembers it, came to the home of Edward Moody above what is now Foscoe.* Here he met

---

* In his geological tour through Ashe in 1828, Dr. Elisha Mitchell speaks of a hunter as living on the head of the Watauga River with the children of his real wife, who was then residing on the Big Sandy, in Kentucky, and his own children by another woman with whom he was then living as his wife. If this refers to James Aldrich, then Betsy Calloway had two children by him after his first wife appeared in the scene, for both Ben and Waightstill were born after 1828.

James Aldridge, and, knowing something of his past, returned to the Big Sandy and told Aldridge's wife what he had discovered. Soon afterwards a woman riding a fine horse stopped at Edward Moody's, asked the way to James Aldridge's house, and was directed there. The next morning, before day, Aldridge came to Moody's and bought a bushel of wheat, which he had ground on Moody's little tub-mill at the mouth of what is still called Moody's Mill Creek, near Foscoe. After it had been ground it was "hand-bolted," that is, sifted through cloth by hand. James explained that "the cat was out of the bag at last," meaning that his wife had appeared on the scene. When asked how Betsy "took it," he answered that she was sulky, but that he himself was treating both women exactly alike, and had no doubt but that Betsy would soon get over it. But she never did. She told Aldridge plainly that he had deceived and outraged her and her children, and that while she had no other home than his, and must perforce remain there in order to rear her children, their relations had ceased. Finding that Betsy was not disposed to contest her rights, Mrs. James Aldridge lost interest in James and returned to her former home on Sandy. Soon afterwards several of her children appeared on the scene, the boys being Sam, Frank and James, while a girl, Rachel, married William Calloway, and remained permanently, the boys returning to Big Sandy. James followed his wife back to Big Sandy, where he remained awhile, but soon came back to Watauga, but finding no welcome from Betsy, he again returned to Big Sandy. It is likely that his real wife would have no more of him either, for Betsy and her oldest son, Harrison, visited his hut there and found him living with a young girl. He threw some bear skins on the floor, where she and her son passed the night, leaving at dawn the next day. James came again to Watauga, when Ben was four years old, gave him a dime and patted him on the head. But he brought two large brindle bear dogs with him, and his little son was afraid to put foot out of doors while they remained. This must have been about 1838, since which time no one has seen James Aldridge in Watauga County. His grandson, James A. Aldridge, says he heard that his grandfather died on Big Sandy during the Civil War, aged 110 years.

Betsy Calloway.—Ben Calloway says that his mother told him that she had dug many a pound of sang with a child strapped to her back. That is, she had had to go into the mountains to dig sang when her youngest children were too small to be left at home, and carried them with her from the necessity of the case. "She was the master sanger you ever seed" is the way one old man expressed her industry and devotion to her children. For sang was the only cash article in those days, and it brought only about ten cents a pound. But Betsy could make a living in no other way, except when, occasionally, she could get a job of scouring or washing to do for some friendly woman for her meals and meals for her children. She was also a master sugar maker, if accounts may be trusted, and worked several "sugar orchards" through the mountains. Her old kettle, in which the sap was boiled, is still to be seen at Foscoe in the yard of the home of former Sheriff W. H. Calloway. The first shoes Ben Aldridge ever had were bought by Betsy with the proceeds of the sale of sang dug by him. She had to take the sang sometimes as far as Abingdon, and this particular sang which Ben had dug was sold by her at Blountville, Tenn. As the sang was gradually becoming scarce, she went to Big Sandy to sang, taking Harrison with her. It was while on this trip that she spent a night at James Aldridge's cabin. She had no feeling against James Aldridge's first wife, but told him, though he had lied to her, to bring his children and she would do the best she could by them. Once when in a sugar camp on Watauga she saw tracks of a bear in the snow and knew that they were those of a she-bear with cubs, as bears do not come out of winter quarters when snow is on the ground except to get sustenance upon which their cubs could draw. Harrison, her eldest son, killed the mother bear and caught the cubs. Betsy sold the maple sugar for ten cents a pound and the syrup for ten cents a gallon. When Harrison was seven years old his mother was baptized in Linville River, near Fred Ledford's, by Rev. Robert Patterson, at the Elkhorn Meeting House. She took care of all preachers who came to her home, and Ben was always glad to see them come, as then he "got something good to eat." He used to put corn into dried bladders and tie the bladders to chickens, which, when they heard the rattle, became frightened and flew across the table at which the preachers were eating. Once he tied such a contrivance to the horns of a "billy-buck," as he terms a goat, and he nearly ran himself to death. Betsy Calloway died about 1900 and is buried in the Moody graveyard above Foscoe.

Delilah Baird.—She was born about 1807, and when eighteen years of age left her home with John Holtsclaw, who had been a member of Three Forks Church and a moderator of that congregation at its meeting in October, 1821. There is evidence also that he was a preacher. He had a wife and seven children living at the time Delilah eloped with him, about the year 1825, for their first child, Alfred B. Baird, was born March 7, 1826.[4] Delilah knew of his marriage, but she went with him, claiming that she believed that he was going to take her to Kentucky. Instead, he took her to the Big Bottoms of Elk, one mile from what is now Banner Elk, where he kept her in a camp at the mouth of a branch which empties into Elk almost directly in front of and about three hundred yards distant from the residence of James W. Whitehead. This was a bark camp, built against the trunk of a large fallen tree. It was here that her first child was born. Later on they moved into a rude cabin lower down the creek and near an apple tree which still stands in Mr. Whitehead's meadow. It was there that she fought wolves with firebrands when they came too near the house, seeking to devour a young calf which she kept in a pen near her chimney. She also "sanged" on the Beech Mountain, and finally recognized one of her father's steers, with a large bell fastened to its neck, and knew that she was not in Kentucky. She soon established communications with her home connections, and would ride up a ridge and across Beech Mountain to get such supplies as she required and sell her sang and maple sugar. She knitted socks and stockings while riding on the road to and from her old home. She brought dried grass in a sheet in order to get seed for the meadow around her new home.

---

[4] According to Mrs. Sallie Hackney, of Neva, Tenn., Delilah Baird was three years younger than her first cousin, Alexander Baird, who was born April 5, 1804.

After awhile poor Fanny Calloway, whose place in her husband's heart and home Delilah had usurped, came, an humble suppliant, to her door, asking to be allowed to spin, weave, wash, hoe or do anything that would provide John Holtsclaw's children with bread. John Holtsclaw was getting old and it behooved him to provide for his real wife before he should go to his long account. Instead, he made a deed to Delilah Baird for 480 acres of land in the Big Bottoms of Elk, which had been granted in 1788 when that part of the State was in Wilkes County. But he made her pay him $250.00 for it.[5] His wife, Fanny, was thus left to the cold charity of the cold world, and his and her children had to make their own way as best they could. That way, we may be sure, was not an easy one, especially for poor Fanny. But nothing is surer in this world than the solemn asseveration of the Bible: "Vengeance is mine, saith the Lord; I will repay." He kept that promise. He always keeps that promise. Among Fanny's children was a girl named Raney. Raney had a hard time at first, but she finally married Abraham Dugger, for years the chief owner and manager of the Cranberry mine. After his death she married Daniel Whitehead, and their son, James W. Whitehead, now owns all the broad acres which John Holtsclaw had deeded to Delilah Baird and away from his own legitimate children, and not one foot of that land or of any of the land nearby which Delilah got from the State belongs to her descendants.[6]

A Sordid, If Belated, Romance.—Sometime in the summer of 1881, when Delilah Baird was seventy-four years old, she spent the night with Ben Dyer's mother on Cove Creek. It was there that she determined to write to Ben, offering him a home and support for his life, and adding, "my folks are lawing me to death," and asking him to come and help her defend her rights. At this time she dressed gaily and was supposed to be demented, but a commission *de lunatico inquirendo*, consisting of Smith Coffey and two others, found that she still had mind enough to manage her own affairs. After the usual manœuvres of courting

---
[5] The deed is dated May 2, 1838, Book N, p. 515, Ashe County.
[6] Deed Books R., p. 274, A., p. 498, and U., p. 98. She had a daughter, named Aurilda, who married Levi Moody.

Photo. by Harris.

AUNT DELILAH'S LAST CABIN HOME.

Showing two bear traps which were made by Abe and George Dugger.

couples, Dyer agreed to come upon the terms stated, and Miss Delilah wrote in September following that she was delighted that he was to come, assuring him again that she had plenty "and all we will have to do is to sit back and enjoy ourselves." But Miss Delilah was too non-committal for Dyer, and he did not come, neither did he write again till November 14th, when he wrote acknowledging her "second letter," indicating that she had written "twice to his once," a thing no coy maiden ever should do. Just what that last missive really contained is not known, for the judgment roll in which this romance is preserved (Judgment Docket A, p. 172, Clerk's Office, Watauga County) does not contain it. But in Dyer's answer he states, "You make me a new proposal in your last letter, which is more than I could expect you to do," adding that he could never repay her except "with my love and kindness towards you." As he himself stated, in 1883, that he was then seventy-two years old, three years Miss Delilah's senior, these old people may be said to have been progressing rapidly and smoothly along the primrose path of love and should, therefore, have known that they were rapidly nearing a precipice.

So, to make a long story short, he came, saw and was not conquered. Neither was she. For she paid him nothing, gave him no home, and allowed him to return to Texas "loveless and forlorn." Then, in May, 1882, in an action before D. B. Dougherty and J. W. Holtsclaw, justices of the peace, he sued Miss Delilah for his expenses going and coming and while here. They gave him exactly $47.50, railroad fare to and from Texas. He appealed, and a jury of "good men and true" gave him exactly the same amount and not one cent more. Moral: Better let the women have their own way. Miss Delilah died about 1890 and is buried in the Baird graveyard at Valle Crucis. Sometime prior to her death, October 20, 1880, she lived with her son, Alfred Burton Baird, in a small log cabin, which still stands directly in front of James W. Whitehead's home. This cabin was shingled with yellow pine shingles when it was built in 1859, and, although it has never been repaired, the roof does not leak to this day.

"Cobb" McCanless.—David Colvert McCanless was a son of James McCanless, whose wife was a Miss Alexander, said to have been nearly related to Hon. Mack Robbins, former congressman from Statesville. James McCanless came from Iredell County to Shull's Mills and resided near the present Robbins hotel at that place. James was a man of education and taught school where Mrs. Martha Phipps now lives. He was also a cabinet-maker, some of his work being still preserved. James and his brother, David, of Burnsville, were both "fine fiddlers." For some reason, now unknown, Phillip Shull refused to grind James' corn for him on his mill. This mill, built about 1835, was washed away about 1861 and never replaced, though the neighborhood still retains its name. McCanless went before a magistrate and got the usual penalty for such refusal to grind corn without good excuse. Shull still refused and McCanless still collected the penalty till at last Shull gave in. Colvert was always called "Colb" or "Cobb," and he was Jack Horton's deputy when the former was sheriff from 1852 to 1856. It was then that "Colb" announced himself as a candidate against Horton. It is said that the oral duel that then ensued, on Meat Camp, was fierce. "Colb" ran and won. He and Horton had frequent fist fights, both being powerful men physically—Horton, of medium height, but thick set, and McCanless tall and well proportioned. McCanless was a strikingly handsome man and a well-behaved, useful citizen till he became involved with a woman not his wife, after which he fell into evil courses. As sheriff he was tax collector and also had in his hands claims in favor of J. M. Weath, a Frenchman, who sold goods throughout this section in job lots. As there was no homestead then, whatever an officer could find in a defendant's possession was subject to levy and sale. January 1, 1859, came and soon afterwards came also a representative from Weath for a settlement with McCanless.

On the morning of January 6th "Colb" set out for Boone, accompanied by Levi L. Coffey, a near neighbor, then about twenty-seven years of age. "Colb" told Weath's man that he had made many collections for Weath, but had offsets against some of them and could settle the balance due only by an interview with Weath himself. Therefore, he would join Weath's man at Blowing Rock the following morning and go with him to Statesville. He and Jack Horton, who was on McCanless' official bond, then took a ride together, after which Horton sold his horse to one of the Hardins and McCanless immediately bought the same horse for the exact price Hardin had paid for it. During the same day McCanless conveyed certain real estate to his brother, J. Leroy McCanless. Subsequently, on the first day of March, 1859, J. L. McCanless conveyed the same land to Jack or John Horton, and on that day Jack Horton conveyed it to Smith Coffey. In a suit between Calvin J. Cowles against Coffey it was alleged and so found by the jury that these conveyances from D. C. to J. L. McCanless and from him to Jack Horton had been given to defraud the creditors of D. C. McCanless (88 N. C. Rep. p. 341). Horton is said also to have secured McCanless' saddle pockets with many claims in them against various people in Watauga County, these pockets having been left by McCanless in a certain store in Boone for that very purpose, thus securing Horton as far as possible from loss by reason of his liability on McCanless' official bond. McCanless also had the proceeds of a claim which as sheriff he held against Wilson Burleson, who then lived near Bull Scrape, now Montezuma, Avery County. This money was due to J. M. Weath also, and which, for safe-keeping, had been placed by McCanless with Jacob Rintels in Boone, in whose store Col. W. L. Bryan was then clerking, then known as the Jack Horton Old Store. Late that sixth of January McCanless called on Rintels for the money, with the request that as much as possible be paid in gold and silver. This was done. McCanless then started on the road to Wilkes County, where he claimed he was to pay the money over to Robert Hayes on an execution, having told Levi Coffey not to wait for him, as he was not going to return home that night. But instead of continuing on to Wilkes, McCanless went only as far as Three Forks Church, where he doubled back and went up the Jack Hodges Creek and through the Hodges Gap to Shull's Mills, where he was joined by a woman. They went together to Johnson City, where their horses and saddles and bridles were sold to Joel Dyer. There they took the train for the West. After D. C. McCanless had been away several months, J. L. McCanless, his brother, followed him, but soon returned and took west with him D. C. McCanless' wife, who was born Mary, daughter of Joseph Greene, her children, her father and mother and his own sisters, who had married Amos Greene and Isaac Greene, sons of Joseph Greene.

"Wild Bill" Kills McCanless.—News came to Watauga during the Civil War that "Colb" McCanless had been killed in Kansas, but it was not till 1883 that the details became known. But in that year D. M. Kelsey published "Our Pioneer Heroes and Their Daring Deeds" (pp. 481, et seq.), Scannel, publishers, from which the following facts were gleaned: that what was known as the McCanless Gang were impressing horses in Kansas, as they claimed, for the Confederate government, but in reality for themselves. James Butler Hicok, otherwise known as "Wild Bill," was connected with a stage line at Rock Creek, fifty miles west of Topeka, Kansas. There he occupied a "dug-out," the back and two sides of which were formed of earth of the hillside, into which a thatched cabin had been built. There, also, on the 16th day of December, 1861, in a fight with ten of McCanless' gang, all but two of the latter were killed by "Wild Bill" and his friends. Among those killed are mentioned Jim and Jack McCanless. It is supposed that one of these was David Colvert McCanless. J. LeRoy McCanless is now living at Florence, Colorado, as a good citizen and highly respected man. Rev. W. C. Franklin, their nephew, resides at Altamont.

Bedent E. Baird.—There is probably no more picturesque character among the pioneers of this section than that of Bedent E. Baird. He was a man of fine education and possessed the best library west of the Blue Ridge. He was what would be called in these days an agnostic, and was independent in thought and deed. He was one of the first to represent Ashe County in the legislature and was for many years a magistrate. He named one of his sons for Euclid, the geometrician. It is said that his testimony was once challenged on the score of his unorthodox belief, and that when he answered that he had taken the oath as a magistrate, the presiding judge at the trial refused to allow the challenger to go behind that statement.

No Water-Power by a Dam-Site.—It is also related of him that he told Bishop Ives, who was looking for a good site for a water power, that he could show him the finest *site* for such a power in the world. The Bishop, keen to develop the country, then followed Squire Baird to the top of the Beech Mountain over the cart-road which Baird had had constructed nearly to the highest point, after which they followed a trail to the north prospect or pinnacle of the Beech. This is a sheer precipice, or rather overhanging shelf of rock, overlooking the head of Beech Creek. "This," remarked Baird to the Bishop, "is the finest *site* for a water power in the mountains." "But where is the water?" asked his Reverence. "That is your part of the business," returned Baird, chuckling; "I have provided the site—all I agreed to do."

Who Were These Old Bairds?—That many of the first settlers of this county came from New Jersey seems to be confirmed by the fact that Dr. Gilbert Tennent, of Asheville, has a book which is called the "History of the Old Tennent Church," compiled by Rev. Frank Symes, its pastor, and printed by George W. Burroughs, at Cranberry, N. J. In it is published a diagram of the pews of the church, one of which in 1750 was held by Zebulon and the other by David Baird. The church was then called the Freehold Church, but is now known as the Tennent Church. It still stands in Monmouth County, New Jersey. Just what relationship these Bairds hold to the Bedent Baird of Watauga and the Bedent and Zebulon Baird of Buncombe in 1790 seems to be a riddle beyond solution at the present day. But that Zeb Vance's mother, who was a Baird, was related to the Bairds of Watauga is about as certain as any unprovable fact can well be, for family names, family traits and physical family resemblances are so marked as to be unmistakable.

A Mysterious Enquiry.—Early in January, 1858, Bedent Baird received a newspaper, on the margin of which was written a few lines, in which the claim was made that Bedent E. Baird was akin to the writer, who, however, failed to sign his name.[1] But he had given his post office, that of Lapland, in Buncombe County, but now called Marshall, the county seat of Madison. Bedent E. Baird, then, in 1858, in his eighty-eighth year, answered this unknown writer, sending his letter to Lapland, but he received no answer. From this letter we learn that John Baird and a brother came from Scotland in the Caledonia and settled in the Jerseys, meaning in New Jersey. This John Baird had married a woman named Mary Bedent, and they named their first child Bedent Baird—the very first of the name "that was ever on the face of the earth." Their seventh son was named Ezekiel and he married Susanna Blodgett, whose father was killed in the ambuscade near Fort Duquesne at the time Braddock also met his death. Ezekiel Baird moved to North Carolina, where Bedent E. Baird was born about 1770. Ezekiel Baird's brother, Bedent, was married three times "and reared three numerous families at or near the German Flats, Canada." Ezekiel Baird's other five brothers also married and reared families "who helped to break the forests and settle five or six of the southwestern States."

Peggy Clawson.—One of the strongest characters of the past was that of Peggy Clawson, who resided in the neighborhood of Elk Cross Roads. She was the wife of William Clawson, though for some time it was doubtful whether this was to be the case, as her evident inclination was to have him simply the *husband* of Peggy Clawson. For, tradition says, in a most friendly spirit, that they occasionally "fell out and kissed again with tears." On one of these occasions, as the story goes, for it is also told of Ezra Stonecypher, she had driven him to take refuge under the bed. Thinking she had him conquered at last, she told him that if he ever said another "crooked word to her, she would kill him." "Ram's Horn, Peggy, if I die for it!" came the prompt and defiant answer to her challenge. She was a member of the Three Forks Church in July, 1832, for at that time she was excommunicated from that church for "beating her son." However, in due time, namely, in the following October,

---

[1] Adolphus E. Baird, an uncle of Governor Z. B. Vance, is now known to have been the one who wrote the unsigned words on the newspaper referred to.

she "made open acknowledgment for her transgression and was restored to full membership." One morning she was near the cliff or bluff between John L. Tatum's present home and Todd, covered with laurel, pines and ivy bushes, making maple sugar. A dog chased a bear into the river, and she got into the canoe tied near by, poled out to the bear swimming in a deep hole at the base of the cliff, and drowned it by holding its head under the water with the canoe pole. After this exploit, it being Saturday, she walked down to the Old Fields Baptist Church in time for morning service.

Some Other Old Stories.—Welborn Waters was employed after the Civil War to exterminate all the wolves from the Virginia line to the Bald Mountain in Yancey. He undertook the task and succeeded, howling in imitation of wolves when on the mountains, and they, unsuspectingly, coming to him, he killed them. It is related, however, of the old Lewises, as the first wolf hunters in these mountains were called, that wishing to get the bounty offered for wolf scalps, they would not kill the grown wolves, especially the females, as they wished them to bear as many litters as possible, the scalp of a young wolf being paid for as well as that of an old one. It is related till this day that the Wolf's Den on Riddle's Knob took its name from the fact that the Lewises went in there in search of wolves and usually found and killed a litter every spring.

Joseph T. Wilson, commonly called "Lucky Joe," was in jail in Boone at the November term of the Superior Court during a very cold spell, and, pretending to have frozen in his cell, was removed in an apparently unconscious state to the Brick Row joining the Critcher hotel, then the old Coffey hotel. Here he was resuscitated by the late Dr. W. B. Councill, but instead of taking him back to jail to freeze all over again, they left him in the Brick Row with a guard. He persuaded that guard to go out and get some more fuel, and while he was gone the frozen man escaped from the room and the State. He was recaptured in Ohio by Alexander Perry, of Burke, however, brought to Elk Park and thence taken by the then sheriff, David F. Baird, to Morganton to jail, where he remained till the next term of Ashe court, to which his lawyers had had his case moved on account of alleged prejudice in Watauga County. He was convicted in Ashe and served ten years in the penitentiary for stealing horses from Alloway and Henry Maines, of North Fork. While in the penitentiary he became superintendent of the prison Sunday School, and by apparent good conduct had earned a reduction from the full term of his sentence. When, however, his belongings were examined it was found that he had pilfered many small articles from the penitentiary itself, and consequently lost what he had earned by good behavior in all other respects. When he got back home he studied law and led an exemplary life till about 1904, when he again came before the court, was convicted and sent to the Iredell County roads for five years' sentence. There he died, aged nearly sixty years.

Elijah Dotson and Alfred Hilliard quarreled once, standing at a safe distance apart, a mile or more, one being in his own field and the other in his own field also. This occurred on Beaver Dams before the Civil War and no telephone wires connected them. This difficulty arose from a cordial and sincere invitation extended by Dotson to Hilliard to visit certain grid-irons "where the worm dieth not and the fire is not 'squinched.'" It is also said that Hilliard and his wife late in life joined the church, and being dissatisfied with their marriage, which contract had been solemnized by an unsaintly justice of the peace, had the knot retied by a minister of the gospel regularly ordained.

An African Romance.—On the 16th day of October, 1849, Mr. and Mrs. William Mast, then living where the Shipleys now live, near Valle Crucis, were poisoned by drinking wild parsnips in their coffee. It was said by some that a slave woman named Mill or Milley had been whipped for having stolen twenty dollars from Andrew Mast, and poisoned William Mast out of revenge. Others say the crime was committed by Mill and her slave lover, Silas Baker, in the hope that if Mill's master and mistress were dead, she would have to be sold, and that Jacob Mast, who was about to marry Miss Elizabeth Baker and move to Texas, would buy her and thus prevent these dusky lovers from future separation. Although there was no direct evidence against either, Mill was sold to John Whittington and taken to Tennessee, while Silas was taken to Texas with his mistress and her husband, Jacob Mast.

James Speer lived on Beaver Dams and had no more brains than were absolutely necessary. He and two others agreed that all three should go to South Carolina, where Jim was to color his face with lampblack and suffer himself to be sold as and for a slave of African parentage, and that after the money had been paid over, he was to remove the lampblack and escape back to Beaver Dams, where the proceeds of the little game were to be *divided* into three equal parts. This may have been done, but as Jim did not get his third, he and one of his partners were heard to quarrel about the division at one of the Big Musters near Boone. It was not a lawyer who insisted that the letter of the bargain had been fully carried out when the proceeds of the sale had been simply *divided* into three equal parts, but one of Jim's own partners, who had never studied law an hour in all his life. Nor was it in accordance with any sentence of any court of record or otherwise that Jim disappeared from the face of the earth and has remained "gone" ever since. A skeleton was found about 1893 in some cliffs, usually called "rock cliffs," in rear of J. K. Perry's residence on Beaver Dams, and some have supposed that these bones used to belong to Jim Speer.

Joshua Pennell manumitted his slaves by his will, and his nephew, Joshua Winkler, as executor, took them to Kansas and set them free. Many still remember their passage through Boone just prior to the Civil War. Joshua Winkler and Joshua Pennell had lived in Wilkes County, but Winkler soon after his return from Kansas bought land in Watauga and removed to this county, where he died. Among other valuable properties acquired by him was the old Noah Mast farm near St. Jude post office, afterwards conveying one-half thereof to his son, William F. Winkler.

Jesse Mullins' "Niggers."—Jesse Mullins and his wife were getting old just prior to the commencement of the Civil War. They owned two negroes in addition to the farm which still goes by the name of the Mullins farm, on the South Fork of

New River, about four miles from Boone. There is also a small hill or mountain which is still known as the Mullins Mountain. There were two "interests" who had their eyes on those slaves, and one night the slaves disappeared. The next heard of them was the arrest of two young men in a Southern city for trying to sell slaves without themselves being able to show how they got them. It is supposed that the "interest" which had been out-generaled by the one abducting the slaves had caused the arrest of these young men. They were released and the slaves returned to their true owners. It is said that the most famous Grecian Sphinx, that of Thebes in Bœotia, once proposed a riddle to the Thebans, and killed all those who tried but failed to give the correct answer. Œdipus solved the riddle, whereupon the Sphinx slew herself. There is many an Œdipus yet living in Watauga County who might solve the riddle of the taking and carrying away of these darkies and of the arrest and imprisonment of their captors. So, too, they might tell who was one of Jim Speer's partners, and whose grave is said still to smoke in a certain church yard in this county of Watauga.

Cross-Cut Saw and Cross-Cut Suit.—Just before the Civil War, how long no one now knows, Noah Mast, claiming that he had loaned Hiram Hix a cross-cut saw, sued him for its recovery. Hix had some affliction of the eye-lids, rendering it necessary that he should prop them open with his fingers in order to see. He and his wife lived under a big cliff near the mouth of Cove Creek, called the Harmon Rock-House.[8] This cliff projected out a considerable distance and the open space was enclosed with boards and other timbers, thus affording some degree of comfort even in winter, the smoke-going out of a flue built against the side of the cliff. Here Hix kept a boat and charged a nickel to put passengers across the river. He also built a sort of cantilever bridge, the first in the world, most probably, using two firm rocks which extended into the stream, thus forming a narrow channel at that point. Based upon these immovable rocks were two long logs, hewn flat on the upper surface, one projecting from each bank toward the other, but not

---

[8] The first white child born in Watauga County is said to have been born in this rock cliff; but its name is not known.

meeting above mid-stream by several feet—too wide a gap to be jumped by ordinary folk. The shore ends of these logs were weighted to the ground by huge stones piled on them. Hix kept a thick and broad plank which was just long enough to bridge this gap between the projecting ends of the two logs. Upon the payment of five cents Hix would place this board in position and the foot-passenger could then pass over dry-shod. This was a "cantilever" because he claimed he couldn't leave her in position. Whether the revenue from his boat and board was sufficient to pay his lawyers in the suit Mast had brought against him for that cross-cut saw or not, Hix managed to keep it in court till he won it, thus throwing Mast in the costs, which is a very undesirable place to be thrown. This was one of the first suits to be tried in the new town of Boone, and a boy who heard one of the lawyers ask a witness what there was that was "peculiar" about that saw, was so struck by the word "peculiar" that he remembers it to this day, when he is an old man.

Absentee Landlords.—Just as the Scotch used to steal cattle and the Irish of the present day complain of the exactions of landlords who do not live in Ireland, so, too, did our Scotch and Irish fellow citizens make trouble for those living east of the Blue Ridge who drove their cattle to the Watauga mountains in the spring and took them back home in the fall. Colonel Edmund Jones used to pasture cattle on the Rich Mountain, General Patterson on Long Hope and the Finley family on the Bald. All these lived east of the Blue Ridge. It is only about one mile from the Wolf's Den on Riddle's Knob to the Long Hope Mountain, in which rises Long Hope Creek. The Bald, or the Big Bald, as it is often called, contains ninety acres without a tree, and it, the Pine Orchard Mountain, Riddle's Knob and Black Mountain, form a sort of basin through which Long Hope Creek flows into the North Fork of New River, near Creston. Most of this used to be covered with forests, though much clearing has been done since the pioneer days. B. R. Brown and Lindsey Patterson own much land there now. Much of it used to belong to Gen. Sam. Patterson, of the Yadkin Valley. Henry Barlow and family used to live in a cabin in this basin, but Lindsey

Triplett had taken his place. A man named Byrd was the first who ever lived there, and his cabin was covered with shingles which were pinned on with wooden pins. The cabin and field around it are still called the Byrd cabin and the Byrd field. Nelson Grimsley also stayed in that cabin, and subsequent to the Civil War came Wayne Miller, after whom followed Thomas Stevens, only to be succeeded by the Greer family, who are there now. Thomas Isbell, of King's Creek, probably owned the Bald first, and then the Finley family. But, whoever owned the land, the people living around resented the pasturing of cattle there by non-resident owners. When W. S. Davis, who was born July 24, 1832, can just remember, probably in 1844 or 1845, a dozen or more men were indicted for killing cattle, among whom were Buckner Tatum, Squire John McGuire, James Greer, Samuel Wilcox and others. According to Mr. Davis, they were tried at Wilkesboro, probably on account of local prejudice against the landowners. So serious were the cases that Buckner Tatum preferred another atmosphere to the free air of Ashe, as it was then, sold out to Elisha Tatum in 1845 and left the country forever, going to Georgia. It is said that Sam. Wilcox killed forty head of cattle on the Bald one rainy morning before breakfast, and then moved hastily and permanently to Kentucky.*

"School Butter."—When W. S. Davis was about eighteen years old, say in 1850, he suffered with his back, but was able to be up and about, though not fit for hard work. About this time the people in the neighborhood of the Lookabill school house on Meat Camp met to agree upon a more convenient point for the school house, and that school district had settled on the site and gone to work cutting the logs for the building. This site was close to where Edmund Miller now lives on Grassy Creek. These log-choppers "threw in" and raised enough money to pay for a gallon of brandy. Someone borrowed a gallon jug from Aunt Katy Moretz, and "put it on" W. S. Davis to go after the brandy, he having been selected because he could not chop logs. The still was at the old Councill place, where the Widow Reagan now lives. Davis set out upon this errand, but meeting Wm.

---

* Finley Greer's statement to C. A. Grubb.

Proffit on the way and learning from him that there was no brandy at the still, he started back, his jug still empty. On the road to the still, however, he had passed the old Lookabill school house, during recess, and thirteen boys then at play there caught hold of his old brown coat and threatened to put him in the branch. Davis asked that the teacher be consulted, and the latter sent word to let Davis alone, which the boys accordingly did. But, on his return trip, Ben Ferguson slipped out of school without permission, tin cup in hand, and asked Davis for a drink of the brandy which Ben thought was in the jug. Davis turned up the jug to prove his statement that there was nothing in it. Then Ferguson asked, "Bill, ain't you afeard to say 'school butter?'" Davis did not know the consequences of saying "school butter," and answered, "No; I'll say 'school butter' whenever I please." Thereupon Ferguson hastened back to the school house and told the assembled boys that Bill Davis had "hollered 'school butter.'" That was enough, for teacher, boys and girls started pell-mell after the offender. When Davis was about twenty steps from the school house he heard a noise, and, looking back, saw the school children running toward him. He ran, but was overtaken, Lorenzo Dow Allen, the school master, having taken a short-cut and headed him off. Davis warned them of what the consequence would be in case anyone touched him. Jackson Miller, being nearest, got the lick which Davis aimed at the head of his foremost assailant. The jug broke, leaving only the handle in Davis' hand. Davis defied the next one to "come on," but he did not come. All this happened on top of the hill, and it is called Jug Hill to this day.

Lee Carmichael.—Davis feed this attorney and he appeared for him, he having been bound over by Squire Eli Brown to the Superior Court, but Carmichael neglected the case and then Davis employed Quincey F. O'Neil, of Jefferson. The case was tried four years later and Davis was acquitted, only one witness, Ben Ferguson, having been examined for the State, and the judge directing acquittal. It had cost Davis over one hundred dollars, however. Burton Craig, of Salisbury, was the solicitor who prosecuted. There are several variants of this story, but the above is from W. S. Davis himself, the only survivor of the incident. This Lee Carmichael loved the cup that first cheers and inebriates a little later on. That, probably, is why Davis had to fee O'Neil. Then Carmichael ran for Congress and was defeated. He died soon afterwards.

The Musterfield Murder.—As an aftermath of the Civil War, say about 1870, there turned up in several of the more secluded sections of the Southern mountains "men with a past." Whence they came and whither went, no one knew. Among these was a man who called himself Green Marshall, who suddenly and without invitation put in an appearance on what is now universally and enthusiastically called Hog Elk, just east of the Blue Ridge, but still in Watauga County. He lived in the family of young Troy Triplett. Together they came to Boone one day and had a quarrel near the court house. Later on that day they left town together, and when they got half a mile away the quarrel was renewed at the old Muster Ground and Marshall stabbed Triplett, wounding him so badly that Triplett died several days later at the house of Henry Hardin, one mile east of Boone. Marshall hid that night in the house of a colored woman named Ailsey Council,[10] her home being beyond the ridge in rear of Prof. D. D. Dougherty's present home, almost south of Boone, ultimately escaping for a time, but being caught later near Hog Elk. He was tried and convicted of manslaughter and served his sentence. No one knows where he came from nor where he went after his term was up. It was remarked after this murder that Marshall had never been seen without an open knife in his hand. Luke Triplett, the dead man's father, put up a rough mountain rock in the shape of a rude slab, four feet high and twelve to fourteen inches broad, on the spot on which his son had been stabbed. He had chiseled on the stone his son's name and a rude effigy, showing the outline of a man's form and a wound from which blood was apparently flowing. It stood there several years, but disappeared. It is said that the blood from the real wound changed the color of the vegetation on which it had fallen for several years.

---

[10] Ailsey Councill is said to have named what is now known as Straddle Gap, between Brushy Fork Baptist Church and Dog Skin Creek, in which a Boone Marker has been placed. This gap used to be called Grave-Yard Gap.

Horton.

HORTON FAMILY ARMS.

EXPLANATION.—A stag's head, silver; attired, gold. Crest out of the waves of the sea proper, a tilting spear, erect, gold; enfiled with dolphin, silver, finned, gold, and charged with a shell. Motto: "*Quod vult, valde vult.*" "What he wills he wills cordially and without stint."

A Belle of Broadway.—Elizabeth Eagles, of New York City, married Nathan Horton in that place July 10, 1783. She was a daughter of John Eagles and a belle of what is now the metropolis of America. They went first to the Jersey Settlement, afterwards moving to Holman's Ford, from which place they came with William Miller and his wife, Mary, and their son, David, and Ebenezer Fairchild and family to what is now Cook's Gap, six miles east of the town of Boone. This is one of the most historic places in America, for whatever may have been his course from there westward, there is no doubt that Daniel Boone and his companions passed through this gap in May, 1769, on their first trip into Kentucky. It is, moreover, one of the loveliest places on the Blue Ridge, being practically a tableland, from whose rolling hills views of unsurpassed loveliness stretch away on every hand. Rome, that "sat on her seven hills and from her throne of beauty ruled the world," had no lovelier outlook than this. It is through this gap, also, that the first railroad to cross the Blue Ridge into Watauga County is most apt to come. But Jonathan Buck, a hunter, had been there before them, as had also Richard Green. These had built hunting camps, Buck on what is still known as Buck's Ridge, and Green at Cook's Gap. All these people had been members of the Jersey Settlement, as had also been James Tompkins and James Jackson, and afterwards became members of Three Forks Church. The grant of 640 acres of land at this place to William Miller bears date May, 1787, and it was doubtless entered some time before. Tompkins' name still adheres to one of the knobs near Deep Gap, and the Jackson Meeting House on Meat Camp Creek will keep his memory alive for years yet to come, for it was the first school house built in this section. Corn and wheat could not be raised in this section at that early time, and these settlers on the Blue Ridge found themselves in the dead of winter without other food than wild meat and Irish potatoes, of which they had garnered a goodly crop. William Miller and Nathan Horton, therefore, took four horses, all they had, and went down to the Yadkin Valley for a supply of grain. When they were gone the fire in Mrs. Horton's house went out, and as she did not know how to kindle another from flint and punk and steel,[11] she and David, the son of William and Mary Miller, set out on foot to go down to the head of Elk Creek to get fire from the Lewis family, who were then her nearest neighbors. The distance is stated to be five and eight miles, either of which was a long, hard journey for this delicately reared lady. But they got there and started back with a chunk of fire, she bearing her baby boy, William, in her arms.[12] But David stumbled just before they got back to the Horton residence and the "chunk" fell into the snow, then ten inches deep on the ground, putting the fire out entirely. It was then that Mrs. Horton sat down on a log and cried. But she took new courage very soon, and they went on, she telling David that they could milk the cows, drink the milk and get between the feather beds and so keep from freezing till Nathan Horton and William Miller should return. But when they approached the home they saw smoke issuing from the chimney, and upon entering found Richard Green sitting contentedly before a blazing fire. "This is my camp, madam," is said to have been Green's first greeting. "It is my home," was Mrs. Horton's ready answer, "as we have patented the land on which it stands, but when my husband returns he will pay you whatever may be right for the improvements you have put upon the land." This was done, Green getting four deer and two bear skins for his camp. Miller also bought out Jonathan Buck, whose camp he had preempted, paying him in furs also.

---

[11] Mrs. Battle Bryan knew better, however. She opened the frizzin which covers the pan of a flint-lock and removed the powder from pan and touch-hole, filling the latter with tallow. She then replaced the powder in the pan and snapped the gun, having placed tow nearby. "Or, a piece of roughened steel" was hooked over the forefinger, and the punk and flint held between thumb and forefinger of other hand was struck against the steel, the spark catching in the punk, commonly called "spunk."

[12] This baby was destined to be the grandfather of William Horton Bower, member of Congress in 1888.

CHAPTER XIV.
Some of Our Show-Places.

Fine Scenery.—The scenery of Watauga County is as fine as any in the mountains of North Carolina. From Blowing Rock, the Grandfather, the Bald, Howard's Knob, Riddle's Knob, Elk Knob, the Buzzard Rocks and Dogs Ears views can be had that are sublime. Between Banner Elk and Montezuma are two immense rocks, called the Chimneys, seventy-five and ninety feet high, which have never been photographed, but which are striking objects of nature. Hanging Rock above Banner Elk and the North Pinnacle of the Beech Mountain are accessible and afford fine views. Dutch Creek Falls, within half a mile of the Mission School at Valle Crucis, slide over a rock which seems to be eighty feet high, and Linville Falls, now in Avery County, have two falls, each about thirty-five feet in height. Elk Falls, three miles from Cranberry, are well worth a visit, while the rapids of Elk Creek below the old Lewis Banner mill are wild and attractive. Watauga Falls, just west of the Tennessee line, and, therefore, in Tennessee, are not really "falls" in the sense of having a sheer fall of water in a perpendicular direction, but they are a series of cascades pouring over gigantic rocks in a gorge grand and gloomy in the extreme. It is rarely visited, however, many people imagining that a post office called Watauga Falls between Beech Creek and Ward's Store are the real falls, while in fact there are no falls there whatever. The turnpike leading from Valle Crucis to Butler, Tenn., passes in less than half a mile from the real falls, which, however, are not visible from the road. The "walks" are a series of natural stepping stones across the Watauga River below Flat Shoals, near the Tennessee line. At all times of ordinary high water one can cross on these stones dry-shod. The Wolf's Den on Riddle's Knob is well worth a visit. From the Rock House at the Jones or Little place, and from Tater Hill, both on Rich Mountain, fine views can be had.

Cove Creek.—From Sugar Grove to the Tennessee line Cove Creek is so thickly settled as to be almost a continuous village. Several creeks come down from Rich Mountain and Fork Ridge, and on such streams many people live and thrive. For Cove Creek is recognized as the Egypt of Watauga County. It contains some of the most fertile land in the State. Its people are progressive and co-operate in all public enterprises. Beginning at Zionville, near the Tennessee line, there is a succession of villages, including Mable, Amantha, Sherwood, Mast and Sugar Grove. Two large flouring mills are on the creek, while there is the first cheese factory ever established in the county in flourishing condition at Sugar Grove. Churches, schools and masonic lodges dot the hillsides. Hospitality reigns in every household. The people are prosperous and happy and helpful. From a point near the mouth of Sharp's Creek, looking toward Rich Mountain, is a view that is as beautiful as any in the mountains. A forest of young lin trees has been set out on one of the worn-out hillsides and will soon be in fine condition; also grafted chestnut trees—that is, native chestnut trees on which have been grafted French and Italian shoots. A sang garden or orchard is flourishing nearby, while the town of Sugar Grove and vicinity is lighted up with electric lights. Bath tubs supplied with clear spring water are found in many of the dwellings, and an air of prosperity and progress pervades the entire community of Cove Creek. Automobiles and the latest improved farm machinery show the temper and spirit of the people. In short, there is no forward step which can be taken at this stage of its growth that Cove Creek has not taken. Silverstone, in the shadow of the Rich Mountain, is one of the loveliest of all the villages of this vicinity, though it is some distance from Cove Creek. It is, however, part and parcel of that locality.

"The Biggest Show on Earth."—This is the boast of the Barnum-Bailey shows, but it falls far short of being as *fine* a show as the wild flowers of Watauga County make from May till December. Nowhere else on earth do the rhododendron, the azalea and the mountain ivy or calico bush called kalmia grow to such perfection as here. Nowhere else on earth do botanists find

A History of Watauga County

so large and fine a variety of wild flowers of all kinds. The *rhododendron maximum* is, as its name indicates, the largest of the rhododendron family, which derives its name from two Greek words meaning a rose tree. Both its leaves and its blooms are larger than any other variety. It is what we call mountain laurel, as distinguished from the ivy or calico bush, which has spotted, bell-shaped blooms. But we make no distinction between it and what botanists call the *rhododendron catawbiense,* which has a smaller leaf and bloom and the bloom being more like the rose in color. The largest trunks of the rhododendron are six inches in diameter and the trees twenty feet high. In her "Carolina Mountains" Miss Morley gives most impassioned and poetic descriptions of the Watauga flowers, saying, among other charming things, that "all flowers are imprisoned sunshine in a figurative sense, but of no others does that seem so literally true as of 'the flame-colored azaleas' (p. 50), to see the perfect fire of which you must come to their mountains." She also calls attention to the fringe bush, and asks how it came to the Grandfather Mountain "when all the other members of its family live in that remote Chinese empire so mysteriously connected with us through the life of the plants?" In this class she places the silver bell tree, the azalea, the fringe bush, the wisteria and ginseng. And she calls attention to the *rhododendron vaseyii,* which sheds its leaves in autumn. This was thought to have become extinct, but it is still found on the north side of the Grandfather (p. 59). But all these flowers are surpassed by the lovely blooms of our apple and cherry trees in May and June, for nowhere in the world are apples and cherries finer or more abundant than here, the Moses H. Cone orchard at Blowing Rock and that at Valle Crucis producing fruit as fine and in greater abundance than almost any other orchards in the world. Kelsey's Highland Nursery at Linville City makes a business of selling all our wild flowers. Rev. W. R. Savage, of Blowing Rock, cultivates many of them in his garden. Mrs. W. W. Stringfellow, of the same town, also takes great pride in cultivating both tame and wild flowers and in distributing bulbs and seeds gratuitously among the mountain people.

Valle Crucis.—According to a tradition well supported by the statements of many reputable cittizens of the present day, Samuel Hix and his son-in-law, James D. Holtsclaw came in 1779 from Cheraw, S. C., through the Deep Gap, to what is now known as Valle Crucis, and erected a palisade of split logs, with their sharpened ends driven into the ground, so as to enclose about an acre and a half surrounding the Maple Spring between the present residence of Finley Mast and that of his brother, Squire W. B. Mast. This was because they feared Indians, not knowing of the agreement between the Watauga settlers and the Cherokees as to the land between the Virginia line and the ridge south of the Watauga River. After a time Hix became uneasy and retired to the wilderness near what is now Banner Elk, where he made a camp and supported himself by hunting and making maple syrup and sugar, thus avoiding service as an American or a Tory. At some time in his career he is said to have had a cabin in a cove in rear of the present residence of Squire W. B. Mast, then to have lived in the bottom above James M. Shull's present farm, afterwards moving down the Watauga River near Ward's Store, where he died long after the Revolutionary War. It is said that he never took the oath of allegiance to the American cause and that whenever he came home for supplies his mischievous sons would frighten him by firing off a pistol made by hollowing out a buck-horn and loading the cavity with powder, the same being "touched off with a live coal." Just here it may be remarked—a fact not generally known—that if a live coal is not allowed to burn itself into ashes, it becomes a dead coal, which yet has elements of immortality in it to such an extent that, unless it is ground to powder, it remains charcoal indefinitely. Such coals, in beds of ashes, are still plowed up near the Lybrook farm, now the Grandfather Orphanage, one mile from Banner's Elk, still called by old people the Hix Improvement, that being the place where Samuel Hix "laid out during the Revolutionary War." Whether he had a grant or other title to the Valle Crucis land seems immaterial now, as he had possession of it when Bedent Baird arrived toward the close of the eighteenth century, for Baird, with a pocketful of money, had to go a mile down the river to get a home in this wilderness

A History of Watauga County 213

of rich land. Then Hix is said to have sold his holdings to Benjamin Ward for a rifle, dog and a sheepskin, Ward selling it later on to Reuben Mast, while Hix moved down to the mouth of Cove Creek. Ward soon got possession of this also, and sold it to a man named Summers, who was living in a cabin on the left bank of Watauga River during a great freshet which lifted the cabin from its foundation and carried it and its inmates, the entire Summers family, to death and oblivion in that night of horrors. A faithful dog belonging to the family swam after the cabin and when it finally lodged against a rock, the dog would allow no one to enter till he had been killed. The Hix Hole, just below David F. Baird's farm, is still so called because of the drowning there of James Hix and a Tester about 1835, when a bull was ridden into the river in order to recover the two bodies. Reuben Mast lived where D. F. Baird now lives, while Joel Mast lived where J. Hardee Talor resides. David Mast lived near where Finley Mast's large mansion now stands. Henry Taylor, whose father was Butler Taylor, came from Davidson County to Sugar Grove about 1849, married Emeline, daughter of John Mast, of that place, and then moved to Valle Crucis in time to get some of the money paid out for the construction of the Caldwell and Watauga turnpike. This road must have been begun prior to October, 1849, for Col. Joseph C. Shull remembers that William Mast had the contract to build the bridge across Watauga River one mile below Shull's Mills, and was at work on it the morning on which he drank the poison the slave girl, Mill, is supposed to have put in his coffee for breakfast, for he came to Col. Joseph C. Shull's father's home for medicine and returned to work on the bridge, but soon had to go home, dying that night at about the same time his wife died. It was to the valley above this that Bishop Ives came in 1843, where he erected the school and brotherhood described elsewhere. This valley was what the editor of the "Life of W. W. Skiles," Susan Fenimore Cooper, a descendant of Fenimore Cooper, author of the "Leather Stocking Tales," says the Indians would call a "one smoke valley" (p. 17), from the fact that but one family dwelt there in 1842. That family was that of Andrew Townsend, the miller, whose descendants still live nearby.

Sugar Grove.—Cutliff Harmon came from Randolph County to this place in 1791 and bought 522 acres of land from James Gwyn, it having been granted to him May 18, 1791. Cutliff married Susan Fouts first and a widow by the name of Elizabeth Parker after the death of his first wife. It is Sugar Grove that is the most progressive of the Cove Creek towns, having electric lights, a roller mill, the first in the county, and a cheese dairy, established 5th June, 1915. It has also one of the finest school houses in the county. It was here also that Camp Mast was located during the Civil War. The land in this section is considered as about the best in the county. Col. Joseph Harrison Mast, who died September 8, 1915, had his residence here. He was in his prime one of the best and most substantial citizens of the county and still holds the respect and affection of all who knew him. The first roller mill in the county was established here. These people know what co-operation means and act accordingly. The cheese factory is the first that was established in the South, and promises to be successful.

Blowing Rock.—From the "Carolina Mountains" (pp. 350, 355) we learn that "from Blowing Rock to Tryon Mountain the Blue Ridge draws a deep curve half encircling a jumble of very wild rocky peaks and cliffs that belong to the foothill formations. Hence, Blowing Rock, lying on one arm of a horseshoe of which Tryon Mountain is the other arm, has the most dramatic outlook of any village in the mountains. Directly in front of it is an enormous bowl filled with a thousand tree-clad hills and ridges that become higher and wilder towards the encircling wall of the Blue Ridge, the conspicuous bare stone summits of Hawk's Bill and Table Rock Mountains rising sharp as dragon's teeth above the rest, while the sheer and shining face of the terrible Lost Cove cliffs, dropping into some unexplored ravine, come to view on a clear day. From far away, beyond this wild bowlful of mountains, one sometimes sees a faintly outlined dome, Tryon Mountain, under which on the other side one likes to remember Traumfest, Fortress of Dreams.

"Off to the left from Blowing Rock, seen between near green knobs, the shoreless sea of the lowlands reaches away to lave

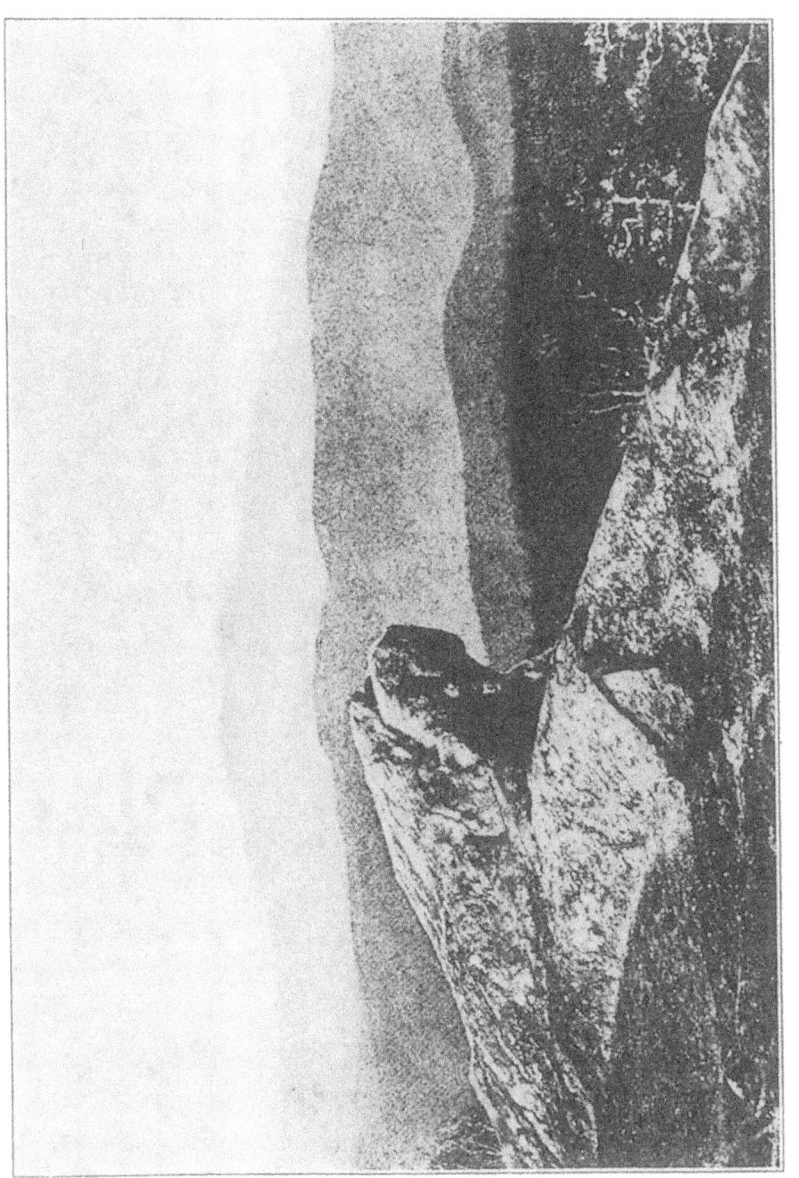

THE BLOWING ROCK.

the edge of the sky. And looking to the right, there lies the calm and noble form of the Grandfather Mountain, its rocky top drawn in a series of curves against the western sky. Long spurs sweep down like buttresses to hold it. Trees clothe it as with a garment to where the black rock surmounts them.

"The view from Blowing Rock changes continually. The atmospheric sea that encloses mountain and valley melts the solid rocks into a thousand enchanting pictures. Those wild shapes in the great basin which at one time look so near, so hard and so terrible, at another time recede and soften, their dark colors transmuted into the tender blue of the Blue Ridge, or again the basin is filled with dreamlike forms immersed in an exquisite sea of mystical light.

"Sometimes the Grandfather Mountain stands solidly out, showing in detail the tapestry of green trees that hangs over its slopes; again it is blue and flat against the sky, or it seems made of mists and shadows. Sometimes the sunset glory penetrates, as it were, into the substance of the mountain, which looks translucent in the sea of light that contains it. As night draws on, it darkens into a noble silhouette against the splendor that often draws the curves of its summit in lines of fire.

"Blowing Rock at times lies above the clouds, with all the world blotted out excepting the Grandfather's summit rising out of the white mists. Sometimes one looks out in the morning to see that great bowl filled to the brim with level clouds that reach away from one's very feet in a floor so firm to the eye that one is tempted to step out on it. Presently this pure white, level floor begins to roll up into billowy masses, deep wells open, down which one looks to little landscapes lying in the bottom, a bit of the lovely John's River Valley, a house and trees, perhaps. The well closes; the higher peaks begin to appear, phantom islands in a phantom sea; the restless ocean of mists swells and rolls, now concealing, now revealing glimpses of the world under it. It breaks apart into fantastic forms that begin to glide up the peaks and mount above them like wraiths. The sun darts sheaves of golden arrows in through the openings, and these in time slay the pale dragons of the air, or drive them fleeing into the far blue caverns of the sky, and the world beneath is visible, only that where the John's River Valley ought to be there often remains a long lake of snowy drift. Sometimes the clouds blotting out the landscape break apart suddenly, the mountains come swiftly forth one after the other until one seems to be watching an act of creation where solid forms resolve themselves out of chaos. The peaceful John's River Valley, winding far below among the wild mountains, is like a glimpse into fairyland, and one has never ventured to go there for fear of dispelling the pleasing illusion.

"Near the village of Blowing Rock, at the beginning of those green knobs between which one looks to the lowlands, is a high cliff, the real Blowing Rock, so named because the rocky walls at this point form a flume through which the northwest wind sweeps with such force that whatever is thrown over the rock is hurled back again. It is said that there are times when a man could not jump over, so tremendous is the force of the wind. It is also said that visitors, having heard the legend of the rock, have been seen to stand there in a dead calm and throw over their possessions and watch them no more in anger than in mirth as they, obedient to the law of gravity instead of that of fancy, disappeared beneath the tree tops far below.

"Blowing Rock, four thousand feet above sea level, is a wonderfully sweet place. The rose-bay and the great white *rhododendron maximum* crowd against the houses and fill the open spaces, excepting where laurel and the flame-colored azaleas have planted their standards. And in their seasons the wild flowers blossom everywhere; also the rocks are covered with those crisp, sweet-smelling herbs that love high places, and sedums and saxifrages trim the crevices and the ledges.

"Blowing Rock is also noted for the great variety of new mushrooms that have been captured there, though one suspects that this renown is due to the fact that the mushroom hunters happened to pitch their tents here instead of somewhere else. For other parts of the mountains can make a showing in mushrooms, too."

Some Blowing Rock Attractions.—Besides the Blowing Rock itself, from which a fine view can be had, there are the Ransom and Grand Views. There are several drives and trails in and near the Rock, some of which surpass in sylvan beauty any to be seen on the Biltmore estate, as the former are through primeval forests, notably the drive between the Stringfellow and Cone Lakes. The Randall Memorial Work Shop was conceived by the late W. G. Randall, who was born in Burke County, North Carolina, and after many hardships obtained an education and became a famous artist in oils. He spent his summers in Blowing Rock, where he died, after living nearly twenty summers there. His remains lie in Washington, D. C. His wife was Miss Anna Goodlow, of Warren County, North Carolina. It is in this Work Shop that the manual industries of the mountain people are preserved and fostered. There are an old-fashioned hand loom, spinning wheels, etc., in this building. The Blowing Rock Exchange is near by, and its object is to afford a greater opportunity to the home people to sell home-made articles, such as woven rugs, coverlids, embroidered bedspreads, laces, articles made of laurel, baskets, etc. In it are a library, a fine collection of Indian relics and mineral specimens. In front of the Work Shop is a garden of rare wild and cultivated plants and one of the two sundials in Watauga County. This garden is the result of the labors of Rev. William Rutherford Savage, who was born in Pass Christian, Miss., October 20, 1854; was graduated at the Episcopal Theological Seminary, Alexandria, Va., and moved to Blowing Rock in September, 1902. He is a worthy successor to the late Rev. W. W. Skiles, of Valle Crucis fame. In the words of Rev. Edgar Tufts, Mr. Savage has done more than any other to create a fraternal feeling among all the denominations of the mountains.

Ante-Bellum Residents.—Col. James Harper, Sr., of Lenoir, built a frame summer residence at what is now the H. W. Weeden Fairview house, about 1858, and spent the summers there till the Civil War began. John Bryant lived where the Blowing Rock hotel stands, on land belonging to Col. James Harper. Edmund Greene lived near the present site of the Greene Park hotel, and Isaac Greene where the Boyden house now stands. Joseph Greene lived near the present site of the German Reformed Church. Amos Greene lived on the opposite side of the road from the present residence of Mrs. Dr. Reeves, and Lot Estes had his home between the present residence of Col. W. W. Stringfellow and the creek. Len Estes, his son, built the mill and dam after the Civil War, but sold out to Colonel Stringfellow and went West. He kept summer boarders and looked like General Grant. William M. Morris bought the Amos Greene place about 1874 and opened a house for summer boarders. He was most successful, and the good things he furnished for his boarders to eat will be forever remembered by all who had the good fortune to sit at his table. He had a most remarkable little bench-legged cow, which gave oceans of the richest milk imaginable. His deep featherbeds were good for tired legs after a day's wading in the creeks fishing for speckled trout. He sold out to Dr. L. C. Reeves, however, and moved east of the Blue Ridge. W. W. Sherrell bought the Harper property and opened two or three small houses for summer boarders about 1877 or 1878 at Fairview. This is now the Weeden place. Robert Greene, father of the late Judge L. L. Greene, lived where the Cone Lake now is. The Kirk Fort was in the Blowing Rock Gap, and trees were felled for some distance down the road so as to give an open view of the country to the east. After Gen. M. W. Ransom became interested in the place, its growth was rapid, and the completion of the Yonahlossee turnpike in 1900 assured its success.

Along the Blue Ridge.—We will now notice the people who originally lived along the Blue Ridge, from Deep Gap to Coffey's Gap. Solomon Green lived in the Deep Gap, and was a good citizen and entertained the traveling public. He was the son of "Flatty" Isaac Green, who lived on Meat Camp near the noted Brown place of 640 acres, the lower part of which is now owned by Lindsey Patterson, of Winston-Salem, and the upper part by L. A. Green, who lives near. L. A. Green is a son of "Little" John Green, who was a son of Richard Green, all of whom are well to do people. The next settled place on the Ridge was called the Old Ellison place, where William Blackburn now lives. The next was the home of the Rev. John Cook, a Baptist minister and a son of Michael Cook, of Cook's Gap, and he lived six

Photo. by *Vannoy.* LAKE AND RESIDENCE OF COLONEL W. W. STRINGFELLOW, BLOWING ROCK.

miles east of Boone, where his grandson, A. B. Cook, now lives, and is better known as "Burt" Cook. From this point, going west along the Ridge, we next reach the home of the old pioneer, Michael Cook, who first settled in the noted Cook's Gap and from whom it took its name. He had six sons, to wit: John, Adam, David, Robert, Michael and William. There were at least two daughters, one of whom married Aaron Hampton and the other Rice Hayes. From this point we go to John and Joshua Storie's, where George Storie now has a store. George is a grandson of John, his father having been Walter, who married a Miss Powell, of Caldwell. Walter lost his life in the Civil War. These two families were hard working and industrious people and owned adjoining farms, the voting place being called Storie's Barn. Jesse, son of John Storie, is probably the only one living of the two old families. This takes us to what is now Blowing Rock, four miles further west, to the old Green settlement, where the two noted brothers, Joseph and Benjamin Green, lived. These brothers were so much alike that their neighbors could scarcely tell them apart. Isaac Green, called "Mountain" Isaac, lived at what is now the Boyden place, where he reared a large family. Amos Green lived where Mrs. Sallie Reeves, widow of the late Dr. L. C. Reeves, now lives. He had a large family. Alexander Green, son of Benjamin, lived where Mr. Lance now lives, one mile east of Blowing Rock. His father used to live there before him, while Joseph Green lived east of Green Park hotel. He was the grandfather of Mrs. W. L. Bryan. A small Reformed Lutheran Church stands on part of the land. Warren Green, youngest son of Joseph, was killed when Stoneman raided Boone. Robert Greene lived where Cone's Lake now is. He was the father of Judge L. L. Greene, his wife having been Chaney Elrod, whose father lived two miles south of Boone, where J. Watts Farthing now lives. Lot Estes married Chaney Green, a daughter of Benjamin Green, and lived where Colonel Stringfellow's house now stands. Five miles west lived McCaleb Coffey at what is called Coffey's Gap. He married Sally Hayes, a sister of Ransom Hayes. They had four boys and no girls. The boys were Jones, Thomas, Ninevah and

John. All were killed in the Civil War except Jones and he was badly wounded. No one else lived on the Blue Ridge from Coffey's Gap west till after the Grandfather was passed. Finley and Jesse Gragg probably moved to the top of the Ridge after the Civil War.

Moses H. Cone.—He began to acquire real estate in the vicinity of Blowing Rock about 1897, and secured over 3,500 acres of land before his death at Baltimore, Md., December 8, 1908. The mansion he erected on Flat Top Mountain is second only to that of George W. Vanderbilt near Asheville. The lake in front of that residence is one of the picture places of the mountains. He died childless and intestate, but his widow and brothers and sisters have joined in the creation of the Moses H. Cone Memorial Park for the public "in perpetuity," after the death of his widow, by donating the above land. Moses H. Cone was born at Jonesboro, Tenn., June 29, 1857. He married Miss Bertha Landau, of Baltimore.

An Established Pleasure Resort.—Blowing Rock went up top as a pleasure resort soon after the completion of the turnpike from Lenoir and Linville City. Many people bought land and built summer homes there. Hotels and boarding houses began to go up and to multiply year by year. Livery stables, bowling alleys, automobiles, drug stores, churches, stores of all sorts soon became numerous and provided for the amusement and needs of a growing summer population. It has a flourishing bank also, a long-distance and local telephone line, several physicians, and everything to make life pleasant for the permanent resident and the transient guest. The views are unsurpassed. Schools provide for the education of the children, and all sorts of games, entertainments and amusements go on from morn till night all seasons of the year. The mails are adequate, and Charlotte and Raleigh papers reach "The Rock," as it is called, on the day they are issued. In other words, everything that is essential to a first-class pleasure resort is provided, and all tastes and purses can be suited, as the range of hotel and boarding house accommodation is extensive. Blowing Rock is established beyond question as one of the finest and most popular pleasure resorts of the South.

Brushy Fork.—John Holtsclaw, son of James D., who was the son-in-law of Samuel Hix, moved from Valle Crucis in 1801, when the road was finished down Brushy Fork and built and operated the Buck Horn tavern, which stood in the field to the left of the road going down the creek opposite Floyd Ward's present home. Buck horns were nailed to a large white oak which stood in front of the old tavern. Valle Crucis was then off the main road to Tennessee, and John had come to Brushy Fork to be in the current of the western movement. Later on a school house was built near this old tavern, which has long since disappeared, and the small mound on which it stood is still pointed out. Marcus Holtsclaw, son of John, lived at several places on Brushy Fork. John also built and operated a grist mill a third of a mile below the Brushy Fork Baptist Church, on the right of the road going down, a sycamore stump still marking the site of the old dam. Almost opposite the old dam site, but to the left of the road, still stands an old stone chimney which furnished a fireplace for a cabin which stood on ten acres of land which John Tomlin in 1830 to 1835 contracted to buy and pay fifty dollars for. He put up the walls of a large log house, Alfred Hately hewing the logs, but Tomlin was unable to finish paying for the property and it fell back to its original owner. Tomlin sold goods at what is now called Vilas. His wife was a daughter of John J. Whittington, but she left him and went to Missouri. What became of him is not known, except that he also left Brushy Fork, never to return. John J. Whittington lived a quarter of a mile below and on the right of the road, and the old Whittington graveyard is on the hill on the right of the road, while the Hagaman graveyard is on the left. John Holtsclaw's youngest son is buried there. He had married Nancy, a daughter of Moses Hateley. There was a sang factory at the Whittington place as far back as W. W. Presnell can remember. It was in charge of Bacchus J. Smith, of Buncombe, who in turn was the agent of Dr. Hailen, of Philadelphia. The sang factory stood just below Joseph Ward's present home. M. Granville Hagaman first lived and sold goods right after the Civil War in a house where Andrew Greer now lives. He also bought sang there, and Col. W. W. Presnell gathered and sold to him $47.00 worth of sang at twenty-five cents a pound in exactly twenty-two days.[1] Where Samuel Flannery now lives is the site of the original home of Thomas Hagaman, who settled there before the Civil War, coming from the Fork Ridge. The Ben Councill house at Vilas, built of brick, was completed about 1845 by a man from Tennessee by the name of Mace, while Polly Cornell cooked for the work hands. In 1827 the parents of Col. W. W. Presnell reached Brushy Fork, coming through the Coffey Gap on the old John's River Road from near Taylorsville. His mother, Mary Munday, was born at the Black Oak Ridge and his father, Solomon Presnell, in Union County in 1810. Where the widow of ex-Sheriff A. J. McBride now lives, nearly opposite the Ben Councill brick house at Vilas, is where the old Tomlin and Ben Councill store house stood. It was built of logs. On the hill above the present residence of Wm. L. Henson is the site of the first Methodist Church that was ever built in Watauga County, but it seems never to have been completed, though Colonel Presnell says that his mother told him services were held there soon after she came to this settlement in 1827. It is at Vilas that Ben Councill built a large mill for that day and time (1845), and from that place the road forked, one prong going through the Councill Gap to Valle Crucis and the other to Sugar Grove, from which point it went through the Mast Gap to Valle Crucis, as well as on down Cove Creek to Watauga River and up the Cove Creek to Tennessee. The Whittington family finally moved to Missouri. The Dugger family of Cove Creek are descendants of Benjamin Dugger, who came from Yadkin Elk in 1793 or 1794 to Brushy Fork and entered land there, and for whom the Dugger Mountain and creek east of the Blue Ridge are named. There were three Dugger brothers who came from Scotland and stopped awhile near Petersburg, Va., named Benjamin, Daniel and Julius. Ben stopped at Yadkin Elk, Daniel went to Kentucky and Julius settled near Fish Springs on the Watauga River, Tennessee. It was from Julius' children that the Banner's Elk Duggers descended.

---

[1] One of the sons of Newton Banner has about a fourth of an acre in ginseng, near Sugar Grove. Others have large patches of it also. Many have very small plots of ground in shaded corners where a few plants are tended.

Shull's Mills.—From this point to the Linville Gap is full of historical incidents and romantic occurrences. It was in the field in front of the Joseph C. Shull home, near the cattle barn, that young Charles Asher was shot by White's men after the Revolutionary War, and soon after he had married a daughter of David Hix and settled in the orchard below the Shull house. Here also came James Aldridge soon after he had left the Big Sandy and his wife and five children to commence life anew with Betsy Calloway, as a hunter and trapper. Rev. Henry H. Prout came there, too, and built Easter Chapel, and it was there that Edward Moody and his wife lived lives of usefulness and inspiration to all who came into contact with them. There, too, came Jesse Boone, a nephew of Daniel, and built a cabin on one prong of Watauga River, which has ever since borne the name of the Boone Fork. Col. Walter W. Lenoir, soldier, lawyer, legislator and philanthropist, settled just above Shull's Mill at the close of the Civil War and built, or, rather, improved a mill there which has ever since been known as Lenoir's Stonewall Mill. The Grandfather Mountain looms above it on one side and the Hanging Rock on the other. It was in this neighborhood that many of the most tragic events of the Civil War occurred, while just across the Linville Gap is the romantic valley of Altamont, the old home of the Palmers and Childses, who had been lured from New York and Massachusetts to pass their days in these enchanting surroundings. It was the broad bottoms and other attractions that made Bishop Ives apply to Phillip Shull, the father of Joseph C., for a deed to what was then Shull's Mills, embracing the present Shull holdings as well as those of Alex. Moody across Lance's Creek. And it is as well to state here that Lance's Creek was so called because Lance Estes first lived on its waters, but sold out to Len. Estes February 8, 1830. The Shull Mills land was granted to Charles Asher in 1788, when it was supposed to be in Washington County, Tennessee, and by him conveyed to Joseph White in 1792, and by Joseph to Benjamin White in 1798. It was from this neighborhood, also, that Cobb McCanless rode to Boone with young Levi L. Coffey on that January morning in 1859, where he was confronted with the agent of the Weyeth's, for whom he had been collecting money, but to return that night and take the fatal step of absconding with trust funds from which there was no return. The old bridge across Watauga River, one mile below Shull's Mills, still called the Old Bridge Place, and on which William Mast had been at work when, in October, 1849, the poison he and his wife had drunk that morning in their coffee began to make its fatal effects felt, fell down in 1909 while Wood Young was passing over it in a wagon drawn by two mules; while Zeb Dana was killed there in 1883 at night when returning with horses which he thought he had borrowed and their owners thought he had stolen. The old Caldwell and Watauga Turnpike crossed the river at this point, but after the Civil War (1870) Col. Joseph C. Shull changed it so as to cross at the present ford and run in front of his residence, instead of in rear, as it had done before, thereby avoiding a moist and boggy place near his well.

Linville Valley.—One scarcely thinks of this region—from Linville Gap to Linville Falls—as a valley, for it is more like a high ridge upon the crest of which a silver stream winds its romantic way, with "here a blossom sailing, and here and there a lusty trout, and here and there a grayling." And, most wonderful, even incredible, it seems, is the fact that its course from Linville Gap to the Linville Falls is *east* of the Blue Ridge. The Humpback Mountain lies between the stream and the eastern lowlands, and looks for all the world like the Blue Ridge, but such is not the case. And more wonderful still is the fact that just over Pisgah Ridge is one prong of the Tow River, flowing into the Gulf of Mexico. Following this ridge out, one comes to the ridge which divided the waters of the Watauga from those of the Toe, and the Cherokee territory to the south from the Watauga Settlement's lands to the north. Indians were seen there under the cliff just above Pisgah Church before the Revolutionary War, to which point they had been chased by troops from below the Blue Ridge. A man named Fullward evidently lived on the branch between the old J. B. Palmer house and the store now occupied by Bickerstaff and Stroup, as that branch is called for in grant No. 1 of Burke County land. This grant is dated December 17, 1778, and is to J. McKnitt Alexander and William Sharp, for 300 acres, covering what will always be known as the Palmer Place on Linville River.[2] It is signed by Governor Caswell and has the old bees-wax seal hanging to the grant by an old ribbon. Who Fullward was no one can now tell, but there was also another early settler whose name even has been forgotten and who lived where M. C. Bickerstaff now resides. William White, after whom the Billy White Creek of this place is called, then lived at the Bickerstaff place, but he moved to Missouri about 1821, when that territory was opened up to settlement. White sold to James Erwin and he to J. B. Palmer. George Crossnore settled what is still called the Crossnore Place, where Benjamin Aldridge now lives, and he was probably a hunter. The postoffice and neighborhood still bear his name. William Davis, a soldier of the Revolution, stole his wife, a Carpenter, from Ashe, and settled at what is still called the Davis Mountain, now the Monroe Franklin place, and which Warsaw Clark now owns, one mile and a half above the Crossnore place, where Kate, the five year old daughter of Davis, is buried under an apple tree. It is said that he first gave the name of the Cow Camp to a creek of that name which runs into Toe River because of the fact that, having no feed for his cattle, he camped near them on that creek and supplied them with lin tree limbs, called laps, from the time the buds began to swell till the grass came. Another reason is given, however, for this name, which is that there was abundance of stagger-weed on the creek, and when the cattle ate it, as they did, their owners camped on the creek in order to doctor them.

The Ollis Family.—John Ollis was one of the first to settle in the Linville country, making his home just above Crossnore, where he cleared a field, still called by some the Ollis Place, while across the Fire-Scald Ridge is a rock called the Ollis

---

[2] Col. J. B. Palmer, afterwards colonel of the 58th North Carolina, came from New York State in 1858, and built a large frame house there. Because of the execution for desertion of some of his soldiers, condemned by court-martial, he could not return there after the Civil War. His widow sold it in 1889 to Mrs. Anna K. Watkins, wife of Maj. G. R. Watkins, of U. S. Navy, retired, and she to C. E. Wood, trustee, in 1908. Kirk having burnt the Palmer house, Major Watkins erected the residence now on the old site.

Deer Stand. He was of German extraction and was a soldier of the War of 1812, but was discharged at Salisbury after serving only sixty days on account of physical disability. His children were Boston, John, Jr., Daniel, James and George, Sarah, who married a Harrel; Elizabeth, who married James Gragg, and Mary, who married Major Gragg. W. H. Ollis, one of John's sons, was born September 22, 1840, and married Melinda Harstin, January 25, 1866.

Other Early Settlers.—Harvey Clark settled near the Harshaw place below Pinola; Andrew Bowers, at the Bowers' Gap; Abe Gwyn lived above Scaly, near Cranberry mines; Rad Ellis lived on the Fork Mountain, while Dr. Wm. Houston lived at what is now called Minneapolis, where he bought sang. Dr. Houston is said to have been seven feet tall. Bayard Benfield now lives where Abram Johnson first put up a forge. It is said that Johnson frequently looked for his jacket, as the vest is called here, while he had it on his person, and that the floor of his home was made of red hickory six inches thick and so closely joined that cracks were invisible. Tilmon Blalock lived on Beaver Creek, near Spruce Pine. Larkin Calloway built a little mill and lived at what is now Linville City, a little above, and his brother-in-law, Torry Webb, lived where the lake now is. Mathias Carpenter came from Pennsylvania and settled on New River in Ashe. It was his daughter who married William Davis. His son, Jacob, moved to Three Mile Creek, where he died July 18, 1856, aged eighty-six years. His son, Jacob, of Altamont, was born January 4, 1833. Henry Dellinger came from Burke about 1834 and settled where Linn Dellinger now lives. Henry salted and tended cattle in the mountains for the Erwins; John Franklin lived at the Old Fields of Toe and was one of Cobb McCanless's deputies. Wesley Johnson, a son of Abraham's, went to Utah and died there in 1880, aged eighty-one years.

Elk Crossroads.—As Elk Creek comes into the South Fork of the New River at this point, it has been a noted place for many years. Riddle and his men passed there with Ben Cleveland after they had captured him at Old Fields in April, 1781.

Wm. Howell, Wm. Ray, Solomon Younce and G. and Joseph Tatum were early settlers. It has always been a stopping place and a noted "stand" for the sale of goods and provisions. James Todd and Hugh A. Dobbins kept a store there before the Civil War and several others have sold goods there since. It is now called Elkland by the Virginia-Carolina Railroad, having for several years borne the name of Todd. Col. E. F. Lovill, of Boone, kept a store there after the Civil War, and then moved to Boone, where he has practiced law ever since. The completion of the Virginia-Carolina Railroad to that place in 1915 promises to make of it a large town in the near future. All of Elkland is now in Ashe County, the legislature making the line follow the creek from its mouth to the Blackburn ford. The Tatum place was first granted to Thomas Farmer in 1788, when this was a part of Wilkes County. Farmer sold to John Lipps in 1796 for £70, "current money." (Deed Book C, p. 598.) Lipps sold to Susanna Holman in 1799 for same amount (E, p. 241), and she sold to William Clawson in 1802 (A, p. 534), who held it till 1835, when he sold it to Ebeneezer Clawson, and he to Buckner Tatum in 1836 (L, p. 122), and in the year 1845 Buckner sold it to Elijah Tatum, the father of John L., its present owner (N, p. 483).

Banner's Elk.—John Holsclaw was the first permanent resident of this place, though Samuel Hix had occupied a place in the laurel a short distance away at what is now the Grandfather Orphanage. Baker King and Ben Dugger at some time had a camp on that very land.[3] It was there, too, during the stormy days of 1863 to 1865 that Lewis and Martin Banner piloted many an escaped Federal prisoner and Union man trying to get through the lines into Tennessee. Only a few in the secret knew of the place—Dan Ellis, of Elizabethton, Tenn.; Harrison Church, another conductor of the underground railroad, and Keith Blalock were admitted into the inner temple. Andrew Bowers lived in what is still known as the Bowers' Gap and gave his name to the Bowers' Mountain between Banner's Elk and Valle Crucis. Down on Elk, Abram Gwyn lived at what is still

---

[3] This camp is called for in deed from John Holtsclaw to Delilah Baird of date May 2, 1838, to the Big Bottoms.

called the Ford of Elk. George Dugger came later on and settled about where the road to Dr. Jenning's hotel leaves the turnpike. This, however, was on the Shawnehaw side of the ridge. There were no clearings of any extent at Banner Elk, except those at the Hix Improvement, which was very small, and at the Big Bottoms, but there were two "deadenings," one called the Moses Deadening, and the other the Lark Chopping. But nearly one hundred years ago Martin Banner had walked through from Surry to Nashville, accompanied by a single companion and having one horse between them. He passed through Banner Elk and determined to return there at some future time. Accordingly, in 1845 he returned with his family, crossing Watauga River at a ford opposite the place Walter Baird now lives, it being then the home of Bedent Baird, and followed his cart way or wagon road to his place on Beech Mountain, where he turned to the left by the Roland clearing and reaching Banner's Elk at what is now called Balm. But he did not stop there, pitching his tent permanently near what is now the Lowe Hotel. His brother, Lewis, came three or four years later and built his cabin where his daughters, Mrs. Wetmore and Miss Nannie Banner, now live, a mile above Martin's home. Levi Moody and Joel Eggers lived above Lewis Banner's house. Martin Banner moved across Sugar Mountain Gap and built a new home near the head of the North Fork of Toe River in 1866. Some time later he was on a visit at Eb Harris's home near what is now Montezuma, where he died as the result of a fall. He was born February 7, 1808, and died February 19, 1895. John Franklin and Marcus Tuttle also lived near Montezuma at that time. It was then called Bull Scrape because, being on the very crest of the Blue Ridge, there is a current of cool air constantly stirring and the cattle on the ranges thereabout used to assemble there in the heat of the day and lie under the trees while the amorous bulls pawed the ground around and locked horns over their bovine love scrapes. Close to what is now Linville City, a rather small city, but remarkably clean and attractive, lived Tyree Webb, then a very old man. The road through the McCanless Gap, reaching from Banner Elk to Linville Gap, was not con-

A History of Watauga County 229

structed till about 1895, though a trail went through there "furder back" than anyone now remembers.⁴ Behind a thick laurel, near where Napoleon Banner now lives, was the camp of a man named Ollis, who was hiding out during the Revolutionary War. Ashes and coals can still be plowed up near that place. He used to live, as did Samuel Hix, by hunting and making a crop of potatoes in a little patch, ekeing out his simple fare with maple syrup and sugar from the maple trees which had made this section their home time out of mind, and which give its name to Sugar Mountain. After awhile Burton Baird, Delilah's son, married the Widow Keller, and her daughter Aurilda, called "Rildy" for short, married Levi Moody. Below Harrison Aldrich's house on head of Watauga River lived Tom Fudge and two old maids, one of whom was named Laudermilk, for whom he milked, tended garden and did other work.⁵ He had a little gun with a very short barrel. He was a little dried-up man, but useful to these two forlorn women. William Baird lived at what is now called Matny. Mike Snider lived at what is now called Elk Park, where he operated a small grist mill. Down at Old Fields of Toe lived James Calloway and the Maxfield family, the Clarks and Braswells living above that place, and there after the Civil War Gen. Robert F. Hoke and associates, James Wilson and Sam. McD. Tate, decided that sheep raising in these mountains would be profitable, got control of the Old Fields of Toe,⁶ imported a genuine Scotch shepherd and a genuine Scotch shepherd dog, several fine bucks, and then bought up over a hundred natives ewes. It did not pay as well as had been expected, native dogs being too much for the one imported collie. Even the tie-tie business for pipe stems was carried on. John Hardin and his son, Jordan, moved from the Hardin place, a mile

---

⁴ Shep. M. Dugger, the distinguished author of the "Balsam Groves of the Grandfather Mountain," and his brother-in-law, J. Erwin Calloway, built the Grandfather hotel, half a mile from Linville Gap, in 1885; but it was burned in 1914. It served a good purpose as a resting-place for tourists to the Grandfather Mountain.

⁵ In 1857 Newton, Ab. and Luther Banner, caught trout in the North Toe River, and ran with them to the head of Banner Elk, crossing at Sugar Gap, replenishing the water as they went, and this stocked Elk Creek above Elk Falls. Rev. H. H. Prout also stocked Linville River above the Falls from head of Watauga River.

⁶ A man named Birchfield was probably among the first settlers at the Old Fields of Toe, dying there of milk-sick many years ago.

east of Boone, and lived at Cranberry forge from about 1850 till after the Civil War, during which Jordan had charge of the property. John Hardin died in 1873. Between these places and Banner's Elk there was constant communication. The rapid development of Banner's Elk and its surrounding country, including all the places named herein, is too recent to need recording here. The coming of the Rev. Edgar Tufts, however, was the most fortunate event in the history of that section. (See chapter on Schools.)

On Foot to Banner's Elk.—Miss Morley gives us this account of her trip to Banner's Elk. Does that "gold tree" still stand we wonder? The only way to find out is to go and see.

"From Valle Crucis to Banner Elk, under the Beech Mountain, is another day's walk, when again you take the longest way up Dutch Creek to see the pretty waterfall there and where the clematis is a white veil over the bushes, and up the steep road by Hanging Rock where the gold tree grows. This is an oak, known far and near because its top is always golden yellow. The leaves come out yellow in the spring, remain so all summer, and in the fall would doubtless turn yellow if they were not already that color. The people say there is a pot of gold buried at the roots, but this pleasant fancy has not taken a serious enough hold to menace the life of the tree.

"Stopping at a picturesque, old time log house to rest, a little girl invites you to go to the top of Hanging Rock, which invitation you gladly accept, thereby getting one of the most enjoyable walks of the summer, your little guide telling you all the way about the flowers and the birds and stopping under an overhanging cliff with great secrecy to show you a round little bird's nest with eggs in it cleverly hidden in the moss. One suspects it was the chance to show this treasure that led the child to propose the long climb to the top of the mountain. The gooseberries of Hanging Rock are without prickles, perhaps because the wild currants growing there have stolen them. Imagine prickly currants! There is plenty of galax on Hanging Rock, the mosses and sedums and all the other growths that make mountain tops so agreeable. The top of Hanging Rock is a slanting ledge, from which the mountain gets its name. At Banner Elk you will want to stay awhile, it is so pretty, and you will also want to climb the beautiful Beech Mountain with its grassy spaces and its charming beech groves.

"From Banner Elk you take the short walk over to 'Calloways,' close under the shadow of the Grandfather, and from here the long and beautiful walk down the Watauga River at the base of the Grandfather, then along the ridges back to Blowing Rock, watching as you go details of the mountain beneath whose northern front you are passing. The open benches, the rocky bluffs and abrupt, tree-clad walls of this side of the mountain, which we call the back of the Grandfather, are not impressive like those long southern slopes sweeping from a summit of a little less than six thousand feet down into the foothills. For the mountain on this side is stopped by the high plateau from which it rises. Yet it is good to be at the back of the Grandfather. From the Watauga road we see the profile from which the mountain is said to have received its name, although one gets a better and far more impressive view of it from a certain point on the mountain itself.

"And so you return to Blowing Rock after days of wandering, only to rest awhile and start again, gaining endurance with every trip until the ten miles' walk that cost you a little weariness becomes the twenty miles' walk that costs you none. You cannot tire of the road, for every mile brings new sights, new sounds, new fragrances, new friends, new flowers, one charm of walking here being the endless variety. No two days are alike; each has its own pleasant adventures."

Meat Camp.—This was one of the first places to be settled in Ashe County, William Miller, the Blackburns and James Jackson going there from the Jersey Settlement as early as 1799, while Ebenezer Fairchild, of the same colony, settled on Howard's Creek, only a short distance away. Jackson's grave is still pointed out in the woods near the site of the old Jackson Meeting House, while the cabin of an old hunter named Abbey stood in what is now the garden of John C. Moretz. Brown got the first grant to land on this creek, part of the Lindsey Patterson farm, before he had ever seen it, having entered it from the natural boundaries furnished him by Daniel Boone and his associates. The cabin in which the old hunters stored their meat and hides when on hunts in this region stood in a rocky patch just above the bend of Moretz's mill pond, the foundation of the old chimney still showing above ground. It was this camp and the use to which it was put as a sort of primitive packing house that gave the name of Meat Camp to the creek. John Moretz and his wife and family came to Meat Camp in September, 1839. There was already an old mill there when he came, which he bought from Samuel Cooper, who then moved to Meadow Creek. The dam of the old mill was of logs, but John Moretz put sixty men to work erecting the stone dam which still stands. With the grinding and other work of the mill was also a carding machine. But late in the fall of 1847 the mill burned, the supposed act of an incendiary, as it occurred just before day. But he rebuilt, leaving out the linseed oil feature only. After his death Alfred J. Moretz tore that mill down and built the one which still stands. Alfred Moretz moved to his present home at Deep Gap in April, 1885.

The Rich Mountain.—This mountain deserves its name, for it is richer than most bottom lands. This is true of the top as well as of the slopes and coves. It is said that Ezra Stonecypher lived in a cabin above T. P. Adams' barn, and ashes and charcoal are still plowed up there. But, like Daniel Boone, Ezra loved plenty of elbow-room, and so, when a man moved on to Cove Creek and settled there, Ezra moved to Norris's Fork of Meat Camp and built a poplar log cabin. This was several miles from the Cove Creek intruder, and Ezra was happy for a time, but only for a time, as another pushing person obtruded himself on Meat Camp and settled there, which was the straw that broke the camel's back, for Ezra pulled up stakes and moved to Kentucky. One of his sons met Col. Thomas Bingham there during the Civil War, and proved that he knew all about Rich Mountain and that section of the county. Then Dr. Calloway, it seems, got a grant to two tracts called the Big and Little Cay-vit (Caveat?), and after awhile, say about 1840 or 1845, Col. Edmund Jones got title to some of the mountain and pastured his cattle there. Several people have lived at what is still called the Jones Place on Rich Mountain, but Allen Beech went there from Caldwell in 1848 and remained several years, his son, Allen W., having been born there February 11, 1854. The late Hon. R. Z. Linney bought the Tater Hill and other land on the Rich Mountain about 1902 and had a turnpike built from the Rich Mountain Gap above Boone to the gap in Rich Mountains above Silverstone, through which a road from Meat Camp passes over to Cove Creek and Zionville. Dr. H. McD. Little owns part of the Rich Mountain and pastures many cattle there. The two-story rock house on Dr. Little's land was built by Col. R. Z. Linney and stands on what is also known as the Jones Place. Part of this rock house fell down in June, 1915.

The Tater Hill.—No one ever makes any apology for calling this striking mountain peak by its real name—Tater Hill. For it was never a potato hill, potatoes being mere ornaments for the skill of French chefs. Taters are what we were "raised" on, while city children were "reared" on potatoes. The first man to see the charm of this lonely spot was one Chapley Wellburn. He entered it in April, 1799, four hundred acres of it, and lived there, probably hunting for a living, the people who live on lower levels being the only ones who indulge in the pastime of earning a "livelihood." Well, he thought he had a title to that land, and in 1876 J. B. Todd, by order of the court, conveyed this title to one of his descendants in Wilkes (Deed Book R, p. 108). But Alfred Adams knew a thing or two, one of them being that adverse possession under color of title would "ripen" that title into an "indefeasible estate of inheritance," or words to that general effect. So he got the very best "color" "the air," to wit, a grant from the sovereign State of North Carolina— not from Sovereign Linn, who was living in this county at that time. Adams occupied about three hundred acres of his grant, and when he locked horns with H. M. and W. N. G. Wellburn, through his grantee, John H. Bingham, about the year 1902, over the entire four hundred acres and other lands also, he won three hundred of them handily. (See Minute Docket E, p. 154, Clerk's Office.) It developed in the trial of that suit that one

Flannery, meaning not necessarily that he had no family, but that he might have been almost *any* Flannery, claimed the land in the flatwoods under Tater Hill, but left about 1849, after which a man named James, but whether John James or James John is not known, came and brought a pack of hounds with him. Hounds have to eat. So do wolves. In the duel to see which should eat the other, the wolves won. James thought his turn might come next, either to eat or to be eaten, so he returned to Alexander County, whence he had come, which, sad as that fate might be, was better than furnishing the funeral baked meat for a lupine holiday. Then, about 1902, came the late Romulus Z. Linney, who, remembering that his old namesake had been "fetched up" by wolves, boldly entered on this demesne and retained possession till his demise, demesne and demise having different meanings. But he built a rock wing to his four-room dwelling, which still stands and in which he spent many happy days. This is the gentleman who, before he had tasted of the delights of the Tater Hill, was offered a high office in Washington, D. C. In declining it, he said that he would not give up his spring rambles in the Brushy Mountains of Wilkes for any office within the gift of the American people. But he gave them up for Tater Hill!

The Grandfather Mountain.—Following is Miss Morley's description of this oldest mountain on earth:

"The path beyond the river [Watauga] is cut through dense kalmia and *rhododendron maximum* (our laurel) that make a wide band along the base of the mountain, then it leads up and up through the more open forest. *There is no sweeter walk in the world than that up Grandfather Mountain,* where the path winds among the trees, a canopy of leaves screening the sky, the forest shutting from view the outer world. Once there were large wild cherry trees on the slopes of the Grandfather, but the wood being valuable . . . there are only saplings left, and a few patriarchs that, though useless for lumber, give an air of dignity to the forest in company with the clear gray shafts of the tulip trees, the grand old chestnuts, the oaks, the maples, beeches, birches, ashes and lindens that mingle their foliage with that of the pines and spruces.

PEAKS OF GRANDFATHER MOUNTAIN

By permission of author and publishers of "The Carolina Mountains."

"You pass beside or under large detached boulders covered with saxifrages, sedums, mosses and ferns, and in whose crevices mountain-ash trees and twisted hemlocks have taken root as though for purposes of decoration, and in the damp hollows away from the path great jack vines hang from tree tops. The rock ledges sometimes make caves where bears were wont to live, for the Grandfather was once a famous place for bears. Squirrels still 'use on the mountain,' as the people say, and a 'boomer' will be apt to bark down at you as you go along. You hear the waters of a stream in the ravine below, and here and there you cross a natural garden of 'balimony' or some other precious herb that the people gather in the season. About two-thirds of the way up you take a path that branches off to the left and leads you over the mossy rocks to an open place on the edge of a gorge, where, looking off, you see the clear-cut profile of the Grandfather sculptured on the edge of a rocky bluff, the bushy hair that rises from the forehead consisting of fir trees that when whitened by the winter snow give a venerable appearance to the stone face. Somewhat above this profile from this point is also visible another, with smaller and rounder features, which of course is the Grandmother.

"Returning to the main path and continuing the ascent, the way grows wilder, and, if possible, sweeter. One has a sense of rising spiritually as well as physically. At the base of a high cliff, framed in foliage and crowned with the rosy-flowered *rhododendron catawbiense,* gushes out the famous Grandfather Spring that is only ten degrees above freezing throughout the summer. Up to this point there is a bridle path; beyond here it is necessary to walk. The rose-bay still in bloom clings to the rocks, in whose crevices little dwarf trees have taken root along with the mosses, ferns and saxifrages.

"The path gets very steep and rocky. You are now among the balsam firs, those trees to name which is to name a perfume, and you go climbing up over their strong red roots. The pathway becomes a staircase winding about moss-trimmed rocks in whose crevices are tiny contorted balsams like Japanese flower-pot trees. Enormous coal-black lichens hang from the cliffs and the ground is softly carpeted with mossy growths and oxalis, out from whose pretty pale leaves look myriads of pink- and white blossoms. Long after the *rhododendron catawbiense* is done blooming below, one finds it in its prime on the high peaks of the Grandfather.

"Up among the balsam firs and about the rocks grow large sour gooseberries and enormous sweet huckleberries, and it was here we found a new and delicious fruit. The bushes crowding the woods in places were loaded with bright red globes the size of a small cherry, each dangling from a slender stem. These delightful berries were mere skins of juice, tiny wine-bottles full of refreshment for a summer day . . . we discovered them on other mountains, though never much below an altitude of six thousand feet . . . Up through the spruces and balsams you mount in the resplendent day, lingering at every step . . . Thus climbing through the resplendent day you reach the summit, 'Calloway's High Peak,' the highest point on the mountain, but from which one cannot command the circle of the horizon. It is necessary to get the view from two points, which is all the better. The rocks at the lookout towards the south being covered with heather, one can lie on the delightful couch studded all over with little white starry flowers, to rest and receive the view . . . In the distance lies White Top, on whose summit three States meet . . .

"Leaving this place and walking on to the point that looks to the south, one shares the feelings and almost the faith of Michaux. The view is very impressive, because of that steep descent of the mountain into the foothills, the long spurs sweeping down in fine lines to a great depth . . . The Black Mountains stand forth very high and very blue, and beyond them, among the many familiar forms, are distinguished what one supposes to be the faint blue line of the Smokies, or is it the nearer Balsams? . . . Sooner or later you will find your way to McRae's, which is to the south side of the Grandfather what Calloway's is to the north side, a farmhouse, where you can stay awhile. There is a trail over the end of the Grandfather by which you can go directly from Calloway's to McRae's, but to strike this trail you have to walk down the Linville River, which, rising in an open space but a stone's throw from the head of the Watauga, flows in quite the opposite direction, and through so narrow a pass that you have to keep crossing and recrossing it, no small matter in a season of rains, for there are no foot logs at all . . . But the Linville is one of the streams you are glad to know through all its sparkling length, from the spring behind the Grandfather to where it escapes in wild glee through the gorge below the falls. There are peacocks at McRae's, and Mr. McRae has not forgotten how to play on the bagpipes that have so stirred the blood of his race . . . But you will have to coax him to do it. McRae's stands on the Yonahlossee road that connects Linville, just below the mountain, with Blowing Rock . . . From McRae's there is a path up the Grandfather . . . to another peak reached by a very sweet climb through the balsams, which, in this region, are smaller and more companionable than the straight giants of the Black Mountains, these of the Grandfather being twisted and friendly and profoundly fragrant. From this peak one can see in all directions, excepting where one of the Grandfather's black summits obstructs the view.

"It is the lichens growing an the rocks that give so sombre an appearance to the top of the Grandfather, those big, black lichens with loose and curled up edges. Grandfather's black, rocky top is eight miles long, and once Mr. Calloway (with the assistance of others) blazed out a rude trail so that we could all take that wonderful knife-edge walk up in the sky over the peaks of the Grandfather, Indian ladders—that is, a tall tree trunk from which the branches have been lopped, leaving protruding ends for steps—helping us up otherwise insurmountable cliffs.

"The Yonahlossee road ought to be followed early in the summer, for then the meadowy tops of the long spurs are like noble parks created for man's pleasure. The *rhododendron catawbiense* lies massed about in effective groups and covered with rosy bloom, beyond which one looks out over a wide landscape of mountains and clouds. From these open, flower-decked spaces the road passes into the shadowy forest, to emerge upon a bushy slope where blazing reaches of flame-colored azaleas astound your senses. There are other flowers along the way, but you scarcely see them, intoxicated as you are with the glory of the rhododendrons, and after them the azaleas, for these marvelous growths almost never blossom within sight of each other. You would say they know, like ladies at a ball, how important it is to avoid each other's colors.

"Under the trees along the roadside the earth is covered with a superb carpet of large and handsome galax leaves, for the Grandfather is distinguished by the great beauty and abundance of its galax. Laurel, too, claims standing room on the side of the grand old mountain, and here, as elsewhere, one notices the apparent capriciousness of the laurel, which forms an impenetrable jungle for long stretches and then stops short, not a laurel bush to be seen for some distance, when with equal suddenness it reappears again.

"The splendid slopes of the Grandfather are enchanting also when autumn colors them—deep red huckleberry balds, trees wreathed in crimson woodbine, vivid sassafras, tall gold and crimson and scarlet forest trees—it seems more like the brilliant display of a northern forest. You would say that the outpouring of fragrance must pass with the summer. Not so. As you walk among the trees in their thin, bright attire you have a feeling of their friendliness. The forest, as it were, breathes upon you, you are drowned in the sweetness of resinous perfumes that distil from a thousand pines, firs and hemlocks. When the leaves of the trees are growing scarce and changing to duller hues, into the open spaces witch-hazel weaves its gold-wreathed wands and brightens the woods like sunshine.

"Turning to the right from the Yonahlossee Road, a short distance up from McRae's, you walk along under the chestnut trees just beginning to open their burs, away from the Grandfather out over a beautiful spur that ends in an open, rounded summit. The road to this place has side paths that lead you to high cliffs, whence you look off towards Blowing Rock, and where the sweetest of mountain growths cling to the crevices

THE YONAHLOSSEE ROAD

By permission of author and publishers of "The Carolina Mountains."

and drape the edges of all the rocks. For some reason the trees here are small, the chestnuts being not much larger than bushes, but the nuts are proportionately large, the largest nuts one ever saw on our native chestnut trees, and they are peculiarly sweet, again a hint to the fruit-makers, who from this could doubtless create a nut as large as the chestnuts of France and as sweet as those of America. The summit of this little mountain of the large chestnuts is one of your favorite places to go for a day of rest and contemplation. It is a lovely, soothing place, as it ought to be, for it is the Grandmother Mountain."

Grafting French Chestnuts.—Mr. Jack Farthing, of Timbered Ridge, demonstrated some years ago that French and Italian chestnuts, when grafted to the native trees, will produce as large chestnuts as those imported as French and Italian, and Newton Banner also has several trees so grafted which are never failing.

Dr. Buxton's Description.—A letter from Rev. Jarvis Buxton, which speaks with greatest admiration of the grand sunrise seen from the top of the Grandfather Rock, is thus quoted in the "Life of Skiles" (p. 50):

"I have seen the glorious sunrise at sea, but nothing of sky at sea ever filled my vision with such deep impressions of glory as came from those gorgeous skies—brilliant hues ever shifting, dissolving and re-combining, ever growing in brightness as the morning advanced, till the vast heavens seemed filled with the glory and flame of color; while below, stretching far away into the azure, the hills still slept their lowly sleep of silence, with the heavens all aglow above them."

Beaver Dams.—There is no more picturesque section than this in all the North Carolina mountains, nor is there any population more self-respecting and law-abiding. It has never known lawlessness, depravity or loose living. Schools and churches have been common since it became sufficiently settled to support them. From an account book kept by the late Dudley Farthing, his son, Col. Henry Harrison Farthing, of Timbered Ridge, can tell most, if not all, of the residents of this section in 1826 and 1827. George Wilson lived on Fork Ridge, which is between

Cove and Beaver Dam creeks; Benjamin Harley lived where Lewis Farthing now lives; Joel Dyer, father of Ben., lived where James Cable now lives; Micajah Lunsford lived up under the Stone Mountain, where the Millsaps and Eggers now live, but his family moved to Tennessee after the death of Micajah; a man named Wallace lived in the "Pick Breeches" country, which is on the right of the Baker's Gap road, going west, between where the Millsaps and Eggers families now live and the top of the mountain.⁷ Col. Phineas Horton told Mr. W. S. Farthing forty years ago (1875) that he had helped to build the road up Beaver Dams and over Baker's Gap, which was the main thoroughfare from North Carolina to Tennessee in 1826, and over which drovers took their stock of all kinds, but principally hogs. Mrs. William W. Farthing, widow of the minister of that name, lived just below Bethel Church, though the house is now gone, and entertained the traveling public. Her husband died there in January, 1827, having lived there only since the previous November. Thomas Curtis lived where Lee Osborn now lives at the foot of the George Gap road on the Cove Creek side, and he said that the first clearing on Beaver Dams was the field in which the Farthing graveyard now is and where a log cabin stood. It was there that the first log-raising and log-rolling, or clearing, took place on Beaver Dams. Curtis's sons went west, but in 1910 a greatgrandson, Webb Mast, by name, came back and had a picture taken of the old Ben Webb house site. The Webb cabin stood above the place where Alfred Trivett now lives, Webb having moved to middle Tennessee after he sold to Rev. W. W. Farthing in 1826. One of Ben Webb's daughters married Reuben Mast and died in that old cabin. Reuben Mast then married one of Thomas Curtis's daughters and moved to Texas. It was in this first cabin that Bishop Asbury stayed on one of his trips through Beaver Dams and when it was covered by only a few boards. When Mrs. W. W. Farthing kept the tavern on Beaver Dams, an old man stayed all night there and

---

⁷ Big and Little Hessian are names given to two peaks on the Tennessee-North Carolina line, near Zionville. They are said not to be really named Hessian, but Hay-Shin, because although they are the shin or shank of the mountain they have hay on them, nevertheless. Some claim that they are named the Big and Little Ration because "out-lyers," during the Civil War got their rations there, the rations being left by friends and relatives living near.

started away the next morning. He was never seen again alive, but some time afterwards a dead body was found at the mouth of the Stone Mountain Branch, and it was supposed to have been his, and it was also thought that he had left the road over the Baker Gap and gone to sleep in the woods, and, waking up, became bewildered and followed the branch to its mouth, where he starved or froze. His name was never learned. The body was buried in the graveyard where Rev. W. W. Farthing and his wife are buried, just above where Alfred Trivett now lives. The first mill on Beaver Dams was one mile above Bethel Church, where an old mill is still running today. The Timbered Ridge, on which Col. H. H. Farthing lives, was so called from the heavy timber which grew there. Behind his house, on a high plateau, is a most commanding view, easily reached by a well graded road, and from which the gorge of the Watauga River, the gloomy slopes of the great Beech Mountain, the valley of Cove Creek, and the Big and Little Hessian, the Bald and the Elk mountains can be plainly seen. It invites a magnificent hotel and summer resort adornments, and for climate is unrivaled.

Boone's Beaver Dams Trail.—The Cable family who first settled on Dry Run, just over the Baker Gap, claim that they were living on Boone's trail into Kentucky. That trail is said to have passed down Cove Creek to the place where Dr. J. B. Phillips now lives, from which point it left Watauga River, passed over Ward's Gap, and then followed a ridge down behind the homes of W. S. and J. H. Farthing, crossing the Beaver Dam Creek near where Alfred Trivett now lives—the old Ward and W. W. Farthing home—and passed on up the ridge by the Star Spring over the Star or Stair Gap to Roan's Creek in Tennessee. The Star Springs are at the foot of the Stone Mountain, one being at the head of the Stone Mountain Branch, which empties into Watauga River near W. A. Smitherman's farm, one mile below the Flat Shoals, the other being at the head of the Little Prong of Beaver Dam Creek, the two springs being scarcely 100 yards apart, but on opposite sides of a ridge. Star is the name given these springs because of particles of mica in them which shine like stars. There is little doubt that this was

Boone's trail, but it seems not probable that he would have gone so much out of his way, when by going across the Grave Yard or Straddle Gap and over the mountain at Zionville, he could have got to Shoun's Crossroads on Roan's Creek, and thence followed the Laurel Creek almost directly to Abingdon, and thence to Cumberland Gap, a route many miles nearer than by going by Sycamore Shoals, and thence to Cumberland Gap, and over a more level country. He did go via Sycamore Shoals in 1775, but not in 1769.

Beech Creek and Poga.—The first man Col. H. H. Farthing remembers as living in the Beech Creek country was a man named Hately, who resided near the mouth of Beech Creek. This was long before the Civil War. I. Valentine Reese has lived a mile below since before the Civil War, where he has carried on a mercantile business. After the turnpike was finished down the river, say about 1854, the country began to settle up slowly, though it was used principally for ranging cattle, hunting and fishing. There was also a Harman settlement near the mouth of Beaver Dam Creek, but on the opposite side of the river, near what is now called the Cow Ford. But Golder Councill Harman and John Tester settled there even before the turnpike was built. The first settlers on Poga were Samuel Trivett, Phillip Church and Vincent Greer, although some man had settled on the Dark Ridge Branch before these came to that section. Vincent Greer lived in the Loggy Gap, he having married Jennie Brewer, "a big, portly woman, sir," to use a quite descriptive phrase of one of the neighbors. All Poga has been cleared within the recollection of men yet living. Poga is said to have derived its name from the alleged fact that a man got lost in that section and wandered around a long time. When found, he said he had been "pokin" around all day—hence poky or pogy. But in his "Rhymes of Southern Rivers," M. V. Moore claims that pogy is nothing but a corruption of boggy, which was also the name of the Elk River.

CHAPTER XV.[1]
Schools.

Ante-Bellum Education.—Much has been written about the want of education of the mountain people. Some of it has been deserved and some undeserved. There have always been schools in Watauga County. Tradition tells of schools as far back as the coming of the first settlers into this country. It is true that education was not general, neither was it of an advanced type. But children were taught the rudiments—the three R's—from time immemorial. The minutes of Three Forks Church show chirography that would be a credit to the best pensman of today,[2] and while the spelling is sometimes erratic and lacks uniformity, the language is terse and plain, leaving no doubt as to its meaning. Some of the phrases are even more forceful than any of the present time, and the tendency to follow Bible language is marked, showing close Bible study. When a member was admitted to the church, the invariable formula was "a door was opened and ———— received into the church." That the church doors are always open to any who would enter, goes without saying, but that "a door" was opened for the reception of that particular person seems far more expressive and forceful. "She confessed her transgression," was another phrase of strength and scriptural authority. And even now we have expressions which transcend any that modern philology has substituted for those of the sixteenth century. "He heired that land," is far more significant and direct than to say "he inherited" it. We "mend" when we improve in health, which is far better than to say that we "get better." "It don't differ" certainly is more economical and quite as expressive as "it makes no difference."

---

[1] Space will not permit the record of public schools, a full account of which can be obtained from the reports of the Superintendent of Education.

[2] John W. Owen appears to have recorded these minutes, which are correct in diction and spelling. Thomas Morris, a kinsman of Mrs. Geo. L. Van Dyke, was a fine scribe also, his copy-book, still preserved by her, showing specimens of his writings when he was a boy of twelve years, being remarkable. All writing of those days was done with a quill pen.

But an adept at such matters has given an entire chapter to our short-comings, as well as to our long-goings in that respect. Hear him:

Peculiarities of Our Speech.—In chapter XIII Mr. Kephart sums up many of the most striking peculiarities of our speech which differentiate us from most people. Following is a condensation of some of them: The insertion of sounds where they do not belong, as musician*er;* the substitution of one sound for another, due to a change of vowels, as *ruther* for rather; difficulty in pronouncing diphthongs, as *brile* for broil; the occasional substitution of consonants, as *atter* for after; the conversion of nouns into verbs of action, as "that bear'll *meat* me a month;" the coining of a verb from an adjective, as *"much* that dog, and see won't he come along;" the creation of nouns from verbs, as "I didn't hear no *give-out* at meetin'," or from an adjective, as "Nance took the biggest *through* at meetin'," and "a person has a *rather,*" meaning preference; the use of corrupt forms of verbs, as *gwine* for going, *het* for heat; the formation of peculiar adjectives from verbs, as "them's the *travelin'est* horses I ever seed;" the use of verbs for adverbs, as "if I'd a been *thoughted* enough;" the use of the old syllabic plural, as in *nesties, posties, beasties;* the great abundance of pleonasms, as "I done done it," and "in this day and time;" the use of double, thribble and even quadruple and quintuple negatives, as "I ain't never seen no men-folks of no kind do no washing;" intensifying expression, as "we had one more *time,*" "we jist pintblank got to do it," etc. Biscuit-bread, ham-meat, rifle-gun, rock-clift, ridin' critter, cow-brute, man-person, women-folks, preacher man, granny-woman and neighbor people are common everywhere in the mountains.

We Are Commended for Much.—This author in the same chapter credits us with seldom being at a loss for words, even if we have to create them. They are, however, always produced from English roots, but if all else fails, we fall back on "spang," a coinage peculiarly our own. The use of the old English past tense of holp, stunk and swum is commended, holp being used both as a preterite and as infinitive, and he gives examples of a strong preterite with dialectical change of the vowel in brung, drap, drug, friz, shet and shuck, and of weak preterites in div, driv, fit, rid, riz, seed, throwed, etc. Even our most illiterate "startle" the "furriner" by the glib use of such words as tutor for rear or train, denote for signify, caviled for quarreled, discern for realize and proffered for offered. He says that cuckold and moon-calf, which have none but a literary usage in America, are often heard in the mountains, and of the much-derided "hit" he says, "His, pronoun hit, antedates English itself, being the Anglo-Saxon neuter of he;" and on another page, 280, he says hit and it are used indifferently, as euphony may seem to require. We use fray for affray or fight, and fraction for rupture, which we find in Troilus and Cressida. "Feathered into them" he says is heard here, and refers to the time when arrows were driven into the flesh up to the feathers. We call married women "mistress" and "miz" for short, and aged men "old grandsir." We still "back" letters, instead of addressing them, as was the custom before envelopes were invented. We call a choleric person "tetchous," and, like Ben Franklin, we "carry" our wives and daughters to different places when we accompany them there. To most of us molasses is "them," and license to marry invariably is called "a pair of licenses." Of some of our idioms he cites: "I swapped hosses, and I'll tell you for why;" "Your name ain't much common;" "You think me of it in the mornin';" "The woman's aimin' to go to meetin';" "I had a head to plow today;" "Reckon Pete was knowin' to the sarcumstance;" "I knowed in reason she'd have the mullygrubs over them doin's," and "You cain't handily blame her."

Place Names.—He gives a number of names of places which have adhered to them for years merely because of some event which happened there. Among these are Dusk Camp Run, Mad Sheep Mountain, Dog Slaughter Creek, Drownin' Creek, Burnt Cabin Branch, Broken Leg, Raw Dough, Burnt Pone and Sandy Mush. The fighting spirit blazes forth in Fighting Creek, Shooting Creek, Gouge-eye, Vengeance, Four-Killer and Disputantia. Personal names are common everywhere, as Jake's Creek, Dick's Creek and Jonathan's Creek. But he had not heard of the Snow Wine Branch of the Beech Mountains, and so did not include it.

Not Guilty in Watauga.—Several words and colloquialisms are recorded which seem strange to some of us in Watauga County, as gin for if, do' for door, dauncy for mincing, doneygal for sweetheart, toddick or taddle for the toll-measure at a mill, swivvet for hurry, upscuddle for quarrel, etc.

Occult Errors.—Both Mr. Kephart and Miss Morley are struck with the use of "soon" for "early," but to most of us there is nothing wrong in this use, and we "fling a rock" in South Carolina as well as in the mountains when to "furriners" we throw a stone. Why, too, should we not ask, "Are you plumb bereft?" if we wish to know if one is entirely bereft of one's senses? What, too, is wrong with "Sam went to Andrews or to Murphy, one," or "I don't much believe the wagon will come today," or "'Tain't powerful long to dinner, I don't reckon?" They may be plainly wrong to others, but to us they are "plumb right." In conclusion, he adds that instead of having a limited vocabulary of three hundred words, he had himself taken down from the lips of Carolina mountaineers some eight hundred dialectical or obsolete words, to say nothing of the much greater number of standard English terms that they command.

No Foreign Words Admitted.—Mr. Kephart has detected only three words of directly foreign origin in the vocabulary of the mountaineers (p. 289)—doney, from Spanish or Italian donna; kraut, from the Germans, and "sashiate" or "sashay," from the French chasse. And he calls attention to the fact that, although the eastern band of Cherokees have lived with the Smoky Mountain highlanders for from seventy to eighty years, the mountain dialect contains not one word of Cherokee origin. Many of the whites, however, do use the word "O-see-you," which is the Cherokee for "Howdy do." What he calls the obsolete title of linkister or interpreter, is nothing but a corruption of the present word linguister.

Our Literary and Moonshine Fame Secure.—Kephart, in his "Southern Highlanders," agrees with us in thinking that ours is the purest English spoken anywhere in the world today. As has been shown, he commends us for very, very much. He condemns us for little, if anything. And to this high praise we can now add that of no less distinguished a literary lion than Mr. Cecil Chesterton, of London, England—not Connecticut. This is how he is quoted in the *Literary Digest* for June 19, 1915 (p. 1469): "I do not want anybody to suppose that I am suggesting that the American language is in any way inferior to ours (the English!). In some ways it has improved upon it in vigor and raciness. In others it adheres more closely to the English of the best period. Thus an American uses the word 'sick' as it is used in the Jacobean Bible—to his not inconsiderable embarrassment sometimes, I should think, when he finds himself in European society. Also he uses old forms like 'gotten,' which we have abbreviated. If you want the purest Shakespearian English, I believe you have to go among the illicit whiskey distillers on the Southern mountains. But I was never fortunate enough (in a double sense) to come in contact with this ancient and delightful race."

Ante-Bellum School Teachers.—Following is a partial list of school teachers who taught at various places in Watauga prior to the Civil War, as remembered by several old men and women at various points in what is now and used to be Watauga County: James McCanless, William Roland, George N. Evans, Vine Thompson, H. H. Prout, Mack McCleard, Culver Wise, Josiah Wise, Levi Chandler, Joseph Culberson, Levi Chandler, John Wise, Alex Dobson, John Patterson, Sterling Sallens, Wm. C. Wise, George Grissom, Isaac and Harvey Wise, ——————— Miller, Wm. Thomas, Pink Matheson, Erastus Longacre, Samuel Watson, a one-armed man; Levi Heath, H. A. McBride, Joel Dyer, Wm., Reuben and James Farthing, William Draughan, ———————Byland, Poovey, Wm. Cannon, T. C. Coffey, Abner C. Farthing, Edward Faucett, Lewis Church, Thomas Hodges, Martin Harrison, Joshua Rominger, Jonathan Norris, Joseph Woodring and Christian Woodring, L. Dow Allen, W. W. Presnell, Hamilton Blackburn, H. B. Blackburn, Charles Lippard, T. C. Land, Carroll McBride, A. F. and H. A. Davis, Timothy Moretz, Leonard Phillips, Thomas Bingham, J. B. Miller, Frank Whittington, Christian Moretz, Dr. ——————— Thurman, David Calton, Geo. Dyer, John Kennedy, Robert Coffey, Elbert Dinkins.

Our Schools.—The public schools of Watauga are matters of record and need no extended mention in these pages. To rescue the story of ante-bellum efforts in education is quite as much as there is occasion for in this work. In old days there were no schools till after the crops were gathered in and secured for the winter. Then men were employed to teach in various localities upon written contract, the teacher boarding among the patrons. There is still preserved among the many valuable old papers of Col. Henry H. Farthing, of Timbered Ridge, a contract duly executed between the subscribers and Alfred Fox for a school to commence on the 9th of November, 1835, and last three months, for which the teacher was to receive $1.50 for each scholar and board for himself, and the subscribers "agree to tolerate him with due and legal authority in school." It is nowhere recorded that any school teacher in these mountains got rich by teaching school, but Massachusetts herself has no such record for any of her ante-bellum pedagogues, either. Then, too, there were what were termed "Saturday and Sunday teachers," who taught on those days, or, sometimes, only on Saturdays, when they were called "Saturday teachers." The coming into Watauga County of Rev. Henry H. Prout in 1843, or 1845, to teach school was a great step forward, and old men now living on upper Watauga speak of him as the most scholarly man they ever met, and credit him with having taught them more than they ever learned from any other teacher. Unfortunately, during the first term of the regular school at Valle Crucis, about 1845-46, several unruly boys were sent there from east of the Blue Ridge, under the impression that the school was a sort of reformatory for recalcitrant youths. This disheartened several of the ladies connected with the mission, and they withdrew one after another (Skiles, p. 20). However, after Mr. Thurston's death, in 1846, Rev. Jarvis Buxton came, after which the school got a good start, Mr. Prout going up to Mrs. Edward Moody's to teach.

"Straights and Pot-Hooks."—Mrs. Battle Bryan used to tell her son, Col. W. L. Bryan, of Boone, that the way in which writing was taught in her girlhood was by requiring the be-

THE APPALACHIAN TRAINING SCHOOL, BOONE, N. C.

Photo. by Vest.

ginner to make numerous vertical lines, one after the other, till a degree of perfection was attained, when the same straight lines were required to be made, but with the addition of small curved lines, turning upward, and called hooks. The arithmetics that preceded Davies' were Pike's, Smiley's and Fowler's, and the spelling book that was the forerunner of Webster's Blue Back was Dillsworth's. A few of these old school teachers are now distinctly remembered by Col. W. L. Bryan, who supplies the following:

Phillip Church.—When about twelve or thirteen years old, he went to Phillip Church, who lived in the edge of Ashe County, near Riverside. He taught at the old Lookabill school house, which stood close to David Lookabill's residence, one mile east of Soda Hill, and on the road leading from the Deep Gap of the Blue Ridge to the Deep Gap between the Snake and Rich mountains where those mountains come together and where the road forks, one prong going to Zionville, N. C., and the other to Trade, in Tennessee. It was a free school, which was usually taught in the fall and winter, after the crops had been gathered and there was little for the children to do. He attended this school about three months, or one session. Soon after the close of that session Church married Samuel Trivett's daughter, and moved with his father-in-law to the Poga Creek settlement between Beech Creek and Ford of Elk, where he died in 1914. Colonel Bryan got as far as "abase" at that time.

Jonathan Norris.—This pedagogue was called "Lame Jonathan," because he had rubbed brimstone—powdered sulphur—over a skin eruption and had then gone in swimming. The result was almost complete bodily paralysis, though his mind remained clear. He taught at the Lookabill school house also, and Colonel Bryan attended his school parts of two terms. Norris lived till he was about sixty years old, when he died at his home near Soda Hill.

Eli M. Farmer.—Colonel Bryan's next teacher was Eli M. Farmer, at the same school house. This gentleman married a Miss Austin, of Caldwell County, and died on Cove Creek about 1890.

Burt Davis.—This was the next teacher, but he taught at Soda Hill school house and at Eli Brown's school house. Davis married Carolina Moretz first, and, after her death, Martha Lookabill. His first wife was a daughter of Squire Johnnie Moretz, and his second the daughter of David Lookabill. The latter still lives on Elk Creek, above Todd. Davis himself, however, died about 1900.

Todd Miller, of Wilkes County, was the next of Colonel Bryan's instructors, and he taught at the Ben Greene school house between the latter gentleman's residence and where his son, Jacob, now lives on the Little Fork of Meat Camp Creek. It was there that he went through Davies' arithmetic and ended his school days. This was in the fall or winter of 1857, and after the Colonel had been clerking for Joseph Councill and Allen Myrick. Before that he had studied Fowler's arithmetic. That and the blue back spelling book were the only books he had during all his school days. His mother told him that Dillsworth's Speller was the spelling book which had preceded the blue back.

The Twisting Temple.—Battle Bryan called the school house on Meat Camp by this name because the frame was not exactly plumb and square, but leant a little to one side. The district has kept that name ever since. The house stood where Frank Reagan lives now. The district has, however, been divided into the Tugman School and the Green Valley School, and a better house has replaced the Twisting Temple. Still, this old Twisting Temple School District has furnished one congressman, E. S. Blackburn; one lawyer, E. S. Blackburn; two teachers, two physicians, the latter being Thomas Blackburn and B. W. Ferguson.

Lees-McRae Institute.—Without the slightest flourishing of trumpets or sounding of the big bass drum, Rev. Edgar Tufts came to Banner's Elk about 1901 and established a boarding and day school for girls. This has been successful from the beginning and continues to flourish. The terms are reasonable and the instruction thorough. Within recent years Grace Hospital was started, Mrs. Helen Hartly Jenkins, of New York, having given more than anyone else. It is equipped with a complete operating room and laboratory. It has several rooms for patients undergoing treatment. The cool and pure mountain air aids much in all surgical operations. The Grandfather Orphanage was started in the spring of 1914, the Lybrook farm having been secured for that purpose. The capacity of the orphanage has been doubled already. Girls are given practical instruction in many useful arts. The key to these benefactions is "IN, OF, FOR," meaning that they are in the mountains, of the mountains and for the mountain people. This tells the entire story most eloquently. The church which is nearing completion will be one of the most attractive architecturally in the State. The two large conglomerate rocks or pudding stones on either side of the entrance are in themselves rare curiosities. The school most sensibly closes during the cold months of winter, and is open during the summer, spring and fall months, opening in the spring and closing in December. The good already accomplished and yet to be achieved is incalculable.

School Teachers in Boone Before Civil War.—Miss Annie Rutledge, from Wilkesboro, taught in the court house. Miss Barber, of Lenoir, taught in the court house. While being driven in a buggy by Joshua Winkler from Lenoir to Boone, with trunk on back of buggy, they met a man named Dooley as they came up the mountain from Patterson towards Blowing Rock. They talked with him and started on. Soon they found that the trunk was missing. Winkler went back, but never got the trunk. It was never recovered.

Col. J. B. Todd also taught in the court house. After the Civil War Henry Dixon, of Alamance, taught in the court house. W. B. and Robert Arrowood and Professor Blake, of Davidson College, their uncle, taught in a small one-room house which stood in the corner of the lot where Dr. J. W. Jones now lives, near the present drug store. Professor Blake started the school, but left it in charge of his nephews when he returned to Davidson. W. B. Arrowood is now a Presbyterian preacher. They boarded with Dr. J. G. Rivers. Miss Margaret Coffey taught in 1869. After the Arrowoods, came Prof. John McEwen, who taught in Masonic Hall. James Warner taught here three months. James H. Hall, of Mount Airy, also taught at Masonic Hall in 1874. Then came Mr. McEwen. J. F. Spainhour and J. F. Hall taught at the academy which stood where Calvin Cottrell's stable now stands. This consisted of two large rooms, one above the other, and had been built but not quite finished by the Three Forks Baptist Association. It turned the building over to the Boone Baptist Church, which finished it. W. F. Shull was another teacher who has not been forgotten.

A Normal School at Boone.—By chapter 229, Laws of 1885, a normal school was authorized at Boone for the training of teachers, and a sum not to exceed $500.00 was appropriated out of the University Normal School Fund with which to pay instructors. This was a small beginning, but it has had a great ending.

Appalachian Training School.—In 1903, Professors B. B. and D. D. Dougherty were teaching a private school at Boone, having succeeded in securing the erection of a large and commodious building for that purpose. But in that year the legislature incorporated the Appalachian Training School and made an appropriation for its support. It had already begun, however, for in 1899 the sum of $1,500.00 had been appropriated on condition that a like sum should be provided by the people. By several yearly appropriations following the first, the present plant was built, consisting of about a dozen buildings, a water power electric light plant and library. There are 500 or more acres of valuable land belonging to the school. There are three sessions annually, with an attendance of from four to five hundred. There is a competent faculty.

T. P. Adams went to Raleigh at his own expense in 1905 and urged the inauguration of the training school, and when in the late fall of the year the science building was about to be left exposed to the elements all winter, he carried mortar and brick for one month till the roof was on. He also insisted on the purchase of the Edmisten farm, containing the present dam and electric light plant, and in the face of much opposition from other directors, succeeded in having the purchase completed before the option expired.

A History of Watauga County

Skyland Institute.—This school was started about 1891 by Miss Emily C. Prudden. She conducted it for a short time, after which it was turned over to the American Missionary Association. About 1912 this association reconveyed it to Miss Prudden, since which time it has not been open. It was a girls' school, with industrial training, and did a vast amount of good. It was located at Blowing Rock.

The Silverstone public school house is now said to be the best in Watauga County, containing four large rooms and an auditorium with a seating capacity of from 800 to 1,000 people. The chief movers and workers in this were John Mast, Larkin Pennell, Newton Mast, A. J. Wilson, A. L. Wilson and T. P. Adams. It cost, without paint or equipment, $2,000.00, all of which is fully paid. The present term is five months, and in another year it will probably be nine full months. Silverstone School District was the first in the State to vote a special tax to continue the school two months and for compulsory attendance.

Walnut Grove Institute.—In December, 1903, Finley P. Mast agreed to give three acres on the Old Meeting House hill, where the Cove Creek Baptist Church used to stand, for a school building and campus. T. C. McBride, J. H. Bingham, D. C., W. H. and J. C. Mast agreeing to give $100.00 each, and to procure all subscriptions possible, began work and finished the school house in August, 1904. It is large and convenient. This district then voted a tax of thirty cents on each hundred dollars of property and ninety cents on each poll for six years, without a dissenting vote. In 1910 the same tax was renewed for five years, with but two votes in the negative. Not one dollar was paid to complete the actual work of construction of the institute, W. E. Dugger, Ben. Dugger, J. C. Smith, D. C., W. H., J. H. and J. C. Mast doing the work themselves.

Other Schools and Academies.—Cove Creek Academy was built about 1885, Enoch Swift, J. H. McBride, W. F. Sherwood and Asa Wilson being active in its inauguration and subsequent support. Rev. Wiley Swift, who is so active in the cause of the factory children's interests, is a son of Enoch Swift. The academy at Valle Crucis was built about 1909, and W. W. Mast,

T. H. Taylor, T. C. Baird, J. M. Shull, D. F. Mast, W. E. Shipley, C. D. Taylor, W. H. Mast and D. F. Baird were its principal promoters.

Valle Crucis School for Girls.—On the site of the old Ives school has been reared several large and convenient buildings in which a school for girls is taught. It was opened about 1903, Rt. Rev. Junius M. Horner, bishop of the Missionary District of Asheville, being ex-officio its head and directing mind. Many of the girls of the neighborhood have taken advantage of this opportunity to gain an education, while at the same time learning many useful lessons in domestic affairs. Great good is being accomplished and the people are coming more and more to appreciate the advantages offered by this school.

First Agricultural Instruction.—From De Rosset's "Church History of North Carolina" we learn that Bishop Ives had a herd of blooded cattle sent to Valle Crucis, from which it was intended to produce a finer breed of cattle in this section. Also, from Haywood's "Bishops of North Carolina," that the Valle Crucis Farm was early put under the direction of a young agriculturist from New York, which was the first practical instruction ever given in any school or college in North Carolina.

Prominent in the Cause.—Messrs. D. D. and B. B. Dougherty, of Boone, have been and still are active in the cause of education, as is also Col. E. F. Lovill, who for years has done yeoman service for the Appalachian Training School without reward or the hope of reward. He has been for years chairman of the board of trustees. These gentlemen also have been active in trying to get railroads to this section, and have not abated one whit of their efforts because of failure. Moses H. Cone, deceased, late of Blowing Rock, not only built a school house there, but agreed to contribute four dollars for every dollar that was given by anyone else. His loss was irreparable.

The Lenoir School Lands.—On the 16th day of February, 1858, the late William Avery Lenoir conveyed to Thomas Farthing, trustee, five tracts of mountain lands, aggregating about two thousand acres, lying principally on Beech Creek and the waters of Curtis's Creek and Elk River. The considerations moving him thereto were his appreciation of "the kind regard

MISSION SCHOOL AT VALLE CRUCIS.

Photo. by Harris.

manifested toward him by the citizens of Watauga County, to promote the settlement of this new county and the education of the children in the same, and Thomas Farthing's promise to execute the trust without charge or deduction except for taxes, etc." Mr. Farthing was the trustee who was to sell such lands as he could and invest the proceeds in interest-bearing securities for fifteen years after the date of the deed, and then turn the sum so resulting over to such a school board as the State might provide, and if none were so provided, to the school authorities of Watauga County for the education of its children. The Civil War came on, however, and Thomas Farthing died without having executed the trust, whereupon his widow and heirs and W. W. Lenoir, representing the estate of W. A. Lenoir, also deceased, on the 11th of August, 1877, joined in a deed conferring this trust on R. H. Farthing, son of Thomas. The lands have been sold and the proceeds applied as directed. (Deed Book L, p. 409.)

School House Loan Fund.—By chapter 372, Laws 1911, a permanent fund was established to aid in the construction of school houses. This fund was provided from the "fines, forfeitures and penalties" in criminal cases, and the same was to be loaned to such school committees as might need such money to aid in the erection of school houses, to be repaid in ten annual instalments, the whole bearing only four per cent. interest.

Samuel Lusk.—This gentleman was not a schoolmaster, but he was a most conscientious stonemason, and was employed to build a chimney for a schoolhouse on Meat Camp. When the chimney was finished it drew well—very well indeed, but it was in the wrong direction, and instead of drawing the smoke from the fireplace up the flue and out at the top of the chimney, it drew the air from the top of the chimney down into the schoolroom, thereby causing the chimney to smoke outrageously. It was said by James Reagan that it even drew the buzzards out of the sky. This hurt Uncle Sammy's feelings inexpressibly. He came from Lincoln County to the Castle Settlement a few miles above what is now called Todd, but afterwards moved to Dutch Creek, near Valle Crucis, where he died, leaving a family of highly respected children.

Col. W. W. Presnell.—This gentleman lost an arm in the Civil War and had to teach thereafter for a livelihood. His wife also lost an arm during the same trying period while helping to feed a cane mill. The first schoolmaster to whom he went was Eli Mast, who taught in one of the sang factories in the meadow just below Joseph Ward's barn on the old Whittington property. This was about 1847 or 1848. Mark Holtsclaw, Thomas Smith, Wm. Carver, Col. Joe B. Todd, Joshua Fletcher, Larkin Pips, Smith Reece, Jacob Hayes, D. C. Harman and Thomas Hodges were other schoolmasters who taught public schools on Brushy Fork from 1848 till the Civil War. Colonel Presnell also tells of a man called "Master" Huff, a school teacher, master being the most common designation for teachers at that time. He taught writing by causing the students to make straight marks, to which were added loops, called pot-hooks. The Dillsworth Speller preceded the Blue Back many years.

The Ablest Schoolmaster.—But first and best among all these schoolmasters was Thomas Lanier Clingman, for, from 1843 till 1861, he was a teacher in every county in his congressional district. He spent a year or more in Watauga, mining in the Beech Mountains (1870, 1871) and is still well remembered by many of our older citizens. He was a fine angler and an unerring shot with rifle or pistol. And, though he did not teach little children in ante-bellum log school houses, he was constantly instructing the "big" children of these mountains around their firesides and on the hustings—not by books, but by word of mouth, enforced and made indelible by apt illustrations and in most practical ways. There may be more book-learning among us now than in former days, but no people were better versed in all useful information concerning crops, plants, woodcraft, the mechanic arts, minerals and the laws of nature than our unlettered ancestors. General Clingman kept them fully informed as to the progress of the outside world in all matters which concerned their material welfare, and at the same time, far more than all others combined, kept the outside world posted as to the wonderful beauty, resources and advantages of this mountain region—its minerals, its physical phenomena and the progress of its inhabitants. Being a frequent contributor to *Appelton's Journal,* the *National Intelligencer* and other widely circulated periodicals, he was the first and only one to tell the world of the passing of the wonderfully brilliant meteor of 1860, of the destructive waterspouts of 1876, and of the apparent earthquake at the head of Fines Creek, which he visited and explored in 1848 and 1851. Years before the United States established its meteorological station on Mitchell's Peak, General Clingman had explained why the climate of the Asheville Plateau is the dryest east of the Rockies, and it was entirely through his influence that Dr. Arnold Guyot, of Princeton College, and Dr. S. B. Buckley visited and measured all the highest mountains in western North Carolina just before the Civil War. Calhoun, as early as 1835, had foretold the existence of the Blacks as the highest mountains east of the Mississippi, and, although Professor Mitchell actually measured them soon afterwards, his services to science were negatived by the uncertain data he took concerning their altitude. Compared with the work of Clingman, Buckley and Guyot among all our mountains, Mitchell's barometrical measurements among the Blacks was inconsiderable.

Statesman, Soldier, Scientist.—When North Carolina makes up her jewels no gem among the brilliants that sparkle in her coronet of achievement will shine with "a purer, serener or a more resplendant light" than that of Thomas Lanier Clingman, for as statesman, soldier and scientist, as well as teacher, guide and friend, he was incorruptible, patriotic and inspiring. But for nothing that he did will his memory be more precious or more richly cherished than for his dignified and noble refusal to contend with an honorable gentleman whose mouth had been closed by death in an effort to establish the truth as to who had first visited and measured the highest peak of the Black Mountain chain.

Country Above Fame.—For at this time the country was torn and rent asunder by the demon of sectionalism, and Clingman found better use for his time and talents than in contending for an honor which, however great, was as dust in the scales when weighed against the welfare of his native State and section.

Then, too, his fame was already secure, for he had met upon the arena of House and Senate the doughtiest and most skilful of the political gladiators of the fifties, and had lowered his sword to none. Looming blue-black on the border of North Carolina and Tennessee, General Clingman knew that there was a yet statelier and more imposing pile than the Blacks, and that at the culmination of this gigantic range his name had been indisputably and forever linked with the grandest mountain of the Appalachian system—Clingman's Dome of the Great Smoky Mountains!

Our Mountain Heights Still Doubtful.—Whether this incomparable mountain be higher or lower than the disputed peak of the Blacks, is still a doubtful point, for we are told by Horace Kephart that all our mountains still remain to be measured accurately. He says (p. 56): "Yet we scarcely know today, to a downright certainty, which peak is supreme among our Southern highlands. The honor is conceded to Mount Mitchell in the Black Mountains, northeast of Asheville. Still, the heights of the Carolina peaks have been taken (with but one exception, so far as I know) only by barometric measurements, and these, even when official, may vary as much as a hundred feet for the same mountain. Since the highest ten or a dozen of our Carolina peaks differ in altitude only one or two hundred feet, their actual rank has not yet been determined. For a long time (p. 57) there was controversy as to whether Mount Mitchell or Clingman Dome was the crowning summit of eastern America. The Coast and Geodetic Survey gave the height of Mount Mitchell as 6,688 feet, but later figures of the United States Geological Survey are 6,711 and 6,712. In 1859 Buckley claimed for Clingman Dome of the Smokies an altitude of 6,941 feet. In recent government reports the Dome appears variously as 6,619 and 6,660 feet. In 1911 I was told by Mr. H. M. Ramsour that when he laid out the route of the railroad from Asheville to Murphy he ran a line of levels from a known datum on this road to the top of Clingman, and that the result was 'four sixes' (6,666 feet above sea level). It is probable that the second place among the peaks of Appalachia may belong either to Clingman Dome or

Photo. by Vest.

HON. THOMAS LANIER CLINGMAN.
Statesman, soldier, scientist.

Guyot or LeConte of the Smokies, or to Balsam Cone of the Black Mountains. In any case the Great Smoky Mountains are the master chain of the Appalachian system, the greatest mass of highland east of the Rockies (p. 58). The most difficult and rugged part of the Smokies (and of the United States east of Colorado) is in the saw-tooth mountains between Collins and Guyot, at the headwaters of Oconalufty River."

Who Measured the Highest Peak?—Dr. Arnold Guyot, of Princeton College (now University), published an article in the *Asheville News,* July 18, 1860, to the effect that Dr. Mitchell's measurements of this mountain failed to agree with each other; that the location of the highest peak had remained indefinite, even in the mind of Dr. Mitchell himself, *"as I learned it from his own mouth in 1856."* At that time, 1860, the peak now called Mitchell's, or Mount Mitchell, was called Clingman's, while the peak now known to some as Clingman's was called Mount Mitchell. Dr. Guyot says of this: "If the honored name of Dr. Mitchell is taken from Mount Mitchell and transferred to the highest peak, it should not be on the ground that *he first made known its true elevation, which he never did, nor himself ever claimed to have done,* for the true height was unknown before my measurement of 1854 . . . Nor should it be on the ground of his having first visited it, for, though after his death evidence which made it probable that he did [came out], *he never could convince himself of it.* Nor, at last, should it be because that peak was, as it is alleged, thus named long before, for I must declare that neither in 1854 nor later during the whole time I was on both sides of the mountain, did I hear of another Mount Mitchell than the one south of the highest, *so long visited under that name,* and that Dr. Mitchell himself, *before ascending the northern peak in 1856,* as I gathered it from a conversation with him, *believed it to be the highest."*

Politics or Public Opinion?—Dr. Guyot further said in the same article that General Clingman "could not possibly know when he first ascended it [the highest peak] that anyone had visited or measured it before him, nor have any intention to do any injustice to Dr. Mitchell." General Clingman in 1884 told

Charles Dudley Warner ("On Horseback," pp. 94 to 96) that he had been the first to discover the highest peak, and he also told this writer later that he had made this discovery by climbing a balsam tree on what was then called Mount Mitchell, the southern peak, and applying a spirit level to the surrounding horizon. Thus, the superior height of the northern peak was disclosed to him, and he then proceeded to measure and claim it. He told others the same story. Dr. Warner states that public sentiment awarded Dr. Mitchell this honor because of his tragic death. (Id. p. 95.) But was that all? Here is what Hon. Z. B. Vance, long Clingman's political opponent, said in a letter to Prof. Charles Phillips, dated Asheville, August, 1857:[2] "Yet there are some who believe that Clingman superintended the creation of those mountains, and, therefore, has a right to know more about them than anyone else. The editor of the *News* [the late Major Marcus Erwin], who expects to go to Clingman when he dies (and perhaps will) . . . is already beginning the war against the dead, as you will see by reference to that sheet of last week. I advised the *Spectator* men to keep perfectly quiet, and would give the same advice to the doctor's friends elsewhere. Let us prepare our case in silence and wait patiently for the good feeling to operate among the mountaineers, which is now going on admirably. In the meantime the proper efforts might be made to rectify Coke's map [which gave Clingman's name to the highest peak] and to push up the *influential journals at a distance,* a thing that the faculty are better able to do than anyone else. Only one thing remains to be done, in my opinion, to make our proof complete—to have the bearings of the High Peak taken from Yeates' Knob and compared with Dr. Mitchell's memorandum thereof. I hope steps will be taken to do this before long, as Clingman intends doing it himself after the election. I understand, though I have not seen it, that Mitchell's map also puts that peak down as Mount Clingman. Is it true? . . ."

In the same letter Senator Vance speaks of certain certificates from Big Tom Wilson and others, but their contents are not disclosed. There was also published in the same paper a copy

---

[2] Published by R. D. W. Connor, secretary N. C. Hist. Com., in *Charlotte Observer*, p. 11, Jan. 24, 1915.

of an address to solicit from citizens of North Carolina and friends of Dr. Mitchell funds for the removal of his body to the highest peak and the erection of a monument there. Five thousand dollars was asked for, but nowhere in that address can be found any claim that Dr. Mitchell either discovered or measured the highest peak. Its language is: "In view of the fact that he was the first to visit these mountains and to make known their superior height to any east of the Rocky Mountains, and that he spent a great portion of his time and finally lost his life in exploring them," the subscriptions were asked. As the result of this appeal, is also published a subscription list containing the names of only ten subscribers, with William Patton at the head for $100.00, and the entire amount aggregating only $195.00.

Big Tom Wilson was with Dr. Mitchell on his first trip, when it is claimed that he measured the highest peak, and his certificate should settle the controversy. But where is it? Where is the data showing the comparison of the "bearings of the High Peak from Yeates' Knob with Dr. Mitchell's memorandum thereof?" Did Mitchell's geography or map concede the highest peak to General Clingman? We are in the dark as to these matters. But we have Judge David Schenck's report of an interview with Big Tom on the subject.

The Crucial Question.—Did Dr. Mitchell ever visit the peak which now bears his name? "Big Tom" Wilson is the only witness, and upon his testimony rests the validity of the claim that he did. What is that testimony? Simply this: that the search party with Wilson first "examined the area of ground on Mitchell's Peak, where the doctor went, and then going to the trail he [the doctor] was directed to take, *and, finding no sign,* they commenced the descent towards the *south* side by the east prong. They had not gone more than a quarter of a mile until Adniram D. Allen found an impression in the moss . . ." This was the first trace of the doctor, and, after following it some distance, they went back to "examine where the track first left the peak . . . and found that the doctor had taken a 'horse trail' by mistake for the trail which led to 'Big Tom's.'" This is every shred of evidence concerning the peak in the interview between Wilson and Judge David Schenck on the 26th day of September, 1877, and which was published in the *Charlotte Democrat* of November 2, 1877. From it can be deduced only that there was no "sign" of the doctor's having been on "the area of ground on Mitchell's peak," but that when "they commenced the descent towards the south side," *the very side on which stood the peak which had always been called Mitchell's,* they found the first sign in the moss "not more than a quarter of a mile away." There is no evidence that they went to the south peak at all, where it is probable the professor went, and from which he was going when they found his track in the moss. What is meant by "where the track first left the peak" and that he took "a horse trail by mistake for the trail which led to Big Tom's," is all that even vaguely points to the fact that the doctor had been on the northern, or highest, peak.

Dr. Kemp P. Battle's Error.—In an article on Dr. Mitchell, written by Dr. Battle, the last survivor of the University Faculty of June, 1857, and published in the Journal of the Elisha Mitchell Scientific Society, March, 1915, he refers (p. 161) to "Letters from the *Raleigh Register* in reply to General Thomas L. Clingman, who claimed that Dr. Mitchell was never on the highest peak of the Black Mountains, but that he, Clingman, was the true discoverer. He caused W. D. Cooke to designate on his wall-map the highest peak as Mt. Clingman. On the death of the Doctor he gracefully surrendered his claim. It is now conceded that Dr. Mitchell was right. He is confirmed by the United States Geological Survey of 1881-'2, the highest and final authority." Dr. Battle is right in saying that Gen. Clingman "gracefully surrendered his claim," but it is *not* generally "conceded that Dr. Mitchell was right," and the United States Survey simply ascertained the highest peak among the Blacks, but did not and could not prove that Dr. Mitchell had ever been upon that spot.

Clingman's "Speeches and Writings."—North Carolina has not yet reared any monument to this one of her greatest sons. But in his "Speeches and Writings," published by himself after the Civil War, he has erected to his own memory a monument more eloquent than "storied urn or animated bust," and more enduring than bronze effigy or marble cenotaph.

CHAPTER XVI.
Gold and Other Mines.

Gold Mining.—Some time in the fifties, Joe Bissell, of Charlotte, worked every branch which runs away from the Muster Field Hill, east of Boone, looking for gold and finding some. The branch running from Joseph Hardin's was worked almost, if not quite, down to the river, especially where it passes through the old Reuben Hartley place, now occupied by Farthing Edmisten. Henry Blair worked the same stream afterwards, just before the Civil War, and sold dust at eighty cents a pennyweight. Blair used a hand-rocker, fifty cents a day being at that time the price of labor. Others also worked the branch running from the Muster Ground southeast by Eli Hartley's. The next work was done by Ison Doby for J. C. Councill about 1858-59 just where the Moretz and Hartzog saw mill now stands, and below the road where Robert Bingham lives. This stopped when the Civil War began, but afterwards John and Dick Haney, brothers, came from about King's Mountain and leased Henry and Joseph Hardin's branch, but failed. Colonel Bryan cashed some of the gold offered by them at first, and it was all right, but later on the dust became mixed with copper filings, and the Haney brothers did not try conclusions with Uncle Sam as to their responsibility for this mistake. This was about 1870-72. Phillip Chandler, from east of the Blue Ridge, worked same stream about 1858-59. Colonel Bryan and George Dugger worked around the edge of the Muster Field, but the dust was too fine. When the former was a boy there was a deep hole or shaft still open on the Muster Field which had been dug by old time miners. Miss Eliza Jordan, youngest daughter of Jordan Councill, the first, is said to have panned out enough gold near Joseph Hardin's to pay for a new silk dress before the Civil War. She afterwards married, first George Phillips, and then Rittenhouse Baird.

First Owners of Cranberry.—Sometime about 1780 Reuben White took out a grant for 100 acres covering the Cranberry iron vein, and Waighstill Avery obtained four small grants surrounding White's grant (100 N. C. Rep. 1, 127 Id. 387). In 1795 William Cathcart was granted 99,000 and 59,000 acres in two tracts, covering almost all of what is now Mitchell and Avery counties. Isaac T. Avery inherited Waightstill Avery's interest in this land and to numerous 640 acre grants along the Toe River. John Brown became agent for the Cathcart grants, and as these conflicted with the Avery lands, a compromise was effected, under which I. T. Avery got a quit claim to about 50,000 acres in 1852, including the Cranberry mines, excepting the Reuben White tract, which had passed to William Dugger by a chain of deeds, he having contracted to sell to John Harding, Miller and another. Hoke, Hutchinson and Sumner got title from Hardin, but had to pay several thousands of dollars to Brown and Avery to settle their claims upon the Cranberry ore bank. The forge-bounty grant to these lands obtained by the Perkinses was sold by order of court for partition at Morganton and bought in by William Dugger; but before getting title to the land, Dugger agreed that I. T. Avery and J. E. Brown, son of John, should each have a one-third interest in the mineral outside the original grant to Reuben White. This agreement, however, was not registered, and the Supreme Court at Morganton, under which the decree of sale for partition had been made, having been abolished after the Civil War, and the clerk of that court, James R. Dodge, having died, an ordinance of the State convention of 1866 empowered the clerk of the Supreme Court at Raleigh to execute the title which Dodge should have made to William Dugger, but made no reference to Brown's and Avery's interests therein. To still further complicate matters, William Dugger had sold his interest without excepting these equitable claims upon the mineral rights in the property. But Brown and Avery gave notice of their claims and compelled the purchasers to pay them for their interest in the minerals.

Iron Forges.—There were three of these in what was Watauga County: Cranberry, Toe River and the Johnson forges. The first grew out of the discovery of the Cranberry metallic

A History of Watauga County 265

ore by Joshua, Ben and Jake Perkins, of Tennessee, who in a rough play at a night feast and frolic at Crab Orchard, Tenn., after a log-rolling, had attempted to remove the new flax shirt and trousers from Wright Moreland, and had injured him sufficiently to arouse his anger and cause him to take out a warrant for them. They escaped to North Carolina, where they supported themselves by digging sang. In search of this herb, they discovered the Cranberry ore, and having been concerned in the Dugger forge on Watauga River four miles above Butler, Tenn., constructed a dam about half way between Elk Park and the Cranberry Company's store, only nearer to the Boone road than to the present railroad. Here they put in a regular forge with all the equipment used in that day, including the water trompe, furnace, goose-nest, hammer, etc. This was about 1821. Soon after they started their forge Abraham Johnson, the agent of John Brown, the land speculator, built a forge on the left bank of the Toe River, three-quarters of a mile above the mouth of White Oak Creek and near the mouth of Cow Camp Creek. He got some of his ore from a deposit near by, but also hauled ore from the Cranberry vein. Still later on, William Buckhannon had a forge built by one Calloway one-half a mile above what is now Minneapolis, on Toe River, but he had little or no ore nearer than that at Cranberry, from which he also drew his supply. After the Perkinses had been at work some time they are said to have applied for and obtained a grant from North Carolina for 3,000 acres of land for having made 3,000 pounds of iron, but shortly thereafter John Brown, who kept a keen eye out for squatters and trespassers on what was then the Tate and Cochran land, though then claimed by him under a junior or Cathcart grant, convinced the Perkinses that he held a superior title to theirs, and they bought his title to the land. They then sold to William and Abe Dugger, who came from the old Dugger forge above Butler and operated the mine till Abe's death, when, being offended with his son, George, for having married Carolina McNabb, a perfectly respectable girl, left his interest in the mine to his three daughters, Mattie, who afterwards married Jerry Green; Nancy, who had married Charles Gaddy, and Elizabeth, who had married Joseph Grubb, leaving George only fifty acres just below the law office of L. D. Lowe, Esq., at Banner's Elk. John Hardin became guardian of Mattie, then unmarried, taking possession of the mine about 1850 and retaining it till sometime during the Civil War. With him went Peter Hardin, then twelve years old, who remained with the Cranberry mine longer than any other in its existence. Peter was the son of a Creek Indian whom Nathaniel Taylor, of Elizabethton, Tenn., had brought with him from the Battle of the Horse Shoe in 1814, and who was named Duffield, after an academy at Elizabethton, according to Dr. Job's reminiscenses of that town. Jordan Hardin, son of John, took possession of the mine during the Civil War and worked from forty to sixty men, making iron for the Confederate government. This iron was in bars for the manufacture of axes and was hauled to Camp Vance, below Morganton, by Peter Hardin, one four-horse load every month, winter as well as summer. It was sometime during or after the possession of the Hardins that a man named Dunn had some connection with Cranberry, but exactly what could not be ascertained accurately. Thomas Carter, who had operated a plant for the manufacture of guns at Linville Falls during the Civil War, and Gen. Robert F. Hoke then obtained an interest in the Cranberry mine and forge, and General Hoke sold the property to the present company, Carter, in May, 1867, having agreed to convey his interest therein to Hoke for $44,-000.00. When, however, Carter tendered Hoke a deed therefor, Hoke gave him a sight draft on a New York bank for the price agreed to be paid. This draft was not paid. The money to meet it was to have been provided by the sale of the property by Hoke to Russell and his associates, who refused to take it because Carter would not deliver the deed for his interest till he had been fully paid. Carter got an injunction against the sale, and the Supreme Court upheld Carter. (Carter v. Hoke, 64 N. C., 348.) Carter and Hoke soon effected a compromise and the title to the property was thus settled. After Hoke and Company sold the property soon after the Civil War it remained in the control of Peter Hardin, who kept the hotel and looked after the property generally for many years. He was allowed to make and sell all the iron he wished and to operate a small saw mill. When the present company began to build the railroad from Johnson City to the forge, Peter Hardin kept a store at Cranberry and was postmaster, keeping all the accounts of the employees of the company and delivering all the mail, etc., although he could not read a line, the clerical work having been done by his wife and her daughters by a former marriage. White people stopped at Pete's hotel and were well entertained by these care-takers. They still live near Elk Park, and have the respect and confidence of all who know them. They are called colored people, but their good names are as white as those of the best people in the State. Abram Johnson died at his home near what is now Vale, on the E. T. & W. N. C. R. R., in the house which stood where Bayard Benfield now lives, near the mouth of White Oak Creek, and is said to have been a soldier in the War of 1812. His wife died there August 18, 1880, and he October 15, 1881, aged about 107 years, according to the record of Jacob Carpenter, of Altamont.

Some Old Hammermen.—Among those who worked at iron mines in this county were Jess Sizemore, at Johnson's forge, and Jack Mayberry, ———— Grandire, Wash Heaton, Elisha Stanley and George Dugger, all at Cranberry.

Gen. Thos. L. Clingman's Mining.—This enterprising gentleman mined on Beech Creek in Watauga County in 1871, and a branch in that locality still bears his name. (Deed Book 3, p. 595.)

Oil and Gas Mining.—About 1901 it was thought that oil had been seen on a pool of water near N. L. Mast's store on Cove Creek, and the Carolina Valley Oil and Gas Company sank a well there, but abandoned it. The flat formation of the rock strata on Cove Creek and about Ward's store on Watauga River seems to indicate petroleum. There were options taken by the Carolina Valley Oil and Gas Company on lands in the vicinity of Sutherland. J. A. Zins and Joseph Bock, of Minnesota, worked a copper mine on Elk Knob in 1899, but they fell out among themselves and quit work.

The Elk Knob Copper Mine.—On the 22d of August, 1900, John Castle agreed to convey to the Zinns-Bach Mining & Lumber Co. 100 acres on Elk Knob, and mining was soon begun there for copper. The scheme was soon abandoned, however. (Book W, p. 495.)

CHAPTER XVII.
Roads and Railroads.

First Roads.—From John Crouch's "Historical Sketches of Wilkes" (1902) we learn that Hamilton Holton (or Helton?) obtained a charter for a turnpike from Holman's Ford to New River in Ashe. This road passed through Deep Gap, Old Fields and on to Jefferson and Virginia and south to Three Forks, Brushy Fork, Cove Creek, and west to Meat Camp, crossing the New River at The Bend, near what is now called the Salmond's place, but which formerly belonged to the Fergusons of Wilkes. From there it went to the top of the ridge between the river as it runs in two directions, thence west, passing Moretz Mill, and on up Meat Camp to the gap between Rich and Snake mountains to Trade in Tennessee. Later came a road from Jefferson to Boone, via Elk Cross Roads, and from Sugar Grove up Beaver Dams over Baker's Gap to Tennessee. The road up Cove Creek probably stopped for a long time at Zionville, and some say that there was only a trail from there to Shoun's Cross Roads for years.

The First Roads Across the Blue Ridge.—According to "The Archibald D. Murphey Papers," published by the State Historical Association, 1915 (Vol. II, p. 185), Wilkesborough may be taken as the point on the Yadkin from which they (roads) diverge in different directions across the mountains. One runs to the north into the counties of Grayson and Wythe in Virginia, passing the Blue Ridge at Elk Spur Gap. Two roads run to the west, one crossing the Ridge at Reddy's River Gap, passes by Ashe court house and, forking, it extends to the northwest into the counties of Russell and Washington in Virginia, and to the west of Jonesborough in East Tennessee. The other, called Horton's Turnpike, passes the Ridge at the Deep Gap, and runs through the southwestern parts of Ashe County, on to Jonesborough. Another road leads from Wilkesborough

Photo. by Vannoy.

THE DEEP GAP.

The gateway to Watauga.

to the southwest, passes Morganton and crosses the Ridge at Swannanoa Gap. The mountain can be easily passed at each of these gaps, and, if the roads were good, the inconvenience of crossing the mountain would be disregarded. The roads have been badly laid out; they are badly made, and the population in many parts is too weak to keep the roads in even tolerable repair. All these roads should be made at the public's expense.

Caldwell and Watauga Turnpike.—The General Assembly of 1846 and 1847 (Ch. CV) passed an act to incorporate the Caldwell and Ashe Turnpike Company, the State to provide $8,000.00 when $5,000.00 had been subscribed, which was altered in 1850-51 so that the name should be the Caldwell and Watauga Turnpike Company, while the capital stock was increased from $10,000.00 to $12,500.00, whatever amount of the increase that might not be subscribed within six months to be taken by the State. The president and directors were authorized to change the route on the Blue Ridge where it exceeded one foot in twenty so as to reduce it to that standard, and otherwise improve the road, while all hands within two miles who were then required to work on roads were required to work on this road, but should not be required to work any other roads or to pay toll on this. This act was ratified January 21, 1851 (Ch. CLXIV, p. 463). By chapter 131, Laws of 1881, the Turnipke Company was authorized to surrender to Watauga County "so much of said turnpike as lies west of the top of the Blue Ridge at the Yadkin Springs," etc. Chapter 445, Laws of 1893, authorized the State to sell its interest in this road and apply the proceeds to the construction of the Boone and Blowing Rock Turnpike. The charter was repealed in 1911, but in 1913 a new charter was granted, the people living along the road not being able to keep it in condition.

The old road passed along the mountain side above the former residence of Smith Coffey at the Old Bridge place, one mile below Shull's Mills, while the turnpike crossed the Watauga River on the old bridge and followed the Woody bottoms to Shull's Mills on the right bank of the river, passing west of Phillip Shull's old house, which was of logs, and faced west. Joseph Shull changed the road so that it crossed the river at the ford near Robbins' store and east of the house, now a frame structure which faces east. Old Albany, nine-passenger stage coaches, swinging on straps, passed over this road from 1855 to 1861, going from Lincolnton, via Lenoir, Blowing Rock, Shull's Mills, Valle Crucis, Sugar Grove, Zionville, Shoun's Cross Roads, Taylorsville—now Mountain City—to Abingdon, Va., and they were operated by a man of the name of Dunn, of Abingdon. It was a daily line each way, with stands at John Mast's at Sugar Grove and at Joseph Shull's, where J. M. Shull now lives.

This road undoubtedly served to open up and encourage the settlement of Watauga County, and was an excellent one for that day. But Blowing Rock, Banner's Elk, Linville City, Boone and Valle Crucis were growing rapidly, and in 1893 an act was passed authorizing the State to sell its interest in the Caldwell and Watauga Turnpike Company and apply the proceeds to the construction of the Boone and Blowing Rock Turnpike Company, in the building of which the late Thomas J. Coffey was very active. This new road diverted much travel from the old turnpike. The turnpike company from Lenoir to Blowing Rock had already absorbed much of the original Caldwell and Watauga turnpike, leaving only the stretch between Blowing Rock and the Tennessee line belonging to the company. By chapter 17, Laws 1911, it was authorized to sell or lease any of its road bed or other property to any other turnpike company, and if such a sale should be made it might wind up its affairs. Section 2 of this act, however, authorized the company to turn over the road from Shull's Mills to Blowing Rock to the county of Watauga, which was done, and the county required to keep it up as a public road. But there were too few people living near it to keep it in good condition, and, accordingly, some of the citizens living near secured a charter for a turnpike company from the Secretary of State, known as the Valle Crucis and Blowing Rock Turnpike Company, to run between those points. Its capital stock is $3,000.00, and its charter was granted June 4, 1914.

A History of Watauga County

Yonahlossee Turnpike Company.—About the year 1890 S. T. Kelsey, formerly of Kansas, but later of Highlands, Macon County, N. C., went to Watauga County, and a turnpike company was chartered to build and maintain a road from Linville City to Blowing Rock, passing clear around the eastern base of the Grandfather Mountain and running along the crest of the Blue Ridge, much of the distance being north and east of that picturesque and ancient mass of stone and earth. The distance is eighteen miles and it cost less than $18,000.00. It is decidedly the best and most level road in the mountains.

Elk Park and Banner's Elk.—A road was constructed between these places about 1895 and serves the country through which it passes admirably.

Early Road Legislation.[1]—In 1850-51 Charles McDowell and Hugh Taylor, of Burke, and John Franklin, of Watauga, were appointed commissioners to lay off a public road from Charles McDowell's in Burke via Upper Creek, Jonas Ridge, Old Fields of Toe River to Cranberry Forge in the county of Watauga. (Ch. CLXXI, p. 473.) In 1852 Alfred Miller, Jonathan Horton, James Ragen, M. T. Coxe and Reuben Mast were appointed commissioners to view, lay off, alter or amend so much of a public road from Holman's Ford by way of Deep Gap at Solomon Green's and the Rich Mountain, near Welch's store, to the Tennessee line as lay within the limits of Watauga County. (Ch. CLIII, p. 579.) In 1854-55 (Ch. 214, p. 216) Reuben Mast, M. F. Cox, James Ragan, Alfred Miller and John Moretz were appointed commissioners to survey and improve the public road from the Wilkes County line by way of Meat Camp Creek to the Tennessee line, at or near Welch's store. At the same session (Ch. 219, p. 222) Michael Snider, Jourdan C. Hardin, for Watauga, and three men from Yancey, were appointed commissioners to lay off a public road from the Tennessee line at Wm. D. Hose's, via Cranberry and Arthur Erwin's to the McDowell County line, near Charles McKinney's, so as to intersect the public road leading from Burnsville to Morganton. At

---

[1] Just prior to the formation of Watauga County (Ch. XCVIII, Laws of 1846-'47) a public road was authorized from Councill's store in Ashe (now Boone) to Bedford Wiseman's in Yancey County, at the mouth of Three Mile Creek.

the same session (Ch. 224, p. 224) it was provided that all public roads to be built in Watauga after the date of the ratification of the act shall not be required to be more than twelve feet wide where side-cutting is necessary and used, and where blasting is necessary and used such roads shall not be required to be more than eight feet wide. The county and superior courts were given concurrent jurisdiction of all indictments against overseers of Watauga County roads. By the laws of 1876-77 (p. 175), John R. Hodges, Daniel Wheeler and John Elrod were authorized to locate the road authorized by the act of 1870 (Ch. 254), and by the same laws (Ch. CLXXXIX, p. 365) the road from Phineas Horton's store in Wilkes was altered by changing the Stony Fork road so as to run to John Key's, and then up Stony Fork at Larkin Bishop's mill, and thence to Deep Gap. By the same laws (Ch. LII, p. 673) the citizens of Watauga and Caldwell counties were allowed to pass free all toll gates of Catawba and Watauga Turnpike Company. By the laws of 1870-71 (Ch. 254, p. 409) a public road was authorized from Phineas and A. H. Horton's store in Wilkes County to Boone, running up Elk Creek and crossing the Blue Ridge by the most practicable route. As seen above, this road was not built till after the laws of 1876-77 had been passed. By chapter 68, laws of 1874-75 (p. 59), a road was authorized to be constructed from Boone to the Caldwell and Watauga Turnpike at a point on the Blue Ridge between Wm. Morris' and L. Henly's, and by the laws of the same year (Ch. 109, p. 601) a road was authorized from a point on the Caldwell and Watauga Turnpike, where the old Morganton road intersects the same in Watauga County, and thence via Wm. Welch's and Elisha Lewis' to M. C. Coffey's, thence with a dividing ridge via Thomas Right's and A. J. McClean's, so as to intersect the Morganton road at the Globe Church in Caldwell County.

The Earliest Stopping Places.—The first and only taverns or inns or public houses, as they were variously called, were Solomon Greene's, which was in Deep Gap, to the right of the old State road running from Wilkesboro through that gap via what is now Boone, Hodges' Gap, Sugar Grove, through George's

A History of Watauga County

Gap and Baker's Gap to Roan's Creek in Tennessee. Squire Wm. P. Welch lives there now. Col. Jonathan Horton kept the next place, which was on New River, one mile below Three Forks Church, where Rudy Vannoy now lives. There were no other stopping places from there to Benjamin Webb's, where Rev. William Farthing afterwards lived and died. It was on Beaver Dams. These were then the places of "entertainment," though private houses then "took in" travelers as they do now. While Webb was keeping this house, it is said that James Ward went there "a-courtin'." Webb arose early and began mowing grass before breakfast, and came in to that meal wet and hungry. Ward was just getting out of his bed, and, "stretching," exclaimed, "I feel like I could stretch a mile." "I wish you would," cried Webb, "and I wish you would stretch it towards your own home, too."

The First Paper Railroads.—In January, 1851, the legislature appropriated twelve thousand dollars to be used in the survey of a route for a railroad from Salisbury to the Tennessee line "at or near the place where the French Broad River passes into the State of Tennessee." This may be said to have been the first of the almost numberless steps to get a railroad across the Blue Ridge. It is evident, however, that it was not then contemplated to build a road through any part of Watauga County, which had just been formed. But at the next session of the legislature, in 1852 (Ch. CXXXVI), the North Carolina and Western Railroad Company was incorporated, and Jordan Councill, Jonathan Horton, Reuben Mast and John Morris, or any three of them, were authorized to open books of subscription to the capital stock in the town of Boone. The road was to commence at Salisbury and run thence by the most practicable route across the Blue Ridge to the Tennessee line. Its capital stock was to be three million dollars. It was not confined to any route, and Watauga County might have stood a chance to profit thereby if the most practicable route over the Blue Ridge had been found within its borders. But it was not, the Swannanoa Gap having been chosen. At the same session another railroad was incorporated, to run so as to follow down the

Little Tennessee River to the Tennessee line. This was called the Blue Ridge Railroad. Neither road came as far as the mountains of North Carolina till after the Civil War. But the door of hope was not entirely closed to Watauga, for in February, 1855 (Ch. 227), the Atlantic, Tennessee and Ohio Railroad was incorporated, to run with one or more tracks and to be operated by steam, animal or other power between Charlotte, N. C., and some point on the East Tennessee and Virginia Railroad, at or near Jonesboro, in Washington County, Tenn., and form such connection by way of Moccasin Gap of Clinch Mountain in the State of Virginia, by the most practicable line to the head waters of Big Sandy River, thence the most eligible route to the Ohio River. Commissioners were appointed to open books of subscription on the first Monday of July, 1854, and be kept open for twenty days, Sundays excepted, between 10 a. m. and 4 p. m. at Boone and many other places, including points in Tennessee and Virginia. This road must have crossed the Blue Ridge near the Coffey Gap and followed the Watauga River to Jonesboro. It has not been built yet, though nature had graded a road-bed for it from the foundation of the world. The track was completed from Charlotte to Statesville before the Civil War, but the iron and cross ties were removed and laid down upon a grade constructed by the government of the Confederate States from Greensboro to Danville, Va., early in the Civil War. The track was relaid between Charlotte and Statesville soon after the close of hostilities, but it has never passed through the Coffey Gap or down the Watauga River, which still opens inviting arms to its construction. By chapter XL (Laws 1871-72) the Charlotte and Taylorsville Railroad Company was authorized to build a road from Troutman's depot on the A. T. & O. R. R., in Iredell County, to Taylorsville, and thence, by or near Lenoir and Boone, the most practicable route, to some point on the Tennessee line. This stopped at Taylorsville, however, and is there yet. Just where the North Western North Carolina Railroad Company, amended by chapter XLVII (Laws 1871-72), was to run is immaterial, as it never came to Watauga or near it under that name. At the same session the upper division of the Yadkin Railroad Company was incorporated to run from Salisbury to Wilkesboro and thence to the Tennessee or Virginia line, but it too stopped before reaching God's country. The Carolina Narrow Guage Railroad Company was chartered to run from the South Carolina line via Dallas, Lincolnton, Newton, Hickory Tavern to the town of Lenoir, but no further. It has observed its original charter and is at Lenoir still—very still. By chapter XXV, Laws 1872-73, the Carolina Narrow Gauge (name spelt right this time without any legislative authority whatever!) was authorized to consolidate with the Chester and Lenoir Narrow Gauge Railroad Company if stockholders of both companies were willing. They were, but Lenoir is still the head of the railroad. The State found good employment for its convicts by making them build railroads, and this policy was continued with general approval till recently, when certain statesmen in the eastern part of the State, having secured all such aid as was required for their immediate needs, tried to discontinue the custom absolutely, but failed. It was in the hope of such aid that some of the enterprising citizens incorporated the Watauga Railway Company (Ch. 411, Pr. Laws, 1905), which, by chapter 408, Laws of 1909, was authorized to be transferred to W. J. Grandin and his associates upon certain conditions; but two years having elapsed and those conditions not having been complied with, the legislature (Ch. 316, Laws 1911) gave Grandin and associates twenty months longer, after which time, if they had not commenced work, etc., the powers and property so assigned were to revert to the original incorporators. By chapter 11, Pr. Laws of 1913, the Watauga Railway Company was authorized to become part of the Watauga and Yadkin River Railroad Company. In 1912 the county of Watauga voted $100,000.00 to aid in the construction of this road, upon certain conditions, which were never fulfilled. At the session of the legislature of 1915 it was determined to continue the convicts on this railroad construction. The East Tennessee and Western North Carolina Railroad was finished to Cranberry in 1882, coming from Johnson City via Elizabethton, Tenn. The Linville Railroad Company extended this line to Pinola or Saginaw in

1900, but it is now under the management of the E. T. & W. N. C. R. R. This road was for several years the nearest to Watauga County, Pinola being only twenty-four miles from Boone, but in May, 1915, the Virginia-Carolina Railway from Abingdon, Va., was completed to Todd, now called Elkland, and is in operation. This is about eleven miles from Boone.

First Railroad Surveys.—Major William Cain, a distinguished member of the faculty of the University of North Carolina, has furnished many valuable facts as to the first surveys for railways made through Watauga County. It seems that in 1859 a line was run from about Patterson, in Caldwell County, known as Kuper's line, which required the tunneling of the Blowing Rock Ridge and Watauga Gap, thence along the north side of the Grandfather to the head of Watauga River, and down that stream to Elizabethton, Tenn. This line would be expensive to construct, but it would eliminate, by the use of deep tunnels, a great deal of the elevation that has to be overcome on the line through Cook's Gap. Nothing was done, however, till the winter of 1881, when General Imboden obtained a charter from the North Carolina legislature for the South Atlantic and Ohio Railway Construction and Operating Company. (Ch. 41, Laws 1881, p. 87.) This charter recited that representations had been made that the Tinsalia Coal and Iron Company of Virginia were the owners of valuable coal mines in Virginia and were building a narrow gauge railroad from their mine in Big Stone Gap to Bristol, Tenn.-Va., and had also obtained a charter from Tennessee to extend their line to some convenient point on the North Carolina State line so as to pass through Watauga and Mitchell counties. Upon these and other representations the above charter was granted for a narrow gauge railway, and C. L. Dwight, a civil engineer of South Carolina, was employed to make the survey. As he was engaged at that time on another survey, the main task of locating the road fell on Major Wm. Cain, and he ran the line so as to come up Elk Creek through Cook's Gap, thence passing two or three miles from Boone through a gap to the Watauga watershed, thence north, grading down along the sides of Rich Mountain with much curving, until finally the line took a westerly direction and reached the level of the Watauga River some few miles before reaching the Tennessee line. There were about 2,000 feet to be overcome from east of the Blue Ridge, with seventeen miles development to make the rise to Cook's Gap, but there were no tunnels. Major Cain was a pioneer in putting the heavier grades on the tangents and the lighter on the curves—a practice then unheard of, but now universal. To reach the valley of the Elk from his initial point near Patterson, he had to wind around many little peaks of the Bull Ruffin Ridge at one point and curve around the heads of several valleys in order to reach Elk Creek, where for a few miles the fall of the creek was greater than his grade, but he eventually caught up with it and reached the valley with his grade line successfully. The average grade was approximately 150 feet to the mile. From Cook's Gap the fall to the Watauga is not so great, its elevation being 3,349, just seventeen feet more than that of Boone, and the Watauga River at Shull's Mills 2,917, and at Valle Crucis 2,726, but the slopes are smoother than the line east of Cook's Gap. He began this line on the 21st of March, 1881, and when near the Tennessee line was called to another road, June 18, 1881, Mr. Dwight then taking charge. But the chief promoter fell out with the president of the road, who had the financial backing, and nothing was done after the survey was finished.

A Great Inter-Montane Road.—There was a road, to run from Sparta to Asheville, planned and partially constructed somewhere about 1868, Coffey Brothers, of Boone, having a contract for the construction of two miles, running from the Musterfield, through the town to the branch above the Blackburn hotel, and thence through the Bryan and Gragg farms to Poplar Grove Church, where it was to follow down Lance's Creek to Shull's Mills. Robert Shearer had the mile running from the Musterfield towards the Three Forks Church. It was during this period that the road was changed just east of the John Hardin home to its present location and beyond the Musterfield so as to run north of its old location. The grade from Todd was also made at this time, the old road going directly up a very steep hill. But the new road from the high hill beyond the Perkins home and between it and Sands was surveyed by T. L. Critcher four years ago and built by the county. One of these days, believer, a railroad will run from Sparta to Jefferson and from there to Boone, or near it, and thence over the Linville Gap and down Linville River to near the falls, thence to the Toe, crossing that stream to Cane River, Weaverville and Asheville. Then the mountain people can go from north to south and from south to north without having to zig-zag across the mountains from east to west and then back again, as at present, without getting to their destination even then. Such a railroad would tap every transmontane railroad and wagon road, would get all the lumber, grain, fruit, minerals, stock and passengers that now have to go miles and miles out of the way to get a few miles north or south. Besides, the public could then learn that all the scenery, climate and pure water of the mountains of Western North Carolina are not confined between Old Fort and Murphy. Then the wonderland of Madison, Yancey, Mitchell, Avery, Watauga, Ashe and Alleghany would be revealed in its unsurpassed loveliness.

SKETCHES OF PROMINENT FAMILIES

(*Alphabetically arranged; not indexed.*)

The Adams Family.—Alfred Adams was born in 1811, July 10th. His wife was Elizabeth Flannery, born in Lee County, Virginia, November 28, 1815. These were married on Cove Creek December 29, 1839. Their children were Sarah, who married Carroll Wilson, who was killed in the Civil War, and, after his death, she married Jacob S. Mast; George F., born December 8, 1842, and was killed in Civil War; Tarleton P. Adams was born March 14, 1846, and married, first, Rebecca Adams, June 7, 1877, and, second, Mollie Tugman, December 15, 1910; Leah E., who married Isaac Dougherty about 1876, and Abner, who married Elizabeth Combs about 1875. The father of Alfred Adams was John, who was born in France of English ancestry and came with Lafayette's soldiers as a drummer boy of sixteen years. He stayed till the Revolutionary War was ended, but when Lafayette's soldiers were about to return, John hid himself in a flour barrel at Philadelphia and escaped. There he joined a whaling ship and went with it two years, after which he apprenticed himself to a cabinet maker for seven years in Philadelphia. It becoming rumored that the French were about to search the city for deserters, John set out for North Carolina and reached the head of the Yadkin, where he met and married Easter Hawkins. Their children were Frank, who married ————————————; Tarleton, who married a Harman; Squire, who married a Greene; Allen, who married a Greene; Alfred, who married Elizabeth Flannery; George, who died at eighteen; Patsy, who married a Williams; Rachel, who married Jehiel Smith, and Elizabeth, who married Enoch Greene.

Tarleton P. Adams was elected a county commissioner in 1878, and was appointed on Board of Education in 1882, and, with the exception of four years, from 1896 to 1900, has been a member ever since and will be six years longer—by far the longest service in the State.

Baird Family.—Ezekiel Baird was the father of Bedent and William Baird, and came to North Carolina from New Jersey. William went West, where he died. Bedent married Mary, a daughter of Cutliff Harman, and lived one mile down the Watauga River from Valle Crucis on its left bank, where Walter Baird now lives, though Bedent's old house has been replaced by the present large frame dwelling. Bedent's sons were Alexander, who married Nancy Vanderpool, and lived on the waters of Brushy Fork; Franklin, who married Catharine Moody, daughter of Edward, who lived at what is now Foscoe. Franklin lived one mile down the Watauga, where James Church now lives, and just above Walter's; Palmer, who married, first, Elizabeth McBride, and lived on Beech Mountain, three miles from Bedent's; Blodgett, who moved to Tennessee and married a lady near Nashville. He was absent forty years before he was heard of at Valle Crucis. The next was Euclid, named for the geometrician, and he married Louisa Councill, daughter of Jordan Councill the first, and lived where ex-Sheriff W. B. Baird now lives.

Franklin's children were: Jackson, who married Tempe Shull; William, who married Sarah McNab; Susan, who married James Lowrance; David F., who married Elizabeth Wagner; Thomas Carroll, who went to Texas, where he died unmarried about 1861.

Alexander's children were: Bedent, who went West and married Susan Jane Merchant; Abram, who married Elizabeth Hartley; Warren, who married Rebecca Hartley; Ezekiel, who married Sarah Wilson; Jonathan, who died in the Civil War; Phœbe, who never married; Elizabeth, who married Hiram Wilson.

Palmer's children were: John, who married Miss Shupe; Andrew, who died in the Civil War, unmarried; Ann, who married Wm. Grimsley; Caroline, who married ———————; Eliza, who never married.

Blodgett's children are not known to his Watauga relatives.

Euclid's children were: Benjamin, who married Celia Gragg; John, who married Emeline Shell; Hiram, who died in the Civil

A History of Watauga County 281

War; Thomas, who went West and died unmarried; Sarah, who married John Hackney; Charlotte, who married Eli Brown; Mary, who married Hiram Gragg.

Rittenhouse's children were: William B., who married Eliza Gragg.

David F.'s children are: Victoria, who married T. H. Taylor; Allie, who married J. M. Shull; Nora, who married D. C. Mast; Susan, who married Jack B. Horton; Emma, who married W. W. Mast; Lula, who married J. C. Moore; Thomas C., who married Emma Mast.

Banner Family.—From Murphey's Papers (Vol. II, p. 381) we learn that Joseph Banner was born in Pennsylvania in 1749 and moved to Stokes County, North Carolina, in 1751. Stokes was then Anson County, and it was there that Joseph's father settled. His home was on Town Fork, near the present village of Germantown, N. C. One of the Banners entered land in Ashe soon after its formation. Banner is a Welsh name and used to be written Bannerman. It seems, however, that Henry Banner was the first of the name to come to America, arriving between 1740 and 1750, and married a Miss Martin from England. They settled on Buffalo Creek, then Rowan, now Stokes County. He bought land from Lord Granville in 1752. There were three sons of this union: Ephriam, Joseph and Benjamin. Ephriam was the father of Joshua, and Joshua of Lewis, and Lewis of Edward J. Banner. Lewis Banner's brothers were Martin, who married Mary Ogburn; Anthony, who married ————————————; John, who married a Miss Shiposh; Edward, Mathew and Joshua, who married, but the surnames of their wives have been forgotten. All these came to Banner's Elk about three years before the Civil War, except Martin, who came in 1849. Martin died at Montezuma, Anthony and John at Banner's Elk, Edward at Elk Park, Mathew in Texas in 1914, and Joshua in Surry County. Martin Banner's children were: Virginia, born in 1832; Napoleon, in 1834; William, in 1836; Oliver, in 1838; Columbia, in 1840; Newton, October 8, 1842; Luther, in 1844; Martin, in 1846; Mary, in 1848, and Missouri, in 1850. Newton Banner married Sophronia Mast in 1866.

Bingham Family.—George M. Bingham was born July 20, 1805, on Reddy's River, Wilkes County, and married Mary Ann Davis, who was born in 1813, on waters of Cove Creek. He died January 21, 1880. They were married in 1833 or 1834. Their children were: William G., born in 1835, and who married Roxanna Presnell; Louisa, who married Marshall Miller in 1856, lived on Cove Creek till 1892 or 1893, when she moved to Idaho, her husband having died during the Civil War. She died in Idaho in 1900. Harvey was the next child, and was born February 13, 1839; died March 17, 1895. He married Nancy Ann Miller in 1861 and went to the war in Young Farthing's company, 37th North Carolina regiment, but was discharged in the latter part of 1862 because of bad health, having been slightly wounded twice. He became major of the battalion at Camp Mast of the Home Guard. After the war he went to Haywood County and taught school at what is now Canton, but was then Ford of Pigeon River. Then he went to school at Sand Hill, Buncombe County, to a Presbyterian minister named Hood. Then he came back to Watauga County and was admitted to the bar in 1869, and practiced here till 1881, when he moved to Statesville, where he taught a school of law and engaged actively in the practice of his profession. The next child was Harrison Bingham, who died in infancy; then came Violet Emeline, who died when barely grown; then came Elliott, who was killed in the Civil War on Beech Mountain; Marshall, who died at thirty-four, unmarried; Isidor, who died when two years old, and Carolina, who married E. L. Presnell. George M. Bingham's father was William, and his wife was Elizabeth McNeil. William was born in Virginia and came to Reddy's River when a young man. Their children were: William, who married; Sarah, who married, first, Thomas Proffitt, and, second, Wm. Case; Nancy, who married Joseph Miller; Joel, who married a Miss Miller in Georgia, and Jemima, who died unmarried when about grown. It is a family tradition that Benjamin Bingham, brother of William, who came from Virginia to Reddy's River, fired the last cannon at Yorktown. Hon. Thomas Bingham thinks that Benjamin was the ancestor of Robert,

MAJOR HARVEY BINGHAM

Soldier and lawyer.

A History of Watauga County

Steven and Duval Bingham, and that Steven was a Methodist preacher and first cousin of George M. Bingham. This Benjamin was a giant in his day, and it is related of him that a noted fighter, wishing to test his strength as a wrestler, came to Reddy's River and lay in the shade of some trees and watched Benjamin lead the reapers in the wheat harvest till sundown, when he made his business known. It was then that Benjamin, without resting or eating, girded his loins and threw his opponent as often as he wished to try conclusions with him.

Thomas Bingham was born February 3, 1845, and he married, first, Sarah Ann Farmer, February 17, 1870, and, second, Laura E. Combs, July 4, 1885. There were two children by the first marriage, one of whom died unmarried, and the other, Etta, married Ed. Madron. There were fourteen children by the second marriage. Thomas Bingham was early elected assistant township clerk, and then to the county board of education; he was then appointed a member of the board of county commissioners in 1895, to fill out the unexpired term of Critt Horton, and was then elected to the legislature in 1880, 1886, 1896, and clerk of the Superior Court in 1902 and in 1906. He was stricken with paralysis October 7, 1910. He was also editor of the *Watauga Enterprise* from February till November, 1888.

John H. Bingham, Esq.—This distinguished attorney was born in 1867, and was a son of William G. Bingham. He married Alice Smith about 1890, and was elected Superior Court clerk in 1898. Filmore and Richard Bingham are physicians, and are brothers of John H. Bingham.

Major Harvey Bingham.—In the winter of 1864-65, the Home Guard battalion of Watauga was camped on Cove Creek near what is now Sugar Grove, the name of their camp having been Camp Mast. Harvey Bingham was the major, and Geo. McGuire, who had been absent from the county for a long while before his return and election, was captain of Company A. Jordan Cook was captain of Company B, of which Col. W. L. Bryan, of Boone, was first lieutenant. Major Bingham and his adjutant, J. P. Mathewson, left camp to go to Ashe to confer with Captain McMillan, who commanded a cavalry company there, about co-operating with his battalion in a raid he then contemplated. During his absence Company B, under command of Lieutenant Bryan, was camped at Boone, and Captain McGuire sent him word about dark that he expected an attack on Camp Mast that night. Lieutenant Bryan, however, did not start for that place till the following morning, and when he got near it, discovered the cabins in smoking ruins and all of Company A absent. McGuire had surrendered them to Colonel Champion, of the Federal army, the night before. They were taken to Camp Chace and kept till the close of the war. It is said, however, that McGuire was not treated as a prisoner, but was allowed a horse and rode away with the officers to whom he had surrendered his men. It was thought at the time that McGuire had betrayed his men to the enemy, and he certainly had surrendered them under the protest of many of his subordinate officers; one of whom, Paul Farthing, told him that if the company was surrendered Farthing's life would be surrendered, meaning that he would not survive captivity. He and a nephew who was surrendered with him shortly afterwards died in Camp Chace. After the war Major Bingham was a candidate for the State Senate before a Democratic convention held at Lenoir, and the late W. B. Farthing stated that Bingham was suspected of complicity with McGuire in the surrender of the troops at Camp Mast, and that if he was nominated the people of Watauga would not support him. This led to his defeat and there was talk of a duel between these two, but both decided it was best to leave the issue to the future rather than to two leaden bullets, and the matter was dropped. But feeling still ran high against Major Bingham, and he and his wife, a daughter of John B. Miller, of Wilkes, left Watauga together and rode on horseback to one of the western counties, where they taught school till a better feeling pervaded their home county, when they returned. He studied law and practiced in Statesville, to which place he soon removed. He died there, a respected citizen and able lawyer, and time has fully vindicated his memory of the unjust suspicion that once drove him from his home, and no one now doubts his entire loyalty to the cause of the Southern Confederacy.

A History of Watauga County

Blackburn Family.—The first of the name to come to this section, according to Mr. Clyde C. Miller, of Sands, N. C., a member of the Blackburn family, was Benjamin, a soldier of the Revolution, who settled on the South Fork of New River at what is now called the Cal Tucker place, near the new town of Riverside. He and another Revolutionary soldier named Jones are buried on the opposite side of the river in the same graveyard. Benjamin had three sons and one daughter, Sarah, who married Levi Morphew or Murphey. Their children were Edmund, Levi and John. Edmund had a daughter who married Joseph Williams, and two sons, one named Benjamin and the other Levi, the latter of whom married a Greer, from whom there were Noah, William, Isaac, Edmund, John and Hampton; his daughters were Rebecca, Hannah, Nancy, Elizabeth and Sarah. Rebecca married Jonathan Miller; Hannah married John Campbell; Nancy married John Gentry and moved to Tennessee; Elizabeth married William Miller, and Sarah, W. S. Davis. Noah Blackburn lived and died in Carter County, Tenn. Among his children were Dr. Larkin Blackburn and Milly Blackburn. William married a Ray and lived in Bald Mountain township. He had a large family, principally of girls, several of whom died in childhood, Margaret living to womanhood and marrying Asa Clawson, and Martha, who married Julius Graham, and Elizabeth, who married Dr. Graham. Isaac Blackburn married Martha Tatum and moved to Missouri. He was killed in the Civil War, leaving three sons, all of whom now live in Missouri. Edmund lived and died on Meat Camp, where he reared a large family, many of whom are still living. His children were: Martha, Mary, Alexander, Smith, Wiley, Manley B., Martitia, Eugene Spencer and Thomas. Martha married Wm. Blackburn and lives at Virgil; Mary married T. B. Miller and lives on Meat Camp; Alexander, who married Rhoda Howell and lives at Elkland. Smith died when young. Wiley married twice, first, Mary Norris, and then Nora Houck, and lives on Meat Camp, near the old home place. Manley B. married Martha Norris and lives at Boone. He has been postmaster, register of deeds and clerk of the Superior Court, succeeding his brother, Eugene, who died unmarried while serving as register of deeds. Martitia married Jonathan Greene and moved to Missouri, where she now lives. E. Spencer became a lawyer and located at Jefferson, and was elected to the legislature from Ashe, becoming speaker of that body. A few years later he was appointed assistant United States District Attorney for the Western District of North Carolina. Then he moved to Wilkesboro, and while residing there was elected twice to represent the Eighth District in Congress. Afterwards he moved to Oklahoma and then to Elizabethton, where he died in 1912. Thomas studied medicine, located at Boone and afterwards became assistant surgeon in the United States navy. He is now practicing medicine at Hickory, N. C. John married a Case, and had three children, Silas, Levi and Mary. Silas is married and lives in Tennessee. Levi is married and lives at his father's place in Ashe. Mary married Mack Edwards and lives at Wilkesboro. Hampton married a Snyder, dying at Todd and leaving two boys and five girls: The boys, Roby and George, are married and live at Todd. Roby studied medicine and is now a practicing physician. Victoria married Shadrach Graham; Florence married B. Bledsoe; Callie married Caleb Green; Rosa died unmarried; Sophronia married K. Edwards and lives in Ashe.

Edmund Spencer Blackburn, born in Watauga County, September 22, 1868; attended common schools and academies, admitted to the bar in May, 1890; was reading clerk of North Carolina Senate 1894-1895; representative in State Legislature 1896-1897; was elected speaker *pro tem* of this Legislature; appointed assistant United States Attorney for western district in 1898, and assisted in the prosecution of Breese and Dickerson in the First National Bank case; elected as Republican to 57th Congress (March 4, 1901-March 3, 1903); re-elected March 4, 1905, and died at Elizabethton, Tenn., March 10, 1912. Interment at Boone, N. C. Edmund Blackburn was the first of his family to settle in Watauga, then Ashe County, and married a relative of Levi Morphew, who died in 1914 on the New River, well up in the nineties. Edmund's children were Levi, Sallie

HON. E. SPENCER BLACKBURN, M. C.

A History of Watauga County

and Edmund, Levi having been the grandfather of E. Spencer and M. B. Blackburn, of Boone. Levi Morphew is a son of Sallie Blackburn. Among the first Methodist Churches in Watauga was the one built by the Blackburn family on Riddle's Fork of Meat Camp Creek, called Hopewell, the Methodists having worshipped in Levi Blackburn's house prior to that time. Henson's Chapel on Cove Creek was probably the first Methodist Church in Watauga. The first church built in Boone was built about 1880. About 1904 Mr. Blackburn married Miss Louise Parker, daughter of Myron T. Parker, of Washington, D. C., from which union two girls were born.

Blair Family.—James Blair came from England and went to the Jamestown Settlement of Virginia at some period of its existence, but exactly when tradition does not state. His wife was a Colvert, she and her and his family having accompanied him over, one of their sons having been named Colvert. This son after awhile returned to England and married a Miss Morgan and returned with her to Virginia. Some of their descendants came to this State and settled in Randolph County, John Blair, Sr., having been born there July 6, 1764, where he married a Miss Hill. Their children were James, who married a Barnes; William, whose wife's name has been lost; Thomas, who married Susannah Edmisten; Colvert, who married a Barnes; Henry, who married Mary Steele, June 28, 1832. Of these, Henry Blair was born April 22, 1806, and Mary Steele February 10, 1806; John Culbison, born April 9, 1833; Nancy Rebecca, born August 26, 1835; Elijah S., born June 14, 1838; Wm. Morgan, born December 27, 1840; James Thompson, born October 16, 1843; George Henry, born March 25, 1847. Of these, James Culbison married Susan C. Powell, June 21, 1871; Nancy Rebecca married Wm. Horton, October 16, 1860; Elijah S. married Corrinna Finley, May 17, 1870; Wm. M., killed in Civil War, having been wounded March 31, 1865, and died April 19, 1865, near Petersburg, Va.; James Thompson was accidentally killed September 25, 1850; George Henry married, first, Mary E. Councill, January 2, 1872, and then Mary A. Rousseau, September 27, 1882.

Thomas Blair was also a son of John Blair, Sr., and his children were: John C., who married Julia A. Conley first and then Lidia Ann Yelton. Their children were Wm. T., who married Mary E. Boyd, April 15, 1866; James B., who married Emeline Curtis; Mary S., who married Wm. Glenn; Julia Caroline, who married L. R. Jones. By John C. Blair's second marriage there were: Sarah Jane, who married Richard Taylor; Alice M. A., who married Valentine Reese; Lou Ellen Rebecca, who married Mathew Hammons; Margaret I., who married John Hammons; Margaret, daughter of Thomas, married Reed Moore, of the Globe.

John was another son of John, Sr., and married Abigail McCreary and lived on Little River.

Morgan was another son of John, Sr., and married Elizabeth McLeod, and lived on Little River. Elijah was still another son, but died unmarried; also William, who married and moved to Virginia, where he died.

Colbert's children were: James B., who married Harriet Coffey; John, who married in Buncombe; Nancy, who married Martin Dougherty; Louisa, who married Robert Greer; Sarah, who married a Harman; Elizabeth, who married Joseph Green, and Polly, not married.

The daughters of John Blair, Sr., were: Frances, who married and moved to Virginia; Elizabeth, who also married, and another who married Martin Cox in Caldwell County.

Brown Family.—James Brown came from Holland to Wilkes County and settled near Holman's Ford of the Yadkin—the Dutch equivalent of Brown sounding very much as the English word is pronounced. He had ten sons, of whom is still remembered Joseph, who settled just below Three Forks Church. He married a Miss Hagler, of the "Big Waters of Pee Dee," in South Carolina. Their children were: Thomas, Elizabeth, Jesse, Sallie, Nancy and James. Thomas married Susan Greene, a daughter of John "Flatty;" Joseph married Nancy Farthing, daughter of Rev. Wm. Farthing; Elizabeth died unmarried; Jesse married a Miss Webb, of Judge James L. Webb's family; Sallie married Reuben P. Farthing; Nancy married Daniel Bradley; James married Harriet Farthing, daughter of Rev. Wm. Farthing. James' sons were Eli, James, Frank, Thomas, Hubbard, Jesse and Ben. Eli and Ben settled in Ashe. Eli had one son, Jesse, who lived on Brushy Fork, and he left a son who now lives there. Benjamin left a son, Asa Brown, who lives near Todd or Elkland, and a daughter, who is now Mrs. Church, and lives at the head of Watauga River. James the second had a son, Eli, who settled in Ashe and married a Miss Sands, and left Newton, who moved to Missouri before the Civil War; Milton, who died on Middle Fork, and married Hannah Shearer, daughter of Jack and granddaughter of Robert Shearer the first. Caroline never married. Nancy married Thomas Brown; David went to Missouri and married a Miss Brown there. Eli, son of James the second, had a number of brothers, of whom Thomas is still remembered. He went to Alabama; William went to Georgia and another brother, whose name has been forgotten, went to Missouri. James, youngest son of Joseph Brown, settled on Roan Creek, Tenn., and married Harriet Farthing. Their children were Hamilton, who was killed by a tree on Roan Creek when fourteen years old; Nancy, who is still living; Captain Bartlett Roby Brown married Callie Wagner, daughter of "Gray Jake;" Stephen Justice married a sister of B. R. Brown's wife and died in 1913; Mary, wife of William Shull, both now dead, left a son, James A., who lives at Neva; Sallie, who died when nine or ten years old; Eva, yet living at Neva; Martha, who married Norman Wills and lives at Silver Lake; James Julian, who died at twenty-one, and Dudley, who married a Miss Williams and lives near Knoxville.

Thomas Brown, eldest son of Joseph and grandson of James the first, was county surveyor of Watauga County, and one morning was out before breakfast making up his field notes while sitting under a tree near Henson's Chapel on Cove Creek, with a number of men around him. There was no wind, but suddenly hearing bark begin to fall, the others ran. But he, waiting to gather his papers, was delayed and unfortunately ran in the direction in which the tree fell. He was caught by its branches and killed. It was an immense tree and prostrated five other trees when it fell. His sons were Richard, Joseph, Bartlett, Daniel, Alfred, who was a baby when his father was killed; Mary, who married Rufus Holtsclaw, and Elizabeth, who married Elisha Green, all now dead. James Brown the first entered 640 acres of land on Meat Camp from a description of its boundaries given by Daniel Boone and his companions while James still lived in Wilkes and before he had even seen the place. Rev. L. W. Farthing, his greatgrandson, surveyed the land by the original grant, which was dated in 1789 or 1790.

John and Lewis Bryan or Bryant.—This name used to be spelt Bryant, but when it was discovered that the "t" was superfluous, it was dropped. Morgan Bryan spelt his name with a "t," as did all who now call themselves Bryan. Battle Bryan, as he was baptized, but changed his name, because the children called him a battling stick, to Bartlett, was the son of Lewis Bryan and Elizabeth White, of Iredell County. Lewis was the first merchant in Jefferson, about 1800, but he had a clerk whose name was Merchison, and on one occasion, when Lewis was absent, purchasing goods, this clerk sold all the goods he could convert into money at a small price, collected all the debts he could at a large discount, and disappeared. When Lewis Bryan returned he remarked to his wife, after looking over his affairs, "Betsy, I'm busted." He returned to Iredell with his wife, and was killed there by a tree which fell on him at a "chopping frolic." Lewis was the son of John Bryan, who was at home on a furlough when the notorious Col. David Fanning, of the Revolutionary period, killed him in cold blood.

From "Murphey's Papers" (Vol. 2, pp. 397, 398) we learn (p. 396) that Wm. Lindley was one of Col. David Fanning's men, but took no part in Fanning's cruelties, being beloved by his neighbors. Towards the close of the Revolutionary War, when the Tories began to think the Whigs would eventually triumph, Lindley, with many others of the Tories, "crossed the Blue Ridge and determined to remain on New River until the fate of the war was determined. But before this he had given offence to two Tories, Wm. White and John Magaherty, and they pursued and killed him on his way over the mountains.

Fanning hanged White and Magaherty for this, both on same limb (p. 397). In trying to save his head from the blow of a sword in the hands of one of his murderers the fingers of one of Lindley's hands were cut off, but his head was wounded notwithstanding. White gave his own wife, who was pregnant, an account of all this, and when the child was born it had marks on its head and the fingers on one hand were declared to be precisely such as White had described (p. 397). Toward the close of the war Fanning did not pretend to fight openly, but went about with from five to fifteen men, murdering, burning and wantonly destroying property of defenceless people. He killed Andrew Balfour in the presence of his wife and daughter and burnt the house of Colonel Collins." From that place they proceeded to John Bryant's. He closed his doors; they called on him to come out and surrender (p. 398). He refused. They then threatened to burn his house. He agreed to surrender himself if they would treat him as a prisoner of war, which they promised to do. Bryant came out, and they instantly shot him down. On the same day they hanged Daniel Clifton, of Virginia, to the same limb on which they had hanged White and Magaherty.

Lewis Bryan's children were John Gilson, a Baptist preacher, who married the daughter of James Norris, of New River, and lived on Meat Camp where Billy Green now lives. He moved to Alexander County and afterwards to Georgia, where he died at the age of ninety-eight. The four girls all married and reared families. Their names were Sarah, Ann, Polly and Fanny. Another of Lewis Bryan's sons was Battle, who married Rebecca Miller, a daughter of Hon. David Miller, and reared twelve children, four boys and eight girls, and, strange to say, there was not a dose of doctor's medicine ever given one of the family until after the youngest child was grown. The other boys in the Civil War, who escaped without a wound, were W. Lewis, John and Joseph.

Battle Bryan's children were John, who married Lydia Ann Holder; Henry M., who was killed at Spotsylvania, Va., having been shot in the center of the forehead; William Lewis, who lives in Boone; Joseph, who married Sallie Hodges, daughter of Thomas Hodges; Polly, who married Lawson Woodring; Susan, who married Amos Green; Nancy, who married David Norris; Elizabeth, who married Jehiel Eggers; Sallie, who married a Raegan; Jane, who married John White; Carolina, who died young and unmarried, and Ann, who married T. J. Brown. He is dead, but she still lives.

William Lewis Bryan.—He was born on Meat Camp November 19, 1837. His father was Battle or Bartlett Bryan and his mother Rebecca Miller. Battle Bryan was a son of Lewis Bryan, and his wife, Elizabeth White, and was born in what is now Alexander County in 1799, dying in 1894. Rebecca Miller was the daughter of Hon. David Miller, and was born in 1806 and died in 1904. Colonel Bryan moved to Boone in 1857, after having attended several schools on Meat Camp and spending one summer in the home of Paul Hartzogg, near the mouth of Phœnix Creek, Ashe, helping Daniel Moretz build an overshot grist mill for George Bower. While in Boone Colonel Bryan clerked for Jacob Rintils, and made shoes for Jack Horton. Rintils having moved to Statesville about 1858, where he married Betty Wallace, a sister of Isaac and David Wallace, Colonel Bryan followed him there, and clerked for him a few months, after which he returned to Boone and carried on business for Rintils in the James H. Tatum store till early in the Civil War. Rintils having withdrawn, Colonel Bryan and Moretz Weisenfeld continued the business at the same stand till Weisenfeld went into the Confederate army, when Colonel Bryan moved the stock to the store room which stood where the J. D. Councill house now stands, buying everything he could that he thought the people needed. Stoneman's men did not molest him or his stock, but robbers who followed that raid stole all he had. He then returned to Meat Camp and tended a crop on shares for his aunt, Mrs. Polly Lookabill. He married Miss Sarah Hayes, a daughter of Ransom Hayes, on the 12th of December, 1865, and went with her to his Meat Camp home, where they resided till the death of her father in 1868. Then they returned to Boone and farmed till March, 1870, when he opened up a mercantile business in the old Councill store for M. V. Moore, buying Moore out in 1873. He continued in this business till his store and dwelling and stock were burned July 4, 1895. Since then he has farmed. He was for years United States commissioner and mayor of Boone. He has done much to preserve local history.

Cable Family.—Kasper Cable came from Germany in the British army during the Revolutionary War, but deserted at the first opportunity and went to Dry Run, in what is now Johnson County, Tenn., where he married a Miss Baker. Their children were Jacob, Benjamin, Joseph, Kasper, Daniel, Conrad and several daughters. Of these children, Conrad had the following sons and daughters: Kasper, who married Lucinda Hamby; John, who married Edith Blevens; Andrew, who married a Miss Bradley; Claiborne, who married Lotta Dugger; Edna, who married William Staunton; Polly, who never married; Sarah, who married Morgan Swift; Rhoda, who married John Dugger, and another daughter who married Elias Swift. T. A. Cable is a son of Claiborne, and was born June 22, 1846. He married Ermine B. Farthing, November 17, 1870.

The Coffey Family.—Thomas Coffey was a son of John Coffey, and his wife Jane Graves, of the Church of England. His grandfather came from Ireland to America, where he died, leaving two sons and three daughters, as follows: John, Elizabeth, Patsy, Anister and Edward. John married Jane Graves, whose parents came from England. They had six sons and two daughters, as follows: James, who married Elizabeth Cleveland; John, who married Dorcas Carter; Edward, who married Nancy Shenalt; Thomas, who married, first, Eliza Smith, and, second, Sally Fields; Reuben, who married Sallie Scott; Benjamin, who married Polly Hayes; William, who married Elizabeth Ashburn; Elizabeth, who married Thomas Fields, and Winifred, who married Nicholas Morrison.

The children of Thomas Coffey and his first wife, Eliza Smith, were Betsy, who married David Allen; John, who married Hannah Wilson; Thomas, who married ——————— Coffey; James, who married Delia Ferguson; Polly, who married William Coffey; Smith, who married Hannah Boone.

The children of Thomas Coffey and his wife, Sallie Fields, were: Martha, who married James Dowell; William, who married Annie Boone, niece of Daniel Boone; Reuben, who married Polly Dowell; Elijah, who married Polly Hull; Sally, who married Samuel Stewart; Jesse, who died unmarried; Lewis, who married Harriet Powell; Larkin, who married Catharine Wilson, and McCaleb, who married Elizabeth Collett.

McCaleb Coffey was born August 22, 1803, and married Elizabeth Collett, February 5, 1828. He died February 17, 1881. His wife was born March 8, 1809, and died July 6, 1887. Their children were Thomas Jefferson Coffey, who married Mollie Greer; Charles L., who married Emily Coffey; Sarah A., who married John Steele; an infant who died unnamed; John E., drowned when a child; Mary L., who married George Nelson; Margaret, who died unmarried; W. Columbus, who married, first, Carrie Curtis, and, second, Mrs. Ada Penn; Martha E., unmarried; Henry C., who married Sophronia Coffey; Carrie, who married David J. Farthing; James E., who died of diphtheria at Petersburg, Va., in 1864; Rachel M., who married Thomas Coffey; Jennie, unmarried; Laura, died when four years old; Buddie, who died when two years old.

Smith Coffey, son of Thomas Coffey and Elizabeth Smith, his first wife, married Hannah Boone, a niece of Daniel Boone and a sister of Anna Boone. Their children were: Squire, who married Ella ————; Morgan, who married ————; Athen, who married ————; Sallie, who married Wm. Puett; Leland, who married Myra Day; Isaac, who married Sallie Estes; Millie, who married, first, Wiley Stanley and then John Tritt.

Abram Collett came from Scotland and married Margaret Wakefield, by whom he had three children: Betsy, who married Thomas Church; Rachel, who married a Mr. Ingmon; Charles, who married Amelia Parks, by whom he had ten children: Margaret, Rachel, Abram, Thomas, John, Mary, James, Elizabeth, Francis and McCoy. Of these, Rachel married William Wakefield; Abram married Mary Stewart; John married Margaret Murphy, who died, and he then married Eliza Jane Cald-

A History of Watauga County 295

well; James, who married Jane Stewart; Elizabeth, who married McCaleb Coffey, and Frances, who married Alfonso McGimpsey.

William Columbus Coffey.—He was born near Patterson in Caldwell County April 3, 1839; went to Butler, Tenn., in April, 1859, where he arrived with only three cents in his pocket. He went into business there, on the left bank of Roan Creek and a little above the present residence of D. J. Farthing, where the store washed away in September, 1861. He waded waist-deep in water trying to save the stock. In April, 1862, he went into the 26th North Carolina regiment, where he remained till 1863, when he got a transfer to the 58th North Carolina, Col. J. B. Palmer, in which he was elected third lieutenant in April, 1864, in which capacity he served till the 58th and 60th regiments were consolidated, when he became second lieutenant. He surrendered at Greensboro with Johnson's army in April, 1865. In November, 1865, he came with his brother, Thomas Jefferson Coffey, to Boone and opened a store in the J. W. Councill store. In June, 1866, he left Boone and opened a branch store of Thos. J. Coffey & Bro. at what is now Zionville, near the head of Cove Creek, where he carried on business in a store room which is now gone, but which stood on Reuben Farthing's land. He returned to Boone and assisted his brother to build the Coffey hotel and store in 1869, and moved into that hotel before it was completed, which was not till 1870. He married Carrie L. Curtis, daughter of Hezekiah Curtis, of Wilkesboro, in 1866. Their children were Edgar S., who married Anna Parks; Thomas Finley, who married, first, Jennie Councill, and, second, Blanche Wells, of Manning, S. C. After the death of his first wife, W. C. Coffey married Mrs. Ada Penn in July, 1908.

Thomas Jefferson Coffey was born near Patterson, Caldwell County, in December, 1828, and died in June, 1901. He taught school at Valle Crucis before the Civil War, but soon went into business at what is now Butler, Tenn. He joined the Confederate army, finally becoming captain of Company E, 58th North Carolina infantry. He married Mollie Greer about 1866. She is still living in Statesville. Their children were Elizabeth, who married Judge W. B. Councill; Margaret, who married Stacy Rambo, of Mountain City, Tenn., and Stewart, who married, first, a Miss Sanborn, and then a Mrs. Roby, and lives at Statesville. Before his death he and brother, W. C., entered into an agreement that whichever survived the other should carry on the firm business as long as he thought fit, and then divide the property. Upon the death of Thos. J., in 1901, W. C. carried on the business as before for about two years and until T. J.'s youngest child became twenty-one years old. He then divided the property into two lots. Lot No. 1 contained the stock of merchandise on hand, the debts due the firm, cash on hand and part of the land. In lot No. 2 were the greater part of the land and the live stock principally. T. J. Coffey's heirs were given choice of the two lots, and chose lot No. 1. Thomas J. Coffey had most to do with the building of the turnpike from Blowing Rock to Boone. He got the charter through the legislature and took the contract to build the road, which contract was given to himself and brother, W. C. Coffey. The survey was made by S. T. Kelsey, the overseeing was done by Alexander McRae, the work was commenced in August, 1893, and the road was finished in October, 1894.

Cottrell Family.—Wm. Cottrell, Sr., settled in Caldwell County, and was the father of several children, among whom was William, Jr., who married Lucy Day. Their children were: John, who married a Triplett, and moved to Mississippi, where both died, leaving children, two of whom live in that State and one in Texas. Thomas and William and several girls were other children of William, Jr., and Lucy Day. One of these girls married a Minton and settled near Wilkesboro, another married Wm. Brown and moved to Georgia, while a third married a Coffey and settled on Mulberry, where they died several years ago, leaving several children in Caldwell County. William Cottrell married Susan Shearer, settled in Caldwell, where they died. James, a brother of William and Thomas, married a Blair and settled in Caldwell. Thomas Cottrell married Louisa Shearer and settled in Watauga. To them were born ten children, all of whom are dead but four. These are: Louisa and

Julia, who live in Caldwell; Susan, who lives with Mr. and Mrs. L. N. Perkins near Boone, and C. J. Cottrell, who married Melissa Norris. This gentleman is a justice of the peace and is connected with the Appalachian Training School. He lost an eye at Resacka in 1864. He is a most worthy and highly respected citizen.

Councill Family.—The following facts have been taken haphazard from the family Bible in possession of Mrs. J. S. Williams. They will be valuable to all who trace their ancestry from this family, the first of whom was Jordan, making three Jordans in succession before 1850. Jordan Councill, who lived at the Buck Horn Tree place, just east of the town of Boone, where Jesse Robbins now lives, was born in 1769, having been the son of Jordan Councill. He married Sallie Howard about 1797, and died December 10, 1839. His son, Jordan Councill, was born September 22, 1799. Sarah Councill was born September 23, 1802.

The children of Jordan Councill, Jr., who married Sallie Bowers, September 3, 1823, were: John C., born August 1, 1824; James W., born December 29, 1826; William Bowers, born February 23, 1829; Elizabeth, born September 29, 1831; Sarah Louise, born December 7, 1841; Martha Adelaide, born December 8, 1845; George R., born October 12, 1849.

Daughters of Jordan Councill, Sr., and his wife, Sallie Howard: 1. Sallie, who married Alfred Martin, of Yadkin County; 2. Lottie, who married John Hardin, Sr.; 3. Elizabeth, who married Willis McGhee; 4. Nancy, who married Col. Euclid Baird; Eliza, who married, first, George Phillips, the father of Dr. J. B. Phillips, and, second, Rittenhouse Baird, the father of ex-Sheriff William B. Baird, who lived below Valle Crucis on the old homestead. George Phillips was the sheriff of Ashe County, and on his return from Raleigh, where he had gone to settle the taxes collected by him, was drowned in the Shallow Ford of the Yadkin. This was long before the Civil War and soon after the birth of his son, Dr. J. B. Phillips.

The children of Dr. W. B. Councill, who married Alice M. Bostwick, June 7, 1854, were: Jefferson Bostwick, born October 3, 1855; William Bower, born August 11, 1857; Margaret, born February 10, 1861; I. Lenoir, born March 25, 1864; Emma A., born June 19, 1866; Mary Virginia, born January 12, 1862.

The children of J. W. Councill, who married M. V. Cocke November 29, 1854, were: Mary Alice, born October 17, 1856; G. W., born December 31, 1859; J. D., born August 21, 1861; R. Lenoir, born April 19, 1864; Sallie M., born September 16, 1866; Bettie Folk, born August 17, 1870; John Hardin, born February 25, 1874; Walter Armfield, born May 14, 1878.

George R. Councill ("Toad") married Anna M. Carter June 28, 1881; S. W. Boyden married Margaret F. Councill February 14, 1882; John S. Williams married Elizabeth F. Councill January 9, 1889; Dr. L. C. Reeves married Sallie M. Councill April 16, 1890; Richard L. Councill married Cora Bryan October —, 1889; Geo. N. Folk married Elizabeth A. Councill October 16, 1853; J. W. Councill died November 19, 1884; Jordan Councill, Jr., died July 24, 1875; Sarah L. Councill died November 26, 1844; Martha A. died November 3, 1856; Sallie B. died April 23, 1877; George R. died July 9, 1891; Mary V. died November 26, 1894.

Jordan Councill the First.—He married Sallie Howard, daughter of Benjamin Howard, and lived on the right hand side of the old road which led from Councill's store to Jefferson, at what is now called the Buck Horn Tree place and where Jesse Robbins in 1914 erected two houses. There is a fine spring near by. Councill's house was of logs. He was a farmer and a man of means. His children were: 1. Jesse, who married Sallie Dixon, of Ashe, and lived where Jerry Ray now lives, nearly two miles east of Boone and off the road to Three Forks. 2. Jordan, who married Sallie Bower, sister of George Bower, and lived at the old Councill home, opposite Richard M. Greene's home in Boone. He was the Father of Boone, and Ransom Hayes, who gave as much land as he, was the Step-father of Boone. 3. Benjamin, who married, first, Lizzie Mast, daughter of Joel Mast, and lived at Vilas, and, second, Tempe Shull, sister of Joseph Shull, Sr., and of Phillip Shull. There were four children by the first and four by the last marriage.

Jordan Councill's Grandchildren.—Jesse's children were: 1. Sallie, who married Jesse Ray and lived on Old Fields Creek; 2. Nancy, who married Thomas Green and lived at the mouth of Meat Camp; 3. Elizabeth, who married Albert P. Wilson and lived on Cove Creek after the Civil War, when he sold the place to Hiram McBride, of Tennessee, and came to Boone, where his wife died. He now lives near Three Forks Baptist Church. 4. Louisa, who married D. B. Ferguson, of Meat Camp, and died when he was in the Civil War. Ferguson still lives in Catawba. 5. John, who died unmarried while in the Confederate army, as did also Jordan. Jordan Councill's children were James W., who married Mollie Cocke, of Sumter, S. C. These were the parents of J. D. Councill, of Boone. Dr. William B. Councill, who married Miss Alice M. Bostwick, of Sumter, S. C.; George R. C. Councill, who married a Miss Carter, of Yadkin Valley; Elizabeth A., who married Col. George N. Folk at Easter Chapel on upper Watauga River, Rev. Henry H. Prout officiating. Benjamin Councill's children were, by his first marriage: Jacob M., who married Sallie Lewis, daughter of Jacob, who lived at the head of Hog Elk and was killed by Stoneman's men, March 28, 1865, aged thirty-five years. Their children were: Mary, who married George W. Blair; Benjamin J., who married Blanche Hagaman, and Mattie, who married John Hardin, of Boone; Joseph C., who married in Texas, where he died; Sallie, who married Eben Smith, son of Jehiel; Elizabeth, who married Holland Hodges, both of whom are living at Hodges Gap, two miles west of Boone. By his second marriage Benjamin Councill had Jordan, who married Polly Horton; Benjamin, who married, first, a Miss Adams, and, second, a Miss Bradley; James, who married Sallie Horton, and Polly, who married James W. Horton, of Cove Creek.

James W. Councill's children were: 1. Alice, who married Samuel Lenoir and still lives in Sumter, S. C., though her husband is now dead; 2. George W. (Bud), who died unmarried in Sumter, S. C.; 3. J. Dudley, who married Emma, daughter of Joshua Winkler, and lives in Boone; 4. Richard L., who married Cora Bryan and died in Boone in October, 1895; 5.

Sallie, who married Dr. L. C. Reeves, who died at Blowing Rock about 1899. She still lives there with two children. 6. Elizabeth, who married John S. Williams and lives near Three Forks Baptist Church; 7. John H., who died unmarried; 8. Walter, who died before reaching manhood. Dr. Wm. Bowers Councill's children were: 1. Jefferson B., a physician, who lives in Salisbury; 2. Judge W. B., who married Elizabeth Coffey, daughter of T. J. Coffey and wife; 3. Margaret, who married Stephen Boyden, of Salisbury. She is dead, leaving four children. 4. Emma, who married James, the son of Henry Taylor, of Valle Crucis. He is dead, but she still lives at Hickory and Blowing Rock. 5. Isaac Lenoir, who is unmarried and lives at Waynesville; 6. Jennie, who was the first wife of Finley Coffey, of Manning, S. C.

Jesse Councill's daughters were: Sarah, who married Jesse Ray; Nancy, who married Thomas Greene; Elizabeth, who married Albert P. Wilson; Louisa, who married Burnett D. Ferguson. His two sons never married. They were John and Jordan, and both died in the Confederate army. Benjamin Councill's first wife was a Miss Mast. Their children were: Jacob, who married Sarah Lewis, of Hog Elk; Joseph, who married a lady in Texas; Sarah, who married Eben Smith and moved to Texas, where both died; Elizabeth, who married Holland Hodges and are still living a few miles west of Boone. Benjamin Councill's second marriage was to Tempe Shull, an aunt of Joseph Shull. Their children were: Jordan, who married Polly Horton and died in Lee's army in Virginia; Benjamin, who married a Miss Bradley, daughter of Daniel Bradley, of Brushy Fork, where he died, and James P., who married Sarah Horton, daughter of Jack Horton, and lived at Vilas; sold out to Finley Holsclaw and moved to Limestone, Tenn., and Polly, only daughter, who married James W. Horton and lived at the old homestead on Cove Creek.

Jordan Councill, Jr.—Was born at the Buck Horn Tree place, Boone, and married Sallie Bower, a sister of George Bower, of Ashe County. His son, James W., married Mary Cocke, of Sumter, S. C.; another son, Dr. William Bower Councill, married Alice Bostwick, of Sumter, S. C.; George

Russeau married Annie Carter, of Caldwell County; Elizabeth, who married George N. Folk, noted lawyer, who lived at Boone where Dr. J. W. Jones now resides, but moved to Asheville shortly before the Civil War, where he entered into a copartnership with one of the Woodfins, but returned to Boone and made up a company of cavalry, which was a part of the First North Carolina Cavalry. When he was in Boone he made a speech to his men from the front of the store which stood on the site of the present residence of W. L. Bryan, and where Wallace, Elias and Rintils were merchandising. J. W. Councill was the first lieutenant; J. B. Todd, second lieutenant, and J. C. Blair was third lieutenant. J. W. Todd, afterwards the distinguished attorney of Jefferson, was the first sergeant.

Critcher Family.—Nathaniel R. Critcher was born in Granville County, North Carolina, September 6, 1803, and married Cynthia A. Clarke, who was born in Orange County, North Carolina, August 9, 1804. They, with her mother and David and Daniel Clarke and Elisha Holder, moved to what is now Watauga in 1840, Nathaniel settling where Abe J. Edmisten now lives, Holder on Howard's Creek and the Clark brothers at the mouth of Roan Creek, now Butler, Tenn. Nathaniel's children were: Guilford A., Sarah J., William J., Nancy C., John C., Thomas A., all of whom are dead except Sarah J. Hodges, John C. having been killed near Richmond, Va., in the Civil War. Guilford A. was born in Orange County, North Carolina, April 28, 1828, and married Frances R. Satterwhite, daughter of Nathan and Lucy, of Granville County, North Carolina, December 29, 1852. In 1858 they settled where Charles L. Cook now lives, and where they both died. Thomas L. Critcher, the oldest living son of Guilford A., was born October 20, 1857. He married Nannie J. Wilson, daughter of Isaac, and she died December 20, 1910. He is a merchant, justice of the peace and civil engineer. He owns part of 640 acres granted to William Miller in May, 1887, and deeded to Nathan Horton May 20, 1898, the deed having been witnessed by Shadrach Brown and Hodges Councill. It is in Cook's Gap of the Blue Ridge in which Thomas, Bethuel and Jonathan Buck, William Miller, Nathan Horton, Robert Greene, the Coffeys, Hayes and Shearers have been settlers, or through which they have passed on their way further West, following in the footsteps of the famous Daniel Boone. James and Alfred Brown, Henry Blair, Nathan Satterwhite, Samuel Brown, Adam Cook, have at various times owned an interest in this land, which could not be bought now for $10,000.00. It is through this gap that the Grandon Railroad is to pass on its way to Boone.

Davis Family.—James Davis was first of this family, and he was born in England and emigrated to America. His son, James, married Nancy Fullbright. He was born and reared in Lincoln County, till Catawba was established, five miles northeast of Newton. James the second moved close to Miller's farm on Meat Camp in 1844 when William S. Davis was thirteen years of age. W. S. married Sarah Blackburn November 30, 1854. The object James had in coming was to run the linseed oil mills for John Moretz. James Davis had four sons, Isaac and David, both of whom died young; Smith, who moved to Texas, and James, father of William S.

H. A. Davis was born in Catawba County July 17, 1840, but in December, 1845, moved to Watauga County with his parents, James Davis and his wife, who was born Nancy Fullbright, their parents having come to North Carolina from Pennsylvania. H. A. Davis was married January 23, 1868, to Mary A. Hodges, daughter of Wm. R. Hodges and Nancy Triplett Hodges, who were born in Watauga and Wilkes counties, respectively. May 17, 1861, he enlisted as a private in Company D, 1st North Carolina cavalry, and was captured by the 16th Pennsylvania cavalry June 9, 1863; exchanged June 30, 1863; was wounded September 22, 1863, near Jackshop, Va. His wife, Mary A., born January 1, 1850, died December 5, 1875. James Davis, father of H. A., died August 30, 1859. Nancy Fullbright Davis, mother of H. A., died March 5, 1895. James Davis' parents were James Davis and Delphia Mahaffa. Nancy Fullbright Davis' parents were Wm. Fullbright and Nancy Plonk. Nancy Triplett Hodges died in May, 1912. Wm. R. Hodges' parents were Jesse Hodges, who was murdered in 1864 by Thomas Roberts, of Johnson County, Tennessee; Polly Clawson, died in 1863.

Dugger Family.—In 1793 or 1794 Benjamin Dugger came to Watauga County from Yadkin Elk, where a creek and mountain still bear his name. He entered land on Brushy Fork, near the present Holtsclaw settlement. His children were Selah, who married Laus Goodin; Daniel Dugger; Cora Ann, who married Samuel Burns; Susannah, who married John Whittington; Mary, who married John Calihan; David and William Dugger. David Dugger bought out the other heirs. The deed is dated November 1, 1815, and calls for two tracts on Brushy Fork. There were three Dugger brothers who came from Scotland to Yadkin Elk, having settled for a time near Petersburg, Va., Benjamin, Daniel and Julius. Ben stopped on Brushy Fork, Daniel went to Kentucky and Julius settled in what was then Carter County, Tennessee, near Fish Spring, where some of his descendants still live. It was from the Julius Dugger family that the Dugger forge and the beginnings of Cranberry forge started. David married Margaret Ernest and their children are: Henry, who married a Green; Polly, who married David Howell; Elizabeth, who married Jehiel Smith, and William, who married Unice Munday. William's children were: Henry, who never married; Franklin, who married Martha Presnell; David, who married Mary Munday; Elizabeth, who never married; John, killed in Civil War; William Eben., married Nannie Wilkerson; Margaret and Mary Jane, not married.

The Eggers Family.—Landrine Eggers came from London to the eastern part of this State first and then to Ashe County. He was born in 1747 and died March 17, 1833. He was married, first, to a lady whose name has been forgotten, and, second, to Joanna Green, whose family lived near Three Forks Church and were members of that body. Children of first marriage have been forgotten, but those of the second are: Hugh, the date of whose birth and the name of whose wife are not now known, and one daughter, Lydia, who was born December 14, 1791, and married James Swift, who died January 8, 1858, leaving the following children: Franklin, born August 11, 1816; Elias, born February 5, 1818; Morgan, born October 23, 1819; James, born December 3, 1821; Martha, born January 1, 1824; Margaret, born August 26, 1826; Elizabeth, born June 20, 1828;

304 A History of Watauga County

Wilburn, born October 7, 1831; Mary, born March 16, 1833; Rebecca, born April 15, 1835. Hugh's children were: Landrine, born September 10, 1805; Malinda, born February 11, 1802; Washington, born August 21, 1808; Nancy, born April 15, 1836; Jehiel S., born October 20, 1834; Martha C., born September 27, 1837, and the following, the dates of whose births are unknown: Cleveland, Abner and Joel. Landrine the second married Ellen McBride, daughter of Wm., of Rowan County, born August 5, 1800; died December 5, 1872. The children of Landrine the second were: Brazilla, born June 10, 1825, married Sarah Isaacs; Ransom, born January 5, 1827, married Rachel Isaacs; Hugh and Sarah, twins, born December 26, 1828, of whom Hugh married Alva Kilby, and Sarah, John Isaacs; Landrine the third, born November 18, 1830; Anna, born July 21, 1832, married Franklin Reese; Richard, born February 1, 1834, married Elizabeth Reese; John, born December 2, 1835, married Martha Stout; Ellen, born January 16, 1839, married Maston Davis. Landrine the third married September 7, 1854, first, Sarah Ward, daughter of James Ward, of Watauga River, who was born November 26, 1834, died July 6, 1867. The children of the first marriage were: Sarah Ellen, born May 17, 1862, married Solomon Grogan. Landrine the third's second wife was Mary Potter. They were married March 8, 1868, she having been born March 15, 1831. Their children were: John L., born July 21, 1870, married, first, Alice Greer; second, Daisy Adams, and, third, the widow Woodring; Omer C., born August 14, 1873, died of diphtheria November, 1887; Luther D., born December 26, 1876, married Emma Jones, daughter of Rev. E. F. Jones, and lives at Post Falls, Idaho; Barton R., born August 17, 1878, died of diphtheria November, 1887; Carroll and Jehiel, twins, born May 30, 1881, died November 9, 1887, and were buried in same grave.

Edmisten Family.—Wm. Wallace Dixon Edmisten was born on Mulberry Creek, Caldwell County, August 29, 1850. He was the son of James Edmisten and Mary Shull, a daughter of Phillip Shull, and they were married September 25, 1848. Their children were W. W. D. and Nancy Carolina, the latter of whom married Frank Read. James Edmisten's father was William and his wife was Nancy Garner. William's father was also named William, and his wife was the widow of ——————— Blair, born Sudderth, a sister of Abraham Sudderth. Her husband, ——————— Blair, was killed at King's Mountain while fighting on the side of the British, and William Edmisten married her after the Revolution. She was then a young widow, but William had fought at King's Mountain, too, where two of his brothers, who were said to have been officers, were killed, but he and they had fought on the American side. These brothers were from Virginia.

Elrod Family.—The first of this family came from France to Pennsylvania and thence to Davie County, North Carolina. From this State they have spread out to Ohio, Tennessee, Kentucky, Virginia and South Dakota, Henry C. Elrod having been governor of the latter State a few years since. Conrad Elrod was the father of William, and died near the present Reformed Church, on the Blue Ridge. He was buried in a hollowed out chestnut log. William married Elizabeth Lowrance, and their children were: Chaney, who married Robert Greene, father of Judge L. L. Greene; Malinda, who married Asa Triplett; Henry, who married Sarah Brookshire; Alexander, who married Polly Shearer; Mary, who married Thomas Cook; Ann, who married Lot Greene; Hardin, who married Temperance Bradshaw; Rachel, who never married, and John, who married Elizabeth Brookshire. Henry Elrod moved to the Watts Farthing place when two years old, traveling over a trail, and having the household articles carried on pack horses for want of a road. He had two children, William and Louisa. William married Chaney Brookshire and Louisa married T. M. Cannon. William remembers that when he was eight years old, on September 27, 1856, there was a snow storm in Watauga County. He also remembers when a wagon was a rare sight in this section. He remembers when the buckhorn which had been nailed on the old oak tree on the old Jordan Council place showed through the bark, and when it was entirely covered by the bark. He saw this when he came to the old Musters before the Civil War. Top buggies were even rarer than wagons, and James W. Councill had what was probably the first in the county in the fifties. Henry Elrod was conscripted after he had moved in 1857 to the Flat Top Mountain, and taken to Camp Vance, after which he was transferred to Camp Mast, where he was captured. He died in 1885. Alex Elrod was captured by Stoneman, but, pretending to have rheumatism, was allowed to escape.

Farthing Family.—Dudley Farthing was born in Virginia, April 6, 1749. He was the son of William Farthing and his wife, Mary. Dudley Farthing died in Wake County February 22, 1826. His wife was Annie, daughter of Wm. Watkins and Phœbe, his wife. She was born July 4, 1747, in Virginia, and died February 13, 1812, in Wake County. Their children were: Phœbe, born November 15, 1778, and she married John Link, February 3, 1803; Mary, born July 3, 1780, and died March 22, 1826; William, born August 25, 1782, married Polly W. Hallyburton, February 9, 1804; John, born September 26, 1784, married Lucy Goss, first, who died April 9, 1827, and then Polly Amos; he died February 29, 1868; Reuben, born September 1, 1787, married ————————; died August 14, 1834; Eliza, born February 22, 1790, and died August 3, 1790. The children of the Rev. William W. Farthing were: Dudley, born November 29, 1804, married Nancy Mast in 1831; he died July 8, 1895, and she September 22, 1882; Patsy, born December 4, 1805, married Thomas Shearer, an uncle of Robert Shearer; they moved to Kansas between 1850 and 1855; Nancy was born February 21, 1807, married Joseph Brown and went to Missouri; Reuben P., born June 28, 1808, married Sallie Brown, and died December 20, 1889; John Atkins, born July 21, 1809, married, first, Melissa Curtis, and, second, Keziah Farthing; William Brown, born December 20, 1810, and married Annie Kindle; Edward F., born April 30, 1812, and died May 3, 1812; Thomas, born May 9, 1813, married Ermine Hallyburton; Annie Watkins, born September 5, 1814, married Wm. Young Farthing, father of W. S. Farthing; Harriet, born March 22, 1816, married James Brown, and died May 16, 1897; Mary Hervey, born February 21, 1818, married Hiram McBride, died May 26,

A History of Watauga County 307

1869; Abner Clopton, born October 6, 1819, and married Mary Narcissus Farthing; Paul, born April 17, 1821, married Rachel Farthing; he died in a Federal prison at Camp Chase in 1865; Stephen, born January 3, 1823, married Margaret Adams, and died January 25, 1882. Dudley Farthing's wife was Nancy, daughter of John Mast and Susan Harman, and she was born May 18, 1809. Their children were: William Judson, born February 6, 1832, and went to Texas in 1859, where he died unmarried September 10, 1865; Susan, born July 12, 1833, and is yet alive; James Martin, born July 25, 1835, and was killed December 13, 1862, in the battle of Fredericksburg, Va.; Mary White, born January 9, 1837, married Newton Moore in 1860 and died May 11, 1914, in Virginia; Thomas Jefferson, born August, 13, 1838, never married, died of pneumonia at Lynchburg May 21, 1862; John Young, born May 17, 1840, married Polly Farthing; Henry Harrison, born October 7, 1841, married Sarah Catharine Baker November 29, 1872; Martha B., born August 24, 1843, died in infancy; Joseph, born August 9, 1844, died in infancy; Lewis Williams, born November 6, 1845, married Nancy McBride, daughter of Hiram; Sarah Carolina, born January 31, 1849, married Warren Greene, first, and then Anderson Cable; Wiley Hill, born March 23, 1850, married Rachel Louisa Farthing, sister of W. S. Farthing, and lives near Blountville, Tenn.; Nancy Emeline, born January 6, 1852, and never married. John Farthing was a brother of Rev. William Watkins Farthing and a son of Dudley the first. He was born in Durham, then in Orange County, July 29, 1812, and in the fall of 1826 came with his brother, W. W., to Beaver Dams, but he lost his wife there and also his brother, W. W. John's first wife was Miss Lucy Goss, and he returned to Durham and married Polly Amos and came back to Watauga in 1831 and settled where Zionville now is, where he owned most of the land. The children by his first wife were: William Young, who married Ann W. Farthing; Dudley, who married Sarah Wilson; Sherman, who was killed by a tree near Zionville just before 1840, thus preventing his expected marriage; Nancy, who married Wm. Ferrall; Rachel W., who married Paul Farthing, a son of Wm. F. Farthing; Mary Narcissus, who married Abner C. Farthing, a son of Wm. W. Farthing; Keziah, who married John A. Farthing, who lived where W. S. Farthing now lives; Lucy White, who never married; Anne, who married Caswell King in Wake County, was an infant when her mother died in Watauga, and was taken back by her father, John Farthing, and reared by Keziah Cozart in Wake County. In her old age she came again to Watauga, where she died.

The children by the second marriage were: Reuben, who married Ellen Wilson, first, and then a Miss Harman; Elijah, who married Amanda Oliver; John, who died when nineteen years of age; Sallie, who married John Adams.

John Farthing's father was Dudley Farthing, who died in Wake, his wife having been Annie Watkins, whom he married February 2, 1778. The first Dudley Farthing had, beside William Watkins and John, the following children: Reuben, who married a Miss Hargus, his descendants still living in and near Durham.

The Farthings came originally from Wales to Pittsylvania County, Virginia, from which they went to Person County, North Carolina, where Annie Watkins was reared. The Rev. William Watkins Farthing was a minister and traveled some for the old Missionary Society of North Carolina, which antedated the Baptist State Convention, and he was traveling and preaching when he first got acquainted with Watauga County. His sons, Reuben, John A., Abner C. and Stephen J., were ministers, the two youngest having been ordained under authority of Bethel and the two elder under that of Cove Creek churches. Rev. J. Harrison Farthing, son of Abner C., is a minister, as are also Calvin S., son of Thomas; Robert Milton, a son of Calvin S., and he preaches in Tennessee, and Rev. L. Whitfield also preaches.

Dudley Farthing was a son of Rev. W. W. Farthing; married Nancy Mast, a daughter of John Mast, who lived where Finley Mast now lives. He had been a member of the Ashe County court prior to the establishment of Watauga County, having been appointed in 1832 to fill out the term of Abram

DUDLEY FARTHING.

Judge of the Court of Pleas and Quarter Sessions.

Vanderpool, and from that time till the Constitution was changed in 1868 he was chairman of the Watauga Court of Pleas and Quarter Sessions. He presided with great dignity and administered his office with sound judgment and ability. No superior court judge who ever came to Watauga County presided over his court with more justness, impartiality or legal learning than Dudley Farthing. He was elected county commissioner after 1868 and became chairman of the board. According to the recollection of his son, Col. Henry H. Farthing, there was reason to suspect that $1,000.00 of the county funds was missing, and Judge Farthing declared that at the next meeting that matter would be investigated. The court house was burned before that meeting and with it all the records except Deed Book F. He was born November 4, 1804, and died July 8, 1895. He was just twenty-two years old when he moved with his father to Watauga County. It is said that when corn was scarce he would not sell it for money, saying that a man with money could get it anywhere, but a man who had no money could get it only where he was known and his needs obvious. He lost little if anything by thus crediting his neighbors in distress. Dudley Farthing lived where Mrs. Susan Farthing lives now, in a frame house built about 1850, three-quarters of a mile southwest from Bethel Church. He and his wife are buried there, Stephen Farthing having inherited the W. W. Farthing home place and objected to additional interments in graveyard above the old home place. There is a graveyard which W. S. Farthing and others have used for burial of their relatives east from the old Farthing graveyard.

Rev. L. Whitfield Farthing was a son of Reuben Pickett and grandson of W. W. Farthing. R. P. Farthing married Sarah Brown, a sister of Thomas Brown, below Three Forks in 1831. Their children were: Thomas Brown, who was born in 1833 and married Celia Greene; William Watkins, who was killed at Brandy Station, Va., in the Civil War; James Hervey, who was born about 1836 and married Lucretia Farthing, but moved West, where they died; L. W., who was born April 18, 1838, and married Nancy Farthing in October, 1866; Joseph

Elmore, who was born April 18, 1840, and married Mary Harman; Mary, born in 1842, but never married; Jesse, born in 1844, but died when twenty or twenty-one years of age; John Watts, who was born February 15, 1848, and married Adeline Rivers in 1876.

Rev. Reuben P. Farthing was the son of Rev. William Watkins Farthing and his wife, Phœbe. He was born June 28, 1808; married Sallie Brown, and died December 20, 1889. He was early admitted to the ministry of the Baptist Church and preached for nearly all his adult years, literally "without money and without price." He was one of the foremost educators of his day, and did much for the advancement of the religious and educational status of the people of Watauga County. He answered every call from all who needed his aid and assistance. His life was one of devotion to duty. When he died the late Major Harvey Bingham paid a tribute to his worth and excellence of which any man might well have been proud. This was published in one of our newspapers and is preserved by the family as a sacred memorial of a great and good man, for in it was said that, while not a college graduate, Reuben Farthing was nevertheless a highly educated and very learned man, having unaided and alone dug out from the classics and from scientific books a store of knowledge that was not only abundant, but practical. A distinguished visitor to his home was struck by his erudition, and was surprised to learn that he had acquired it all by dint of hard work and unremitting study.

Franklin Family.—Levi Franklin was the father of Lawson A., and resided at what is now Altamont on Linville River when that was a part of Watauga County. His sister married Leroy McCanless, who is now a resident of Florence, Colorado, and a brother of D. Colvard McCanless. Rev. William Colvard Franklin, of Altamont, bears part of his name, and is now about sixty years of age.

Gragg Family.—William Gragg was of Irish descent and settled, first, in West Virginia, from which he came with his wife, born Elizabeth Pulliam, to John's River, Caldwell County, soon after the Revolutionary War, in which he had been a soldier

A History of Watauga County 311

under Washington, having fought from the first to the last battle of the war. Their children were: John, born September 7, 1781, in Virginia; William, Obediah, Robert, James, Benjamin, Susan and Elizabeth. Of these, John married, first, Elizabeth Majors, and, second, Susannah Barrier. The children by the first marriage were: Tilmon, John, Tipton, Major, Elisha, Nelson and Hamilton. Those by the second marriage were Harvey, Empsey, Alexander and William Waightstill. There was one daughter by the first marriage, Nicie, and six by the second, Irene, Elvira, Margaret, Eliza and twins, Adeline and Carolina.

William married Celia Boone, a grandniece of Daniel; Obediah married Elizabeth Webb; Robert married Rhoda Humphrey; James married Nancy Humphrey; Benjamin married Nancy Dyer; Susan married Isaac Green; Elizabeth married Alfred Pritchett.

Tilmon married, first, Hila Layell, and, second, Jane McNeely; John married a Miss Morris in Georgia; Tipton married Rachel Greene; Major married Celia Wilson, first, and Polly Ollis, second; Elisha married Selina Piercey; Nelson married Violet Greene; Hamilton married, first, a Cobb, then a House, and, third, Martha Strickland, and Harvey married Melinda McLeard. Empsey married Serena Ford, first, and then Susan Barrier; Alexander married Carolina Munday; William W. married Martha McGhinnis, first, and, second, a lady in the State of Washington.

Nicie married James Calloway; Irene married Samuel Barrier; Elvira married Wiley Holtsclaw; Adeline married W. W. Pressly; Carolina married Madison Gragg; Margaret married Archibald Qualls; Eliza died young and unmarried.

Greene Family.—From "The Greene Family of Watauga," by Rev. G. W. Greene, we learn that the first Greene to come to America came from Wiltshire, England, to Massachusetts about 1635. His name was John, but he was a Quaker and soon joined Roger Williams in Rhode Island, and from him in the fifth generation sprang Gen. Nathaniel Greene, of the Revolution. Early in the eighteenth century one branch of this family went to New York State and settled near Brooklyn, but soon passed on to New Jersey, where many of its members became prominent. But about the middle of the eighteenth century Jeremiah Greene came to North Carolina with the Jersey settlers and bought 541 acres of land on the waters of Pee Dee, near Linwood. This was about 1762. Jeremiah's son, Isaac, and himself remained in the Jersey settlement, but "Stephen Greene, who was probably a younger son of Jeremiah Greene, in 1784 settled in the Forks of the Yadkin, and has left in Davie County a large and honorable progeny." Soon after the Revolution three sons and two daughters of Jeremiah Greene left the Jersey Settlement and moved to what is now Watauga, then a part of Wilkes. These brothers were Richard, Jeremiah and John, all then married, as were their sisters, Joanna, to Landrine Eggers, and Sarah, to a man named Wilson. Richard, the eldest, settled at Blowing Rock and was accompanied by his father-in-law, an old man named Sullivan. He brought a tombstone with him and died February 27, 1794. His coffin was hewed out of a poplar tree when the wood was frozen hard. The stone still stands in the graveyard of the German Reformed Church, one mile from Blowing Rock. This is the inscription:

E. E. S 1794.

It will be noticed that the S is upside down. But, according to Mr. Greene's sketch, the inscription is:

F 27
1794.

If he is right, then F probably stands for February and 27 for the day of that month on which he died.

The brothers, Jeremiah and John, settled in the middle or the eastern part of the county, while the sisters, Mr. Greene thinks, probably lived nearer the borders of Tennessee, which is true of the one who married Landrine Eggers, at least, and possibly of the other also, according to the Wilson she married. Richard Greene's children were eight in number, the first five of whom had twelve each, two others had ten each, while one had to be contented with seven. Jeremiah Greene, whose wife was Polly Wiseman, an aunt of J. W. Wiseman, of Farmington, had

HON. L. L. GREENE.

Judge of the Superior Court.

A History of Watauga County

eleven children, his oldest son, Isaac, living to be seventy-nine years old. At his death he counted eleven children, 102 grandchildren and 100 great-grandchildren. Isaac's son, Solomon, lived to be quite old, eighty-five, and had twenty-one children, 160 grandchildren and 160 great-grandchildren, and two or three of the fifth generation. This was in 1886, and he lived two or three years longer. His eldest sister, Mrs. Elizabeth Norris, was then ninety-two years old. John "Moccasin" Greene with part of his family moved to Mitchell, then a part of Burke, while his brother moved to Rutherford. John "Moccasin" died in Madison County in 1852 when more than ninety years old. The most noted member of the family was Judge L. L. Greene, of the Superior Court, of whom a sketch is given below.

Judge Leonidas L. Greene.—He was born in Watauga County, at Blowing Rock, on the 11th day of November, 1845, and was elected judge of the Superior Court in 1896 and served till his death in 1898. He was a son of Robert Greene and his wife, Chaney Elrod. He was a consummate politician and managed party affairs adroitly. On March 1, 1876, he married Martha Horton, a daughter of Col. Jack Horton, who survives him. Judge Greene's portrait hangs over the judge's desk in the county court house in Boone. He left two children, Albina, who married Frank Mandefield, of Duluth, and Wilhelmetta, unmarried. Judge Greene was also United States commissioner. He was considered a good lawyer and enjoyed a large practice. He was a good neighbor and well liked.

Greer Family.—Benjamin Greer was a soldier of the Revolution. His wife was a Miss Wilcox, and their children were: John, who married Nancy Owen; William, who married Hannah Cartright and died when 103 years of age; Jesse, who married Mary Morris; Thomas, who married a Ketron; James, who married a Hampton; David, who married Nancy Hodges; Samuel, who married Sallie Church; Joshua, who married Jennie Church; Rachel, who married Robert Judd and moved to Kentucky; Ann, who married Thomas Holman and went West.

Benjamin Greer married a second time, after the death of his first wife, Mrs. Sallie Atkinson Jones, widow of Thomas Jones, who died from a wound received in the Revolution. She reared children by both husbands. They moved to Green River, Ky., where he died in 1810. Samuel Greer has three children living here: Elizabeth Hendrix, now ninety-four years of age; Finley Greer, ninety-two years of age; Riley Greer, ninety years old.

Mary Ray Greer was born September 22, 1813, and died March 26, 1906, at the Critcher hotel. Her grave is in the cemetery at Boone. She was the daughter of William Ray, of Elk Creek, above Todd, and the wife of Thomas Greer. Her daughter, Jennie, married J. L. Phillips, while Evelyn became the wife of George Grubb; Martha the wife of Julius Elliott, of Rowan, and Millie the wife of Thos. J. Coffey. Her son, Larkin, was killed in the Civil War. The latter was about to marry Sarah Ferguson, of Meat Camp, when he was at home once during the Civil War on furlough, and was on the way to the magistrate's to be married when they were met by her sister, Martha Ann, who faced them about and prevented the marriage. Sarah afterwards married Zachariah Moretz. Martha Ann never married.

The Grider Family.—John Grider married Agnes Flowers in 1844 and their children were: Adolphus, killed in Civil War; Mary, born in 1848 and married George P. Sherrill; Sarah, who married Duke Glenn, and Martha, who married Monroe Harman. John's father was John, who married Nancy Gibbs, of Alexander County, and their children were: William, who married Amanda Rector after the death of his first wife; Cameline, who married; Rufus, who married Betsy White; Wiley, who married Malinda ———; Sally, who did not marry, and Betsy, who did not marry; Pinckney, who married Becky Pool. All these lived in Alexander County, near Taylorsville.

Grubb Family.—The first of this family were a Grubb and his wife who started from Germany with their children, but the parents died at sea. Their sons, George and John, married two sisters of the name of Leonard and went to Indiana, while Henry, another son, married a Miss Michael, first, and then a Miss McBride; Jacob married Susannah Hedrick; Conrad and David were twins, David marrying a Young and Conrad a

Hedrick; Frederick married a Gordon; Daniel married a Thistle, first, and then a Miss Grubb, and Jacob, whose son, John, married Martha, a daughter of John Morphew.

Hagaman Family.—Thomas Hagaman married Sarah Reese, and their children were: John, who married Mary Shoun; Hamilton, who was killed in the Civil War; M. Granville, who married Mary Winkler, a daughter of Joshua; Thomas, who married a Miss Blackwelder; Joseph, who married a Crawford; Louisa, who married Captain A. J. Critcher; James Roby, who married a Crocker of Lincolnton, and Epsey, who married Jerome Moretz. Joseph Hagaman was a brother of Thomas, but never married. Thomas was born, according to his tombstone on Brushy Fork, in 1810, and died about 1876. Isaac Hagaman married Joanna Reese, and his son, Hugh, married Elizabeth Wilson, daughter of Alexander. Their children were: Smith, who married Blanche Sherrill; Millard, who married Grace Isaacs; Emmett, who married Florence Cook; America, who married Wm. Smith; Ennis, who married Roy Dotson; Alice, who married Ellis Moody, and Nancy, not married. Isaac Hagaman was the father of Theron, who married, first, a Greene, a sister of Jeremy on Cove Creek, and, second, Mary Dougherty, daughter of Elijah and sister of D. B. Dougherty. The children by the first marriage were: Rev. Jacob G., who married Helen Hayes; Brazilla C., who married Dilly Scott, and W. Jasper, who married Amanda Wilson, daughter of Alexander. Children of the second marriage were: Raleigh, who died at about twenty years of age, was unmarried; Isaac Hagaman, Jr., married Hilah Dougherty and moved away long ago, their three children, Annie, John and Carey, living near Asheville for awhile and then moving to South Carolina. Jacob Hagaman, son of Theron, had the following children: George, who married Margaret Sherrill, and Cora, who married Lee Qualls and lives in Tennessee. John Hagaman, son of Isaac, had the following children: Alexander, who married Anna Farthing; Daniel, who married Mary Harmon; Hugh, who married ———————; Thomas, who married ———————; Francis, who married a Gambill; also two daughters, names not recalled by informant.

Hardin Family.—Henry Hardin came from England and settled in Pennsylvania. His sons were: Wilburn, John and Richard. His daughter was named Catharine.

Wilburn married and lived on Beaver Creek, Ashe County. His children were: John, who married a Ray; Joseph, who married ——————————; Martin, who married a Hawthorne; Marcus, who married ——————————; William, who married ——————————, and Catharine, who married a Burkett, who was killed in the Civil War.

John, who lived at the old Hardin place east of Boone, married Charlotte, sister of the first Jordan Councill. On a tombstone in the Boone cemetery is found: "Charlotte Hardin, born April 16, 1795, died November 1, 1843." Their children were: Henry W., born December 29, 1821, died January 11, 1904; his wife was Nancy Lucinda Horton, born May 27, 1824, died March 8, 1909; Sarah, who married George Snider; Martha, who married John Snider; Elizabeth, who married John Powell, and Jordan C., who married Julia Williams.

Richard married a Ray(?) and settled on Beaver Creek in Ashe County. Their children were: Hence, who married an Oliver; Frank, who married Rhoda Howell; George, who married a Ray; Catharine, who married a Graybeal; John, who married a Goodman, and Ida, who married a Reeves.

Catharine, who married Thomas Sudderth, settled in Caldwell County. Their children were: Wilburn, Tolliver and John.

Henry C. Hardin's children were: James H., born October 19, 1847, married Emma Sutherland; John F., born February 1, 1850, married Martha H. Councill; William H., born February 13, 1852, married Sarah Wilkler; Jordan C., born May 17, 1854, married Nannie Kitzmiller; H. Joseph, born October 24, 1857, married Alice McRary; L. Cornelia, born April 19, 1859, married, first, Wm. Church, and then John Snider; Ida B., who was born October 13, 1862, and married Wm. Spainhour.

Harman Family.—In 1791 Cutliff Harman came from Randolph County and bought 522 acres of land on Cove Creek from James Gwyn, to whom it had been granted August 6, 1791, according to Malden C. Harman in *Watauga Democrat* of April, 1891.

A History of Watauga County 317

Cutliff married Susan Fouts, and was about ninety years of age when he died in 1838, his wife having died several years before, and he having married Elizabeth Parker, a widow. He had ten children by his first marriage; none by his second. Among his children were: Mary, who married Bedent Baird; Andrew, who married Sabra Hix; Eli, who married the widow Rhoda Dyer (born Dugger); Mathias, who married and moved to Indiana; Catherine, who married Benjamin Ward, and went west; Rebecca, who married Frank Adams and moved to Indiana; Rachel, who married Holden Davis; Sarah, who married John Mast; Nancy, who married Thomas Curtis; Rev. D. C. Harman was a son of Eli Harman and was born April 17, 1826, and died December 23, 1904.

Hartley Family.—Waightstill Hartley came to America from Shropshire, England, in 1740, and settled near Frederick, Md. His children were: John, who married Elizabeth Becket; Mahala, who married John Dinwiddie, and Nancy, who married David Tucker. It is said that Elizabeth nursed Thomas Jefferson. John Hartley had seven children: Nancy, who married George Tucker; Elizabeth, who married General Wilson; Ava, who did not marry; Finley, who married Sarah Brooks; George, who married Elizabeth Davis; James, who married Anna McCrary; Reuben, who married Jane Fullenwider. John Hartley was a weaver and died in Virginia, after which his family came to North Carolina in 1783, finally settling in Rowan, while others of the connection settled in Caldwell and Burke. George had six children: Clinton, Larkin, George, Alfred, Waightstill and Mahala. George Hartley, Sr., was a saddle and harness maker. He died in 1834, aged seventy-two. Clinton never married. He was a colonel of the militia and sheriff of Burke and one of the commissioners who located Lenoir. He was a Whig, and died at the age of ninety-five. Larkin never married. He was a blacksmith and a great hunter, and died at the age of fifty-three. George married Catharine Fincannon, and they had five children: Rufus, Jason, John, Polly and Mahala. Rufus married Piety Kirby, and they had four children: Jason married Sarah Ann, daughter of Waightstill Hartley; Polly, daughter of

John W. Hartley, married W. W. Sherrill, and her son, George P. Sherrill, now lives on Beaver Dams, Watauga County.

Hayes Family.—Ransom Hayes died in March, 1868, aged about sixty-three years. He married Sallie Greene, daughter of Joseph. Joseph Green had married Elizabeth, daughter of Robert Shearer, Sr. Ransom Hayes' children were: 1. Joseph, who died in 1911, aged about seventy-five, on Brushy Fork. He married Eliza, daughter of Larkin Hodges, of Poplar Grove. His son, Joseph, now lives there. 2. Elizabeth, who married Thomas Storie, son of Joshua, and died in 1875. 3. Robert, who married Rebecca Hately, daughter of William, who lived about Watauga Falls postoffice. 4. John, who married Eliza Cook, daughter of Rev. John Cook, of Vergil. John died in the army at Richmond, Va. His widow is still living. Their one son, John Lee, was one of the builders of Blowing Rock. 5. William, who married Benjamin Brown's daughter, Clorinda, and lived near Todd. William lived near Poplar Grove, but went first to Tennessee and then to Oregon, where he died about 1900. 6. Thomas, who was killed in the second battle of Manassas in the 37th North Carolina regiment. He never married. 7. Nancy, who married Harvey Dougherty, of Johnson County, Tennessee. He was a brother of D. B. Dougherty. Nancy died in Blount County, Tennessee, in May, 1913. 8. Sarah, who married W. L. Bryan December 12, 1865. They moved to Meat Camp in 1865 within a mile of Soda Hill, where farming was carried on till the fall of 1868, when they returned to Boone. 9. George, who married, first, Emily, daughter of Riley and Violet Hodges, and, second, Louisa Bumgarner, of Howard's Creek. They live near Boone. 10. Ransom, who was born in 1846 and married a lady in Texas. He died in 1910, his wife having died several years before. They had two daughters, one of whom died young and without having married, and the other, Nannie, now Mrs. Yeagel, lives in Dallas, Texas. 11. Richard, born about May, 1849, and married Delphia Hayes, a distant cousin, of Caldwell County. After having lived in Mitchell County, they returned to Caldwell and now reside in the Globe.

Hodges Family.—Thomas Hodges came from Virginia and settled at Hodges Gap, two miles west of Boone, during the

A History of Watauga County 319

Revolutionary War. He was a Tory. His family came with him. His son, Gilbert, married Robert Shearer's daughter. Robert died about 1845.

Gilbert Hodges lived where I. W. Gross now lives, about one-half mile east of Hodges Gap. His children were: 1. Thomas, who married Mary Ingraham. 2. Robert, who died in the summer of 1914 near Hodges Gap, at the home of George Teague, who had married his niece. His wife was Peggy Ingraham. 3. Holland, who was born July 18, 1827, and still lives near the place of his birth. In 1856 he helped Jordan McGhee kill 432 rattlesnakes on Rich Mountain. 4. Riley, who is still alive and lives on the waters of Laurel Fork. He married Violet Moody, of Watauga. 5. Elizabeth, who married Edward Clawson, her cousin. 6. Louisa, who married John Greene. He was killed in the Civil War. She afterwards married John Dougherty, who still lives, having married Martha Cook after the death of his first wife. 7. Larkin, who married Miss Eliza Gragg, a daughter of John Gragg, who lived where David F. Baird now lives at Valle Crucis. Larkin Hodges lives in Buncombe County.

William Hodges lived a quarter of a mile east of the cabin in which Jacob M. Councill was killed by Stoneman's men in March, 1865. That cabin is still called the Mark Hodges house, as William's son, Mark, built it. It is almost due north from Benjamin Councill's present residence. William was a brother of Gilbert Hodges, and married a Miss Mullins, sister of Jesse Mullins, who was a great hunter and lived on the South Fork of New River three miles from Boone. His children were: 1. Larkin, a preacher, who married Miss Polly Moody. 2. Adam, who married twice. He lived and died in Knox County, Tennessee. 3. William, who married Miss Morris, of New River, and lived near Todd. 4. John or Jack, who married Fanny Morris, sister of William's wife, and lived near Boone. 5. Burton, who married Miss Northern and lives in Tennessee. 6. Jesse, who married and lives in Knox County, Tennessee. 7. Demarcus, who married a Miss Calloway, daughter of Isom Calloway, who lived on Elk above Todd. 8. A daughter, who married Solomon Green. 9. Sallie, who married Rev. John Cook, son of Michael, Sr. 10. Delphia, who married Adam Cook, brother of John.

Jesse Hodges was a brother of William and Gilbert, and married Polly Clawson. He lived a mile and a half north of Soda Hill, at the head of Little Grassy Creek. His children were: Frank, who married Nancy Ingraham; William, who married Nancy Triplett; Elbert, who married Katie Davis; Larkin, who died young and unmarried; Jack, who was killed by bushwhackers during the Civil War; Thomas, who died in the Confederate army unmarried; Patsy, who married Jesse Stanberry; Cynthia, who married Edmund Blackburn; Elizabeth, who married Jacob Jones, first, and then Captain William Miller, son of Hon. David Miller, and moved to Middle Tennessee, where they died. Jones, her first husband, was lost in the Confederate army; Nancy, who married Thomas Griever, of Johnson County, Tennessee.

Jesse Hodges sold his farm to David Lookabill about 1858 and moved to Johnson County, Tennessee, where he and his son, Jack or John, were killed by renegades in the Civil War.

Holtzclaw Family.[2]—James T. Holtzclaw came from Germany and settled first in Virginia, near what is now Gordonsville, about 1735 or 1740, where John Holtzclaw was born, and his brothers, Henry, William, Joseph and Benjamin. John Holtzclaw served in the Revolutionary War under a Captain Lewis, after which he settled on Watauga River, near Valle Crucis, where he married Catharine Hicks (sometimes spelt Hix). Their children were: John Hicks, Henry, Benjamin, Marcus and William, Agnes and Nancy. Of these, John married Lurana Dugger and lived on Banner's Elk; John Hicks married Sallie Hartley and lived near Watauga River; Henry moved to Albany on the Ohio River below Louisville, Ky.; Joseph moved to Alabama and settled near what is now Birmingham; Benjamin married Nancy Hately and settled on waters of Watauga River; Marcus married Lena Green and settled on Brushy Fork four miles west of Boone; William

---

[2] This was the original spelling, but it came to be spelt Holtsclaw.

married a Miss Smith and lived near Cranberry Forge; Agnes married William Dugger and lived in Johnson County, Tennessee; Nancy married James Morgan and lived in Ashe till the death of her husband, when she moved to Tennessee. To John Holtzclaw and Lurana was born one son, Rufus, and to Benjamin Holtzclaw and Nancy were born Wiley, Rufus, William and Sally. To Marcus and Laura were born Pemberton, Crawford and Wesley, Catharine, Agnes and Lena, and by Marcus' third wife, whose name was Elizabeth Munday, were born Thomas C., Lafayette, Eliza, Mary, Laura and Nancy. Pemberton married Catharine Pharr and lived in Haywood County, North Carolina; John Wesley married Martha Williams and made his home mostly in Watauga County; Thomas C. married Carrie Munday, first, and, second, a Miss Cairns, and lives in Transylvania, N. C.

Horton Family.—Nathan Horton settled in Rowan, near the Jersey Settlement, but afterwards moved to a farm near Holman's Ford in Wilkes County. Then he came to Cook's Gap in the Blue Ridge, the very gap through which Daniel Boone, in May, 1769, had passed on his first trip to Kentucky. With Horton came also his own wife and William Miller and wife, Mary, and their son, David Miller, and Ebenezer Fairchild and family. Horton went into a hunter's camp at Cook's Gap, Miller into another hunter's camp at Buck's Gap, while Fairchild went on to what is now called Howard's Creek. All these became members of Three Forks Baptist Church, which had been organized in November, 1790. There is a tradition in the Horton family to the effect that the camp into which Nathan went belonged to Richard Green, and that on one occasion, when the fire went out and Mrs. Horton went to a neighbor's several miles distant to get some live coals, she found this Green in possession of this camp, which was their first acquaintance with each other. But there are among the Fairchild papers receipts from Jonathan Tompkins,[3] tax collector for 1780, showing that he collected taxes in this settlement at that early date. There is also a knob of the Blue Ridge, near Deep Gap, which bears his

---

[3] Wm. Temple Coles collected taxes from E. Fairchild in 1769.

name. There is also a tradition that the Greens were members of the Jersey Settlement, and that James Jackson, William Miller, the three Bucks, Tompkins and Horton himself were members of the Jersey Settlement. They were all members of the Three Forks Church between 1790 and 1800, and the probability seems that Richard Green told Horton where his camp was and invited him to take possession of it and that Buck extended the same invitation to Miller with regard to his own camp near by. Nathan Horton lost his little daughter, Hannah, at Hagerstown, Md., on his way from New Jersey, she having sickened and died there. William Horton was an infant in arms when the family arrived at Cook's Gap, and he became the grandfather of Hon. Horton Bower, afterwards member of Congress, William having married Millie Dula and settled at Elkville, Wilkes County. James, another of Nathan's sons, married a daughter of James Webb and settled where Noah Brooksher now lives on South Fork of New River, half a mile below Three Forks Church. David Eagles, named for his mother, who was born Elizabeth Eagles, married Sallie Dula and settled one mile above Elkville. Phineas, another son, married Rebecca Councill, daughter of the first Jordan Councill, and settled on the land now occupied by J. C. Horton, his house having stood in the bottom in front of J. C. Horton's present home, though Phineas afterwards built a log house on the ridge, just above the present J. C. Horton home. Sarah and John, two of Nathan's children, died when children, while Jonathan, another of Nathan's sons, married Malinda Hartzog and settled where R. F. Vannoy now lives. Elizabeth, daughter of Nathan, married Zephaniah Horton, of Yancey County.

William Horton, of Elkville, had eleven children.

James Horton's children were: Colonel Jack, who married, first, Rebecca Mast, and then Mary Swift; Lucinda, who married Henry W. Hardin and lived where Joseph Hardin now lives; Elvira, who married Mathias Bledsoe near Todd; Eveline, who married Hamilton Ray, of Roan Mountain Station, Tenn.; William, who married a Shull and lived on Cove Creek, afterwards removing to Roan Creek, Tenn.; Polly, who married Thomas Ray, of Three Tops, Ashe County.

Photo. by Vest.

COLONEL JONATHAN HORTON.

The children of David Eagles Horton were: Thomas, who married Clara Perkins and lived in Burke; David, who married Jane Young, of Yancey, and now lives on the Yadkin one mile from Elkville; Adeline, who married C. P. Jones and lives on the Yadkin above Elkville; Larkin L., who married Louisa Isbell and lived on King's Creek; John and Jane died unmarried; James, who married Rosa Lynch, of Yadkin County; Louisa, who married James M. Isbell, of King's Creek.

Phineas' children were: William, who married Rebecca Blair and settled at the J. C. Horton place; Nathan, who married Juliette Gentry, of Jefferson, and settled on the opposite side of New River from the J. C. Horton place; Jonathan and James died in the Civil War.

Jonathan Horton had no children and died in Boone November 24, 1895. His widow, Malinda, died April 17, 1911.

Elizabeth's children were: Nathan, James and David, and lived near Burnsville, Yancey County.

The children of William, son of Phineas Horton, were: James Crittenden, who married Mary Elrod, of New River; Jonathan Blair, who married Miss Smith, of Elkin; Julia, who died unmarried; Wm. Phineas, who married Emma Wyn, of Warren County, North Carolina; Emma, who married Lewis P. Moore, of High Point; Addie Elizabeth, who married J. S. Winkler, of Boone; Henry Walter, who married Susan Usher, of Charlotte, and lives in North Wilkesboro; Sallie Hill, who died when eight years old.

Col. Jack Horton's children were: James W., who married a Miss Councill, and David, who married a Miss Mast, and Mattie, who married Judge L. L. Greene.

Col. Nathan Horton was born at Chester, N. J., February 25, 1757, and married Elizabeth Eagles in New York City July 10, 1783. She was a daughter of John Eagles. Nathan and wife removed to North Carolina about 1785. Elizabeth Eagles was born in New York City December 1, 1766, and Hannah, their first child, was born at Chester, N. J., October 15, 1784; William, their second child, was born on New River August 15, 1786; James was born there February 28, 1789; David Eagles was born there May 5, 1792, as was Phineas January 9, 1795; Sarah was born September 19, 1794; John was born June 11, 1800; Elizabeth, September 15, 1803; Jonathan, February 26, 1806. Malinda, Jonathan's wife, was born May 10, 1820. Col. Nathan Horton died on New River July 22, 1824, and his wife died there May 19, 1854. Nathan Horton bought in Richmond, Va., in 1803, a negro boy fourteen years of age, and Vinie, a girl, eleven years old. Vinie's first child was born in 1806 when Vinie was only fourteen years old. This child was named Tempe. Among J. C. Horton's heirlooms is a grandfather clock seven feet high, with a mahogany case and a face showing the rising and setting of the moon, a hand to mark all the seasons and several other devices. This was Nathan Horton's property, which he hauled all the way from New Jersey to North Carolina on his journey down. There is still in the family a shot gun or rifle with a bore capable of chambering three buck shot, on top of which a bullet the size of the barrel was rammed home encased in buckskin, thus making a load that was apt to "git 'em, both a-goin' and a-comin'." It has a flint-lock, and it was used by Nathan in guarding Major Andre when the latter was executed as a spy. Col. Nathan Horton was buried in Three Forks churchyard, and on his tombstone is carved the fact that he was a soldier of the Revolutionary War. He was several times in the legislature, and built the wagon road through Cook's Gap and on the Beaver Dams, called Horton's Turnpike.

Horton Family Genealogy.—In 1876 the Home Circle Publishing Company, Philadelphia, Pa., published the "Horton Genealogy, or Chronicles of the Descendants of Barnibas Horton, of Southold, L. I., 1640." It was compiled by George F. Horton, M. D. There is a picture of the old Horton homestead, erected by Barnibas Horton, Esq., in 1660, and was still standing at Southold, L. I., in June, 1873. Barnabas was probably the son of Joseph Horton, of Leicestershire, England, and was born in the little hamlet of Mouseley of that shire. He came over in the ship "Swallow" in 1633-38 and landed at Hampton, Mass., but in 1640 he and his wife and two children were in New Haven, Conn., in company with Rev. John Youngs, Wm. Welles,

A History of Watauga County 325

Peter Hollock, John Tuthill, Richard Terry, Thomas Mapes, Mathias Corwin, Robert Ackerly, Jacob Corey, John Conklin, Isaac Arnold and John Budd. There, on the 21st day of October, 1640, they formed a Congregational Church and sailed for the east end of Long Island, now Southold. They had all been members of Puritan churches in England. These were the first to settle the east end of Long Island. The genealogy of the family is then traced down to 1876 and includes the North Carolina family whose history has been given above.

Ingram Family.—David Ingram was reared in New England, from which section he came to North Carolina before anyone now living remembers. He married a Miss Frieze from near Winston-Salem. His son, Jacob, was born near Jefferson and married Peggy, daughter of John Greene, who then lived half a mile from Sand's Postoffice, Watauga County. John Ingram, son of Jacob, was born on New River one mile from Sands December 24, 1823. John Greene, father of Jacob's wife, was a soldier of the Revolutionary War. Besides John, Jacob had a son, Richard, who died in Texas during the Civil War unmarried, and Susan, who married Daniel Miller, of Ashe; Eliza, who married Ben. Greer; Mary, who married Thomas Hodges; Hannah, who married Isaac Greer; John, who married, first, Martha Ray, of Ashe, and, second, Louisa Gragg, widow of Edward Hodges; Nancy, who married Franklin Hodges, and Peggy, who married Robert Hodges.

Isaacs Family.—Richard Isaacs was the first of this family and came from Ireland about 1790, and his wife was a Miss Robbins, of Randolph County, from which place he moved to settle in the Cherokee country. but when he got to Morganton he heard of Watauga River and especially of Cove Creek, when he came through Linville Gap up Elk and Beech Mountain to Hiram Hix's ford of Watauga, from which place he struck up Cove Creek to the Cove Creek Church, where Wm. Williams' family now lives, close to the old graveyard. Their children were: James, born 1791, married Rachel Reese; Richard, born 1793, married Lily Swift; Solomon, born 1795, April 1st, and married Lily Giles, first, and, after her death, Sarah Eggers, a daughter of Hugh Eggers; Massy and Mary, twins, born in 1789, of whom Massy married Samuel Swift and Mary a man named Massagee, but they left this section and went west before Hugh M. Isaacs was born.

Solomon was married twice. The children by his first wife were: Elijah, who married Sally Hartly; Peggy, who married Milton Davis; William, who married a Norris in Missouri. His second wife's children were: Hugh M., born May 13, 1839, and married, first, Nancy Thompson, and, second, Leona Presnell; Martha, born June 17, 1841, and married, first, John Wilson, who was killed at Chickamauga, and, second, Sherman Swift; Solomon, born June 2, 1845, and Richard, born August 15, 1847. Hugh M. joined Company I, 58th North Carolina; William Miller, captain, and Fred. Toby, adjutant.

Walter W. Lenoir.—He was born in Caldwell County about 1823 and died at Shull's Mills, Watauga County, July 26, 1890. He graduated with high honors at the North Carolina University, studied law and was admitted to the bar in 1845, and married Miss Cornelia Christian, of Staunton, Va., in 1856, but she died soon afterward. He lost a leg in the Civil War at the battle of Ox Hill, September, 1862. He was a descendant of Gen. William Lenoir, a lieutenant in Rutherford's expedition against the Cherokees in 1776; was a captain at King's Mountain battle; was first president of the board of trustees of the University of North Carolina; was president of the Senate in 1790-94; was a member of the constitutional conventions of 1788-89; was chairman of the county court of Wilkes; was major-general of militia.[4]

Lewis Family.—The sons of Richard Lewis the first were: Jacob, who married Hannah Waters and lived on Yadkin Elk. Their children were: 1. Betsy, who married Abraham Younce; Allie, who married Charles Hayse; Nancy, who married Abraham Lewis; Sallie, who married Jacob Council. 2. Daniel, who married Sallie Allen, their children being: James, who went to Texas in 1840; David, grandfather of P. C. Younce. By his second wife (Betsy Vanderpool) Daniel Lewis had Abraham,

---

[4] Note by Dr. K. P. Battle, of U. N. C., pp. 40-41, No. 6, of Sprunt Hist. Monograph series.

and John, who went to Texas in 1840; Richard, who went to Arkansas; Jonathan, who went to California in 1849; Daniel, who married Martha Hendricks; Louisa, who married A. Younce. By his third wife, Louisa Franklin, Daniel had Andrew, who married Victoria Reese; Elizabeth, who went to Georgia; Emeline and Columbus, who also went to Georgia. 3. David Lewis married Polly Hendricks, and their children were: Sallie, who married Daniel Brown; Betsy, who married Alfred Simmons; Minerva, who married Joseph Bingham. 4. Richard Lewis married Phœbe Vanderpool, and their children were: Rebecca, who married Thomas Robbins; Nancy, who did not marry; Malinda, who married a Day, and William. Margaret Lewis was buried at Cove Creek Church. Daniel Lewis settled where Jacob Lewis now lives, one mile from Sherwood on the Vanderpool Mill Creek, where the Vanderpools lived and where Lewis married a lady of that house. Lewis is said to have come to this section prior to 1800. Jonathan Lewis, son of Daniel, left Zionville for California in 1848, settled at Fresno, Cal., and became rich.

Romulus Z. Linney.—He was born in Rutherford County December 26, 1841; was educated in the common schools of the country, at York's Collegiate Institute, and at Dr. Millen's school at Taylorsville; he served as a private in the Confederate army until the battle of Chancellorsville, where he was severely wounded, and was discharged. He then joined a class in Dr. Millen's school at Taylorsville, of which Hon. W. H. Bower was a member; studied law with the late Judge Armfield; was admitted to practice by the Supreme Court in 1868; was elected to the State Senate in 1870, 1872, 1874, and again in 1882; was elected to the 54th, 55th and 56th Congresses as a Republican, receiving 19,419 votes against 18,006 for Rufus A. Doughton, Democrat, and 640 for Wm. M. White, Prohibitionist. He married Dorcas Stephenson in Taylorsville. In 1880 he became interested in Watauga so much that he bought property there, and in September, 1902, he bought a tract of land he called Tater Hill on Rich Mountain, where he built two rock houses. He was influential in getting a wagon road built along the top of the Rich Mountain range from the gap above Boone to a gap just north of Silverstone. He contributed $500 to the Appalachian Training School. Above the front door of the chief building of this college is written in marble the following quotation from one of his speeches delivered July 4, 1903: "Learning, the Handmaid of Loyalty and Liberty. A Vote Governs Better than a Crown." He died at Taylorsville, April 15, 1910. His mother was a sister of the late Judge John Baxter.

Col. Edward F. Lovill.—He was born in Surry County February 10, 1842, married Miss Josephine Marion, of the same county, February 15, 1866, and moved to Boone in 1874. He was admitted to the bar in February, 1885, and was commissioner to the Chippewa Indians from 1893 to 1897. He was captain of Company A of the 28th North Carolina Infantry, and on the second day of Chancellorsville commanded that regiment in the absence of Col. Samuel D. Low. Of this incident Colonel Lowe reported: "While absent, General Stuart again commanded the line forward, and my regiment charged through the same terrible artillery firing the third time, led by Captain (Edward F.) Lovill, of Company A, to the support of our batteries which I had just got into position on the hill from which those of the enemy had been driven." Captain Lovill had commanded the same regiment during the midnight attack of the night before. Upon the death of Col. Asbury Speer at Reems Station and the resignation of Major Samuel Stowe, Captain Lovill was senior officer of the 28th till the surrender at Appomattox, and commanded the regiment at the battle of Jones' farm near Petersburg in the fall of 1864, where he was severely wounded. He returned to duty in March, 1865, and was recommended for promotion to the colonelcy of his regiment at the time that James Lineberger was recommended for the lieutenant-colonelcy and George McCauley for the majority, but the end came before these appointments were published. He was wounded in the right arm at Gettysburg. At Fredericksburg "Captain Lovill, of Company A, the right company of the regiment, stood on the railroad track all the time, waving his hat and cheering his men, and neither he nor Martin (who had just

COLONEL ROMULUS Z. LINNEY, M. C.

shot down the Federal color bearer) was struck." Soon after the battle of Jericho Ford, in September, 1864, Natt Nixon, a seventeen-year-old boy of Mitchell's River, Surry, was desperately wounded, and at night Captain Lovill and Private M. H. Freeman, a cobbler of Dobson, went to get him, as he had been left within the enemy's lines. They called him and he answered, saying the Federals were between him and them, but had been to him and given him water. Freeman put down his gun and accoutrements and shouting in a loud voice, "Natt, I'm coming after you. I am coming unarmed, and any man who shoots me is a damned coward," started. It was night, but no one fired at him, and he brought his stricken comrade back to Captain Lovill, but the poor boy died near a farm house to which he had been borne before daylight. Colonel Lovill is a director of the Oxford Orphanage, having been appointed by Governor Aycock. He is chairman of the board of trustees of the Appalachian Training School and a lawyer of ability.

McBride Family.—John McBride came from the north of Ireland and settled in New Jersey, from which place he moved to Rowan County with the New Jersey settlers. He married Mary Baird in Rowan, and their children were: Brazilla, who married Rachel Wilson in Rowan; Timothy, who went to Missouri, where he remained, and William, who married a Miss Swicegood in Rowan and died there. One of the daughters married Levi Heath; Ellen married Landrine Eggers, while another daughter married David Goss, who moved to Missouri. Brazilla was in the War of 1812 and named his first son for Andrew Jackson.

Brazilla's children were: Andrew Jackson, who married Polly Green; Hiram, who married Mary Farthing; Silas, who married Emily Green; Brazilla Carroll, who married Catharine Brinkley, of West Tennessee; Sarah, who married Harrison Johnson; Ann, who married Squire Green; Mary Amanda, who married John Combs; Emily, who married Jonathan Green.

Brazilla's second wife was Elizabeth Eggers, and their children were: Manly, who married Martha Norris; John, who married Miss Greer; Rachel, who married George Hilliard;

330   *A History of Watauga County*

Ellen, who married Bruce Harman; Louisa, who married Jacob Younce; Martha, who died unmarried at the age of sixteen; Nancy, who married William Church; Elizabeth, who married Richard McGuire.

From the gravestones in the Cove Creek graveyard the following was taken: Rev. Brazilla McBride was born September 27, 1790, and died December 10, 1858; Hiram McBride was born August 9, 1818, died July 30, 1880; Mary, wife of Hiram, born February 21, 1818, died May 26, 1869; Rachel, wife of Brazilla McBride, born February 15, 1797, died August 18, 1839.

From the A. J. McBride graveyard the following was taken: Rev. Andrew J. McBride was born November 27, 1822, and died November 12, 1891; Silas McBride was born November 18, 1827, and when he died he was aged seventy-two years, six months and twenty days; Elijah Green was born November 4, 1800, died July 15, 1882. His wife was born October 10, 1803, and died January 8, 1879.

Willis McGhee came to this county early in the nineteenth century and resided with Jordan Councill, bringing with him a fine stallion and a negro man slave. McGhee married Bettie, daughter of Jordan Councill, Sr., and settled in Hodges Gap of the Rich Mountain. Their children were: Jordan C., James H. and Willis, Jr., Eveline, Carolina, Louisa, Elvira and Mary. Jordan C. married Eliza Todd, a daughter of James Todd; James H. married Vina Vandyke; Willis, Jr., married a Miss Hall of Wilkes; Eveline married Bart Wood, a brick mason; Carolina married Col. J. B. Todd; Louisa married, first, Nathan Hartley, but he died in the Civil War, and then she married J. B. Clark. She still lives; Elvira never married; Mary married Thomas Triplett. Jordan C. was a brick mason, but has been in a hospital on account of poor health for many years.

Mast Family.—Joseph Mast, the first of the name to come to Valle Crucis, Watauga County, was born in Randolph County, North Carolina, March 25, 1764, and on the 30th of May, 1783, married Eve Bowers, who had been born between the Saluda and Broad rivers, South Carolina, December 30, 1758. Joseph was a son of John, who was brother of the Jacob Mast who

A History of Watauga County

became bishop of the Amish Mennonite Church in Conestoga, Pa., in 1788. They had left their native Switzerland together and sailed from Rotterdam in the ship "Brotherhood," which reached Philadelphia November 3, 1750. John Mast was born in 1740, and shortly after becoming twenty years of age left his brother, Jacob, who had married and was living near the site of what is now Elverson, Pa. John wandered on foot through many lonely forests, but finally settled in Randolph County, where Joseph was born. There he married a lady whose given name was Barbara. From Joseph and Eve Mast have descended many of the most substantial and worthy citizens of Western North Carolina, while the Mast family generally are people of influence and standing in Pennsylvania, Ohio, Nebraska, Iowa, Montana, Oregon, Florida, Illinois, Missouri, California, Kansas, and, in fact, nearly every State in the Union. C. Z. Mast, of Elverson, Pa., in 1911 published a volume of nearly a thousand pages, all of which are devoted to an excellent record of all the Masts in America. John A. Mast was born on Brushy Creek September 22, 1829. He married Martha Moore, of John's River, December 5, 1850. He died February 6, 1892. His paternal grandfather, John Mast, and maternal grandfather, Cutliff Harman, were among the pioneers of this section and were Germans, settling on Cove Creek. His wife, Martha Mast, was born April 13, 1833. She died February 15, 1905.

Joseph Harrison Mast.—His father was John Mast and his mother, Susan Harman, who are buried at the Taylor buryingground at Valle Crucis. John Mast's father was Joseph, and he lived where Finley Mast now lives, while Cutliff Harman lived where David Harman now lives. Joseph H. Mast was born April 9, 1829, and married Clarissa P. Moore October 12, 1848. Her father was Daniel Moore, of the Globe, Caldwell County. Their children were: Sophronia, wife of Newton Banner, born July 15, 1850; Andrew J., born February 25, 1852; Leona, born December 2, 1853; Martha V., born April 20, 1856; John H., born October 10, 1858; Allie J., born May 8, 1861; Sarah C., born August 19, 1863; Daniel H., born June 26, 1866; Joseph C., born May 8, 1869. He settled at his present home at Sugar

Grove in 1848, and built the dam and grist mill of the present Mast mill before the Civil War, bolting the ground wheat by an old reel still in existence, though J. C. and J. H. Mast, his sons, changed that old mill into the first roller mill in Watauga County in 1897, E. F. Bingham building the second half a mile above. His children married as follows: Andrew Jackson married Joana King; Leona A. married Robert Mast; Martha V. married Thomas Sullivan; John H. married, first, Eleline, daughter of Hiram McBride, and, second, Nancy, daughter of Hiram Wilson; Alice J. married Finley Mast; Sarah C. married John Smith; Daniel H. married Ruia Lowrance; Joseph C. married, first, Nora Phillips, and, second, Ada Madron, of Bristol, Va. Joseph H. Mast, Sr., died September 8, 1915.

The brothers and a sister of J. H. Mast, Sr., were: Noah, who married Elizabeth Roland; Leson, who married Sally Dugger; Eli, who married Callie Dugger; Jack, who married Martha Moore, of the Globe, and Finley P., who married Rhoda Smith.

Miller Family.—According to Clyde C. Miller, of Sands, N. C., there is a tradition that, several years before the Revolutionary War, three young men, a Horton, a Miller and Baird, all married sisters named Eldridge and moved to the upper Yadkin from Pennsylvania. They probably came with the Jersey settlers. Tradition also gives this Miller the name of William and credits him with having fought in the Revolution. His son, David, was one of the first settlers in the bounds of what is now Watauga County, near Meat Camp Creek. David Miller and Levi Murphey or Morphew were constables and called the first court in Watauga to order. David had twelve children, seven sons and five daughters: Wayne, David, John, William, Joseph, Ephriam and Jonathan; Lydia, who married a Bingham; Rebecca, who married Battle Bryan; Polly, who married a Lookabill; Elizabeth, who married an Allison, and Nancy, who married a Lewis.

Wayne's sons were: William, James, Daniel, Jonathan and Alfred. David, a brother of Wayne, was the father of Clingman, who has been for years in the State of Washington; George, Mrs. L. D. Cole and Mrs. George Moody were also children of Wayne. Daniel lived and died on Cove Creek.

John lived on Meat Camp and was the father of three boys and four girls: Jonathan, Calvin, Thomas, Myra, Katharine, Carolina and Angeline, all the boys having been in the Confederate army. Calvin lived at Sutherland and died in the summer of 1913; J. B. Miller lived on Meat Camp and died December 14, 1914; Myra married a Greer and moved to Kentucky; Caroline married John Norris and moved to Kentucky; Katharine married B. F. Burkett, and Angeline married C. P. Todd. All have been dead a number of years.

William Miller, captain of Company I, 58th North Carolina, was the father of Ephriam, Harrison, Silas, John, Wayne, David and Levi.

Joseph married Sally, daughter of Edmund Blackburn, and had two sons, Lorenzo Dow, who lives near Zionville, and Frank, who lives on Meat Camp. Ephriam also was a soldier in the Confederate army, and had two sons, Alexander and David, the latter living in Tennessee. Jonathan also served in the Civil War and is the only one of these brothers still living. He is in good health and lives on Howard's Creek, although ninety-odd years of age. He married Rebecca, daughter of Levi Blackburn, and is the father of Edmund and Henry and of Carolina, who married Ben Tugman; of Neomi, who married Marsh Tugman, and of Martha, who married Pat Hodges, all of whom are yet living.

Moretz Family.—John Moretz was born in Randolph County, North Carolina, about 1788. His first wife was a Miss Moser, and to this union were born nine children. John's second wife was Catharine Hefner, and from this marriage there were sixteen children, eight boys and eight girls, Alfred Jacob Moretz, of Deep Gap, having been the eighth child. The first John Moretz's father came from Pennsylvania, and he and his wife were full-blooded Germans. John Moretz and his second wife and family came from Randolph County in September, 1839, and there Alfred Jacob was born the following October. John bought land and the original mill on Meat Camp from Samuel Cooper, who then moved to Meadow Creek. John's eldest son first moved west, but returned and lived at Soda Hill, which he bought from a Norris. He died September 12, 1868. Alfred

J. married Mary Emeline Lutz, who was born in Burke and reared in Caldwell. She was a daughter of Ambrose L. Lutz, who had moved from Lincoln to Burke and then to Caldwell, near Rutherford College. With John Moretz also came one son and two daughters by his first marriage. He reared three daughters and two sons by the first wife, and seven girls and seven boys by the second lived to be grown, although there were four of his daughters who died of diphtheria during the Civil War within a few days of each other. Of John's children, Christian, now dead, married a Miss Stirwalt; John, Miss Jane Miller; William, a Miss Condor; Jonathan, a Miss Norris; Zachariah Taylor married, first, a Miss Bowman and then a Miss Ferguson; Joseph L. married a Miss Miller, a sister of John Moretz's wife; Sallie, who married Jacob Winebarger; Carolina, who married A. S. Davis; Mary, who married a Miller, the three youngest of John's daughters having died young and before marrying. Joseph L. Moretz was the father of J. M. Moretz, of Boone.

Morphew Family.—Joseph Morphew married Mary Burke, a sister of the Tory colonel, Benjamin Burke, who was killed at the battle of the Shallow Ford. Their children were: Mary, who married Ephriam Norris; Naomi, who married Ephriam Allison; James, who married and one of whose children, Mary, married Thomas Robbins, Sr., the rest of the children going to Butler County, Ohio, before the Civil War, about 1820; Silas married Elizabeth England about 1775. The Morphews were Quakers and Tories, and Silas was hanged, but a woman held him up by the legs till help came and he was cut down and his life saved. This happened in Rowan, probably. The children of Silas and Elizabeth were: Uriah, born about 1780 and married a Fairchild; Obediah, born about 1782 and married a Berry; Silas, who married Matilda Cayton; John M., who married Sarah Blackburn in 1813; James, who never married; Aaron, who married Nancy Sample; Rhoda, who married Samuel Todd; Jennie, who married George Wells. Peggy, Kizzy and Sallie never married. All left this country long ago, except John Morphew, grandfather of Cyrus A. Grubb.

A History of Watauga County 335

The Norris Family.—John Norris came to North Carolina from Pennsylvania before the Revolutionary War and was probably a loyalist. His son, John, was born in Wilkes County, and his wife was Nancy Brown, of the same county. They moved to Ashe, now Watauga, and settled on Meat Camp and there their son, Ephriam, was born, July 12, 1819. This son was killed March 28, 1865, at Boone by Stoneman's men. He had married Margaret Greene in 1842. Captain Elijah J. Norris was born at the same place as Ephriam September 4, 1843, and married Mary E. Norris, whose father was first cousin to Ephriam, his name having been John. Their children were: Emma B., born November 20, 1869, and married W. R. Greene; Jackson Ephriam, who was born April 25, 1877, and married, first, Zenna Brown in 1904, and, second, Maggy Hardy in 1913; Mollie A., born March 30, 1887, not married. Captain E. J. Norris joined Col. J. B. Palmer's regiment at Johnson City, Tenn., July 12, 1862. He was wounded five times, the last time desperately through the hips, September 4, 1864. He was in Boone when Stoneman passed through in March, 1865, and told his father to run when he became sure the men were regular troops and not Jim Hartley's crowd, whom the Home Guard expected to attack them that day. These were native Union men who claimed to be in the service of the Union. The Home Guard had met that morning in Boone and elected Jordan Cook captain and himself (E. J. Norris) a lieutenant, to keep order and prevent depredations by marauders. Stoneman got to Boone about 11 a. m. and burned the jail that night. In 1910 E. J. Norris was elected commander of the Nimrod Triplett Camp U. C. V. No. 1273.

John Norris, a son of William, Sr., married Rachel Sands, a sister of David, and reared a family of seven children: Sallie, who never married; Anna, who married Joseph Hayes; Lucinda, who married George Brown; Susan, who married John H. Brown; Mary, who married E. J. Norris; Joel S., who married Sarah Hopkins; William D., who married, first, Bartlett Brown's daughter, and, second, Miss Parlier. They lived three miles east of Boone on the Jefferson road, and used to operate a carding machine for carding wool into rolls. Joel Norris, son of

William, Sr., lived near Soda Hill, which he owned and is famous and much admired. He married Polly Griffa and reared three children: Granville, Millard and Bittie. Bittie married Ed. Gragg and moved to Oregon. Joel and wife are both dead, while all their children are still iving.

William Norris, Sr.—He lived on Brushy Fork, near its mouth, where it empties into Meat Camp Creek, and married, first, a Miss Case and their child married Isaac Greer and moved to Kentucky. His second wife was Eunice Shinn, from which union were five boys, Samuel, Levi, Joel, Jonathan and David, and three girls, Rebecca, Anna and Myra, all of whom matried and reared families. Samuel married a lady near Ducktown, Tenn.; Levi married Margaret Morphew, daughter of John; Joel married a lady of the name of Griffith; Jonathan married Ailsey Proffitt; David married Matilda Proffitt; Rebecca married Samuel Trivette; Anna married Michael Cook; Myra married Jacob Cook. Of the last marriage about eighteen children were reared, the eldest daughter marrying John Hartley. He was a son of Eli and Delphia Hartley, and was born on the 8th day of February, 1835, "The Cold Saturday."

A. W. Penley, who lived on the southeast side of the Blue Ridge, about twelve miles from Boone, on Joe's Fork of Buffalo Creek, was the first county court clerk of Watauga County elected by the people. He was a man of great intelligence, and a magistrate for many years. He was also postmaster at Penly Postoffice several years. He married, first, Rena Triplett, to which union were born two boys, Avery and Jasper, and one girl, Mary Ann. His second marriage was to Elizabeth Triplett, to whom there were born Adolphus, Robey and Alice. He was a clever man, went through the Civil War and returned without a wound. He was also a member of the county court for several years, and a great hunter.

The Perkins Family.—L. N. Perkins, who lives on the Jefferson Road, two miles from Boone, is a worthy representative of this distinguished family. Joseph and Timothy Perkins were the first of the name in these mountains, and came from one of the New England States, where they had been tax-gatherers just prior to the commencement of the Revolutionary War. But being loyalists, they were not welcome there after that great struggle began. They moved to Old Fields in Ashe County, retaining their allegiance to the British crown all during that struggle, Timothy losing his life in a skirmish in Ashe. He left several sons and one daughter, Lucy, who married a Young. Joseph also left sons and daughters. Granny Skritch, who lived with one of her Perkins relatives on Little Wilson, remained loyal to King George even when she had reached a great age.

Presnell Family.—Solomon Presnell was born in Chatham County in 1810 and came to Watauga County in 1827. His wife was Mary Mundy, who was born in what is now Alexander County in 1813. Their children were: Melvin, who died in infancy; Carolina, who died when three years old; Wesley Wayne, who was born July 22, 1837, on Cove Creek road at the Vanderpool place. He married Susan Adeline Gragg March 17, 1861. The next child was Amanda, who married Holden Moody; Benjamin, who was killed at Bentonville; Squire Adams, who married, first, Catharine Hartley, and, second, Mattie Fox; James M., who married Rebecca Greene; Rufus W., who married Sallie VanDyke; N. Jerome, who married Caroline Hodges; Mary A., who married David Fox. Solomon's father was Nathan Presnell, and his wife was Mary Whitehead. He came and settled near Lenoir in 1814. She was probably reared in Union or Chatham County. Besides Solomon, their children were: William, who married a Miss Watkins, of Alexander County; Elijah, who married and had several children, but lived in Alexander County. Mary Whitehead had a brother who went to Tennessee and settled on Elk Creek.

Asa Reese, Pioneer.—Valentine Reese came from Germany to America about 1750 and married Christina Harman, settling at the old Bowers Place, now called Trade, Tenn. Their children were: John, born in 1770 and married Sarah Eggers, John dying at age seventy and his wife at age ninety-six. They reared ten children: Hiram, born in 1798, married Rhoda Smith and settled in Watauga. They had six children, and after Rhoda's death Hiram married Martha McCall, six children having blessed this union. A divorce followed, and two years later Hiram married his third wife, Jane Widby, by whom he had one child, a daughter. Hiram died July 9, 1872, aged seventy-four years. Asa, son of Hiram and Rhoda, was born May 9, 1820, and married Catharine Wagner February 27, 1845, settling two miles from what is now Mountain City, Tenn. His wife joined the Baptist Church in February, 1872, and he in December, 1876. They had ten children, one of whom, a girl, dying in childhood. Asa died November 27, 1898, and was buried near his home and daughter, Rhoda. Asa's children were Jehiel, Asa, John, Nelson, Cinderella, Mahetebel. After the death of his first wife Hiram Reese moved his family to what was known as the old Jim Reese house, below Phillip Greer's on Cove Creek, in 1830. In 1832, during a cold spell, a family named Hutchinson, with their team, were added to the family of fourteen already at the small house, where they remained till warm weather, without money and without price. During this time Asa and his brother had to sleep on the open porch, with a snow coverlet frequently to keep them warm. In copartnership with Samuel Reese, of Buncombe, Hiram Reese lost much money wagoning to South Carolina, and the sheriff sold him out for debt about 1834-35, and the family was broken up. In the fall of 1838 Asa, with Alfred Adams (father of T. P. Adams) and Sarah Mast, took a trip to Sequachy Valley, Tenn., near Collins River, Warren County, Asa's father having consented that the boy should keep all he earned after reaching nineteen years of age. In the fall of 1840 Asa, with Hiram McBride, Riley Wilson, two of Asa's uncles, a girl named Roland, and two daughters of Jacob Reese, went to the Platt Purchase, Mo., 300 miles west of the Mississippi River, where he stopped with his uncle, James Webb, crossing the Platt River at New Market. But McBride got home-sick and returned. Asa returned to this State in the spring of 1844 in company with John Ellington and Reuben Sutherland, going to his uncle, Bennett Smith's, and his cousins, George and Polly Hayes. In the summer of 1844 he worked for awhile with the Fairchild ladies on Howard's Creek, where he flirted with a girl named Winkler whom these ladies had hired to weave for them, much to their disgust. But Asa concluded that "old maids are the most jealous, superstitious, whining old things that belong to the human family." He decided not to enlist for the Mexican War, visiting his father in Russell County, Virginia, and finding him in poverty, but he declared he loved him as much and reverenced him more than if he had given him a couple of thousands of dollars, adding that children who are aided by their parents often forget them, and sometimes their God, as well. While Asa was a small boy he and his brother attended Sunday School in a small old log house which stood at the mouth of a hollow, just below where the widow, Ann Farthing, used to live on Beaver Dams. This must have been about 1828, and was undoubtedly the first Sunday School of which there is any record known to this writer. Thus, to the many other good deeds, the Farthings have the glory of having instituted Sunday Schools, now universal, then unknown. The house in which Asa was born stood on a branch of Sharpe's Creek and was built of logs, with puncheon floor, the chimney of which was built of stone inside and of wood outside to the top of the mantelpiece, above which it was of sticks and clay. It was covered with old-fashioned clap-boards. His father had a smoke house for his meat, though many hung their meat in the gables of their homes, thus giving all kinds of meat a chance to become smoked yellow, including hog, beef, bear, venison, coon, etc.

Col. J. J. T. Reese, eldest son of Asa Reese, was born near Mountain City (then Taylorsville), Tenn., June 21, 1849, where he was educated, and afterwards taught school at Butler and elsewhere. He was in the mercantile business at Butler in co-partnership with L. L. Maples, afterwards moving to his farm on Beaver Dams, N. C., where he remained three years. He married Margaret N. Wagner, daughter of N. T. Wagner, Esq., near Shouns, Tenn., April 19, 1880. She was a granddaughter of David Wagner, who came from Davie County, North Carolina, partly cutting his way through the mountains to Roan Creek, where he settled and became owner of a thousand acres of that fertile land. After his marriage, J. J. T. Reese moved permanently to his Beaver Dams farm, where he farmed and dealt in live stock for a time, afterwards engaging in the lumber and timber business. He has refused all offices except that of justice of the peace, preferring a quiet life to politics. Five children bless this union, the entire family being members of the Baptist Church.

Rivers Family.—Dr. James Gray Rivers was a son of Samuel and Rebecca Rivers, who were Virginians by birth. Rebecca Rivers was born Grey, while Samuel Rivers was a descendant of one of three brothers who came to America from England, landing at Edisto Island, S. C., one of them having been named Horace, as is evidenced by his name engraved on a heavy silver ladle now in the possession of Rev. Dr. Murray and wife, of Spencer, N. C., Mrs. Murray having been a Rivers before her marriage. Dr. James Grey Rivers married Miss Lucretia Jane Rhea, who was born at Clarksburg, W. Va., near the Ohio River. Her father was R. P. Rhea, also born in West Virginia, and a graduate of the Naval Academy at Annapolis, Md. He became a teacher of great note, and had the honor of having taught Gen. T. J. (Stonewall) Jackson, as will be seen from any authentic life of that great Confederate soldier. He was a dull student, according to Mr. Rhea. Dr. J. G. Rivers refugeed from Carter County, Tennessee, to Watauga County, North Carolina, during the Civil War, serving in the Home Guard till the capture of Camp Mast in February, 1865. He suffered many hardships and lost much property, living as he did on the border line between Tennessee and North Carolina. He moved to Boone in 1865, where he practiced his profession of medicine till his death in 1878. He left four children, all of whom are living except one. R. C. Rivers, Miss Nannie Rivers and the wife of J. W. Farthing survive.

Sands Family.—David Sands was born April 4, 1791, and died June 30, 1884. His father was Joseph Sands, who was born in 1743 and died October 15, 1821. He came from Scotland. The Sands family lived about three miles east of Boone, and a postoffice of that name still recalls the family name. David was a son of Joseph. Of David Dr. Elisha Mitchell has this to say in letters to his wife, published by the University of North

Carolina, 1905 (p. 56): "Rode from Shearer's down to David Sands, Esq., a bachelor with three or four sisters, and his mother with him. He showed me some ore from Tennessee which he supposed to be antimony, but which proved to be micaceous oxide of iron. Walked with him to see a white substance in the creek on his land. It was the porcelain clay. Sands rode down with me to Esquire Miller's. We passed through a meadow, beautiful like those of Yankeeland." This was David Miller's.

Shearer Family.—Robert Shearer the first was a Scotchman and came to Ashe before the county was formed from Wilkes. He settled near Three Forks Church, to the left of the road and at the foot of a hill still called Shearer's Hill. Just when he was born or the maiden name of his wife are not known now. He lived to a great age and his grave is in the graveyard of Three Forks Baptist Church, of which he was a consistent member. There were eight children: John Shearer, born August 9, 1792; died January 2, 1858. He married Mary Greene, April 27, 1815. She was born August 15, 1797, and died August 30, 1868. Louisa Shearer, born May 7, 1817, married Thomas Cottrell and died January 31, 1896. Susannah Shearer was born December 10, 1818, married William Cottrell and died December —, 1896. Robert Shearer was born July 24, 1823; married, first, Myra Coffey, November 26, 1854, and, second, Martha Estes, February 19, 1860. He died December 2, 1895. His widow survives. John Shearer was born May 5, 1828; died January 11, 1908. William Shearer, born June 28, 1830, and moved to the West. Sarah Shearer, born March 7, 1843, and moved to the West. Hannah Shearer was born May 11, 1838; married Milton Brown, who is dead, but she survives and lives on New River. Mary Shearer, born May 15, 1843; died April 25, 1844. The daughters of the first Robert Shearer were: 1. Elizabeth, who married Joseph Greene; 2. Sallie, who married Gilbert Hodges; 3. Polly, who married Richard Greene; 4. Nancy, who married Daniel Greene, brother of Richard. Robert Shearer's sons were: Jack, who married Mary Greene, sister of David and Richard; Thomas, who married Patsy Farthing, daughter of Rev. William.

Children of Robert Shearer, the Second.—Milton Shearer was born September 4, 1855; married Mary Ann Estes, September 25, 1884, and lives in Lenoir. Mary Shearer was born October 31, 1861; married L. N. Perkins, May 18, 1889, and lives at the old Shearer homestead, near Boone. Myra Shearer, born November 8, 1863; married J. G. Pulliam, July 24, 1888, and lives in the West.

Sherrill Family.—William W. Sherrill was born January 23, 1828, in Caldwell County, and he married Mary Hartley, who was born August 14, 1830, in Caldwell County. William W. died January 11, 1903, while his widow still survives. They were married in 1849. Their children were: George P., who was born December 9, 1850, at Deals Mills, Caldwell County, and married Mary Grider, March 28, 1869. Their second son was David, who went to Texas, where he died; Louisa married Wade Sherrill; Jason married Titia Wilson; Vienna married William Edmisten; Zeb Vance married Free Love Cole; George M. married Rebecca Payne and went first to Cherokee and then to Kansas, where he married a second time; William, who married Mary Hartley; Thomas, who married, first, Polly Wilson, and, second, a Satterwhite, and, third, a Sherrill; Sarah, who married William Wilson; Amanda, who married Miles Bowman. Still another married a White and moved to Cherokee. The father of David was William, who was born in 1733 and died in 1829. He had at least two children, David and William. Tradition says these were English people who came first to New York and thence to North Carolina, settling on Catawba River, at Sherrill's Ford, below Newton. William was a farmer and wagonmaker and a man of all work.

Shull Family.—From the genealogy of Simon Shull and family, taken on Watauga River, Ashe County, North Carolina, January 30, 1814, the following is culled: Simon was son of Frederick and Charity, born in Lincoln County October 24, 1767. Mary Sheifler, daughter of Philip and Mary Ormatenfer Sheifler, was born May 5, 1772, in Loudoun County, Virginia. Simon Shull's children were Elizabeth, born on John's River, March 6, 1791; the rest were born on Watauga River; Mary, born March 19, 1793; Sarah, born March 2, 1795; Phillip, born February 15, 1797; John, born March 24, 1799; Joseph, born April 22, 1801; Temperance, born October 16, 1804; Elizabeth, born April 10, 1808. Simon Shull married Mary Sheifler on Upper Creek of Catawba River, March 25, 1790, Wm. Penland officiating. Elizabeth Shull died February 15, 1794, two years and eleven months old; Joseph died April 7, 1886; Elizabeth died January 2, 1897; Adeline Taylor died April 15, 1894. Joseph Shull married Lizzie Mast October 28, 1835; W. F. Shull married Mary Brown September 28, 1869; Temperance Shull married W. H. Horton March 24, 1861; N. S. Shull married Mary Gilmore; P. P. Shull married Cindy Gragg March 26, 1866; B. C. Shull married Ollie Berry; John T. Shull married Chaney Hayes November 5, 1874; J. M. Shull married Sarah Greene January 12, 1882, and after her death he married Allie Baird August 30, 1888; John T. Taylor married Addie Shull March 28, 1878; Mary married David Mast; Sarah married James Ward; Phillip married Phœbe Ward; Joseph married Lizzie Mast; Temperance married Ben Councill; Elizabeth married Noah Mast. Joseph Shull's children were: William F., born September 18, 1836; Temperance C., born August 7, 1838; Noah S., born April 15, 1840; Phillip P., born July 20, 1842; Ben. C., born October 23, 1845; John T., born October 27, 1853; James M., born May 23, 1859; Mary Adeline, born March 28, 1861.

Phillip Shull's Family.—Phillip married Phœbe Ward and their children were: Elizabeth, who married Wm. Cannon; N. Canada, who married Elmyra Green; Matilda, who married Jesse Gragg; Thomas, who married Polly Spainhour; Polly, who married James Edmisten; Rhoda, who died unmarried; Sarah, who married Phillip Duvall; Temperance, who married A. J. Baird; William, who married Eugenia Campbell; Carolina, who married Alexander Ward; Simon, who married Martha Baird; Joseph Carroll, who married Eliza I. Mast; Phœbe Sophina, who married Peter Dana.

Smith Family.—George Smith was the first of this family to come to these mountains, arriving about 1780. According to his

Bible, he died April 30, 1838, aged ninety-one years and fifty days. Elizabeth, his wife, died March 8, 1842, aged ninety-two years and ———— days. Their children were: Abner, died May 20, 1850, aged sixty-nine years. He had two sons, Bennett and Jehiel; Bennett died November 15, 1844, aged forty-two years, eight months and twenty-two days; Abner. Mehetabel was the wife of Abner. She was born Fairchild and died March 3, 1855, aged eighty-four years, nine months and sixteen days; Bennett Smith married Elizabeth Moody December 23, 1824. Bennett Smith's children were: Abner, who married Chaney Green; Polly, who married George Hayes. Abner's children were: Bennett, who married a Kimes; Polly, who married James Rayfield; Elijah, who married Emma Austin; Elizabeth, not married; Sally, who married Pink Henson; George, who married, first, Emma Price, and, second, Mary Bingham; Rebecca, who married Julius Isenhour. The daughters of the first Abner were: Rhoda, born August 27, 1799; Mary, born February 27, 1802; Elizabeth, who married Jacob Reese, March 17, 1825; Susannah, who married Jacob Moody April 28, 1831; Rebecca, who married Jacob Norris March 27, 1835; Mary, who married Wm. Roland June 6, 1835. Jehiel was born September 16, 1806, and died January 10, 1885. He was twice married, his first wife having been Rachel Adams and his second wife Elizabeth Dugger, whom he married September 15, 1835.

Jehiel's children were: Ebenezer, born March 3, 1828; Bennett, born January 29, 1835, and married Jane Green December 6, 1856; Wiley, born June 27, 1836, never married; Carolina, born January 5, 1838, never married; Rhoda, born March 22, 1839, married Finley P. Mast; Henry, born March 3, 1841, never married; William, born September 18, 1842, never married; Mary, born October 9, 1845, married Tillett Combs; Martha, born June 15, 1847, and Jehiel, born October 27, 1849. Martha married D. J. Lowrance.

Bennett Smith married Jane Green December 6, 1856, and their children were: Carolina, born May 3, 1857, and died April 26, 1859; John C. Smith, born January 28, 1861, and married Sarah C. Mast January 2, 1881. Abner and Bennett

Smith settled at Silverstone, Abner having been in the legislature in 1821 and 1825, while his great-grandson, Abner W., was sent there in 1914.

Story Family.—This name is also spelt Storie. The first of the family who came to Western North Carolina was Jesse, who settled on King's Creek. He came from Pennsylvania and married Frances Bradley. Their children were Joshua, John and Eli, all of whom married and reared large families, Eli moving with his family to Missouri many years ago. About 1815 Joshua and John were living on the old Thomas Lenoir place on the Yadkin River, both having married Greens, but about 1825 they removed with their families to Ashe County, following members of their wives' families, one of whom settled at the Wm. Gragg place and the other at Blowing Rock, near the present store of Mr. Holtshouser, while a third settled at what is now Green Park. The Storys, however, settled at what is now known as Bailey's Camp, where Thomas H. Story, son of Joshua, was born. The nearest mill to their home at that time was what is now known as Winkler's, two miles south of Boone. The children of Joshua were: Elvira, William, Thomas, Lucy, Channie, Jesse, Amos, Isaac, Rufus, Martha and Noah. John's children were: Walter, Bettie, Ann, Jonathan, Rachel, Eliza, Sena, Mary and Jesse. William, Noah and Jesse (son of John) were in the Federal army in the Civil War, while Walter, Jonathan, Rufus, Jesse (son of Joshua) and Amos were conscripted into the Southern army. Isaac was in the Home Guard. Some of the others tried to enlist in the Federal army, but could not get through the lines. The homes of the Storys were open to the Federal soldiers and sympathisers, and the women of the families often waded the streams to carry food to outlyers, Bettie and Lucy once taking a wounded Yankee to Coffey's Gap in the night on an old horse, while on another occasion they hunted and found the body of a man named Hines, who had been killed by the Home Guard, and buried it decently. Jesse, son of John, is the only survivor. It is said that the *Toledo Blade* a few years ago stated that the Story family came to America on the *Mayflower* in 1620, but afterwards moved to

Pennsylvania. This is a very prolific family, the single school district of Aho having out of 105 children of school age, twenty-nine Storys. Of the present family, Mr. G. L. Story has been active in promoting good roads in Watauga County.

Swift Family.—Samuel Swift came from Germany and settled where Joseph Johnson now owns on Cove Creek. His children were: Samuel, who married ——————————; Hila, who married Berryman Fletcher; Rhoda, who married James Lewis; Polly, who married Jack Horton, sheriff; Sarah, who married William Proffitt; Emily, who married Bartlett Hilliard; Massy, who married Calvin Moody, and Nancy, who married Hugh Harman; Thomas, who married a Greene; Elias, who married an Adams, a daughter of Squire Adams.

Thomas' children were: Richard, born in 1845 and died in the Civil War; Enoch, born in 1847 and married Martha McBride; Clarissa, born in 1849 and married J. C. Davis; George, born in 1851 and married Jane McBride. Enoch is the father of Wiley, the distinguished friend of factory children. Samuel Swift deeded the land for the Cove Creek Baptist Church.

Tatum Family.—Elijah Tatum was born April 16, 1816, and married a cousin, S. Goodin Tatum, November 21, 1852, near Old Fields, in Ashe. She was a daughter of Joseph Tatum and wife, Sarah Pearson. Joseph was reared in Ashe, but Miss Pearson came from Burke. Elijah's father was George and was reared in Ashe and was a brother of Joseph. Their home was what is now Riverside. George married Delphia Jennings, of Old Fields. The father of George and Joseph was James and a soldier of the Revolutionary War. James' wife was a Miss Sheppard, of Ashe. James was born in Rowan County, from which he came to Ashe before the Revolutionary War when he was about fourteen years old. His father had come to America from England. Elijah had nine children. Only two of his boys lived to be grown—George and John. George married a daughter of Jacob Walters, of Burke, and John married Zora C. Tugman about 1880. Her father was Thomas Tugman and his wife was Anzanette Davis, daughter of W. S. Davis. Elijah's children were: James, who married Julia, and Senter, who married

Evelyn Tatum, sisters, and daughters of Joseph Tatum. George Tatum had two brothers, Joseph and Buckner, the latter having married a Miss Sheriff of Ashe. John Lee Tatum is a son of Elisha, and has an old sword which tradition says was used by James Tatum in the Revolutionary War. James is buried in Ashe County, near Riverside, the new railroad station. James and Senter, sons of Elijah, moved to Newtonia, Mo., where James died about 1907. Buckner moved to Georgia about 1845.

Tester Family.—Samuel Tester came from Scotland and settled at the mouth of Cove Creek before 1840. His wife was a Miss Foster. Their children were: Robin and Ransom, Jennie, who married Hiram Hix; Ellen, who died young, and another who married a man in Tennessee. Robin married first a daughter of David Hix and their children were Finley, Harman and Elizabeth. Robin's second wife was Katie Ward, daughter of Duke, and their children were Robin, Duke, James and Samuel; Sarah, who married Councill Harman, and another daughter who married Waightstill Davis; Celie, who married a Panther, and still another who married Link Pressly. Ransom married Fannie Hix, daughter of Harman, and their children were Harman, Samuel, Ellen and Polly.

Thomas Family.—William Thomas was the first of the name and was born in Salem, N. C., and married Sarah Sutherland, of Ashe County. Their children were Alfred, Margaret, Sarah, Joseph, Steven and William. By a second marriage to Mary Greer, there were the following children: William K., Thomas, Wiley and Elizabeth. Alfred was born in 1823 and married Malinda Wilson; Joseph was born in 1825 and married Sarah Wilson; Stephen was born in 1837 and married Lidia Porter; Sarah was born in 1828 and married Alexander Osborn; Margaret was born in 1821 and married Reuben Potter; William, born in 1834, married a Miss Potter; Alexander, born January 26, 1830, at Sutherland, and married Elmira M. Ward in 1853. Alex. ran away from his uncle, Joseph, when the former was about eighteen years of age, going to Missouri, where he remained about eighteen months, and then crossed the plains to California in 1849. He returned via the Panama route in 1853.

He married Elmira M. Ward in 1853 or 1854 and settled at the old Samuel Baker farm on lower Watauga River, where Samuel Baker had lived till about 1909. (Ashe County Deed Book D, pp. 207, 210.) He died December 13, 1909, and was buried at St. John's Church.

Col. Joe B. Todd.—He was born September 2, 1822, and died December 11, 1903. From the old Todd family Bible, printed in Edinborough by Mark and Charles Kerr, MDCCXCI, it is learned that James Todd was born July 31, 1757, and Margaret Erwin, his wife, October 14, 1759. These were married March 11, 1784; and that John Sharp Todd, father of James, was born December 11, 1724, and his wife, Nancy, was born June 7, 1739. James Todd died November 17, 1814. He was a soldier of the Revolution, and Mrs. Lizzie McGhee, of Boone, has the old powder-horn he used in that war.

Col. Joe B. Todd's first wife was Caroline McGhee, a daughter of the first Jordan Councill, and wife of William McGhee, who was born December 5, 1830, and died September 1, 1873. Two of their children are buried in the cemetery at Boone: Joe C. Todd, born November 8, 1855, and died November 1, 1858, and Maggie E., born July 7, 1853, and died February 12, 1858. James Polk Todd and Mary, wife of F. P. Moore, and William G. Todd, three of his children, survive him.

Colonel Todd's second wife was Mrs. Eliza Edmisten, widow of Harrison Edmisten and a daughter of Mr. Dancey, of Wilkes County.

Colonel Todd was a non-commissioned officer in the Mexican War, having first volunteered in Boone, but, there being delay in calling out the volunteers from Ashe County, he went to Cabarrass County, joined a company there and went to Mexico with them, participating in several battles. He received a pension till the Civil War, and it was restored long after the close of that struggle. He was colonel of the 98th North Carolina militia.

He was a candidate for clerk of the Superior Court in August, 1852, but was defeated by George M. Bingham, who, however, resigned, owing to an impediment in his speech, and a young lawyer named Clewell was appointed in his place. Upon

Clewell's removal from Watauga, Col. Joe B. Todd was appointed by the court, and he was sent for in the night, his residence then being at Dugger, now Penly Postoffice, east of the Blue Ridge. He was first lieutenant in Company D of the 1st North Carolina cavalry in the Civil War, but resigned on account of heart disease and returned home. He re-entered the service soon, however, joining the 37th North Carolina Infantry. After the close of the war, he was elected clerk of the Superior Court and served till the arrival of Judge J. L. Henry, when he was removed because he could not take the iron-clad oath. He was elected to the legislature in 1872, and then in 1882 to the office of clerk of the Superior Court, which office he held for twelve years after the close of the Civil War. With his ten years' service before the Civil War, this makes the longest service of anyone in this office in Watauga County. Colonel Todd was highly esteemed by all. He was a fine sportsman, delighting in hunting and fishing.

Trivett Family.—The great-great-grandfather of Larkin M. Trivett lived in Pennsylvania before the Revolutionary War, in which he was a soldier and during which he was killed in battle. His widow with two sons moved to Surry County, North Carolina, where one of these sons married and reared a large family of six or seven boys, two of whom settled in what is now Watauga County. One of these was named John, who settled on the south side of the Blue Ridge on Stony Fork, near the Wilkes line. He married Sallie Elrod, daughter of Adam Elrod, and reared one son and two daughters. The son was named Elijah, and he married Irena Carleton, daughter of Wyatt Carleton and his wife, Nancy Livingston. Elijah was the father of thirteen children, ten of whom are still living. One of the daughters of John Trivett, of Stony Fork, married Larkin Greene, son of Solomon, and they reared a large family of boys and girls. The other daughter of John Trivett married David Adams, son of Allen Adams, and his wife, Maggie Greene (familiarly known as Aunt Peggy Adams), and they reared a large family. John Trivett, of Stony Fork, had a brother whose name was Samuel, and he settled in the western part of Watauga

County near the Tennessee line on a creek known as Poga. He married Rebecca Norris, daughter of William Norris, and to them were born nine children, four boys and five girls. Larkin M. Trivett, the author of this sketch, is a civil engineer and a man of ability.

Tugman Family.—Micajah Tugman was born about 1820 and married Nancy Greer in 1843. They had six children, five boys and one girl, all of whom lived to be grown, except one boy, who did not survive his fourteenth year. James M. died at Richmond in August, 1862, in the Confederate service, unmarried; Benjamin married Carolina Miller and died in January, 1900; William L., who died at fourteen; Thomas J., who married Anzonette Davis, was born on Riddle's Fork March 5, 1851; Mary married L. Frank Ragan and died August 31, 1910; Marshall E., who married Neomi Miller and is still living. Micajah Tugman's father was William and his mother Mary Hawkins, both of Mecklenburg County, while William's father was James and his mother Elizabeth ─────, both of whom came from England to America. Micajah Tugman had a brother, James, who married Lemedy Hendrix, and two sisters, Nancy and Jennie. Nancy married Ben. Brown, father of Rev. Asa Brown and Jennie, who married Wilburn Groman. Of these, James lived in Wilkes, Jennie in Caldwell and Nancy in Watauga.

Van Dyke Family.—A widow Van Dyke came from Pennsylvania to Catawba County with her parents and her one child, a son, named William, where, after rearing him to manhood, she died. This son moved to Watauga in 1846, after marrying Sarah Herman, of Catawba County, and settled where George L. Van Dyke, his son, now lives, one mile from Three Forks Church. William's children were: Demarcus, born in Catawba about 1834; Emanuel, born about 1837; Luvina, born about 1840, and George L., born January 17, 1843. George L. married Mildred Morris April 4, 1867. He was a sergeant in Company I, 58th North Carolina Regiment, having enlisted in November, 1862, remaining in the service till the close of the war. His children are: Ada Cornelia; Alice Delona, who married John C. Brown; William Thomas, who married Nevada

Elrod, and Clara Ella, who married Leonard Cook. For fine housekeeping, this family is rivaled only by those of John K. Perry and J. J. T. Reese, of Beaver Dams.

Vannoy Family.—Jesse Vannoy married Elizabeth Fairchild. Their children were: Ann, who married, first, Adam Greene, and, second, Reuben Isaacs; John M., who married Martha Byers; Melvin, who married Amanda Eggers; Matilda, who married George Younce; Clarinda, who married Jacob Norris; Elizabeth, who married Jonas Winebarger.

Ward Family.—Among the first to settle on lower Watauga at what is now called Watauga Falls Postoffice (though the actual falls are just across the border in Tennessee), was Benjamin Ward, who had seven sons; Duke, Daniel, Benjamin, Nicodemus, McCaleb, Jesse and James. He also had three daughters, one of whom was named Celia. Benjamin Ward, Sr., was a most enterprising and worthy man, and his widow lived to be 105 years of age, while their son, Dan, lived to be 110. Duke married Sabra, widow of Andrew Harmon, and moved to Illinois. Ben., Jr., went to Cumberland Gap, and his son, Duke, came back and married Lucy Tester, while Amos, son of Duke, Sr., came back from Illinois and married Sally, sister of Lucy Tester. They had two sons, L. D. and John, the latter having been killed before Richmond in 1863.

Watson Family.—David Watson was a soldier of the Revolutionary War, and on a retreat escaped because his horse jumped a ditch which his pursuer's nag could not get over. David probably came from Scotland, but it is certain that he married a Miss Hamby and settled in Wake County, where twelve children were born, moving afterwards to the old Davis Place, near Holman's Ford. Their children were: Elizabeth, James, Gillie, Thomas, Bedie, John, Elihu, Mary, Sarah, David, Willis and Daniel. Of these Elihu married Celie Sherrill, of Burke, she having been born in June and he in August, 1803. Their children were: Mary, George, Nancy, Melinda, Susannah, Ann, Lucy, John, who died in the Civil War; Smith, Sarah, Elizabeth and Catharine. Of these George W. Watson was born in 1823 and married Keziah Morphew, who was born March 10, 1831, June 7, 1849.

Their children were: Isaac S., John, Sarah and Celie. Isaac S. was born October 4, 1850, and married Mary C. Proffitt April 20, 1873, twelve children having been born to them.

Welch Family.—William Welch, of Ireland, married Elizabeth Roper about 1823, and of this marriage Wm. P. Welch, of Deep Gap, was born, October 22, 1837, at High Point, Guilford County, N. C. Wm. P. Welch moved to Deep Gap in 1863 and married Margaret Bradley about that time. They have eight children. Solomon Greene had lived where W. P. settled, and his house had long been a famous stand or stopping place for travelers and stock drovers from Tennessee to Kentucky. But he sold out to his son-in-law, Larkin Greene, and W. P. Welch bought him out and has remained ever since. The country was all in woods when Welch came, and with the exception of the Murphy old place at the foot of the mountain, where Wilson Bros. have a store and house now, and the old David Greene place, Welch's home was the only house in that section.

Wilson Family.—Charles Wilson came to North Carolina from Pennsylvania about the time of the Revolutionary War. His wife is said to have been a sister of Gen. Nathaniel Greene, of Rhode Island. Charles was in General Greene's army and was killed at Guilford. Hiram Wilson married a Miss Smith and they settled on Cove Creek about 1815. Their children were: John, who married Mary Mast; Lucretia, who married Isaac Wilson, a distant kinsman; Sarah, who married Dudley Farthing; Isaac, who married Miss Caroline Greer; Ellen, who married Reuben Farthing; Albert P., who was born April 14, 1826, and married Elizabeth Councill, a daughter of Jesse; Clarissa, who married George Younce; Hiram, who married Alex. Baird, and Wm. Carroll, who married a Miss Adams, a daughter of Alfred Adams. Hiram, Isaac and Carroll were killed in the Civil War, and Albert P. was wounded twice, John having died just prior to the Civil War.

Another Wilson Family.—A. J. Wilson was the head of this family, and it is said that he "came over in the *Mayflower.*" Isaac Wilson, a son of A. J. Wilson, is said to have been killed at Lexington, N. C., in the Revolutionary War. His children were: Boyd, Isaac, John and Hiram. Boyd went to Middle Tennessee; Isaac settled at Sutherland and was killed by a tree falling on him; John married and lived on Sawyer's Creek, as did Hiram, who lived lower down that creek. Hiram's children were: John, Crissy, Sarah, Albert, Clarissa, Hiram and Carroll. John's children were: Betsy, Hannah and Susan, William, Alexander and John. This family of Wilsons came about 1817, when John Wilson, who was born in 1815, was two years old.

Lemuel, John and Hiram Wilson came from Rowan and Lemuel settled at Sutherland and John and Hiram near John Mast's present home.

Lemuel Wilson lived near the Tennessee line and near the dividing line between Watauga and Ashe. His children were: Andrew, who is yet living in that neighborhood, and Alexander, who was in the Civil War. Lemuel had two daughters, one of whom married Alfred and the other Joseph Thomas, sons of William Thomas, of that section. Rev. Leonard C. Wilson, of Beaver Dams, is a son of Lemuel Wilson and grandson of Lemuel Wilson. William Thomas was a school teacher on Sharp's Creek, just below T. P. Adam's present home. He had a number of rules, among which was one that no scholar should nickname another scholar, but this rule did not apply to the pedagogue himself. He nicknamed T. P. Adams when he was six years old because he said he reminded him of pictures of President John Tyler. This nickname clung till T. P. was grown.

Isaac Wilson, son of Hiram, known as Little Isaac, was "bushwhacked" during the Civil War and killed. His son, Rev. W. A. Wilson, a missionary of the M. E. Church, South, has been stationed at Huoshima, Japan, a number of years.

George Wilson, of Fork Ridge, was the father of Lucky Joe Wilson, but not related to the other Wilson families.

Jacob Winebarger married Sallie, daughter of John Moretz; lived on Meat Camp Creek and reared a good sized family. He was a good carpenter and millright and owned a good grist and sawmill. He came from Lincoln County, was a good citizen, and was about sixty years old when he died about 1895. John,

Hiram, Levi and Abel Winebarger also came from Lincoln and settled on Meat Camp and New River about 1850, where their descendants still reside. These were carpenters and farmers and excellent citizens.

Joshua Winkler was born in Wilkes County and in 1856 bought the farm two miles south of Boone on which his son, George, now lives. He married Carolina Pearson, and they reared ten children, five boys and five girls. He kept a grist and saw mill on what is now known as Winkler's Creek, the same stream that was formerly called Flannery's Fork. He introduced the first burrs into his mill for grinding wheat. He was a good farmer and stock raiser and a most estimable citizen. His death was caused by a hurt received from a cow, followed by measles.

Woodring Family.—Lincoln also gave Watauga another good citizen of German blood in the person of John Woodring, who settled on Meat Camp. He and his sons were farmers and hard workers, and accumulated much wealth. The boys were Daniel, Joseph, Alfred, Lawson, Rufus, Noah and Marcus. All have died but Marcus, who yet lives on Riddle's Fork. His one daughter was named Kate, and she married Ephriam Miller, but died in childbirth.

Yountz Family.—According to Phillip C. Yountz or Younce, of Mabel, N. C., Phillip was the first of the name to come to America, he having emigrated from Holland about 1700. He settled in New York. It is said he had one noted son, John, born in 1748, a blacksmith, who shod horses for Washington's army during the Revolutionary War, was twice captured by the British, and twice rescued. After the war he moved to Germantown, near Winston, N. C., coming thence to what is now Watauga, at the head of the New River. He married Rhoda Foutz and died while crossing Elk Ridge on a very cold day when he was about 100 years old. Their children were: Andrew, who moved to Macon County; Phillip and John, who settled in Miami County, Ohio; David and Elijah remaining in Ashe, while Solomon came to what is now Watauga. Solomon was born August 19, 1798, and married Sallie Rollen near Jefferson. She was born in 1802. Their children were: John, born December 15, 1818, married Hannah Lowrance, and to them were born twelve children; Abraham, born December 10, 1820, married Betsy Lewis, four children. After the death of his first wife, Solomon married Louisa Lewis, whose children were: Charlotte, born August 2, 1823, married Franklin Greer, seven children; Phillip, born October 3, 1825, married Margaret Musgrave, six children; Pollie, born March 11, 1828, married David Roten, ten children; George, born March 19, 1830, married Clarissa Wilson, eight children; Barbary, born August 19, 1834, married Isaiah Greer, five children; Sabra, born July 26, 1836, married Hugh Reese, eight children; Hannah, born July 10, 1838, married Henry Grogan, five children; William, born August 1, 1840, died when a small boy; Rhoda, born August 6, 1842, married Elijah Grogan, five children; Nancy, born November 18, 1845, married Rev. E. F. Jones, seven children. This family is very musical, pious and independent in thought.

INDEX

Sketches of prominent families and of individuals are alphabetically arranged from page 279 onward to the end, and are not included in this index.

	PAGE
Absentee landlords,—Killing of the cattle of	203, 204
Adams, Col. T. P. Active in school work	252, 253
Agriculture,—Facts about	138
—First instruction in	254
Aldridge,—Sketch of	187 to 190
Altitudes of various mountains and places	138
of mountains still doubtful	258
Ancestry of our mountain people	3 to 5
Character of our	74, 97
Appalachian Training School,—Some facts about	252
Apples. Facts about orchards	211
Argonauts. Forty-niners from Watauga	131
Arthur, J. P.,—Poem by	x
Asbury, Bishop Francis. Extracts from his journal	103 to 106
Asher, Charles,—Killing of	64
Avery County,—Establishment and lines of	125
Baird, Bedent E.,—Anecdotes of	196 to 198
Baird, Delilah. Elopes with Holtsclaw	191
Lives in camp, etc.	192
Her ridiculous romance with Dyer	192, 193
Banks,—Facts about	140
Banner's Elk,—Some account of	227 to 231
Battle on the Beech,—Some account of	174
Beaver Dams,—Some account of	239 to 242
Boone's Trail through	241, 242
Beech Creek,—Some account of	242
Belle of Broadway. Mrs. Horton's experience in the wilds	207, 208
Big Glades. Battle fought there in Revolutionary War	70
Blalock, "Keith." His part in Civil War	160, 161
Refused to shoot Wm. Coffey	166
Attack on Lott Greene's home	167, 168
His threat against Boyd	184
Kills Boyd	185
Blowing Rock. Described by Miss Morley	214 to 216
Its advantages and attractions	216 to 220
Boone, Daniel. No descendants from in Watauga	29
His relatives in Watauga	29, 30
His creed	30
Marking trail of	32
Monument on his cabin site	33
Colonel Bryan finds his trail	34
Cumberland Gap pedestal	35
His trail in other States	35

357

INDEX

	PAGE
Boone, Daniel. National monument to, advocated	36
Trail had been lost	37
Was a hunter, not a farmer	38
The Boone Tree inscription discussed	40, 41, 42
First trip across mountains	41
At Fort Prince George	41, 42
Trail through Beaver Dams	241, 242
Gave James Brown description of lands	290
Boone, Jesse and Jonathan. Members of Three Forks Church	30
Get into trouble with church	31, 32
Boone, Town of. Incorporation and attractions	142
Miss Morley's visit to	143 to 146
Map of old town	146
First residents of	147
First builders of	147 to 150
Hotels of	150
First merchants of	151 to 154
Post bellum town	154 to 156
Population of	157
Boundary Lines. State and county given	117 to 121, 123, 124
Braswell, Wm. Jonas. Soldier of Revolution; grave, etc.	65, 66
Bright, Samuel,—Former home and lands of	53, 54
Pilferings of his wife	55
Took oath of allegiance	55
His spring on the Yellow	56
His "trace" or trail	56, 59
Brown, James. Entered land described by Boone	290
Brown, Thomas. Killed by tree	289
Brushy Fork,—Some account of	221, 222
Buckwheat of Watauga won prizes at Columbian Exposition	139
Cabbages,—Facts about	139
Caldwell and Watauga Turnpike,—Facts about	269, 270
Calloway Sisters. Sad lives of Fanny and Betsy	186 to 192
Carmichael, Lee. Defended Davis	205
Cattle. Killing of those of absentee landlords	203, 204
Fine cattle introduced by Ives	254
Lived on lin limbs in spring	225
Character of mountain people	3 to 5, 74
Cheese Factories,—Facts about	139, 214
Chestnuts. Grafting French and Italian shoots on native stock	210, 239
Chimneys, The. Described	209
Churches. Three Forks Baptist	71 to 79
Character of people of early churches	97
Pioneer Baptists	98
Various churches of Baptist faith	100 to 103
Excerpts from Asbury's journal	103 to 105
Methodist churches	105 to 111
Primitive Baptists	111
Presbyterian	112
Lutherans	112
Episcopalians	85, 113
Civil War Period,—Volunteers in	159, 160
Danger from Tennessee	162

INDEX

	PAGE
Civil War Period. Longstreet's withdrawal	163
Kirk's Camp Vance raid	164
Various activities of Unionists	167
Michiganders escape	169
Killing of Levi Guy	169 to 171
Killing of Thomas Stout	171
Amazons "arrest" a Johnny Reb	172
Camp Mast and Beech Mountain battle	173 to 177
Stoneman's Raid	177 to 180
Home Guard	180
Robbing Mrs. Horton	180
Post bellum troubles	182 to 185
Fort Hamby, attack and capture of	183 to 184
Blalock kills Blair	184, 185
Clawson, Mrs. Peggy,—Stories of	198
Cleveland, Col. Ben. Not descended from Cromwell	60
His capture and rescue	60, 61
Executed Riddle and others; his grave	63
Clingman's Dome. Name of undisputed	258
Clingman, Hon. Thomas L. Greatest school master	256
Statesman, soldier, scientist	257
Refused controversy with the dead	257
Mount Mitchell controversy	257 to 262
Mined on Beech Creek	257, 267
Coffey, Austin,—Murder of	166
Coffey Brothers. Four in Civil War troubles	161
Coffey Brothers. Merchants of Boone	156
Their enterprises	156, 157
Coffey, William,—Killing of	165
Cone, Moses H.,—Sketch of	220
Active in school work	254
Confederate Soldiers,—Facts about	135
Cook's Gap. Most lovely section of county	207
Facts about	207
Council, Jordan, Jr. His influence in forming Watauga County	114, 115
Counterfeiters,—Facts about	157
Courts,—First terms of	129
Court Houses,—Facts about	126, 127
Cousins, John and Ellington,—Facts about	149, 150
Cove Creek,—Some account of	210
Cranberry Iron Mine,—Facts about	264 to 267
Davis, William. Revolutionary soldier; grave, etc.	67
His wife's courage	68
Davis, W. S. "Hollered School Butter"	204, 205
Dotson, Elijah. Long-distance quarrel	200
Dougherty, D. D. and B. B. Active in school work	254
Active in railroad work	254
Dutch Creek Falls,—Facts about	209
Easter Chapel,—Establishment and ruin of	82
Elkland. Railroad name for Todd	227
Elk Creek Falls described	209
Elk Cross Roads,—Some account of	226, 227

INDEX

	PAGE
Elk Knob Copper Mine,—Facts about	268
English, Mrs. Jemimah. Preserved traditions	56
Episcopal Church. Activities in Watauga	85, 86
Fairchild, Ebenezer. His diary	89 to 93
Appointed "Insigne"	93
Left old documents	94
Old church letter concerning	95
His daughters	95, 96
Not allowed to "spark" hired girl	339
Farthing, Dudley. Judge of County Court	308, 309
Farthing Family. One of preachers and good works	99
Established first Sunday School	339
Farthing, Paul and Reuben. Their troubles in Civil War	170
Paul's home attacked	170
Predicted death if surrendered	176
Farthing, Rev. Reuben P.,—Sketch of	310
Fish,—Laws for protection of	128
Supplying streams with trout	Note 5, p. 229
Flowers,—Some account of our wild	210, 211
Mrs. W. W. Stringfellow and Mr. Savage cultivate	211
Forests,—Facts about	139
Forts,—Location of early	17
Fort Hamby,—Attack on and capture of	183, 184
Gaines, Joseph C.,—Facts about	154
Gano, Rev. John. Preached at Jersey Settlement	89
His journey there and back	89 to 93
Ginseng,—Facts about	190, 221, 222
Grandfather Mountain described by Miss Morley	234 to 239
Grandmother Mountain visited by Miss Morley	239
Grant family referred to	56
Greer, Benjamin. Helped rescue Cleveland	61
Gave and received "hints"	61, 62
Helped kill Ferguson	62
Guy, Levi,—Killing of	169, 170
Hammermen. Names of some still remembered	267
Harrison, Rev. Joseph,—Sketch of	100
Henderson, Col. Richard. Relations with Boone considered	42 to 52
His daughter married Judge McCay	127
Hessian, The Big and Little. Name accounted for	Note 7, p. 240
Hix, Hiram. His ferry, bridge, and cross-cut saw	202, 203
Horton, Mrs. Jonathan,—Robbing of	180, 181
Horton, Mrs. Nathan. Belle of Broadway in wilderness	207, 208
Horton, Nathan. Helped guard Andre; his gun and clock	70, 324
Hospitality of pioneers exemplified by Asa Reese	338
Howard, Benjamin. First boarder in Boone	64
His knob and rock house	64
Indians resembled Hebrews	12, 13
First settlers of Watauga	15
Kept treaty with settlers	16

INDEX

	PAGE
Indians. Incursions by	17, 18
Relics of preserved by Messrs. Savage and Farthing. Note 2, p. 16	
Ives, Bishop L. S. Established school and brotherhood	78 to 81
Sketch of life	79, 80

Jackson, James. Came from Jersey Settlement 207, 332
                Gave land for meeting house................. 207
Jails,—Facts about 127
Jersey Settlement. Little known about 87, 88
                Rev. Gano's connection with 89
"Jug Hill." Why so called 204, 205

King's Mountain Men. Route through Watauga 59
                Incidents on the way 58, 59
Kirk's Camp Vance Raid,—Some account of 164, 165
                Stationed at Boone in 1865 178

Land Warrants for military services 118, 119
Lin Trees,—Facts about 15, 210, 225
Linville Country,—Some account of 224, 225
Linville Falls. Why so named 15, 19, 20
Linville Family,—Facts about 20
Lookabill School House,—Facts about 204, 249
Lovill, Col. E. F. Active in school and railroad work.......... 254
                Sketch of 328
Lusk, Samuel,—Sketch of 255

McCanless, "Cobb." Account of his defalcation and flight...... 194-5
                Killed by Wild Bill 196
Maple Trees,—Sugar and syrup made from 190
Mast, Mr. and Mrs. William,—Poisoning of 200, 201
Meat Camp,—Some account of 231, 232
Mexican War,—Soldiers of 137
Miller, Hon. David,—Facts about 207, 208, 117, 120, 332, 291
Mines and Mining,—Some account of .... 263 to 267
Mitchell, Dr. Elisha. Visited Watauga in 1828 .... 115, 116
                Controversy as to Mount Mitchell....... 257 to 262
Moody, Edward. His gravestone. Revolutionary soldier 65
                His widow's fine character 83
Moonshining. An inheritance? 9, 10
Moore, M. V. Wrote "Rhymes of Southern Rivers".......... 13
                Former merchant in Boone 13
Mountains. Altitudes of given 138
                Altitudes of still doubtful 258
                Rich, Long Hope, The Bald, Black, Riddle's Knob 203
Mount Mitchell Controversy,—Some new facts regarding....... 257, 252
Mullins, Jesse. Lost and recovered slaves 201, 202
Musterfield Murder. Triplett killed by Marshall 206
                Marshall spent night at Ailsey Councill's.
                                    Note 10, p. 206

Newspapers,—Some account of 157

	PAGE
Officers of Watauga County	132 to 134
Oil and Gas,—Boring for, etc.	267
Ollis Family,—Sketch of	225, 226
Ollis, Col. W. H. Furnished valuable information	58
Order of the Holy Cross,—Brotherhood of established	78 to 82

Palmer, Col. John B. In command of Western North Carolina..	165
Home burned by Kirk	165
Facts about his residence in Mitchell	225
Pennell, Joshua. Manumitted slaves	201
Pioneers of mountains in Revolution	6
Character of	3 to 5
Not poor whites of the South	7
McKamie Wiseman's views of	8
Descendants of have ceased to co-operate	9
Poga,—Some account of	242
Population,—Facts about	136, 157
Potatoes flourish in Watauga	139
Powder Mill. Run by Oaks; bounty for making	59
Presnell, Col. W. W. Recollections of "Old Masters"	256
Gave information about Confederates....	139
Prout, Rev. Henry H. Facts about connection with Valle Crucis	82, 83
Put trout in Linville River	Note 5, p. 229
Scholarly man	248

Railroads,—Some account of efforts to secure	273 to 278
Randall, W. G. Eminent artist in oils	217
Records of Ashe County; acts to restore lost	127, 128
Revolutionary Soldiers,—Facts about	65 to 70
Rich Mountain,—Some account of	232, 233
Riddle's Knob. Where Cleveland was rescued	61
Riddle, Captain Wm. Captured Cleveland	60, 61, 62
Death of	63
Roads. Great Pennsylvania described	3
Some account of first through Watauga	268 to 273
Rollins, Major W. W. Built fort at Blowing Rock	178
Root Crops. All kinds flourish in Watauga	139

Savage, Rev. W. R.,—Sketch of	217
Cultivates flowers	211
Has Indian relics	Note 2, p. 16
Scenery in Watauga County referred to	209, 210, 217
School Butter,—Penalty for "hollerin'"	204, 205
School House Loan Fund,—Establishment of	255
School lands donated by W. A. Lenoir	254
School Teachers,—Ancient and modern	243 to 258
Seal. Old one described	54, 225
Shelving Rock. Where King's Mountain men camped	56 to 58
Inscription on	58
Sheep,—Laws for protection of	128
Shull's Mills,—Some account of	223, 224
Silverstone,—Facts about	210
Has fine school house	253

INDEX 363

PAGE

Skiles, Rev. Wm. West. Connection with Valle Crucis.......... 83, 84
        Sketch of 86
Spangenberg, Bishop. Visited Watauga 21, 22
        Description of Three Forks .... 22 to 28
Speer, James,—"Sale" and disappearance of 201
Stair Gap. Proper name for Star Gap. Note 4, p. 104.......... 241
Stock. All kinds flourish in Watauga 131, 138, 139
Stoneman's Raid,—Some account of ....177 to 180
Stopping Places. Some of the earliest ones 272
Stout, Thomas,—Tragic death of 171
Sugar Grove,—Some account of 214
      Walnut Grove Institute 253
      Has first cheese factory 139, 214
Sunday Schools established first in Watauga 339

"Tater Hill,"—Some account of 233
Three Forks,—Spangenberg's description of .... 22 to 28
Three Forks Baptist Church. Facts from minutes .... 71 to 77
Todd. New name for Elk Cross Roads 227
Tories,—Some facts about 53, 56
     Execution of several 63
     Two "Tory Knobs" 69
Tufts, Rev. Edgar. His good works at Banner Elk............. 112, 230
"Twisting Temple." Why so called 250

Valle Crucis. Order of Holy Cross established there........... 78 to 81
     Some account of 212, 213
     Mission School 254
     Fine public school 254

Walnut Grove Institute,—Facts about 253
Walks, The,—Described 209
Washington County, Tenn., embraced part of Watauga County.
                     16, 57, 64, 223
Watauga County. Indians never lived here in memory of whites 15
      First white settlers of 18
      First visited by Spangenberg .... 22 to 28
      Once part of Watauga Settlement.......16, 57, 64, 223
      Formation of ....114 to 117
      Boundary lines of ....117 to 123
      Changes in lines of 124, 126
      Avery County cut off 125
      Line changed at Todd 126
      Jails and court houses 126, 127
      Ashe County records 127
      Lost records restored 128
      People of 130
      Officers and representatives of ....132 to 134
      Finances of 134
      Sent soldiers to Civil War 135
      Agriculture and other facts ....138 to 141
      Population of 136
      Mexican War soldiers 137
      Taxation of 138
      Altitudes of 138

364 INDEX

	PAGE
Watauga Falls,—Facts about	209
Watauga Settlement. Leased and bought Indian lands	15, 16
Once embraced what is now Watauga County	16, 57, 64, 223
Weather,—Facts about	138
Whiskey Rebellion of Pennsylvania suppressed	10, 11
White, Joseph. Asher killed by his men	Note 4, p. 64
Wilson, Isaac,—Murder of	170
Wilson, "Lucky Joe,"—Stories of	199, 200
Wiseman, McKamie. Views of first settlers	8
Death of	8
Wiseman, William,—Sketch of	55
Tried and convicted Mrs. Bright	55
Wolf's Den,—Cleveland rescued from	62
Knife found there by Micajah Tugman	61
Words. Derivation of some Indian words	14, 15
Yarber, Moses. Soldier of War of 1812	68
Yarber, Jemimah and Catharine,—Facts about	69
Yellow Mountain. King's Mountain men did not camp there	60
Yonahlossee Road,—Miss Morley's description of	237

www.ingramcontent.com/pod-product-compliance
Lightning Source LLC
Chambersburg PA
CBHW071227290426
44108CB00013B/1314